MARTIN NOTH

NUMBERS

THE OLD TESTAMENT LIBRARY

MARTIN NOTH

NUMBERS

A Commentary

The Westminster Press

PHILADELPHIA

Translated by James D. Martin from the German
Das vierte Buch Mose, Numeri
(Das Alte Testament Deutsch 7)
published 1966 by Vandenhoeck & Ruprecht,
Göttingen

Standard Book No. 664–20841–X
Library of Congress Catalog Card No. 69–12129

PUBLISHED BY THE WESTMINSTER PRESS®

PHILADELPHIA, PENNSYLVANIA

PRINTED IN THE UNITED STATES OF AMERICA

To my friends in Jerusalem
Crystal M. Bennett
R. P. Pierre Benoit
Paul W. and Nancy R. Lapp
R. P. Roland de Vaux
in gratitude and respect

Martin Noth, Director of the German Evangelical *Institut für Altertumswissenschaft des Heiligen Landes*, died suddenly on 30 May 1968, during the printing of this translation of the last of his group of three commentaries in this Series – Exodus, Leviticus, Numbers. The General Editors of the Series wish to pay their tribute to the memory of one of the greatest names in modern Old Testament scholarship, whose contributions to the understanding of the history and life of the world in which the Old Testament was created have been and are so deeply influential. We would honour not only a great scholar but also a man of deep faith and kindliness.

THE EDITORS

CONTENTS

PREFACE

THIS BOOK has been written almost entirely in Jerusalem in the difficult circumstances of a temporary residence and without an extensive library of my own. It would have been impossible to carry out and finish the work on this book had not good friends in Jerusalem helped, in various ways, to facilitate living and working in Jerusalem. My gratitude for this is expressed in the dedication.

For help with proof-reading I am indebted to my wife and Dr Ute Lux.

Jerusalem, August 1966   MARTIN NOTH

TRANSLATOR'S PREFACE

IN THE ORIGINAL German series from which this commentary is taken, the individual authors have provided their own translation of the Hebrew text. In this English translation the text of the RSV has been printed, except in a few places where the differences between Noth's translation and the RSV have been too great or too extensive to be noted, as has been the usual practice, by means of a translator's footnote (Tr.) in the body of the commentary. In these few cases the textual variants from the RSV have been explained by means of footnotes to the text. Noth's usual practice in such footnotes has been to refer simply to BH (Kittel's *Biblia Hebraica*, 3rd edition), and these references have been expanded in this translation from the textual apparatus in BH. Passages within square brackets in the biblical text are those which Noth regards as secondary. These are usually, but not always, discussed in the commentary. When, in the body of the commentary, a biblical reference is preceded by a paragraph mark (¶), the reference is to what Noth considers to have been the original form of the passage in question.

In the body of the commentary, Noth makes frequent reference to his two earlier volumes on Exodus and Leviticus. These have already been published in this series, *Exodus* in 1962 and *Leviticus* in 1965. Where the titles *Exodus* and *Leviticus* appear in the footnotes without indication of author or date, it is to these volumes that reference is being made.

I

INTRODUCTION

1. NAME AND CONTENTS OF THE BOOK

IN THE HEBREW Synagogue tradition, the 'Fourth Book of Moses' is not called by the first main word of the first sentence, as are the other books of the Pentateuch, according to widespread ancient near-Eastern usage, but by a prominent word from the first sentence, *bammidbār* (='in the wilderness'). In this case, too, the Greek translation of the Old Testament, the Septuagint, has introduced a factual designation derived from the contents in place of the purely formal one. There the title of the book is *Arithmoi* (='numbers'). In this case the Latin translation has not taken over the Greek designation as a loanword, as it does in the other books of the Pentateuch, but has translated the Greek word, 'Numeri'. This Latin title is the one commonly used in scholarly language, abbreviated as Num. This designation derives from the fact that the book provides us with many numbers or numerical lists. Right at the beginning we have the census figures of the Israelite tribes (1.20–46) and of the various groups of Levites (3.14–51). Then we have the lists, complete with measurements and figures, of gifts brought by the representatives of the Israelite tribes for the dedication of the altar (7.10–83); the second account of the census figures of the Israelite tribes (26.5–51); the list, again provided with exact figures, of the offerings to be brought on feast days and festivals throughout the year (28.1–29.38); and lastly the enumeration of the booty from the war against the Midianites (31.32–52).

From the point of view of its contents, the book lacks unity, and it is difficult to see any pattern in its construction. Seen as a whole, it is a piece of narrative, but this narrative is interrupted

I

again and again by the communication of more or less comprehensive
regulations and lists which are only loosely linked to the narrative
thread by the short, stereotyped introductory formula, 'Yahweh
said to Moses' ('in the wilderness of Sinai' or 'in the plains of Moab').
The course of the narrative is as follows. At the beginning of the book
Israel is 'in the wilderness of Sinai' (1.1), that is in the vicinity of the
mountain of the theophany and the law-giving. 10.11–36 reports the
departure from Sinai and thereafter Israel begins a wilderness
wandering in the course of which a first attempt is made, from the
south, to take possession of the land west of the Jordan (ch. 13–14).
The attempt is abortive, but here, at this early stage, the theme of
the conquest is introduced. 20.14–21 is the beginning of the march to
the southern part of the territory east of the Jordan. There the first
victories over the earlier indigenous population take place (21.21–31),
and there a beginning is made with the allocation of land to the
Israelite tribes (32.1ff.). At the end of the book, Israel is established
east of the Jordan, ready to cross the Jordan and enter the land to the
west, the land she regards as the one promised her by her God. From
this indication of the contents it is already clear that the book is not
a self-contained unit. At the beginning, Israel is depicted as sojourning at Sinai, but there is no indication as to how Israel arrived there
or as to what had happened to her there. The book of Numbers is
part of the total narrative of the Pentateuch and must be looked at
within that wider framework.

For the above sketch of the course of the narrative in Numbers, a
few sections have been selected in which the stages in Israel's journey
are fairly clearly marked. Viewed in the context of the whole book,
these sections stand out in no particularly obvious or striking fashion.
There are long stretches where the thread of the narrative fades so
much into the background that it is almost lost to view. What then
appear in the foreground are not larger, self-contained units but, for
the most part, collections of very varied material with little inner
cohesion. The first four chapters form a larger complex. In them the
Israelite tribes and the Levites, in the context of a census, are given
exact instructions about the allocation of camping sites, about the
order of the march and (for the Levites) about the organization of
the cult. There, too, the furnishing of the wilderness sanctuary as it
is described in Ex. 25ff. is presupposed. This complex, which, although it displays various secondary additions, has a comparatively
comprehensive and unified basic form, is followed, in 5.1–6.27 and

NAME AND CONTENTS OF THE BOOK

then again in 8.1–9.14, by unsystematized collections of divine
ordinances on a wide range of subjects. Between these two sections
there stands, in ch. 7, the list of gifts brought for the sanctuary by
the tribal 'leaders', a list which, in its wide range and its monotony,
borders on the fanciful. In 9.15 the theme of the departure from Sinai
begins and we have for the first time a somewhat longer stretch of
narrative proper, consisting of a series of independent narrative units
which have, partly at least, the common theme of life in the wilderness to the south of Palestine (ch. 11, 12, 13–14). With ch. 15 the
flow of the narrative is again halted and there follows a collection of
cultic-ritual prescriptions which have no connection with either the
preceding or the following narrative. The account of the rebellion
against Moses in ch. 16 gives rise to a series of varied cultic-ritual
regulations. Chapter 20 sees the beginning of another narrative
section. This section begins with a typical wilderness story (20.1–13),
which is followed by further independent narratives, some of which
are located west of the *wādi el-ʿaraba* (20.14–21) or even on the
southern edge of the land of Canaan (21.1–3), while others are
located east of the Jordan (21.21–35) or else still in the wilderness
(21.4–9) or are now no longer capable of being located at all
(20.22–29). The 'itinerary' in 21.10–20 can only be described as a
collection of varied material which does not belong together and
part of which can be shown to have been borrowed from various
other parts of the Old Testament. So this complex offers a picture of
great confusion and it is possible to establish a factual connection
only between 20.14–21 and 21.21ff. Then, in ch. 22–24, we have the
longest connected narrative complex of the whole book, the Balaam
story, which presupposes Israel in a situation which has only a very
tentative connection with the earlier narrative. This is followed by the
short narrative concerning Baal of Peor (25.1–5) to which various
expansions have become loosely attached (25.6–19). Again, ch. 26,
with its census information about tribes and individuals, stands
completely on its own, and to one particular item of information
given in it (26.33) there is attached 27.1–11. 27.12–23, with its
announcement of the imminent death of Moses, is a striking passage.
The remainder of the book concerns duties still to be fulfilled by
Moses before his death—the transmission of further regulations
concerning offerings and vows (ch. 28–30), the prosecution of a war
of revenge against the Midianites (ch. 31), the first allocation of land
east of the Jordan (ch. 32), the writing down of the stages of the

journey accomplished hitherto (33.1–49), the giving of further instructions for the future allocation of land to the Israelite tribes west of the Jordan and for the setting up of cities of refuge in Canaan (33.50–35.34), and, finally, the settling of a question of inheritance (ch. 36).

2. THE GROWTH OF THE BOOK
(Literary Criticism and the History of Traditions)

There can be no question of the unity of the book of Numbers, nor of its originating from the hand of a single author. This is already clear from the confusion and lack of order in its contents. It is also clear from the juxtaposition of quite varied styles and methods of presentation, as well as from the repeated confrontation of factually contradictory concepts in one and the same situation. It is also clear, finally, from the relationship of secondary dependence which can sometimes be established between one section and another. These facts are so self-evident that the assertion of the disunity of the book does not require exhaustive proof. It is, however, more difficult to provide any obvious explanation for the facts of the case before us. It is, to be sure, as good as certain, and scarcely ever contested, that the disunity of the book goes back to its origins, that is to a presumably long and complicated history of its origins. But to say this is not really to provide an explanation of the facts. If we compare Numbers with the other books of the Pentateuch, what strikes us most of all here is the lack of longer complexes. Various different elements in the composition can be distinguished comparatively easily from each other. The stories in detailed and lively narrative style, which give the impression of coming directly from an older, originally orally transmitted, narrative source (e.g. the Balaam stories), stand out clearly from those general directives whose purpose is to introduce exact rules and ordinances, which are presumably to be thought of as coming from a fairly late period. But even within these various strata it is difficult to discern any definite lines of continuity. If we were to take the book of Numbers on its own, then we would think not so much of 'continuous sources' as of an unsystematic collection of innumerable pieces of tradition of very varied content, age and character ('Fragment Hypothesis'). But it would be contrary to the facts of the matter, as will already be clear from the account of the contents of the book, to treat Numbers in isolation. From the first, the book has belonged, in the Old Testament canon, to the larger whole of the Pentateuch, and scholarly work on the book has consistently maintained that it must be seen in this wider context. It is, therefore, justifiable to approach the book of Numbers with the results of Pentateuchal analysis achieved elsewhere* and to expect the continuing Pentateuchal 'sources' here, too, even if, as we have said, the situation in Numbers, of itself, does not exactly lead us to these results. In view of the peculiar nature of Numbers, however, the application of these results must be carried through with caution and restraint. It is certainly not practicable simply to proceed to a division of the textual material among the Pentateuchal sources J, E and P (and, in any event, it would have to be a question of secondary forms of these sources). We must, rather, keep in mind the peculiar position and function of the book within the framework of the Pentateuch as a whole. Only thus can we explain the peculiar nature of the book of Numbers.

Numbers participates only marginally in the great themes of the Pentateuchal tradition. The first ten chapters belong to the great 'Theophany at Sinai', but the essentials of this theme have already been treated in the second part of Exodus. The Sinai narrative is continued in a short section of Leviticus where we also find the exposition of numerous, detailed ordinances of a cultic-ritual nature such as are usually connected, from the point of view of time and place of delivery, with Sinai.† We can expect what follows this in Numbers to be little more than a supplement to the Sinai theme. Since, from Ex. 25 onwards, the P narrative (interrupted only by Ex. 32–34) dominates the account of the Sinai events, what we should most readily expect in Numbers 1ff. is the continuation of the P narrative, and this is, in fact, what we find. Following on the ordinances for the building and furnishing of the single sanctuary for Israel and her cult (Ex. 25ff.), P determines, in addition, the classification of Israel's tribes and the cultic duties of the Levites with regard to the external care of the sanctuary. This (with some secondary additions) is what we find in Numbers 1–4, but with this, for P, the 'Sinai' subject was concluded. The account of the departure from Sinai begins in the P narrative with 10.11 (or, if we take the secondary additions into consideration, with 9.15). This point of rupture in the narrative must have appeared suitable for all kinds of later insertions. Since the Sinai revelation was, for ancient Israel, the

* Cf. *Exodus*, pp. 12f. † Cf. *Leviticus*, pp. 10f.

classic place of the proclamation of the divine will and since, therefore, all ordinances which appeared to be authentic were, as far as
possible, read back into the Sinai revelation, it is understandable that
the need was felt, even after the actual conclusion of the Pentateuch,
to include various additional items of this kind within the Sinai
pericope. The easiest place for this to be done was at the end of that
pericope. So, at a very late stage, but before the Pentateuch achieved
canonical status, thereby becoming unalterable, all kinds of material
were added in 5.1–9.14, material which can no longer be regarded
as belonging to the various 'sources'. This material consists of
numerous individual units, having no connection with one another
and in whose sequence no factual arrangement can be discerned. The
simplest hypothesis is that in the course of time these units gradually
became attached to each other. But it is impossible to prove such
a hypothesis, since it is in the nature of these various units that they
are no longer, even in a tentative fashion, capable of being dated.

With the departure from Sinai, which is reported from 10.11
onwards, to begin with in the style and with the presuppositions of
the P narrative, the 'old sources' of the Pentateuch, which have not
been in evidence since Ex. 32–34, find expression for the first time
in Numbers. It is clear and uncontested that 10.29–36—and this is
equally true of ch. 11 and 12—is earlier than the P document.
Clearly, these passages are not, in themselves, smooth and uniform,
but an attempt simply to divide their contents into parallel narrative
variants does not work. It is tempting to assume that we encounter here
the J and E sources which we know from Genesis and Exodus, and this
assumption usually forms the basis of literary analysis. But this is to
do violence to the facts as we encounter them in Numbers. These
facts reveal, rather, a basic form in which we see not doublets and
variants but a gathering together of varied and disparate material
which has been subjected also to comparatively late additions. That
this basic form is probably to be regarded as Yahwistic (J) is indicated
by the general results of Pentateuchal analysis, but, apart from the
consistent use of the divine name Yahweh, there is no positive proof
for such an assumption. This J-narrative is continued in the story of
the spies in ch. 13–14. In this section the juxtaposition of two narrative variants is clear, though not on the plane of the 'old sources'.
The case is, rather, that the basic literary form has been provided
by the P-narrative, which here follows the old Pentateuchal tradition,
and that there has been connected with this an old narrative which,

from what has been said, should be designated as 'J'. Why, in ch.15, another collection of quite disparate cultic-ritual ordinances should follow this comparatively extensive narrative complex is difficult to say. Perhaps the case of the 'Sabbath breaker' (15.32–36) formed the kernel of this collection, for this case occurred 'while the people of Israel were in the wilderness' (v. 32a), i.e. in the situation to which, according to ch. 13–14, they had been condemned. The other parts of ch. 15 will then have become loosely joined to this kernel. What is probably a typical state of affairs is to be found again in the complex of ch. 16–19. The point of departure here is the 'old' narrative (J) of the revolt of the Reubenites Dathan and Abiram against Moses' claim to leadership. Another narrative is quite loosely interwoven with this one. It, too, has a revolt as its subject-matter, but this is not really a variant of the other, since here a completely different personage, Korah, plays the part of the rebel. From its style, this second narrative obviously belongs to P, but it is not a single unit, there being also a variant of it which, however, seems to represent not an independent unit but rather an expansion of it and which is, therefore, to be considered as a secondary expansion within P. The Korah narrative, with its expansion, is obviously 'tendentious', that is, an old tradition about a revolt against Moses (by Dathan and Abiram) has been reworked to form a refutation of specific attacks, now no longer known to us, against the priestly responsibilities and privileges of the Aaronites. This theme was interesting and important for a later age, and for this reason it has been expanded, in ch. 17–18, by a variety of loosely attached additions after the narrative proper has ended in ch. 16. Thus, after rules and ordinances have appeared at this point and in this way, ch. 19 introduces a ritual of distinct character, without there being any obvious reason why it should stand at this precise point.

With the bringing together of narrative sections in ch. 20–21, the Pentateuch draws to a close. This happens on the different literary planes in different ways. The situation in P is comparatively clear. In 20.1–13 there appears the story of a water miracle whose basic form clearly belongs to P (this basic form has subsequently been supplemented by borrowings from the very similar story of Ex. 17.1–7). The P author has placed the story in this position, thereby re-interpreting it to accord with his own conceptions, in order to make it the reason why Moses and Aaron are not to enter the promised land but are soon to die. So there follows in P, in 20.22b–29,

the account of the death of Aaron and, in 27.12–14(15–23), the
announcement of the imminent death of Moses. The actual intimation
of the latter's death, which is lacking at this point, falls outside the
book of Numbers, and with it the P-narrative reaches its final conclusion. The situation is different in the 'old sources'. In 20.14–21
and 21.21ff. there appears the account of the march on the southern
part of the territory east of the Jordan and of the first victories and
conquests north of the Arnon. In this way the transition from the
Pentateuchal theme of the wilderness wandering to that of the conquest of Canaan is achieved. This transition was undoubtedly the
occasion for the secondary insertion of the following individual units
which are completely without context: 21.1–3, 21.4–9 and 21.10–20.
In 20.14–21 and 21.21ff. the Pentateuchal 'source' E seems to appear
for the first time in Numbers. The situation in 20.14–21 leads us to
suppose the juxtaposition of two variants which cannot, it is true, be
separated with any certainty, but whose existence can none the less
be accepted as a fact. In any case they are earlier than the priestly
source and, from the general results of Pentateuchal analysis, J and E
spring to mind. With regard to 21.21–31 (v. 32 is an editorial addition
and vv. 33–35 are a deuteronomistic expansion) there is no motivation
for a separation on the grounds of literary criticism. As for the
decision between the two alternatives, J or E (it is certainly a question
of one or other of the old sources), there is a slight hint in the general
use of the name 'Amorites', which testifies to E. We would, then,
perhaps have, in 21.21–31 on the one hand and in 32.1 on the other,
the two different versions of the beginning of the conquest in E and J
respectively.

In the extensive narrative complex of the Balaam stories in ch.
22–24 we are aware—apart from the later additions in 24.20–24—of
two versions which are usually, correctly, divided between J and E.
In the narrative context, apart from the poetical discourses of
Balaam which are independent units, we encounter a characteristic
of the E-source, namely the use of the word 'God' in place of the
divine name 'Yahweh' (22.9, 10, 12, 20, 38; 23.4, 27), but the way in
which God is designated is no sure guide for literary criticism, since
the textual transmission is not entirely reliable. However, E does have
a substantial share in the Balaam story, especially in 22.41–23.26;
indeed, this is the longest E-section in the book of Numbers. Next,
the short independent narrative of 25.1–5 belongs to the 'old sources'
and is probably to be attributed to J (cf. the divine name). To it, in

vv. 6–18, various late additions have been joined. Finally, the 'old sources' appear once more in ch. 32 (v. 1, perhaps also vv. 16–19) and in such a way that there is no certain indication that it is a question of several versions. For everything in ch. 32, apart from the verses already mentioned, is later expansion, stemming above all from the deuteronomistic account of the conquest. The original basis of ch. 32 is probably 'Yahwistic' and is perhaps the Yahwistic parallel to the Elohistic narrative of 21.21–31. In addition, the remaining contents of the last eleven chapters of Numbers, apart from the above-mentioned few verses in ch. 32, comprise material from a later period which is not susceptible of division among the sources, and this, again, is to be explained by the position of these chapters within the Pentateuch as a whole.

At the end of Numbers there is a deep incision. For with Deut. 1.1 there begins the deuteronomistic historical work which fundamentally has nothing to do with the Pentateuch and became attached to it from the literary point of view only later, and in such a way that in the last four chapters of Deuteronomy the Pentateuchal narrative reappears to answer the need for depicting the chronological sequence of events. The problem of the continuation of the narrative in the old sources, whose account of the conquest theme began in Num. 21–32, must remain unanswered here. The fact that at the end of Numbers the Pentateuch has almost reached its conclusion and that later this was to become the point where the deuteronomistic history was joined to it, is important for the explanation of the situation in the last third of our book. Here again was a place where later insertions could be made, and this in two respects. On the one hand, any ordinances and actions which had to be attributed to Moses would have to be inserted here; on the other, this was the place for a variety of allusions to the approaching conquest, which was then described in detail in the deuteronomistic historical work. The great roll-call of the Israelite tribes in ch. 26 is already regarded, though certainly in opposition to its original sphere of reference according to v. 4b, as the basis for the future division of the land of Canaan (vv. 52–56, 63–65). At a later stage, the independent section 27.1–11 was added in view of its connection with 26.33. Looking forward to the deuteronomistic historical work, the account of the commissioning of Joshua (27.15–23) was added to the announcement of the death of Moses (27.12–14). In ch. 28–30 there is attributed to Moses a last, long series of directions, given at Yahweh's command, concerning offerings and vows. Such, too, is the case in ch. 31, where the narrative of the expedition to take revenge on the Midianites, with its accompanying account of the division of the booty, is seen as the last significant action carried out by Moses at Yahweh's command. The statements about the role played in the conquest by those already settled east of the Jordan (ch. 32) are connected to the old conquest traditions, and they are followed in 33.1–49 by yet another section (itinerary) which is specifically carried back to Moses. Then follow, in 33.50–35. 34, ordinances for the future conquest which are dependent on the deuteronomistic historical work and which, at the same time, have the deuteronomistic narrative of the conquest in view. These are certainly to be attributed to a redactor who either undertook the linking of the Pentateuch with the deuteronomistic historical work or else pre-supposed such a link. Finally, with ch. 36, there appeared what is a very definite addition. No proper sequence is maintained in this whole complex of later additions. We shall have to reckon with the fact that the individual units were simply added one after the other in the order in which they appeared.

The book of Numbers contains an extraordinary amount of late material and this material must in every case have been literary in origin; that is, it must have been written down from the first. It is not possible in every case to give it an exact date, but it certainly originated in the post-exilic cultic community in Jerusalem and is of interest and importance for our knowledge of the ordinances and concepts prevalent in that late period. In this respect, we must always reckon, in view of the conservative nature of cult and ritual, with the fact that even in late contexts we find older material, with the reservation that in individual cases this is scarcely now susceptible of hard and fast proof. It is scarcely to be doubted, for example, that the ritual of ch. 19 has its roots in very ancient concepts and practices. More enigmatic is the fact that even outside the cultic-ritual sphere material from older traditions seems to have been preserved, which, from the literary point of view, first makes its appearance in later contexts (P or Pent[s]).* These facts are difficult to explain; they can only be stated. They concern above all several ancient Israelite tribal traditions. Since other indications are lacking, it is at least very

---

* Noth uses the siglum P[s] to denote secondary additions to the P-narrative (cf., e.g., M. Noth, *Überlieferungsgeschichte des Pentateuch*, Stuttgart, 1948, p. 11, footnote 24). By analogy, Pent[s] must indicate secondary additions to the Pentateuch as a whole. Tr.

probable that the census data of 1.20–46(P) go back to a census tradition from a period before the Israelite tribes were moulded into a political entity, even if it was later misinterpreted (see below pp. 20–23). The same holds good for the figures in 26.4b–51 which, from a literary point of view, is undoubtedly secondary. And it holds good even more for the quite unique list of tribal names in the same section, 26.4b–51.

There is no doubt that the 'old sources', in so far as they find expression in Numbers, go back to very early traditions which, to begin with, would be transmitted orally before they found their way into the narrative works J and E. This holds good for some of the longer narrative complexes, above all for the 'spy' story in ch. 13–14 which, from a traditio-historical point of view, goes back to a Calebite tradition from Hebron of the occupation of Hebron by Caleb, and also for the Balaam story in ch. 22–24 which probably originated in the sanctuary of Baal-Peor in the southern part of the territory east of the Jordan and which presents the nature and appearance of a 'seer' in a unique and very original way. The Balaam discourses, at any rate those of ch. 24, are comparatively old poetical pieces. Several other poetical sections, which have been inserted into the narrative context of the 'old sources', are probably older still. We think of the 'ark sayings' in 10.35–36 which, from the traditio-historical point of view, are perhaps the oldest items of information about the ark in the Old Testament and which therefore give us the oldest provable and thus, perhaps, the original conception of that famous sacred symbol. We think, further, of the poetical 'summons' in 21.27b–30 which is probably a noteworthy source for an approach to the early history of the town Heshbon.

3. THE SIGNIFICANCE OF THE BOOK

We can scarcely speak of a specific significance peculiar to the book of Numbers. It has its significance—even more so than is the case with the other books of the Pentateuch—within the framework and context of the greater Pentateuchal whole. Indeed, within that whole it is indispensable. In the book of Numbers, in the first place, the great central theme of the Pentateuch, that of the 'theophany at Sinai', is brought to its conclusion, not, it is true, with any particularly important material, yet with details concerning the classification of the twelve tribes which round off the subject of the definitive constitution of the cult and life of Israel as this is presented by P. There follows, further, again as a kind of transition (cf. Ex. 15.22–18.27) making use of what are, in part, old traditions, material concerning the continued sojourn of Israel in the wilderness. Here, the necessity for the prolonged sojourn of Israel in the wilderness is explained by the 'spy' story, and thereby the wilderness sojourn of Israel is raised to the rank of an independent theme in the Pentateuchal tradition. The theme of the conquest, a new element, has its beginnings in Numbers. In this respect, the question as to how this theme is actually treated in the different literary strata is an important one. From the point of view of bulk, what stands out most noticeably is the completely secondary material which foreshadows the conquest narrative of the deuteronomistic historical work and which was first added in the course of the editorial conflation of Pentateuch and deuteronomistic historical work. As a result of this substantial addition there comes to light the strange fact that in P it is impossible to discern any positive interest in the conquest. The latter appears in P only in the negative assertion that Moses and Aaron are not to enter the promised land nor lead Israel into it (20.12), but are to die beforehand. From that point on, nothing more is known of P. The situation with regard to the 'old sources' is different. In 21.21–31 and 32.1ff., they introduce the first positive conquest narratives. These can be understood only as preliminary accounts, but they indicate that the 'old sources' contained the conquest theme, which rounded off the Pentateuch as a whole in that it reported the fulfilment of the promises made to the patriarchs. How the conquest narrative is continued in the 'old sources', and whether and where it may still be delineated outwith the Pentateuch, are questions which are very difficult to answer and which need not be discussed here. At all events the conquest narrative in the first half of the book of Joshua is, in all probability, not derived from the Pentateuchal 'sources'. It is, therefore, all the more important that in Numbers, within the sphere of the 'old sources', we undoubtedly find the beginnings of the conquest theme. These show, at the same time, that the subsequent conquest by Israel (21.21ff.) or by individual Israelite tribes (32.1ff.) began in the southern part of the territory east of the Jordan and that, therefore, Canaan proper, which in any event would have to figure largely in an Israelite tradition about the conquest, was occupied from that starting-point, that is in a westerly direction across the lower Jordan valley (cf. Joshua 1–12).

II

FURTHER ORDINANCES OF GOD
AT SINAI

1.1–6.27

IN NUMBERS 1.1ff. the priestly narrative (P) is continued. According to the basic form of this narrative, immediately after the arrival of Israel at Sinai, Moses ascended the cloud-covered sacred mountain for forty days and forty nights (Ex. 24.15b–18) to receive the divine ordinances concerning the setting up and the furnishing of the cultic sanctuary (Ex. 25–28). The carrying out of these ordinances, probably* recorded in Ex. 39.32, 42, 43; 40.17, provided the necessary preliminary for the offering of Israel's first sacrifices which is recorded in Lev. 9.† After Israel's cultic worship had been thus legislated for and introduced, there was a need for certain regulations concerning the outward life of an Israel divided into twelve tribes. The narrative in Num. 1.1 takes up this theme. The relative ordinances are received by Moses no longer on the sacred mountain but, according to Num. 1.1, in the 'tent of meeting' which had been erected in the interval (Lev. 1.1 is somewhat different).

1. THE ORGANIZATION OF THE COMMUNITY OF THE TWELVE TRIBES: 1.1–2.34

1 ¹The LORD spoke to Moses in the wilderness of Sinai, in the tent of meeting, on the first day of the second month, in the second year after they had come out of the land of Egypt, saying, ²"Take a census of all the congregation of the people of Israel, by families, by fathers' houses, according to the number of names, every male head by head; ³from

* Cf. *Exodus*, pp. 280ff.   † Cf. *Leviticus*, pp. 74ff.

13

twenty years old and upward, all in Israel who are able to go forth to war, you and Aaron shall number them, company by company. 4And there shall be with you a man from each tribe, each man being the head of the house of his fathers. 5And these are the names of the men who shall attend you. From Reuben, Elizur the son of Shedeur; 6from Simeon, Shelumiel the son of Zurishaddai; 7from Judah, Nahshon the son of Amminadab; 8from Issachar, Nethanel the son of Zuar; 9from Zebulun, Eliab the son of Helon; 10from the sons of Joseph, from Ephraim, Elishama the son of Ammihud, and from Manasseh, Gamaliel the son of Pedahzur; 11from Benjamin, Abidan the son of Gideoni; 12from Dan, Ahiezer the son of Ammishaddai; 13from Asher, Pagiel the son of Ochran; 14from Gad, Eliasaph the son of Deuel; 15from Naphtali, Ahira the son of Enan.' 16These were the ones chosen from the congregation, the leaders of their ancestral tribes, the heads of the clans of Israel.

17 Moses and Aaron took these men who have been named, 18and on the first day of the second month, they assembled the whole congregation together, who registered themselves by families, by fathers' houses, according to the number of names from twenty years old and upward, head by head, 19as the LORD commanded Moses. So he numbered them in the wilderness of Sinai.

20 The people of Reuben, Israel's first-born, their generations, by their families, by their fathers' houses, according to the number of names, head by head, every male from twenty years old and upward, all who were able to go forth to war: 21the number of the tribe of Reuben was forty-six thousand five hundred.

22 Of the people of Simeon, their generations, by their families, by their fathers' houses, [those of them that were numbered,] according to the number of names, head by head, every male from twenty years old and upward, all who were able to go forth to war: 23the number of the tribe of Simeon was fifty-nine thousand three hundred.

24 Of the people of Gad, their generations, by their families, by their fathers' houses, according to the number of the names, from twenty years old and upward, all who were able to go forth to war: 25the number of the tribe of Gad was forty-five thousand six hundred and fifty.

26 Of the people of Judah, their generations, by their families, by their fathers' houses, according to the number of names, from twenty years old and upward, every man able to go forth to war: 27the number of the tribe of Judah was seventy-four thousand six hundred.

28 Of the people of Issachar, their generations, by their families, by their fathers' houses, according to the number of names, from twenty years old and upward, every man able to go forth to war: 29the number of the tribe of Issachar was fifty-four thousand four hundred.

30 Of the people of Zebulun, their generations, by their families, by their fathers' houses, according to the number of names, from twenty years old and upward, every man able to go forth to war: 31the

number of the tribe of Zebulun was fifty-seven thousand four hundred.

32 Of the people of Joseph, namely, of the people of Ephraim, their generations, by their families, by their fathers' houses, according to the number of names, from twenty years old and upward, every man able to go forth to war: ³³the number of the tribe of Ephraim was forty thousand five hundred.

34 Of the people of Manasseh, their generations, by their families, by their fathers' houses, according to the number of names, from twenty years old and upward, every man able to go forth to war: ³⁵the number of the tribe of Manasseh was thirty-two thousand two hundred.

36 Of the people of Benjamin, their generations, by their families, by their fathers' houses, according to the number of names, from twenty years old and upward, every man able to go forth to war: ³⁷the number of the tribe of Benjamin was thirty-five thousand four hundred.

38 Of the people of Dan, their generations, by their families, by their fathers' houses, according to the number of names, from twenty years old and upward, every man able to go forth to war: ³⁹the number of the tribe of Dan was sixty-two thousand seven hundred.

40 Of the people of Asher, their generations, by their families, by their fathers' houses, according to the number of names, from twenty years old and upward, every man able to go forth to war: ⁴¹the number of the tribe of Asher was forty-one thousand five hundred.

42 Of the people of Naphtali, their generations, by their families, by their fathers' houses, according to the number of names, from twenty years old and upward, every man able to go forth to war: ⁴³the number of the tribe of Naphtali was fifty-three thousand four hundred.

44 These are those who were numbered, whom Moses and Aaron numbered with the help of the leaders of Israel, twelve men, each representing his fathers' house. ⁴⁵So the whole number of the people of Israel, by their fathers' houses, from twenty years old and upward, every man able to go forth to war in Israel—⁴⁶their whole number was six hundred and three thousand five hundred and fifty.

47 But the Levites were not numbered by their ancestral tribe along with them. ⁴⁸For the LORD said to Moses, ⁴⁹'Only the tribe of Levi you shall not number, and you shall not take a census of them among the people of Israel; ⁵⁰but appoint the Levites over the tabernacle of the testimony, and over all its furnishings, and over all that belongs to it; they are to carry the tabernacle and all its furnishings, and they shall tend it, and shall encamp around the tabernacle. ⁵¹When the tabernacle is to set out, the Levites shall take it down; and when the tabernacle is to be pitched, the Levites shall set it up. And if any one else comes near, he shall be put to death. ⁵²The people of Israel shall pitch their tents by their companies, every man by his own camp and every man by his own standard; ⁵³but the Levites shall encamp around the tabernacle of the testimony, that there may be no wrath upon the congregation of the people of Israel; and the Levites shall keep charge

of the tabernacle of the testimony.' 54Thus did the people of Israel; they did according to all that the LORD commanded Moses.

2 1The LORD said to Moses and Aaron, 2"The people of Israel shall encamp each by his own standard, with the ensigns of their fathers' houses; they shall encamp facing the tent of meeting on every side. 3Those to encamp on the east side toward the sunrise shall be of the standard of the camp of Judah by their companies, the leader of the people of Judah being Nahshon the son of Amminadab, 4his host as numbered being seventy-four thousand six hundred. 5Those to encamp next to him shall be the tribe of Issachar, the leader of the people of Issachar being Nethanel the son of Zuar, 6his host as numbered being fifty-four thousand four hundred. 7Then the tribe of Zebulun, the leader of the people of Zebulun being Eliab the son of Helon, 8his host as numbered being fifty-seven thousand four hundred. 9The whole number of the camp of Judah, by their companies, is a hundred and eighty-six thousand four hundred. They shall set out first on the march.

10 'On the south side shall be the standard of the camp of Reuben by their companies, the leader of the people of Reuben being Elizur the son of Shedeur, 11his host as numbered being forty-six thousand five hundred. 12And those to encamp next to him shall be the tribe of Simeon, the leader of the people of Simeon being Shelumiel the son of Zurishaddai, 13his host as numbered being fifty-nine thousand three hundred. 14Then the tribe of Gad, the leader of the people of Gad being Eliasaph the son of Reuel, 15his host as numbered being forty-five thousand six hundred and fifty. 16The whole number of the camp of Reuben, by their companies, is a hundred and fifty-one thousand four hundred and fifty. They shall set out second.

17 'Then the tent of meeting shall set out, with the camp of the Levites in the midst of the camps; as they encamp, so shall they set out, each in position, standard by standard.

18 'On the west side shall be the standard of the camp of Ephraim by their companies, the leader of the people of Ephraim being Elishama the son of Ammihud, 19his host as numbered being forty thousand five hundred. 20And next to him shall be the tribe of Manasseh, the leader of the people of Manasseh being Gamaliel the son of Pedahzur, 21his host as numbered being thirty-two thousand two hundred. 22Then the tribe of Benjamin, the leader of the people of Benjamin being Abidan the son of Gideoni, 23his host as numbered being thirty-five thousand four hundred. 24The whole number of the camp of Ephraim, by their companies, is a hundred and eight thousand one hundred. They shall set out third on the march.

25 'On the north side shall be the standard of the camp of Dan by their companies, the leader of the people of Dan being Ahiezer the son of Ammishaddai, 26his host as numbered being sixty-two thousand seven hundred. 27And those to encamp next to him shall be the tribe of Asher, the leader of the people of Asher being Pagiel the son of Ochran, 28his host as numbered being forty-one thousand five hundred. 29Then the tribe of Naphtali, the leader of the people of Naphtali being Ahira

the son of Enan, ³⁰his host as numbered being fifty-three thousand four hundred. ³¹The whole number of the camp of Dan is a hundred and fifty-seven thousand six hundred. They shall set out last, standard by standard.'

32 These are the people of Israel as numbered by their fathers' houses; all in the camps who were numbered by their companies were six hundred and three thousand five hundred and fifty. ³³But the Levites were not numbered among the people of Israel, as the LORD commanded Moses.

34 Thus did the people of Israel. According to all that the LORD commanded Moses, so they encamped by their standards, and so they set out, every one in his family, according to his fathers' house.

It is generally recognized, in so far as the division into sources is accepted, that this whole section belongs to the Priestly narrative-source of the Pentateuch and the schematization of phraseology and structure points to such a conclusion, as does also the interest in system and order. There is no significant argument against accepting the fact that the section already belongs to the basic form of this source (P) and that, on the whole, it is a literary unit. [1.48–54] Only 1.48–54, which is dependent on the remark made in 1.47 and, on the other hand, anticipates a theme introduced only later, namely, the organization of the camp and of the Levites, is from a later writer who wanted to see the special position of the Levites at least briefly mentioned and envisaged at this point.

The organization of the community of the twelve tribes of Israel, as it is constituted at Sinai according to this section, is concerned only with purely external matters, namely, first of all its numerical strength at this particular point in time on the basis of the division into twelve tribes and then the subsequent rules for the allocation of tribal camping sites, valid for this period in the wilderness and for the order of the march when they moved on. The existence of an internal division into twelve tribes, genealogically derived from the sons of Jacob (cf. Ex. 1.2–4P) is presupposed in the stereotyped mention of 'families' and 'fathers' houses'. Not until the list in Num. 26.5–51, which in turn lies at the basis of the secondary passage Gen. 46.8–27,* are these 'families' explained as being the posterity of the descendants of Jacob. Nowhere in P is any explanation found of the term 'fathers' houses', that is the descendants who live together of forefathers who are still alive.

Within the framework of the stereotyped P formulae which are

* Cf. Gerhard von Rad, *Genesis*, E.T. (Revised) 1963, pp. 397f.

constantly repeated in every detail, the section before us contains strikingly factual material (names and figures). The question thus arises as to whether P could go back to older, and perhaps even very much older, traditions. This question, at least in some cases, is in all probability to be answered in the affirmative, although it still has to be explained how P could have had access to such old traditional material. [1.5–15] This is the case in the first place with the list of names in 1.5–15. In the present context this has a somewhat surprising effect. It is clear that Moses and Aaron would need helpers for the task of making a census of the people, but it is less obvious that their names would have to be enumerated *in extenso*. Besides, the list is not smoothly attached to 1.4. The instruction regarding the selection of the census helpers in 1.4 would be superfluous if, in the divine ordinance, the list of names followed immediately. The supposition is therefore confirmed that P has inserted in his narrative, at a point which seemed to be reasonably suitable, an old traditional list of names. This supposition is supported by the fact that these names give a definite impression of antiquity. There is a total lack of formations with the divine name 'Yahweh', as later became the practice in Israel. It is true that this could be due to conscious reflection, in view of the fact that the revelation of the divine name Yahweh lies in the fairly recent past (Ex. 6.2, 3P). More important, therefore, is the fact that there is a striking frequency of the occurrence of name-elements (especially '-zur' and 'ammi', each three times) which now, in the light of the texts from Mari,* are shown to have been current in a stratum of population which had many relationships with ancient Israel.† The list of names is then closely linked with a census of the Israelite tribes which presents a special form of the twelve-tribe system which, if the above conclusion concerning the proper names is correct, must also go back to an old tradition. This special form differs from the enumeration of the sons of Jacob which goes back to Gen. 29.31–30.24 (JE) and which is also usual in P (Gen. 35.22b–29; Ex. 1.2–4), in one respect, namely that Levi is omitted (cf. 1.47; 3.5ff.). In spite of this, however, the number twelve is maintained by means of a division of Joseph into Ephraim and Manasseh (they appear of equal status with the other tribes; the

---

* Cf. W. Röllig, *Religion in Geschichte und Gegenwart* (3rd edition), Vol. IV, col. 744–7.
† Cf. M. Noth, *Mari und Israel: Beiträge zur historischen Theologie* 16, 1953, pp. 127–52.

mention of the name Joseph in v. 10 is a compensatory addition). There is also the additional difference that the last four tribes mentioned (vv. 12–15) appear in a different order. The order of the tribes in 1.5–15 is unique in the Old Testament, but it has very close connections with the order in 1.20ff. and 26.5ff. Since it is unlikely that P, of himself, would have provided the twelve-tribe system with a special form differing from the traditional one, the conclusion is forced upon us once more that this goes back to an old tradition. The connection between the persons introduced by name in 1.5–15 and the tribal system is made in 1.16 by means of several technical terms, of which the most important would seem to be the one which contains the term 'tribes'. While the expression 'the ones chosen from the congregation' is probably a P-formulation, and the expression 'the heads of the clans of Israel' sounds very vague and also recurs from time to time (apart from Num. 10.4, also in Josh. 22.21, 30), the expression 'the leaders of their ancestral tribes' is unique in this form and one might expect that it has not been artificially created by P but has been taken over along with the preceding list. The word 'leader' translates the Hebrew word *nāsī'*.* It must, then, be accepted that in 1.5–15(16) P is citing an old list of the *n^{e}sī'īm* of the twelve Israelite tribes. These *n^{e}sī'īm* were, therefore, at one time in the early period of Israel's history, officials and not simply helpers called in to assist in the isolated, passing occasion of a census, for they appear also in 2.3ff.—and there only with the title *nāsī'*—as permanent and perhaps lifelong tribal representatives. The *n^{e}sī'īm* list, if it is authentic, must go back to the time of the separate existence of the tribes as members of the totality of Israel. Since the togetherness of the twelve tribes is presupposed, the period after the conquest is the earliest possible one that comes to mind. Since on the other hand, however, the individual significance of the tribes ceased with the formation of the state under David, we must very probably think of the pre-Davidic period.

[1.1–3] The real theme of ch. 1 is the census of the people which is commanded by Yahweh. Whatever thoughts there may have been against such a census as the verification of the extent of the divine blessing (cf. II Sam. 24.1, 3, 10ff. and also the secondary 'P'-section Ex. 30.11–16), they are not expressed nor even hinted at. According to Num. 1 the census is part of the constitution of the external

* Noth throughout translates *nāsī'* as 'spokesman'. Tr. For this technical term, as found already in the Book of the Covenant (Ex. 22.27), see *Exodus*, pp. 187f.

organization of Israel, just as similar kinds of surveys were probably usual among confederated communities in ancient times, such as are, for example, expressly testified to in the state of Mari.* The date in v. 1b is in accordance with P's dating, that is, from the time of the exodus from Egypt (cf. Ex. 19.1; 40.17). Its repetition in v. 18 indicates that the divine command was implemented on the same day as it was given. According to vv. 2–3, all men of twenty years old and upward are to be enumerated. According to the reference to military service in v. 3, repeated, along with the reference to twenty years old, in stereotyped form from v. 20 onwards, it would appear to be a census of those who are capable of bearing arms. In fact, already in the ancient East such censuses must have been undertaken in the interests of the orderly presentation of military forces (cf. also I Sam. 11.8 and the role of the military commander and his officers in II Sam. 24.2ff.). It is true that in the continuation of P's narrative there is no question of any military activity on the part of the Israelite tribes and clearly the census, carried out from the military point of view, is for him simply one element in the external organization of the people. [1.18] There is an apparent inconsistency between the reference to the ability to bear arms and the strange expression in v. 18 which derives from the verb 'to be born'† and seems to refer to a 'register of births' in which new-born children would be entered. But perhaps this expression is here simply meant to be understood in the general sense of receiving and entering names.

[1.20–46] In 1.20–46 the result of the census is given within the framework of an extensive scheme which contains the constant repetition of the formulae of v. 3. In this section we have a form of the twelve-tribe system which agrees almost exactly with that which appears in 26.5–51 which also concerns a census, but with one difference, namely that the tribes of Ephraim and Manasseh are introduced in the reverse order (cf. Gen. 48.13–20). These two last-named forms (i.e. in 1.20–46 and 26.5–51) differ from that in the *neśi'îm* list of 1.5–15 in that in them Gad appears in third place, that is in the place occupied in the traditional system by Levi, who, naturally, does not figure either in 1.20–46 or in 26.5–51. The figure twelve is again preserved by means of the independent position of

---

* Cf. J.-R. Kupper in *Studia Mariana*, 1950, pp. 99–110.

† The word in question, *wayyityal^edu*, is translated by 'registered themselves' in RSV. Noth's translation, 'so that they could be entered in the register of births', is perhaps closer to the Hebrew. Tr.

Ephraim and Manasseh (the reference at the beginning of v. 32 to the 'people of Joseph' is a reconciliatory editorial addition). This fact is evidence that here, too, we are dealing with a twelve-tribe system stemming from an early period and taken over by P.

The main problem of the section 1.20–46 consists in the figures that are given. Their size, as is generally recognized, lies outside the sphere of what is historically acceptable. In no sense do they bear even a tolerable relationship to what we otherwise know of the strength of military conscription in the ancient East. Even the suggestion that the figures, contrary to the statement of the text, originally included the women and children and were only later, erroneously, transferred to those capable of bearing arms, does not help much, since even then we have a mass of population which is contrary to all historical probability. Are we, then, dealing with figures which have simply been invented? This supposition has against it the fact that the figures give a very realistic impression. It is true that they are round figures (to the nearest hundred, in one case to fifty), but otherwise they appear quite distinctive; above all, the division among the individual tribes seems uncontrived in so far as some tribes who, as we know from the later course of Israelite history in Palestine, played no decisive role, are credited with strikingly high numbers (e.g. Simeon and Dan). Some have therefore thought that in the whole system there is hidden some kind of numerical speculation behind which might somehow lie the numerical value of the consonants of the Hebrew alphabet. To this we can only say that no attempt along these lines has so far succeeded in throwing even a tentative light on the recorded figures. The difficulty is increased by the fact that such an attempt would have to be authenticated also with regard to the figures in 26.5–51, which in individual cases differ completely from those given in 1.20–46, but which over all provide a very similar picture. If, then, we must very probably abandon this attempt at an explanation, there still remains the assumption, which has already been noted more than once, that in the lists of figures the Hebrew word *'elep* originally did not mean 'thousand' but was intended to denote a (military) unit (something like 'troop'). There is no certain proof for such an original meaning, but it cannot be regarded as out of the question that just as the word for 'a large number' came to have the numerical significance 'ten thousand', so a word with the basic meaning of 'troop' has developed into the numerical word 'thousand'. It is also noteworthy that the numerals up to and including 'hundred' are common to all the Semitic languages, but that beyond that point the various languages have gone their separate ways (Akkadian has a quite different word for 'thousand') and have, in all probability, chosen words which were not numerals from very ancient ('primitive Semitic') times, but which originally had some other definite meaning. If we take, for the sake of argument, in Num. ch. 1 and 26, *'elep* in the sense of 'troop' (the question of its relationship to the common Semitic and Hebrew word *'elep*=herd complicates the matter still further), then that would signify that in the original form of the census list there is given first for each tribe the number of 'troops' which are set up from within it and then the rounded figure of those individuals capable of bearing arms who belonged to the 'troops'. Therefore, for example (vv. 20–21), 'Reuben: forty-six troops, five hundred (men)'. We must be clear that in this we are departing from the text, for as it stands *'elep* is meant to be taken in the sense of 'thousand', as we can see from the total given in v. 46 and also from the regular recurrence of 'and' between the thousands and the hundreds. It would not, however, be very surprising if the old meaning of *'elep*='troop' had been lost to a later age and had become unknown, so that they could understand *'elep* only in the sense of 'thousand' even in a document handed down from a very early time. The hypothesis advanced here has the merit of presenting, in the original form of the census list, figures which, for Israel's early period, appear to be completely probable, so that the suggestion of fabricated or contrived figures is rendered superfluous. This hypothesis can also be credited with the fact that the figures given for the 'troops' and for those capable of bearing arms associated with them bear a tolerably suitable relationship to each other, a fact which is by no means self-evident and which is, in addition, valid also for the corresponding list in Num. 26. As the total figure for the twelve tribes there would result that of five hundred and ninety-eight 'troops' and five thousand five hundred and fifty capable of bearing arms. On the average, therefore, each 'troop' would be made up of nine or ten men. The consequent smallness of the military unit of a 'troop' need cause no surprise if we look, by way of comparison, at a few figures from the El-Amarna tablets (the edition of J. A. Knudtzon).* According to them, for example, the king Rib-Addi of Byblos asked from the

* J. A. Knudtzon, *Die El-Amarna Tafeln*, Leipzig, 1907–15. The two letters referred to do not figure in the selection given in James B. Pritchard, *Ancient Near Eastern Texts Relating to the Old Testament*, Princeton, 2nd ed. 1955. Tr.

great Egyptian Pharaoh for the defence of his city against outside enemies on one occasion (108.66ff.) an emergency contingent of troops of twenty men each from Nubia and from Egypt, and on another occasion (133.16f.) for only ten men from Nubia. The departures from this average figure of nine to ten men to each 'troop' are no greater than is to be expected from the setting up of tribal conscriptions according to the given genealogical and geographical relationships. In Num. 1 the extremes are found in Simeon, where on the average we have only slightly more than five men per 'troop' and in Gad, where the corresponding average figure lies at a little under fifteen. If the suggested hypothesis fits the situation presented in the census lists of Num. 1, then the latter must stem from a comparatively early period. It is true that the twelve tribes are presumed to be living together on Palestinian soil, but their independent existence before they were moulded into a single state is also presumed. After the formation of the state, statistics are given and calculated in relation to the political entities 'Israel' and 'Judah' (cf. I Sam. 11.8; II Sam. 24.9) and not according to the tribal system. It is not in itself unlikely that, in this period of the individual existence of the tribes before the formation of the state, statistics of a conscription should have been drawn up, even if we have only the testimony of the late P-narrative which does not usually provide us with precise dates.

[2.1–31] The only thing in ch. 2 that is of a peculiar nature is the organization of the camp and the march. All the specific separate elements originate from ch. 1 or its basic form. That Israel, as it camped and wandered in the wilderness, must have had and did have a hard and fast set of rules for rest and movement and that this set of rules could only have gone back to a detailed, divine ordinance, is again set forth by P with great diffuseness. The idea of the organization of a camp can be based either on the concept of a military camp or else on the concept of a pilgrim camp on the occasion of some cultic festival. In the present chapter elements of both concepts are present. The catchword 'host' (ṣābā'), which occurs with each tribe and which, from time to time, includes 'those who are mustered',* is reminiscent of a military camp. The grouping together on each occasion of the 'hosts' of three tribes under one 'standard' doubtless

* Noth renders what appears in the RSV as 'his host as numbered' by 'his host and those who are mustered' (e.g. v. 4), reading, with the Samaritan, upᵉqūdāw instead of MT upᵉqūdēhem. Tr.

also belongs in the same context. The Hebrew word for this (*degel*), in the only place in which it occurs in the Old Testament (S. of S. 2.4), apart from the present chapter and those passages influenced by it (Num. 1.52; 10.14ff.), apparently means 'flag'. From this it is easy to proceed to the meaning of a division of an army gathered round a flag. Finally, the repetition of the conscript figures from ch. 1 also points to the idea of a military camp. On the whole, however, ch. 2 makes one think, rather, of a pilgrim camp, with the reservation that, with regard to the concept that the P-narrative has of Israel sojourning in the wilderness, it is by no means a question of an either-or point of view. The organization of the tribes around the central sanctuary, which is not at all suitable for a serious war, conjures up the picture of a pilgrimage festival at a great sanctuary at which the vast crowds of pilgrims set up their tents round the central cultic point. It is highly likely that such festival camps existed in ancient Israel at the period of the conquest and, indeed, there are examples of such a practice from the most recent Palestinian past.* Therefore in Num. 2, P is in contact with an actual fact, but has, according to his own concepts, strongly schematized the details.

The twelve tribes are ranged in groups ('standards'), three to each of the cardinal points—the latter determined from the central sanctuary—but nothing is said about their positioning within these groups. At the basis of this there is precisely the same twelve-tribe system as in 1.20–42. In this system Judah is in fourth place, that is, at the head of the second quarter. From this it was easy for P to show his intended preference for the tribe of Judah. In P this preference is perhaps not so much based on the fact that the Davidic dynasty, which had also been rulers of Jerusalem, had been Judaic, but rather on the fact that after 721 BC the state of Judah had alone been left as a comparatively independent political power in the territory of old Israel and that therefore the tribe of Judah, as the most important element in the state of Judah, seemed called to represent the totality of Israel and also, after the disaster of 587 BC, remained substantially the bearer of the traditions that were handed down. The preference of P for the tribe of Judah finds expression in the fact that the 'standard' borne by Judah, to which, according to the system in 1.20–42, the tribes of Issachar and Zebulun also belonged, is mentioned first (vv. 3–9) and has designated as its place the front of the whole camp complex, that is, according to the usual orientation, the

* Cf. H.-J. Kraus, *Worship in Israel*, E.T. 1966, pp. 130ff.

east side, and has the leading position in the order of the march (v. 9). Everything else follows from this, namely that, starting from the east, the rest of the cardinal points are enumerated in a clockwise direction. Thus the first group of the tribal system of 1.20–42, the 'standard of the camp of Reuben' along with the tribes of Simeon and Gad, is positioned on the south side and is allocated the second position in the order of the march (vv. 10–16); the third group, the 'standard of the camp of Ephraim' along with the tribes of Manasseh and Benjamin, came on the west side and had to march in third place (vv. 18–24); so there remained finally for the last group, the 'standard of the camp of Dan' along with the tribes of Asher and Naphtali, the north side and the last position in the order of the march (vv. 25–31). The allocation of these positions follows in schematic fashion from the preceding tribal enumeration and has absolutely nothing to do with the position of the (later) tribal possessions west of the Jordan. The last group, the northern one, is, it is true, made up of those tribes which settled furthest away in northern Palestine. But this agreement is purely coincidental, for there is otherwise no question of such agreement (cf. especially Issachar and Zebulun). The mention of the tent of meeting in v. 17 is of doubtful authenticity. That the tent of meeting should form the centre of the entire camp has already been mentioned in v. 2 and is self-evident. In v. 17 it is only laid down, with regard to the order of the march, that even on the way the sanctuary should be in the centre of the tribal 'camps' and from the position of v. 17 it is to be understood that the first two 'standards' are to precede the tent of meeting and the last two to follow it. This idea was obvious and must have commended itself by the fact that, thereby, *en route* the sanctuary was protected by a great vanguard and a great rearguard. For all that, the short note in v. 17a (v. 17b gives a quite general reason for it) gives the impression of being an addition, especially in view of the mention of the 'camp of the Levites' which anticipates the detailed organization of the Levites in ch. 3–4. The short notices concerning the order of the march in vv. 9b, 16b, 24b and 31b may have occasioned the later inclusion of the sanctuary in this order.

The wearisome repetition of all the names of the tribal 'leaders' from 1.5–15 as well as the figures of all those who were 'mustered' from 1.20–42 and which are totalled once more for the four 'standards' (vv. 9a, 16a, 24a, 31a)—these additions, too, presume the understanding of the word *'elep* as the numeral 'thousand' (cf. above

p. 21f.)—all this is to show that the statistical enumeration of the organization and effective strength of the tribes according to ch. 1 formed the basis for the definitive organization of the life and sojourn of Israel in the wilderness. It shows, too, that the office of 'leader', although instituted in the first place for the carrying out of the census, came to be a permanent institution.

[2.32–34] The recapitulatory final section in vv. 32–34, which once again gives the total number and stresses the exclusion of the Levites from the conscription of the other Israelites, ends, in v. 34, with a concise conclusion to the directions which began at 2.1.

2. THE ORGANIZATION OF THE LEVITES: 3.1–4.49

3 [1]These are the generations of Aaron and Moses at the time when the LORD spoke with Moses on Mount Sinai. [2]These are the names of the sons of Aaron: Nadab the first-born, and Abihu, Eleazar, and Itha-mar; [3]these are the names of the sons of Aaron, the anointed priests, whom he ordained to minister in the priest's office. [4]But Nadab and Abihu died before the LORD when they offered unholy fire before the LORD in the wilderness of Sinai; and they had no children. So Eleazar and Ithamar served as priests in the lifetime of Aaron their father.

5 And the LORD said to Moses, [6]'Bring the tribe of Levi near, and set them before Aaron the priest, that they may minister to him. [7]They shall perform duties for him and for the whole congregation before the tent of meeting, as they minister at the tabernacle; [8]they shall have charge of all the furnishings of the tent of meeting, and attend to the duties for the people of Israel as they minister at the tabernacle. [9]And you shall give the Levites to Aaron and his sons; they are wholly given to him from among the people of Israel. [10]And you shall appoint Aaron and his sons, and they shall attend to their priesthood; but if any one else comes near, he shall be put to death.'

11 And the LORD said to Moses, [12]'Behold, I have taken the Levites from among the people of Israel instead of every first-born that opens the womb among the people of Israel. The Levites shall be mine, [13]for all the first-born are mine; on the day that I slew all the first-born in the land of Egypt, I consecrated for my own all the first-born in Israel, both of man and of beast; they shall be mine: I am the LORD.'

14 And the LORD said to Moses in the wilderness of Sinai, [15]'Number the sons of Levi, by fathers' houses and by families; every male from a month old and upward you shall number.' [16]So Moses numbered them according to the word of the LORD, as he was commanded. [17]And these were the sons of Levi by their names: Gershon and Kohath and Merari. [18]And these are the names of the sons of Gershon by their families: Libni and Shimei. [19]And the sons of Kohath by their families: Amram, Izhar, Hebron, and Uzziel. [20]And the sons of Merari by their families: Mahli and Mushi. These are the families of the Levites, by their fathers' houses.

21 Of Gershon were the family of the Libnites and the family of the Shimeites; these were the families of the Gershonites. ²²Their number according to the number of all the males from a month old and upward was seven thousand five hundred. ²³The families of the Gershonites were to encamp behind the tabernacle on the west, ²⁴with Eliasaph the son of Lael as head of the fathers' house of the Gershonites. ²⁵And the charge of the sons of Gershon in the tent of meeting was to be the tabernacle, the tent with its covering, the screen for the door of the tent of meeting, ²⁶the hangings of the court, [the screen for the door of the court which is around the tabernacle and the altar, and its cords;] all the service pertaining to these.

27 Of Kohath were the family of the Amramites, and the family of the Izharites, and the family of the Hebronites, and the family of the Uzzielites; these are the families of the Kohathites. ²⁸According to the number of all the males, from a month old and upward, there were eight thousand three* hundred, attending to the duties of the sanctuary. ²⁹The families of the sons of Kohath were to encamp on the south side of the tabernacle, ³⁰with Elizaphan the son of Uzziel as head of the fathers' house of the families of the Kohathites. ³¹And their charge was to be the ark, the table, the lampstand, the altars, the vessels of the sanctuary with which the priests minister, and the screen; all the service pertaining to these. ³²[And Eleazar the son of Aaron the priest was to be chief over the leaders of the Levites, and to have oversight of those who had charge of the sanctuary.]

33 Of Merari were the family of the Mahlites and the family of the Mushites: these are the families of Merari. ³⁴Their number according to the number of all the males from a month old and upward was six thousand two hundred. ³⁵And the head of the fathers' house of the families of Merari was Zuriel the son of Abihail; they were to encamp on the north side of the tabernacle. ³⁶And the appointed charge of the sons of Merari was to be the frames of the tabernacle, the bars, the pillars, the bases, and all their accessories; all the service pertaining to these. ³⁷Also the pillars of the court round about, with their bases and pegs and cords.

38 And those to encamp before the tabernacle on the east, before the tent of meeting toward the sunrise, were Moses and Aaron and his sons, having charge of the rites within the sanctuary, whatever had to be done for the people of Israel; and any one else who came near was to be put to death. ²⁹All who were numbered of the Levites, whom Moses and Aaron numbered at the commandment of the LORD, by families, all the males from a month old and upward, were twenty-two thousand.

40 And the LORD said to Moses, 'Number all the first-born males of the people of Israel, from a month old and upward, taking their number by names. ⁴¹And you shall take the Levites for me—I am the LORD—

---

* Instead of the present figure 'eight thousand six hundred', we must surely read with several Septuagint MSS, in view of the total in v. 39, 'eight thousand three hundred' (Hebrew *wšlš* instead of *wšš*).

instead of all the first-born among the people of Israel, and the cattle of the Levites instead of all the firstlings among the cattle of the people of Israel.' ⁴²So Moses numbered all the first-born among the people of Israel, as the LORD commanded him. ⁴³And all the first-born males, according to the number of names, from a month old and upward as numbered were twenty-two thousand two hundred and seventy-three.

44 And the LORD said to Moses, ⁴⁵'Take the Levites instead of all the first-born among the people of Israel, and the cattle of the Levites instead of their cattle; and the Levites shall be mine: I am the LORD. ⁴⁶And for the redemption of the two hundred and seventy-three of the first-born of the people of Israel, over and above the number of the male Levites, ⁴⁷you shall take five shekels apiece; reckoning by the shekel of the sanctuary, the shekel of twenty gerahs, you shall take them, ⁴⁸and give the money by which the excess number of them is redeemed to Aaron and his sons.' ⁴⁹So Moses took the redemption money from those who were over and above those redeemed by the Levites; ⁵⁰from the first-born of the people of Israel he took the money, one thousand three hundred and sixty-five shekels, reckoned by the shekel of the sanctuary; ⁵¹and Moses gave the redemption money to Aaron and his sons, according to the word of the LORD, as the LORD commanded Moses.

4 ¹The LORD said to Moses and Aaron, ²'Take a census of the sons of Kohath from among the sons of Levi, by their families and their fathers' houses, ³from thirty years old up to fifty years old, all who can enter the service, to do the work in the tent of meeting. ⁴This is the service of the sons of Kohath in the tent of meeting: the most holy things. ⁵When the camp is to set out, Aaron and his sons shall go in and take down the veil of the screen, and cover the ark of the testimony with it; ⁶then they shall put on it a covering of goatskin, and spread over that a cloth all of blue, and shall put in its poles. ⁷And over the table of the bread of the Presence they shall spread a cloth of blue, and put upon it the plates, the dishes for incense, the bowls, and the flagons for the drink offering; the continual bread also shall be on it; ⁸then they shall spread over them a cloth of scarlet, and cover the same with a covering of goatskin, and shall put in its poles. ⁹And they shall take a cloth of blue, and cover the lampstand for the light, with its lamps, its snuffers, its trays, and all the vessels for oil with which it is supplied: ¹⁰and they shall put it with all its utensils in a covering of goatskin and put it upon the carrying frame. ¹¹And over the golden altar they shall spread a cloth of blue, and cover it with a covering of goatskin, and shall put in its poles; ¹²and they shall take all the vessels of the service which are used in the sanctuary, and put them in a cloth of blue, and cover them with a covering of goatskin, and put them on the carrying frame. ¹³And they shall take away the ashes from the altar, and spread a purple cloth over it; ¹⁴and they shall put on it all the utensils of the altar, which are used for the service there, the firepans, the forks, the shovels, and the basins, all the utensils of the altar; and they shall spread upon it a covering of goatskin, and shall put in its poles. ¹⁵And when Aaron and his sons have finished covering the sanctuary and all

the furnishings of the sanctuary, as the camp sets out, after that the sons of Kohath shall come to carry these, but they must not touch the holy things lest they die. These are the things of the tent of meeting which the sons of Kohath are to carry.

[16 'And Eleazar the son of Aaron the priest shall have charge of the oil for the light, the fragrant incense, the continual cereal offering, and the anointing oil, with the oversight of all the tabernacle and all that is in it, of the sanctuary and its vessels.'

17 The LORD said to Moses and Aaron, 18'Let not the tribe of the families of the Kohathites be destroyed from among the Levites; 19but deal thus with them, that they may live and not die when they come near to the most holy things: Aaron and his sons shall go in and appoint them each to his task and to his burden, 20but they shall not go in to look upon the holy things even for a moment, lest they die.']

21 The LORD said to Moses, 22'Take a census of the sons of Gershon also, by their families and their fathers' houses; 23from thirty years old up to fifty years old, you shall number them, all who can enter for service, to do the work in the tent of meeting. 24This is the service of the families of the Gershonites, in serving and bearing burdens: 25they shall carry the curtains of the tabernacle, and the tent of meeting with its covering, and the covering of sheepskin that is on top of it, and the screen for the door of the tent of meeting, 26and the hangings of the court, and the screen for the entrance of the gate of the court which is around the tabernacle and the altar, and their cords, and all the equipment for their service; and they shall do all that needs to be done with regard to them. 27All the service of the sons of the Gershonites shall be at the command of Aaron and his sons, in all that they are to carry, and in all that they have to do; and you shall assign to their charge all that they are to carry. 28This is the service of the families of the sons of the Gershonites in the tent of meeting, [and their work is to be under the oversight of Ithamar the son of Aaron the priest.]

29 'As for the sons of Merari, you shall number them by their families and their fathers' houses; 30from thirty years old up to fifty years old, you shall number them, every one that can enter the service, to do the work of the tent of meeting. 31And this is what they are charged to carry, as the whole of their service in the tent of meeting: the frames of the tabernacle, with its bars, pillars, and bases, 32and the pillars of the court round about with their bases, pegs, and cords, with all their equipment and all their accessories, and you shall assign by name the objects which they are required to carry. 33This is the service of the families of the sons of Merari, the whole of their service in the tent of meeting, [under the hand of Ithamar the son of Aaron the priest.']

34 And Moses and Aaron and the leaders of the congregation numbered the sons of the Kohathites, by their families and their fathers' houses, 35from thirty years old up to fifty years old, every one that could enter the service, for work in the tent of meeting; 36and their number by families was two thousand seven hundred and fifty. 37This was the number of the families of the Kohathites, all who served

in the tent of meeting, whom Moses and Aaron numbered according to the commandment of the LORD by Moses.

38 The number of the sons of Gershon, by their families and their fathers' houses, 39from thirty years old up to fifty years old, every one that could enter the service for work in the tent of meeting—40their number by their families and their fathers' houses was two thousand six hundred and thirty. 41This was the number of the families of the sons of Gershon, all who served in the tent of meeting, whom Moses and Aaron numbered according to the commandment of the LORD.

42 The number of the families of the sons of Merari, by their families and their fathers' houses, 43from thirty years old up to fifty years old, every one that could enter the service, for work in the tent of meeting—44their number by families was three thousand two hundred. 45These are those who were numbered of the families of the sons of Merari, whom Moses and Aaron numbered according to the commandment of the LORD by Moses.

46 All those who were numbered of the Levites, whom Moses and Aaron and the leaders of Israel numbered, by their families and their fathers' houses, 47from thirty years old up to fifty years old, every one that could enter to do the work of service and the work of bearing burdens in the tent of meeting, 48those who were numbered of them were eight thousand five hundred and eighty. 49According to the commandment of the LORD through Moses they were appointed, each to his task of serving or carrying; thus they were numbered by him, as the LORD commanded Moses.

The present extensive section is closely linked with the preceding one in so far as in it those statements which, in the first two chapters, had pertained to the twelve tribes of Israel are now applied to the distinctive group 'the Levites'. In addition, for 'the Levites', a genealogical structure is also provided and on the basis of this structure there follows a numerical review, 'leaders' of the groups of Levites are mentioned by name and their positions in the camp are given. The style, too, is the same, with its schematization, its circumstantiality and its predilection for wearisome repetition. It is, therefore, not to be doubted that ch. 3 and 4 also belong within the compass of the P-narrative. The peculiar nature of the Levites has occasioned the emergence into the foreground of a theme which has no place in the treatment of the Israelite tribes, namely the theme of their peculiar tasks and duties. In the present section this theme takes the most prominent place.

It is, of course, well known that the complex of ch. 3 and 4 is not a literary unit, at least less so than the section concerning the Israelite tribes. Besides smaller signs of this lack of unity, there are the following indications: the isolatedness of the passage 3.1–4; the repeated new beginning in 3.5, 11, 14; the later resumption of the substance of 3.11–13 in 3.40–51; the different formulation of the same material in 3.18–20 on the one hand and in 3.21, 27, 33 on the other; the repetition of the substance of 3.25f., 31, 36f. in 4.4ff. It is now no longer possible to reconstruct, even with minimal certainty, the literary development of this complex of tradition and there is a lack of reliable points of reference even for the construction of a relative chronology of the individual elements. Probability would suggest that the theme of the classification of the Levites and the determining of the duties of the different groups, which, although not a unit even within itself, is treated so exhaustively, formed the basis and that further elements have become attached to it. This, however, does not answer the question of the relationship of this basis to the P-narrative. It can be taken as highly probable that the P-narrative, having, in ch. 1–2 and on the basis of a twelve-tribe system that had been handed down (cf. above pp. 18f., 20f.), dealt with the Israelite tribes with the exception of Levi, then went on to give, concerning 'the Levites' and their peculiar position, what appeared to be the requisite information; in other words the original P-narrative is to be credited with part of Num. 3–4 and that part is to be found in the basic form mentioned above. There must also be taken into account the possibility that, as in ch. 1–2, older, traditional material has been taken up and used in the P-narrative, not necessarily word for word, but as far as the substance of such material goes. A hard and fast judgment is particularly difficult, because the early and even the late history of the Levitical office is obscure. That the heart of Num. 3–4 is part of the P-narrative and has been subject to later expansion can be seen partly from an analysis of these chapters themselves and partly also from many obvious connections with other secondary P-elements, especially in Exodus.

[3.1–4] The very first section, 3.1–4, is to be regarded as secondary. It falls outside the framework and is added only because, in what follows, 'Aaron and his sons' are again mentioned. The introduction (v. 1) mentions Moses along with Aaron, although the former is not mentioned again, and gives what is, in the context, a completely meaningless indication of time. Aaron and Moses are never otherwise linked in a Levitical genealogy (contrast 26.57ff. and Ex. 6.16ff.). It is precisely only the sons of Aaron who are to be numbered and this follows in a stereotyped list (cf., too, Ex. 28.1) in which, in first place, there are the names of Nadab and Abihu, who appear in an old

tradition in Ex. 24.1, 9 (without, it is true, an express connection with
Aaron), who thus at one time were clearly classified as sons of Aaron
and, therefore, as priests, but who were again removed from this
position in the narrative of Lev. 10.1–7, to which passage verbal
reference is made in this present section (v. 4a). So there remained
the two sons of Aaron, Eleazar and Ithamar, who regularly appear as
such in the later period. They are both designated in v. 3 as 'the
anointed priests', and here anointing and the solemn action of
'filling the hand' seem to be presupposed as signs of installation
in office for all priests and not only for the high priest.* That Eleazar
and Ithamar, according to v. 4b, are said to have fulfilled their
priestly office 'before Aaron their father',† surely refers to the oversight of Aaron as high priest over the rest of the priests.

[3.5–10] In 3.5–10 we have what was probably in the original
P-narrative the introduction to what follows, introducing the 'tribe
of Levi' after the 'tribes' who were dealt with in ch. 1–2 (maṭṭē lēwî
like maṭṭē rǝ'ūbēn etc., 1.21ff.). Without any further preamble the
'tribe' of Levi is presumed to be on hand beside the twelve 'tribes' of
ch. 1–2, in a special position, it is true, that of 'ministering' before
'Aaron the priest', who here represents the priesthood as a whole and
who, strangely enough, is in no way genealogically linked with the
'tribe of Levi', but who is also simply there. The P-narrative has
already presupposed Moses (Ex. 6.2) and 'his brother' Aaron (Ex.
7.1) as persons previously known and does not feel that they need
any special introduction; it now leaves completely open the question
of the relationship between the 'secular tribe' Levi, derived from one
of the sons of Jacob (cf. Ex. 1.2), and the group charged with
particular tasks and known as the 'Levites', as well as the question
of how the relationship between 'priests' and 'Levites' arose and it
reads back, without being aware of any discrepancy, concepts of its
own period into its view of the Sinai period. The 'tribe of Levi', then,
was there (v. 6) and, through a free decision of Yahweh's, they were
set apart for service to the priests and the cultic community in the
sanctuary (v. 7). All that is said of this service is that they are to
'have charge of all the furnishings of the tent of meeting' (v. 8).
In what follows (3.21ff. and 4.4ff.) the service of the various Levitical
groups is made more precise and is confined to the external furnishings

---

* Cf., further, *Exodus*, pp. 230f., on Ex. 29.7 and *Leviticus*, pp. 153ff. on Lev.
21.10.
† So Noth's translation. RSV has 'in the lifetime of Aaron their father'. Tr.

of the wilderness sanctuary and, more especially, to its dismantling and transportation whenever Israel strikes camp during its wilderness wandering. This is exceedingly remarkable, since by the time of the P-narrative the presuppositions for such service no longer obtained. The fixing of the tasks of the Levites is, then, in P purely theoretical and is referred to the desert period of ancient Israel. There is no mention of any kind of participation in the sacrificial cult such as is envisaged in Ezek. 44.10–14, according to which the Levites are to 'slay the burnt offering and the sacrifice for the people'. Now Ezek. 44, in which the 'Levites' (v. 10), in accordance with the deuteronomic law, seem to be contrasted with 'the Levitical priests, the sons of Zadok' who have, therefore, not yet been linked genealogically with Aaron—Ezek. 44 is certainly to be put earlier than P. It follows, therefore, that P presumes the existence of the 'Levites', but denies to them even the modest cultic functions of Ezek. 44 and writes them off with theoretical tasks which can have had meaning only in Israel's former wilderness period. P could not disregard the Levites entirely, for they existed in his own day and their functions had presumably been defined in a definite way. This seems to follow from v. 9, in which P seems to be making use of a traditional formula. According to this 'the Levites' (so here instead of 'the tribe of Levi' in v. 6) were 'wholly' (this is presumably the significance of the verbal repetition)* 'given', i.e. assigned as a possession, and Aaron (as the representative of the priesthood) is designated as the possessor (otherwise in 8.16 where, in an almost identically worded sentence, Yahweh appears as the possessor). Persons said to be similarly 'given' (with the Aramaic technical term $n^e\underline{t}\bar{i}n\bar{i}m$ instead of the $n^e\underline{t}\bar{u}n\bar{i}m$ which is found here) appear alongside the Levites in the ranks of minor cultic personnel in the lists of Ezra 2.43, 58, 70=Neh. 7.46, 60, 73 and in other places of the chronicler's work. The origin of this idea must surely have been that persons are 'given' or 'assigned' to a sanctuary (so Josh. 9.27). P debases the Levites so much that he allows them to be 'given', 'made over' to the Aaronite priesthood, which alone has priestly rights (v. 10a), with the result that the stereotyped phrase about the death penalty for unauthorized approach extends to the Levites as well (v. 10b).

[3.11–13] A different view of the Levites is given in 3.11–13, where it is unusually strongly emphasized that they belong to Yahweh (vv. 12aɑb, 13b). This sounds like a favourably disposed correction

* The word 'given' ($n^e\underline{t}\bar{u}n\bar{i}m$) is repeated in the Hebrew. Tr.

of the preceding and is surely to be seen in this sense as a later addition. At the same time expression is given to the strange thought that Yahweh claims right of possession of the Levites as substitutes for his true right, namely the possession of the first-born males among all the Israelite tribes. That each first-born male (of man and beast) is to be 'given' to Yahweh is demanded in principle in Ex. 13.2; 22.27b, 28, and the idea is obviously that of the sacrifice of the first-born. Yet it is unlikely, and in any case not susceptible of proof, that the sacrifice of human first-born was ever practised in Israel. In Ex. 13.13; 34.20abα there is immediately added to this demand in principle the direction that the human first-born are to be 'redeemed' by—as can be deduced from the context—an animal sacrifice. That other ways of 'giving' the first-born, such as assigning him to a sanctuary, were ever customary in Israel cannot be proved (I Sam. 1.28 is concerned with the fulfilment of a special vow). It must, therefore, be an idea which exists only in the mind, that, according to the present passage, 'the Levites' (so in vv. 11, 12, in agreement with v. 9) as Yahweh's possession are the substitute for what is Yahweh's true right, the first-born of the rest of the Israelite tribes. In view of this idea, the animal sacrifice demanded as compensation in Ex. 13.13; 34.20abα would have been superfluous. One might even consider whether perhaps this late idea were not originally meant to provide a reason for a falling away in the offering of this animal sacrifice. In any case one cannot say that in this present passage the peculiar position of the Levites finds its basis. That position is, rather, presupposed as a given fact, based on the will of Yahweh, and here interpreted with emphasis on its significance as a dedication to Yahweh. Only from this starting-point did there follow the reference to the first-born.

[3.14–39] V. 14 is the start of the main part of this chapter and the substance of it is the directions for the division of the tribe of Levi and for the tasks of the individual groups. The division results in three groups (so, too, 26.57; otherwise in 26.58a) with additional sub-groups. This division is described in two different ways. [3.17–20] In vv. 17–20 it appears in the form of a genealogy of the tribal ancestors, as is usual in surveys of the Israelite tribes and families (cf., e.g., Gen. 46.9ff.). [3.21, 27, 33] On the other hand, the same names appear in vv. 21, 27 (33), not as personal names but as (derived) collectives, with only a very tentative assimilation to the first scheme. So, for example, v. 21 might be thought of as going back to the following basic form: 'These were the families of the Gershonites: the family of the Libnites and the family of the Shimeites.' The same would be true of v. 27 (the family of the Kohathites). The formulation of v. 33 (the families of Merari) is slightly different, because the name 'Merari' already has the gentilic ending -ī. Now, the genealogical presentation of vv. 17–20 corresponds, as has been noted, to the usual form and is probably to be attributed to P, who, in accordance with ch. 1–2, treats Levi as another Israelite 'tribe' (cf. v. 6). In contrast to vv. 17–20, the collective formulation of vv. 21, 27, 33 appears to be older and more original. It follows that P has presumably appropriated older material for the account of the division of the Levites and has anticipated its contents in his own formulation in vv. 17–20. The origin and significance of this division of the Levites is certainly very obscure. All that is certain is that a number of hard facts emerge from it which, for their part, have a similar, more or less complex history; for in 26.58a there occurs a division which partly agrees and partly disagrees with this one and which, with its simple juxtaposition of five 'families of Levi' gives the impression of being older than the division into three main groups and additional subgroups which is found in the present passage. The Levites, therefore, obviously had a history, from a 'sociological' point of view, going back earlier than the priestly narrative. Unfortunately, whatever may be the facts expressed by this division, the names of the main groups and the subgroups cannot be recognized with any certainty. Amongst the names of the main groups, Kohath and Merari are unintelligible and bear no recognizable relationship to anything. In the case of Gershon there is an obvious identification with that Gershom who, according to Ex. 2.22 *et al.*, was a son of Moses and, according to Judg. 18.30 was the father of the ancestor of the Danite priesthood. This identification would also seem to be correct in so far as there is probably a connection, even if the levitical Gershonites reveal nothing of a derivation from Moses (according to P, v. 17, Gershon was a son of Levi); the tracing back of Gershon/Gershom to Moses was, rather, an isolated peculiarity of the tradition. Since Gershon/Gershom in Judg. 18.30 appears, from a genealogical point of view, at the head of a priesthood and therefore occupies a fairly prominent position, the hypothesis might be hazarded that under the name 'Gershonites' there united those (priestly and non-priestly) levitical groups who had some kind of connection (real or fictitious) with the Danite priesthood and who

thus lived, presumably, in some kind of territorial proximity to the
Danite sanctuary, that is within the territory of the northern tribes
of Israel. Since, according to Judg. 18.30, the descendants of the son
of Gershom held priestly office only until the deportation of 733 BC,
the formation of the 'Gershonite' group in these circumstances must
be dated prior to that and the division of the Levites in Num. 26.58a,
in which the name Gershon is still lacking, is to be placed even
earlier. In the list of the subgroups the name of the 'Hebronites' in v.
27 (a subgroup of the Kohathites) is especially noteworthy, for it is
difficult in this connection not to think of the town of Hebron and
thus to accept the existence of a (sub)group of Levites dwelling in the
mountains of southern Judah in and around Hebron and linked
together from the point of view of their territorial proximity. The
subgroup of the 'Libnites' in v. 21 (belonging to the Gershonites)
also reminds us of a place-name. One could, at any rate, associate
them with the town of Libna in the west Judaean hill country. It is
true, however, that in this case the association is not so clear and
compelling, and the fact that the Libnites are part of the Gershonites
would, from what has been said above, suggest rather a northern
habitat, if geographical considerations have played any part at all in
the division of the Levites. Leaving aside connections which cannot
be substantiated, the rest of the names of the subgroups tell us nothing
and cannot be related to anything in particular. What is worth
noticing is the fact that some of these names very probably go back to
personal names and this is especially true of the Amramites and the
Uzzielites (v. 27 among the Kohathites) and probably of the
Shimeites (v. 21 among the Gershonites). From this it would appear
that personal and regional relationships lie behind the present division of the Levites. For the P-narrative, which made use of this
division as traditional material, questions of the history of the
Levites had, of course, no place. For it this division was simply there
as the posterity of Levi, son of Jacob, founded over the generations,
and all that remained for it to do was to furnish this posterity with an
ordered relationship to the rest of the Israelite tribes and its individual
groups with clearly defined duties. This it did by means of unequivocal ordinances given to Moses by Yahweh (v. 14).

[3.15–16] With regard to the organization of the tribe of Levi, too,
there was a 'numbering', i.e. a census (v. 15). The prohibition of
1.47 (1.49, cf. 2.33) had reference, not to a census of the Levites as
such, but expressly only to a census of them 'among the people of

Israel' (i.e. among the 'secular' tribes), that is along with them and according to the same principle, which would have resulted in 'the Levites' being added in with them. According to the divine command there took place, rather, a separate 'numbering' of the Levites (v. 16). In their case it is not men of twenty years of age and upwards and fit for military service (1.3) who are included, but the entire male population from the age of one month and upward (v. 15b). In their case, too, it was not a question of fitness for military service; they were, rather, 'given' (3.9) from birth, even when they were actually able to take up their particular duties only from the age of thirty (4.3 et al.). The idea of 'one month' is certainly to be understood in the sense of the completion of one month of life and is to be explained from the idea that only a month after birth does a child show itself to be capable of life and therefore as really 'alive', a fact which is understandable in view of the high rate of infant mortality obtaining in primitive conditions.

[3.22, 28, 34, 39] The census data is given by sections in vv. 22, 28, 34 (with a total in v. 39). Here, too, there is the question of the origin of these figures (cf. above, pp. 21ff.). Since here, too, the idea of an esoteric numerical speculation does not lead to any particularly illuminating results, such an attempt at explanation must probably, in this case too, be abandoned. On the other hand, the possibility must be taken into consideration that here we have artificially contrived numbers. It is true that the individual components are not more noticeably rounded than in 1.20–43, but the total provides a remarkably round figure, except that it is not clear how it has been divided into three components. It follows that the solution of the problem that is certainly possible in 1.20–43 (cf. above, pp. 21ff.) scarcely comes into question for the Levites, since a division into (military) 'troops' in the case of the Levites would hardly at any time have been a reality in view of the fact that in their case it is precisely not the military man-power alone (from twenty years old and upwards) which is 'numbered'. One can scarcely avoid the conclusion that, on the analogy of the 'secular' tribes, a census, which had to result in definite numerical data, was postulated by P for the Levites, too. The total for the Levites (v. 39) appears remarkably low in the light of the figures given for the other tribes in 1.20–43, and this disparity is all the greater when it is remembered that in the case of Levi those between the ages of one and twenty are included in this figure, for whom, at a rough estimate, one would have to allow a third of the total. Nevertheless, even the figures which are given for the Levites would seem considerably to exceed what is historically acceptable.

[3.23, 29, 35, 38] To this artificial assimilation to the other tribes there belong also the details concerning the camping places of the Levitical 'families' in vv. 23, 29, 35b, 38a which appear in apparently arbitrary succession. The specially favoured eastern side was, according to v. 38a, reserved for Moses and Aaron and the latter's sons, that is for quite a small group, which appears strange in this context; but this was necessary in view of the fact that, with the traditional grouping of the Levites into three, one of the four sides would otherwise have remained unoccupied. That the Kohathites, who, in the traditional scheme (vv. 17–20), appear only in second place, should receive the side following the east in a clockwise direction, that is the south side (v. 29; cf. 2.3ff.), may have as its reason the fact that, according to 3.31 and 4.2ff., they had to perform particularly important duties. This organization of the camping places certainly does not rest on an established event such as the division of territory in Canaan among the individual groups of Levites, even if such an event ever actually took place. Moreover, this assigning of camping places is in line with the organization for the tribes in the camp (2.2–31). One must suppose, although this is never unequivocally stated in the text, that the Levites were to camp in the immediate vicinity of the sanctuary, while the corresponding 'standard' of each group of three tribes was to be placed somewhat further away.

[3.24, 30, 35] An artificial assimilation also produces the mention of 'leaders' for the three Levitical groups (vv. 24, 30, 35a—in the first two cases after the indication of the camping position, in the last case before it), where the tradition of 1.5–15, which is concerned with tribes, is transferred to the three Levitical groups. The names mentioned do not, of themselves, give the impression of having been artificially constructed, but whether they come from some Levitical tradition or other is unfortunately no longer ascertainable. All that is certain is that the 'chief over the leaders' for the Levites as a whole, an office apparently held by Eleazar son of Aaron, has been added only subsequently.

[3.25f., 31, 36f.] The details concerning the spheres of duty for the three Levitical groups in vv. 25, 26, 31, 36, 37 must be reckoned as part of the essential basic form of the P-narrative. The objects with which the Levites concerned were to deal are introduced only as catchwords, without any more specific directions being given about the particular kind of 'service' required. It is a question of the wilderness sanctuary of Ex. 25.10ff. with its various furnishings and, more particularly, of its external construction. It follows, therefore, that there is no explicit thought of cultic activities. Thus, the Levites were to ensure only that externally everything was 'in order'. According to vv. 25–26, the Gershonites were entrusted with the whole of the actual tent itself, namely the tent-like 'tabernacle' (cf. Ex. 26.1ff.) together with its 'covering' (Ex. 26.14), the screen for the door of the tent (Ex. 26.36) and the hangings which formed the entrance court (Ex. 27.9ff.). The text of vv. 25–26 is somewhat complicated and not quite intact. What is clearly meant by the traditional technical term 'tent of meeting' is the wilderness sanctuary as a whole. To the Gershonites there is assigned in particular the 'tabernacle', i.e. the external tent construction, and this term 'tabernacle' is then made more precise by the mention of intrinsic elements. According to v. 26, the 'hangings of the court' were also part of the 'tabernacle'. The other catchwords in v. 26 prove, by their form (we find, contrary to the rules, the Hebrew *nota accusativi*), to be later additions. According to v. 31, the Kohathites were to deal with the sacred contents of the wilderness sanctuary and were, thereby, entrusted with the most important and most difficult duty. Why P should show a preference in this way for a Levitical group which appears in the traditional scheme only in second place is unknown. They were to care for the ark (cf. Ex. 25.10ff.), the table (Ex. 25.23ff.), the lampstand (Ex. 25.31ff.) and the 'vessels of the sanctuary' necessary for the cultic observances. The mention in this context of the 'altars' is problematical, since all that can be meant are the altar (of burnt offerings) of Ex. 27.1ff. and the incense altar of Ex. 30.1ff. Since the latter was only a secondary inclusion in the P-narrative, the present text must be reckoned as one of the additions to P. It is, however, probable that the plural 'altars' was introduced only later, precisely in view of Ex. 30.1ff., and that originally the singular 'altar' stood in the text, as the textual evidence of the Syriac translation indicates. The reference to the 'screen', which is not more specifically defined, at the end of the enumeration in v. 31, proves from its very position (after the generalized reference to the 'vessels of the sanctuary') to be very probably an addition. What is meant by it must be the 'veil of the screen' of Ex. 35.12 *et al.*, which in the tent divided the 'holy place' from the 'holy of holies'. The Merarites,

according to vv. 36–37, had the least important duty, for to them fell
the care of the poles of the whole tent, of the 'frames' of the 'tabernacle' (cf. Ex. 26.15ff.), of the supporting 'bars' (Ex. 26.26ff.), of
those 'pillars' and their 'bases' which carried the entrance curtain
(Ex. 26.37) as well as the 'pillars' and 'bases' of the curtain that
enclosed the entrance court (Ex. 27.10ff.) and of the 'pegs' (Ex. 27.19)
and 'cords' (these only in Ex. 25.18; 39.40) which held the tent fast.

[3.40–51] From 3.40 onwards there follow various additions to the
P-narrative. This is particularly clear in the case of 3.40–51. Here
the theme of 3.11–13 is taken up again, namely the redemption of the
first-born, who belong to Yahweh, by the Levites. If 3.11–13 is to be
adjudged an addition, then this is even more true of 3.40–51, for this
latter passage is secondary even to the former. Whereas in 3.11–13
the fact that Yahweh accepts the Levites as compensation for his
right to the first-born is discussed as a general principle, in 3.40–51
the subject-matter is calculated in detail. That 'calculation' is the
point at issue here, for the whole passage culminates in a precisely
calculated payment to 'Aaron and his sons' (vv. 48ff.). The results of
the census of the Levites (v. 39) are presupposed. According to vv.
40–43, all the first-born males were, by divine command, counted
from the age of one month and upwards (cf. above pp. 37f.). The result
of this census (v. 43)—twenty-two thousand two hundred and seventy-
three—is remarkable enough and bears no acceptable relationship
to the other figures given in Num. 1ff. If one were to relate it to the
total given in 1.46 of the Israelites who were fit for military service,
then the impossible conclusion is arrived at, that at that time every
Israelite family must have had, on the average, some forty male
children. The supposition that the concept of the 'first-born' is to be
referred to the mothers (different wives of one man), a supposition
which is unlikely, would not lead to an acceptable result either.
The figure twenty-two thousand two hundred and seventy-three,
which seems so uncontrived and yet so unrealistic, is probably best
explained by understanding it as a fabricated number which, in
conjunction with v. 39, aims at squaring with the two hundred and
seventy-three 'over and above' referred to in vv. 46ff. The mention
of the Levites' cattle as a substitute for the first-born of the cattle in
the Israelite sphere (v. 41b, cf. v. 45aβ) is quite outside the present
context. Factually this can scarcely be justified, since human first-
born in Israel have always been 'redeemed' in one way or another
(cf. above p. 34), while animal first-born were still being sacrificed

even in the late period (cf. 18.17). The reference to the 'cattle of the Levites' in the present passage is, therefore, purely theoretical, indeed perhaps a later addition. According to vv. 46ff., for the two hundred and seventy-three first-born 'over and above' there was to be made a payment of five shekels apiece (for the 'shekel of the sanctuary'= twenty gerahs—gerah meaning, in fact, 'grain, seed'—cf. Ex. 30.13; Lev. 27.25; Ezek. 45.12). According to the wording of vv. 49–50, this sum was levied on the first-born 'over and above' themselves. Since this can scarcely be accepted (otherwise the two hundred and seventy-three in question would have to have been selected by some means or another), the sense must be that the total of 1,365 shekels was to be raised amongst Israel as a whole. The payment was to be made to Aaron and his sons, that is to the priests. One must suppose that this whole passage is meant to provide for this payment a reason in accordance with 3.11–13, and that at some time or another the sum of 1,365 shekels was to be paid over by 'Israel' to the priests. The real basis for this payment and the circumstances of it are unknown.

[4.1–33] The following section, too, 4.1–33, is to be considered as part of the secondary stratum of P. This is clear not only from the fact that in it a subject is dealt with which has already been under discussion in 3.25, 26, 31, 36, 37, but also from the fact that again there are special connections with Ex. 25ff. (which is not the case in 3.25, 26, 31, 37, 38). Once more the theme is that of the duties of the individual groups of Levites. In contrast to ch. 3, however, these duties are still further delimited in so far as reference is made simply to the striking of the camp and the further wanderings of Israel in the wilderness, in which circumstances the Levites have to dismantle the sanctuary and transport the various parts of it. Emphasis is also laid, in vv. 5–20, on the fact that the Levites are not to approach too close to the 'holy things'. The tendency, already discernible in the basic form of the P-narrative, to entrust the Levites with only very unassuming tasks (cf. above p. 33), appears more emphatically in the present section. The introductions to the subsections (vv. 2–3, 22–23, 29–30) contain divine commands for yet another census ('numbering') of the Levites (cf. 3.15ff.). This time, however, only the (male) Levites between the ages of thirty and fifty are to be counted, that is within the age-group in which they could and must carry out their (cultic) functions (otherwise in 8.24, according to which the Levites were to begin their duties of service at the age of twenty-five). Their service is designated by the word for 'service in war' (ṣābā') which, however, is immediately interpreted in the sense of 'work in the tent of meeting' (vv. 3, 23, 30). The carrying out of this command for a census and the census results are not recorded until vv. 34ff. Before that, in conjunction with the mention of the 'work in the tent of meeting', the sphere of duties of the Levitical groups is defined. Only at the beginning is this sphere of duty specifically referred to the situation 'when the camp is to set out' (vv. 5, 15), but everything that follows makes it clear that it is the situation of the wilderness wandering that is being envisaged, thus a presupposition of a type of 'service' on the part of the Levites which, for all practical purposes, no longer obtains after the conquest. The Kohathites come first, in vv. 4–20, because, for the author of this addition, they were the most prominent Levitical group, since they had to deal with 'the most holy things' (v. 4b; cf. 3.31 and above, p. 39). But these very circumstances, envisaged already in 3.31, result in their duties being spoken of, in what follows, in a purely negative way. Direct contact with 'the most holy things' was reserved exclusively for the priests even when the camp was being struck and the tent-sanctuary had to be dismantled. First and foremost, then, this Kohathite section in vv. 5–15 is concerned exclusively with 'Aaron and his sons' who are carefully to pack the 'most holy' objects for transportation. In this context there are found various formulae from Ex. 35ff. which indicate that this whole passage belongs to the secondary stratum of P, but also several peculiar expressions from which it follows that the author of this passage is not simply to be identified with that of Ex. 35ff. With the 'veil of the screen' (v. 5), cf. Ex. 35.12 et al. The phrase 'put in its poles' (v. 6) contradicts the ruling of Ex. 25.15, which says that the poles were on no account to be removed. The abbreviated expression 'the table of the Presence'* (instead of 'the table of the bread of the Presence') †️ is peculiar, as is the expression 'the continual bread' (v. 7) which is derived from the formula of Ex. 25.30. With the 'lampstand' of v. 9, cf. Ex. 35.14. By 'the golden altar' (v. 11) is meant here, as in Ex. 39.38, the (incense) altar overlaid with gold of Ex. 30.1ff. which first appears in additions to the P-narrative.‡️ By contrast, the 'altar' (pure and simple) mentioned in vv. 13–14 without further definition, refers to the altar for burnt offerings of Ex. 27.1ff. which, after its use

* So MT. RSV has expanded it in translation. Tr.
†️ Cf. Ex. 25.23ff. and *Exodus*, pp. 205f.
‡️ Cf. *Exodus*, pp. 234f.

for animal sacrifices, has to be cleaned of its 'ashes'* before it is made
ready for transportation. Only after 'Aaron and his sons' have
prepared for transportation all these cultic furnishings, together with
all their appurtenances, wrapped in all sorts of costly materials and
skins (thereby hiding them from view), and provided with their
carrying poles (vv. 6b, 8b, 11b, 14b) or laid on a carrying frame
(vv. 10b, 12b), only then, according to v. 15, are the Kohathites to
'come' (into the sanctuary) and take over the 'carrying' of them, but,
in so doing, are yet—upon pain of death which would certainly be
immediately inflicted by Yahweh himself (cf. II Sam. 6.6f.)—to
beware of touching 'the holy things'. After the closing formula of the
Kohathite section (v. 15b), there follows, in vv. 16–20, what is
obviously a still more recent addition which contains a notice about
the priest Eleazar, who is to be in charge of some of the particularly
important cultic materials (cf. Ex. 27.20; 30.22ff., 34ff., et al.; 'the
continual cereal offering' is found elsewhere only in Neh. 10.34) and
who is to supervise particularly 'all the tabernacle' with all its contents
(v. 16). There follows, in vv. 17–20, a broad exposition of the warning
given in v. 15a about touching the 'holy things' (the Kohathites,
without looking on the holy things which they are to carry when the
camp breaks up, are to be led to them by Aaron and his sons).
The 'service' of the Gershonites (vv. 24–28a) concerns, as in 3.25–26,
the tent cloth and the curtains of the wilderness sanctuary, except
that in the present context the concern is particularly with 'carrying'
these when the camp is struck and the march continues. Only after
the particularly sacred contents have been removed from the
'sanctuary' by the Aaronites and the Kohathites, could the tent
cloth ('the curtains of the tabernacle') be taken down and removed,
since no particularly precautionary measures were necessary with
regard to it. In the details, substantially the same objects as in
3.25–26 are mentioned (3.26—cf. above p. 39—has been retrospectively elaborated under the influence of 4.26). In this case Aaron
and his sons have no part to play (as opposed to vv. 5ff.), but are to
supervise the whole operation (v. 27). The note in v. 28b, which
concerns the special responsibility of Ithamar, son of Aaron, and
which comes after the concluding formula of v. 28a, is likely to be
additional (as is v. 16b). After the tent cloth has been taken down, the
whole framework could also finally be removed; this, according to
vv. 31–33a, was the task of the Merarites. The statements of 3.36–37

* Cf. *Leviticus*, pp. 53f.

reappear verbatim in this context, except that here the reference is to the 'carrying' of them. After the concluding formula (v. 33a), there is once more a secondary reference to Ithamar (v. 33b, cf. v. 28b).

[4.34-49] In 4.34-49 there appear finally, with the constant repetition of the same formulae, the results of the census, instigated in 4.2-3, of the thirty- to fifty-year-old Levites. According to vv. 34 and 46 (this remark is not repeated in the intervening passages), the 'leaders of the community' or the 'leaders of Israel' (cf. on 1.16) were present along with Moses and Aaron at the carrying out of this 'numbering' of the Levites. The figures given in vv. 36, 40 and 44 stand in a tolerable relationship to those given in 3.22, 28, 34 for all the Levites (from one month old and upward). In the case of the Kohathites and the Gershonites the thirty- to fifty-year-olds make up about one-third of the total (in the case of the Merarites, it is true, a little more than half). Just as the figures of 3.22, 28, 34 could not be explained as to their origin (cf. above, pp. 37f.), so, too, is the case with the present figures. It is, of course, possible that they go back to a census of active Levites (between the ages of thirty and fifty), but it could be a question of such a census only with regard to the post-exilic Temple, since it is scarcely possible that such a comprehensive organization of 'Levites' existed prior to that. But for the late period, just as much as for some hypothetical early period, the figures given are certainly much too high, as is clear from a comparison with the modest figures for 'Levites' and other lesser Temple personnel in the list (unfortunately obscure from the point of view of its origin) in Ezra 2.40-58=Neh. 7.43-60. One is forced, therefore, in this case, too, to the conclusion, which is by no means satisfactory, that the figures are in some way artificial.

3. VARIOUS DIVINE ORDINANCES: 5.1-6.27

In ch. 5-6 several ordinances of very varied scope and very varied contents have been juxtaposed, with no recognizably close relationships, as far as subject-matter is concerned, either with each other or with what precedes and follows. The result is the typical picture of additions joined together without any particular plan. By this time the narrative is nearing the conclusion of the whole Sinai story, so this was the obvious place (as was also 8.1-9.14) for introducing additional 'legal' material which was to be retrospectively attributed to the great theophany at Sinai. The framework of the individual sections follows the style of the P-narrative and in their present form they come from a comparatively late period, even if they do contain older traditional material.

(a) THE EXCLUSION OF THE UNCLEAN FROM THE CAMP: 5.1–4

5 [1]The LORD said to Moses, [2]'Command the people of Israel that they put out of the camp every leper, and every one having a discharge, and every one that is unclean through contact with the dead; [3][you shall put out both male and female, putting them outside the camp,] that they may not defile their camp, in the midst of which I dwell.' [4]And the people of Israel did so, and drove them outside the camp; as the LORD said to Moses, so the people of Israel did.

This passage is concerned with the preservation of the 'camp' from cultic uncleanness, which may not be tolerated in view of the presence of Yahweh (v. 3). A material understanding of cultic 'cleanness' lies at the basis of this; the thought of dangerous possibilities of contamination which, in any case, is relevant only in the case of the first of the categories mentioned in v. 2, is not the deciding factor. So, too, social or charitable considerations have no part in this. Those affected are simply 'put out' for as long as they remain unclean (this, it is true, is not explicitly stated, but is to be understood), without its being asked how they are to survive 'outside'. Interest is expressed only in the cleanness of the camp, as this is already demanded for the military camp in the deuteronomic law (Deut. 23.10–15) and which must already have long been regarded as important. The Israelite camp in the wilderness period, as it is conceived of in the present passage, could and must have been the prototype both of Israel's later settlements in Canaan and of the circle of the post-exilic community. For the cultic uncleanness of 'leprosy', for the meaning of the term 'leprosy' and for the question of its curability, compare especially Lev. 13–14,* where a separation 'outside the camp' is also demanded (13.46). The uncleanness of bodily 'discharges' (of a 'normal' or morbid variety) is dealt with explicitly in Lev. 15,† where, however, no provision is made for exclusion from the community. Uncleanness 'through contact with the dead', i.e. the uncleanness that is occasioned by some kind of bodily contact with a corpse, was, if certain purificatory rites were performed, only for a stipulated period (cf. 19.11) and only in this present passage has it the consequence of the person being 'put out'. Obviously in this section what is presumably a

* *Leviticus*, pp. 103ff.   † *Leviticus*, pp. 113f.

post-exilic practice is validated by a Sinai ordinance. The double phrase in v. 3a disrupts the context by its use of the second person and is thereby shown to be an addition.

(b) THE RESTORATION OF MISAPPROPRIATED PROPERTY:
5.5–10

5 5And the LORD said to Moses, 6'Say to the people of Israel, When a man or woman commits any of the sins that men commit by breaking faith with the LORD, and that person is guilty, 7he shall confess his sin which he has committed; and he shall make full restitution for his wrong, adding a fifth to it, and giving it to him to whom he did the wrong. 8But if the man has no kinsman to whom restitution may be made for the wrong, the restitution for wrong shall go to the LORD for the priest, in addition to the ram of atonement with which atonement is made for him. 9And every offering, all the holy things of the people of Israel, which they bring to the priest, shall be his; 10and every man's holy things shall be his; whatever any man gives to the priest shall be his.'

This ordinance links up with those cases envisaged in Lev. 6.1–7 (*Hebr.* 5.20–26); it is even probable that the text of that passage underlies the present exposition, since the unusual formulations of v. 6 are best explained in this way. This is especially true of the expression 'any of the (possible) sins that men commit', which looks like a contraction of the formulation of Lev. 6.3b ('any of all the things which men do and sin therein'). If this view is adopted, then the problem as to whether the Hebrew genitive relationship (lit. 'sin of a man') is to be understood as a subjective genitive ('sin on the part of a man') or as an objective genitive ('sin against a man') is solved in favour of the former,* even though, as is shown by what follows, what is meant are lapses detrimental to others (various possibilities are envisaged and listed in Lev. 6.2–3). Even the meaning given to such lapses, namely 'breaches of faith with Yahweh', has its prototype in Lev. 6.2. The demand for the restitution of the amount by which another has been wronged with the addition of a fifth (the restitution, therefore, in 'cash') corresponds partly verbatim (cf. especially the technical term 'in full') to the ruling in Lev. 6.5. What is new in this passage *vis-à-vis* Lev. 6 comes in v. 8. According to it,

---

* The RSV translation ('sins that men commit') takes the Hebrew in the sense of a subjective genitive. Noth's German translation preserves, to some extent, the ambiguity of the Hebrew. Tr.

the restitution money, if the wronged person has no 'redeemer',*
should not simply remain unpaid but should go to the priest. The
mention of the 'redeemer' presupposes that the wronged person has
lost his legal and economic independence—either by incurring debt
or by emigration—and thus is apparently no longer entitled to receive
the restitution money. In this case a more or less close relative would
have to stand in for him as 'redeemer'. If, as is here supposed, no
such 'redeemer' is available, then the restitution is to be made in
favour of the priest. The somewhat difficult phraseology of v. 8
mentions as recipient, in the first place Yahweh and then, immediately
and without intervention, 'the priest', which no doubt means that the
payment is made in principle to Yahweh, but in practice, however,
to the priest. That it is 'the priest' who is mentioned here and not, as
one would expect in a P-context, Aaron or one of his sons, again goes
back to Lev. 6.6–7. The 'apart from'† with regard to the ram of
atonement (v. 8b) does not mean that this ram, which is also
demanded in Lev. 6.6–7, was not to be offered, but that nothing
special need be said about it, since the ram (in money value, too)‡
was, according to Lev. 6.6–7, to be given to the priest in payment for
the atonement rite that was requested. Joined to v. 8, there is,
finally, in vv. 9–10, a quite general ordinance to the effect that all
sacred offerings of the Israelites, which they present to Yahweh as
gifts by 'lifting them up' (with the hands), always become the
property of 'the priest' (so here, too, instead of Aaron).

(c) THE DIVINE JUDGMENT IN CASES OF SUSPECTED ADULTERY: 5.11–31

5 ¹¹And the LORD said to Moses, ¹²'Say to the people of Israel, If
any man's wife goes astray and acts unfaithfully against him, ¹³if a
man lies with her carnally, and it is hidden from the eyes of her husband,
and she is undetected though she has defiled herself, and there is no
witness against her, since she was not taken in the act; ¹⁴and if the
spirit of jealousy comes upon him, and he is jealous of his wife who has
defiled herself; or if the spirit of jealousy comes upon him, and he is
jealous of his wife, though she has not defiled herself; ¹⁵then the man
shall bring his wife to the priest, and bring the offering required of her,
a tenth of an ephah of barley meal; he shall pour no oil upon it and

* Noth translates thus, both in text and commentary, what appears in the
RSV as 'kinsman'. The latter is interpretation, rather than translation, of the
Hebrew gō'ēl. Tr.
† So Noth for the Hebrew which RSV translates as 'in addition to'. Tr.
‡ Cf. Leviticus, pp. 46f.

put no frankincense on it, for it is a cereal offering of jealousy, a cereal offering of remembrance, bringing iniquity to remembrance.

16 'And the priest shall bring her near, and set her before the LORD; [17]and the priest shall take holy water in an earthen vessel, and take some of the dust that is on the floor of the tabernacle and put it into the water. [18]And the priest shall set the woman before the LORD, and unbind the hair of the woman's head, and place in her hands the cereal offering of remembrance, [which is the cereal offering of jealousy.] And in his hand the priest shall have the water of bitterness that brings the curse. [19]Then the priest shall make her take an oath, saying, "If no man has lain with you, and if you have not turned aside to uncleanness, while you were under your husband's authority, be free from this water of bitterness that brings the curse. [20]But if you have gone astray, though you are under your husband's authority, and if you have defiled yourself, and some man other than your husband has lain with you, [21]then" (let the priest make the woman take the oath of the curse, and say to the woman) "the LORD make you an execration and an oath among your people, when the LORD makes your thigh fall away and your body swell; [22]may this water that brings the curse pass into your bowels and make your body swell and your thigh fall away." And the woman shall say, "Amen, Amen."

23 'Then the priest shall write these curses in a book, and wash them off into the water of bitterness; [24]and he shall make the woman drink the water of bitterness that brings the curse, and the water that brings the curse shall enter into her and cause bitter pain. [25]And the priest shall take the cereal offering of jealousy out of the woman's hand, and shall wave the cereal offering before the LORD and bring it to the altar; [26]and the priest shall take a handful of the cereal offering, as its memorial portion, and burn it upon the altar, [and afterward shall make the woman drink the water.] [27]And when he has made her drink the water, then, if she has defiled herself and has acted unfaithfully against her husband, the water that brings the curse shall enter into her and cause bitter pain, and her body shall swell, and her thigh shall fall away, and the woman shall become an execration among her people. [28]But if the woman has not defiled herself and is clean, then she shall be free and shall conceive children.

29 'This is the law in cases of jealousy, when a wife, though under her husband's authority, goes astray and defiles herself, [30]or when the spirit of jealousy comes upon a man and he is jealous of his wife; then he shall set the woman before the LORD, and the priest shall execute upon her all this law. [31]The man shall be free from iniquity, but the woman shall bear her iniquity.'

This text provides the most exhaustive law of procedure that has been preserved in the Old Testament for the carrying out of a so-called divine judgment. Such a divine judgment was envisaged for those cases in which the question of guilt or innocence could not be clarified by human means. Such a case, as is clearly set out in the introduction (vv. 12b–14), is in question here. Divine judgments of this kind were known throughout the ancient Near East, especially in Mesopotamia. Nowhere, however, is there found an exact parallel to the present legislation. The whole gives a markedly primitive impression and certainly goes back to a fairly ancient practice. For the present context, what is obviously a traditional text has been lightly reworked, namely by the addition of the introductory sentences in vv. 11–12a and by the use of the term 'tabernacle' (v. 17), which refers to the wilderness sanctuary of the P-narrative. An older stratum, probably already in literary form, appears in the constant reference to the cultic official as 'the priest', which is reminiscent of the rituals of Lev. 1ff.* and which very probably goes back to a time at which the scene was envisaged as being one of the many local sanctuaries with the priest who officiated at it. Prior to that the contents of the section obviously had a pre-literary history. For in the present version of the procedure two or even three different kinds of divine judgment are so closely amalgamated that they can no longer, from the literary point of view, be separated. On the one hand there is the powerful effect, certainly originally thought of as spontaneous, of 'holy' water whose secret 'power' was further strengthened by the addition of dust particles from the floor of the sanctuary (v. 17). In the case where the suspicion is justified, this water, once it is drunk, causes bodily deformities concerned with conception and child-bearing (the opposite is the case in v. 28). On the other hand there is the oath in the form of a curse (the Hebrew technical term 'ālā), which becomes effective in the case of the woman's being guilty and which was again originally thought of as being spontaneous (cf. Ex. 22.8);† it is in this sense that the direction that the priest is to 'make her take an oath' is to be understood (vv. 19, 21). As a third element there is also in v. 23 the fact that the priest is to write certain words in a book. The original sense of this measure could have been that the suspected person should, by eating the book (cf. Ezek. 2.8–3.3), consume these words which, again, were thought of as effective in themselves and which are to be thought of as a curse formula. In the present context this last element acts as a link between the water which is to be drunk and in which the written words have been 'washed off' and the oath of anathema which has been written in the book.

* Cf. *Leviticus*, pp. 20f.   † Cf., on this point, *Exodus*, pp. 184f.

[5.12–16] First of all the case is described in the style of a ritual (protasis in vv. 12b–14 with *ki* and the subject in first place; cf. Lev. 1.2 *et al.*) and the introduction to the proceedings is regulated (vv. 15–16). This is that the man brings the wife who is suspected of adultery 'to the priest', that is to the sanctuary or (as originally) to one of the numerous sanctuaries (normally the sanctuary of the place where they lived), together with a cereal offering befitting the divine judge whose decision is to be sought. This cereal offering is brought by the man who, in this respect, is the cultic representative of his wife, who, since the divine decision is sought on her behalf, is the one who really brings it. It is to consist of a small amount (cf. Lev. 5.11)* of barley meal, but without the addition of oil and frankincense envisaged in the usual cereal offering ritual (Lev. 2.2), since it is not a joyful sacrifice but an offering to bring about a divine judgment. Then the priest brings the woman 'before Yahweh', that is before the place, however this was thought of, of his presence. With the mention of the name of Yahweh, the procedure, wherever its origin is to be sought, is drawn into the realm of the Old Testament conception of faith.

[5.17–18] After these preliminaries, the action proper begins with the priest's taking 'holy water' (this expression, which occurs only here, means, presumably, water from a container in the sanctuary), mixed with holy earth (v. 17) in a vessel that is to hand and places the woman, with her hair loosened and falling down in disarray (this 'dress', otherwise known—Lev. 10.6; 21.10—only as part of mourning customs, perhaps signifies disfigurement such as might be effected in expectation of a judgment that is to be passed 'without respect of persons') and with the cereal offering taken from the husband's hand and now given to the wife, 'before Yahweh' (the anticipation of this last directive in v. 16b could have the general significance that before the action proper begins the woman is at that point presented to Yahweh). The expression 'the water of bitterness that brings the curse', which is repeated several times in what follows in these or similar words, attributes to the water of v. 17 a potential curse-effect. The Hebrew word *mārīm*, translated as 'bitter(ness)' is difficult from the point of view both of language and of sense. It can scarcely be doubted that it belongs to the root *mrr*='to be bitter'. At all events what we have here could be (and this is linguistically the most obvious solution), in spite of the construct relationship in v. 19 *et al.* and of the exceptional phraseology in vv. 24, 27, the plural of the

* Cf. also *Leviticus*, pp. 45f.

adjective *mar* = 'bitter' in a simple adjectival sense. It is, however, mostly taken as a plural with abstract meaning (hence the above translation). A literal understanding of the use of the expression 'bitter' with regard to 'water' is the most obvious one, yet, in the present text at any rate, and especially in view of the phraseology of vv. 24, 27, a figurative meaning is to be seen such as is also frequently attested for the Hebrew root *mrr*. So the sense is as, for example, in I Sam. 15.32 of the 'bitterness' of death. On this assumption the thought here, too, is of a potential fatal effect of the water.

[5.19–23] According to vv. 19, 21, the priest is now to make the woman 'take an oath'. No oath on the part of the woman is, however, given. Either the words of the woman's oath are not reported, since they could have consisted only of a 'denial upon oath' of the crime imputed to her, or else—and this is more likely—the words of the priest that follow and which the woman must affirm (v. 22b), are to be regarded as containing implicitly the woman's 'oath'. These words of the priest (vv. 19aβb, 20) refer to the (twofold) effect of the water and are meant to imbue the water with this effect. The sentence structure of the priest's words is incomplete in that in the case of the second alternative of the protasis, the corresponding apodosis is missing. Yet it is not necessary to posit a textual error (a secondary omission of the apodosis or the secondary addition of the following clause in v. 21aα); rather the second apodosis is left unexpressed, but is self-evidently understood. V. 21 is no longer concerned with the divine judgment as such, but with its effect as an admonitory example, in which the woman's guilt is taken for granted. The latter is also the case in v. 22a, which harks back to the divine judgment which has actually already preceded it. What is meant by the words of the curse which, according to v. 23, the priest is finally to write down and 'wash off' into the water, is not clear from the context; one could think of vv. 19aβb, 20.

[5.24–28] While the water that is drunk (v. 24) is working in the woman's body (the additional phrase in v. 26b makes the drinking follow the sacrifice), her offering is 'presented' before Yahweh by the priest,* and then a certain part of it, designated by the no longer comprehensible technical term *'azkārā*,† is burnt (vv. 25, 26a). The two possible outcomes of the divine judgment are represented in the following verses (27–28). Here there appear in an emphatic position the expressions 'unclean/clean', which have already been used

* For the cultic technical term 'wave', cf. *Exodus*, p. 232.   † Cf. *Leviticus*, p. 27.

repeatedly in what has gone before. From this it might appear that these are to be understood here in an ethical sense and not in their originally cultic sense, since, from the latter point of view, not only illegitimate but also legitimate sexual intercourse makes a person 'unclean' (cf., e.g., Ex. 19.15). It is, however, unlikely that in what is otherwise a very ancient text the term 'cleanness' is used in what is certainly a later and more subtle sense, namely the ethical one. It must be accepted that in this whole passage there is no thought of the possibility of legitimate intercourse, and that what is being dealt with is simply the question of intercourse with another man* which would have made the woman 'unclean', as would have any sexual intercourse (on occasion).

[5.29–31] The concluding passage, vv. 29–31, is remarkably detailed and repeats what has already been said. In v. 31 the only case envisaged is that the woman is guilty. Its consequence, which is only hinted at in v. 31bβ, but not explicitly stated, since in what has gone before it has been a question of a decision between 'innocent' and 'guilty' and not of the actual judgment, must have been capital punishment for both parties to the crime (cf. Lev. 20.10; Deut. 22.22 *et al.*), presumably carried out by means of a public stoning (cf. Deut. 22.21; John 8.7). There is no indication of any punishment for the man who, in the case of the woman's being innocent, has entertained, out of 'jealousy', an unjustified suspicion (v. 14b); perhaps he simply went free.

(d) THE LAW FOR A NAZIRITE: 6.1–21

6 ¹And the LORD said to Moses, ²'Say to the people of Israel, When either a man or a woman makes a special vow, the vow of a Nazirite, to separate himself to the LORD, ³he shall separate himself from wine and strong drink; he shall drink no vinegar made from wine or strong drink, and shall not drink any juice of grapes or eat grapes, fresh or dried. ⁴All the days of his separation he shall eat nothing that is produced by the grapevine, not even the seeds or the skins.

5 'All the days of his vow of separation no razor shall come upon his head; until the time is completed for which he separates himself to the LORD, he shall be holy; he shall let the locks of hair of his head grow long.

6 'All the days that he separates himself to the LORD he shall not go

* Noth translates the phrase in vv. 19, 20 (cf. also v. 29), which the RSV gives as 'while you were under your husband's authority', by 'with someone other than your own husband'. Tr.

near a dead body. [7]Neither for his father nor for his mother, nor for brother or sister, if they die, shall he make himself unclean; because his separation to God is upon his head. [8]All the days of his separation he is holy to the LORD.

9 'And if any man dies very suddenly beside him, and he defiles his consecrated head, then he shall shave his head on the day of his cleansing; on the seventh day he shall shave it. [10]On the eighth day he shall bring two turtledoves or two young pigeons to the priest to the door of the tent of meeting, [11]and the priest shall offer one for a sin offering and the other for a burnt offering, and make atonement for him, because he sinned by reason of the dead body. And he shall consecrate his head that same day, [12]and separate himself to the LORD for the days of his separation, and bring a male lamb a year old for a guilt offering; but the former time shall be void, because his separation was defiled.

13 'And this is the law for the Nazirite, when the time of his separation has been completed: he shall be brought to the door of the tent of meeting, [14]and he shall offer his gift to the LORD, one male lamb a year old without blemish for a burnt offering, and one ewe lamb a year old without blemish as a sin offering, and one ram without blemish as a peace offering, [15]and a basket of unleavened bread, cakes of fine flour mixed with oil, and unleavened wafers spread with oil, and their cereal offering and their drink offerings. [16]And the priest shall present them before the LORD and offer his sin offering and his burnt offering, [17]and he shall offer the ram as a sacrifice of peace offering to the LORD, with the basket of unleavened bread; the priest shall offer also its cereal offering and its drink offering. [18]And the Nazirite shall shave his consecrated head at the door of the tent of meeting, and shall take the hair from his consecrated head and put it on the fire which is under the sacrifice of the peace offering. [19]And the priest shall take the shoulder of the ram, when it is boiled, and one unleavened cake out of the basket, and one unleavened wafer, and shall put them upon the hands of the Nazirite, after he has shaven the hair of his consecration, [20]and the priest shall wave them for a wave offering before the LORD; they are a holy portion for the priest, together with the breast that is waved and the thigh that is offered; and after that the Nazirite may drink wine.

21 'This is the law for the Nazirite who takes a vow. His offering to the LORD shall be according to his vow as a Nazirite, apart from what else he can afford; in accordance with the vow which he takes, so shall he do according to the law for his separation as a Nazirite.'

This section, too, has been adapted to the ideas of the P-narrative, as is shown, outside the introduction (vv.1–2a), above all by the repeated mention of the tent of meeting. An older basic form is also indicated by the presence of 'the priest' (vv. 11, 16ff.—without reference to Aaron and his sons) and individual details, especially in the concluding description of the sacrifice (vv. 14ff.), are reminiscent of the sphere of operation of the rituals of Lev. 1ff. The subject which is treated here, namely the figure of a 'consecrated person',* is, in itself, an old phenomenon in Israel. A 'consecrated person' = Hebrew *nāzîr* (with various nominal and verbal derivatives of the same root) = 'Nazirite' (the rendering that has become usual), was a person given to God. According to old Israelite tradition, there had been Nazirites in the early period, chosen and appointed as such by the God of Israel himself, remaining 'consecrated' for the whole of their life and regarded as a 'gift' of God to his people (Amos 2.11). As a concrete example there appears in the Old Testament the figure of Samson, who, even before his birth, was predestined as 'consecrated to God' (Judg. 13.5; 16.17) and remained such for the whole of his life 'to the day of his death' (Judg. 13.7). What distinguished him in this respect was his readiness to receive the 'spirit of Yahweh' (Judg. 13.25 *et al.*), which effected in him an amazing physical strength. To achieve this a Nazirite had to impose upon himself certain abstinencies. The hair of his head was not to be cut (Judg. 13.5 *et al.*), presumably because this would have been an incursion into the integrity of his person; he was not allowed to drink wine or any other intoxicating beverage (Amos 2.12; in the case of Samson this restriction was only put on his mother before his birth, Judg. 13.4, 7), had perhaps also to abstain from 'unclean' food (this again in the case of Samson's mother according to Judg. 13.4, 7) in order above all to keep himself from anything that had been 'changed' in any unnatural or artificial way. For Israel, such Nazirites were bearers of a particular kind of divine presence in the midst of the people and, as such, were symbols and mediators of divine grace. The 'Nazirite Law' of Num. 6 is far removed from this old, original type of Naziriteship. According to it, any Israelite (according to the present text of v. 2 any Israelite woman, too) could, by a personal decision, take a vow to become a Nazirite for a certain period, perhaps even a period determined by himself, and would then, for this period, have to take upon himself the old, traditional Nazirite abstinencies (renouncing the cutting of the hair of his head, the taking of wine and strong drink, and contact with what was 'unclean'). This could scarcely still have been of any general significance for the community; it could have relevance for the individuals involved only in the sense of good and meritorious works. There is no hint of

---

* In his translation of the biblical text Noth never uses the word 'Nazirite' to render the Hebrew *nāzîr*, but always the German *weihen* (= 'to consecrate') and its derivatives. Cf. the footnote in RSV to Num. 6.2. Tr.

any role played by such a Nazirite. This late law, still valid in New Testament times (Acts 18.18; 21.23–26), must have emerged at a time that can no longer be determined. The addition to the P-narrative that we have in Num. 6.1ff. has certainly not introduced it for the first time, but has found it as a traditional practice.

[6.2–5] In v. 2 the initiative of the individual concerned is strongly emphasized and in this respect a phrase is used which is perhaps intended to express the unusualness of such a vow (similar phraseology in Lev. 22.21; 27.2; Num. 15.3, 8)* in that it uses the expression 'marvellous' or 'astonishing' (it is, at any rate, difficult to separate the root *pl'* from the usual Old Testament root for 'to be marvellous'). The person who has decided to be a Nazirite had to follow, according to vv. 3ff., the old traditional rules of abstinence. The avoidance of wine and strong drink appears in vv. 3–4, presumably in opposition to the original rule which is thereby intensified, in a form which suggests that not only those products produced by fermentation but all products of the vine are prohibited (some of the special words used here are *hapax legomena* and their meaning can no longer be determined with any certainty). With the prohibition of the cutting of the hair there is closely bound up, in v. 5, the idea of being 'holy' to Yahweh.

[6.6–12] The theme of 'uncleanness' is treated in a particularly detailed way in vv. 6–12, not, certainly, in relation to the eating of 'unclean' food, which was certainly understood to be avoided, but in relation to 'uncleanness' through a dead body which could result from contact with such or even, as the expression in v. 6 seems to indicate, from entering a room in which a dead body lay. In this respect the same rules held for the Nazirite as are applied to the high priest in Lev. 21.11, without our being able to deduce from this any kind of cultic functions on the part of a Nazirite (in both cases the rules are particularly strict). However, while the observance of the other prescriptions for abstinence were essentially within the grasp of the individual concerned, the case could arise that, quite beyond his control, he might come into contact with or proximity to a corpse. To meet this eventuality, extremely detailed instructions are given in vv. 9–12, on the assumption that such 'uncleanness' nullifies the whole Nazirite consecration, with the result that a new beginning must be made. After such an eventuality has occurred, a period of seven days must first elapse which, according to 19.11, 14, 16, is

* This similarity is evident in the RSV only here and in Lev. 27.2. Tr.

applicable in general terms to 'uncleanness' due to a corpse. At the conclusion of this period the hair of the head is cut (v. 9b), thereby removing the outward sign of the condition of 'consecration' now ended, and by means of a sacrifice (vv. 10–11a) the 'sin' of which, from the subjective point of view, he was not guilty, but which, from the objective point of view, is a fact, is 'atoned for' with the help of the priest. The sacrifice demanded here corresponds to the lesser offering which a woman at childbirth had to bring at the conclusion of her period of uncleanness (Lev. 12.8) as well as to the purification offering of a leper (Lev. 14.22, 30f.) and of someone who has had a discharge (Lev. 15.14–15). In all of these cases one dove serves as a 'sin offering' and the other as a 'burnt offering', and with these offerings the necessary 'atonement' is achieved. With this, the ground is cleared for a renewed 'consecration' (v. 11b) and for a recommencement of the Naziriteship for the same period as had been envisaged when the vow of 'consecration' was first taken and which now starts again. With regard to this new beginning a 'guilt offering' had to be brought, since through the nullification of the first 'consecration' something had been removed from Yahweh which, on the basis of the vow, was his due (v. 12).

[6.13–20] Vv. 13–20 deal with the completion of the period of 'consecration' at which time an extensive sacrificial ritual was performed. The sentence in v. 13a, which, in the present context, serves as an introduction, but which must originally have been a concluding formula (it is identical with v. 21aα), tends to suggest that the whole of vv. 13–20 is an addition which accommodates itself to what is perhaps a later practice concerning the cultic termination of the time of 'consecration'. According to it there belonged to this termination, in the first place, a complicated sacrificial offering, the description of which does not appear to be entirely a literary unit. The person who wishes now to be released from his 'consecration' has to bring a number of sacrificial animals (v. 14) as well as the wherewithal for a cereal offering (v. 15, cf. Lev. 2.4) and the priest offers the sacrifices. The reference to 'their cereal offering and their drink offerings' (v. 15b, cf. v. 17b) fits badly into the present context, since the cereal offering has already been explicitly mentioned, but, on the other hand, nothing at all has been said about drink offerings. After the offerings comes the cutting off of the hair of the head which, together with the last of the offerings presented, the peace offering,*

* For this kind of offering, cf. *Leviticus*, pp. 30f.

is burnt in the fire on the altar (v. 18). This last action is scarcely
to be understood as a 'hair offering', such as could be shown in a
whole series of examples from comparative religion. It signifies,
rather, the annihilation of a 'consecrated' thing once it has fulfilled
its function. The fact that the hair was allowed to grow freely was a
particular sign of the state of 'consecration' (v. 6) and this destruction
of it removes it from the danger of being profaned or being misused
in a superstitious way. In vv. 19–20 the priest's share of the offerings
that are brought is determined (cf. Lev. 7.8–10, 28–36) and in this
respect it is, naturally, a question of the peace offering and the cereal
offering. This share is first of all (v. 19) placed in the hands of the
person bringing the offering, so that he can present it as a gift and
then (v. 20a) offered by the priest, with the gesture of 'waving', to
Yahweh, finally, however (v. 20aβ), given to the priest. This is, of
course, in addition to those portions of every burnt offering which,
according to Lev. 7.34, are his due, namely the breast that is 'waved'
and the thigh that is 'offered'. The return to the drinking of wine
which, at the end (v. 20b), is expressly allowed or, rather, enjoined,
signifies, after the cutting of the hair, the definitive conclusion of the
period of 'consecration'.

The conclusion of the whole section (v. 21) is very awkwardly
phrased and is perhaps not in its entirety from the same source. In
its present form it emphasizes the fact that the voluntary vow of
'consecration', once it is laid aside, demands the observance of the
relevant rules. It also indicates that the 'consecration' is, to be sure,
an offering to Yahweh, but as such it does not replace, or absolve
from, other offerings which the person concerned may have to make.

(e) THE PRIESTLY BLESSING: 6.22–27

6 ²²The Lord said to Moses, ²³'Say to Aaron and his sons, Thus
you shall bless the people of Israel: you shall say to them,
²⁴The Lord bless you and keep you:
²⁵The Lord make his face to shine upon you, and be gracious to you:
²⁶The Lord lift up his countenance upon you, and give you peace.
27 'So shall they put my name upon the people of Israel, and I will
bless them.'

The introduction (v. 23) places the blessing of vv. 24–26 on the lips
of the priests, represented by 'Aaron and his sons'. That the act of
'blessing' was part of the priests' duties is stated by the deuteronomic
law (Deut. 21.5; cf. also the secondary deuteronomic passage in

Deut. 10.8 which entrusts the whole 'tribe of Levi' with the duty of 'blessing'). When kings such as David (cf. II Sam. 6.18; cf., too, Solomon according to I Kings 8.14, 55) blessed the people, then they were taking upon themselves priestly functions. Blessing had its place within the sanctuary; it could be imparted to those who entered the sanctuary to take part in an act of worship (so Ps. 118.26) or else it was bestowed at the end when the participants were being dismissed (so II Sam. 6.18; Lev. 9.22). The phrases of the introduction (vv. 22–23), couched though they are in language characteristic of the P-narrative, do not prove that the blessing of vv. 24–26 makes its first appearance only in the late, post-exilic period. It may well belong to the traditions handed down from the earlier period and its simplicity of expression would even argue for great antiquity. It is, of course, impossible even approximately to date its emergence.

The blessing itself (vv. 24–26) consists of three lines which, although they reveal no metrical symmetry, yet from the point of view both of form and content are parallel. Each of them consists of two jussive clauses, in the first of which the divine name Yahweh stands as subject immediately after the predicate which is usually placed first in a verbal sentence. This divine name then forms the subject, without, however, its being repeated, of the second jussive clause, which expresses a consequence of the first. By means of this threefold repetition of the divine name, a usage which is not in itself necessary, God is strongly emphasized as the bestower of the blessing. There can be no question here of a spontaneous formula of blessing; even an impersonal formulation, not in itself impossible, such as is found in Ps. 118.26 ('blessed be . . .') and in which Yahweh is only implicitly the author, is avoided in order to leave no doubt as to the fact that God alone is operative and that the priest is merely the mediator. This point is convincingly brought out by the concluding sentence (v. 27), which no longer belongs to the blessing itself. There the priests are charged with pronouncing the name of Yahweh over Israel, but emphasis is again laid at the end on the fact that Yahweh himself is operative.

The statements of the blessing in vv. 24–26 are short and simple, and their contents in this very form are comprehensive in that they admit of a wealth of references. The second person singular address leaves open the alternatives of a collective or an individual field of reference. Presumably it is not a question of an either-or; rather, those who are addressed by the blessing are the participants in the blessing of God intended for the whole of Israel as well as individuals. In the first line (v. 24), the concept of 'blessing' which, according to the understanding of the Old Testament, includes all of God's good gifts, is, in the second clause, specially referred to protection, which means the help of God in the face of every misfortune and disaster. The second line (v. 25), in a quite unselfconscious anthropomorphism, uses the phrase 'make his face to shine' which occurs frequently in the devotional language of the Psalms (cf. Pss. 31.16; 80.3, 7, 19 *et al.*). The 'shining face' is an obvious figure of speech for benevolence and favour and the fact of its being turned upon those addressed (in Hebrew, the preposition *'ēlekā* = 'towards you') is here the object of the wish expressed in the blessing. It is followed by the wish that he may 'be gracious', which, although it does not exactly stress the possibility of justified 'displeasure', yet at least suggests it. The third line (v. 26) begins with a biblical figure of speech similar to the one in v. 25. The 'lifting up' of the face 'upon someone' (*'ēlekā* again in Hebrew) means first of all quite simply 'to look at someone' (if anyone in anger does not wish to see someone else, he 'lets his face fall'; cf. Gen. 4.5–6; Jer. 3.12) in the sense of turning towards them in friendship. V. 26 goes on to say that such a move would bring *šālōm*. The word *šālōm* is correctly, though not comprehensively enough, translated by 'peace', since, although 'peace', in the broadest sense, is included within it, it has a wider range of meaning. Basically, it designates the state of 'wholeness' and from this it has acquired the meaning of 'absolute well-being'. However comprehensive this meaning may be, yet one must not, on the other hand, lose sight of the fact that by it, in the Old Testament, it is earthly well-being that is meant. And this limitation holds good for the whole blessing in its original sense; it is dealing with God's good gifts in this earthly life.

4. THE OFFERINGS OF THE ISRAELITE TRIBAL REPRESENTATIVES: 7.1–89

7 ¹On the day when Moses had finished setting up the tabernacle, and had anointed and consecrated it with all its furnishings, and had anointed and consecrated the altar with all its utensils, ²the leaders of Israel, heads of their fathers' houses, the leaders of the tribes, who were over those who were numbered, ³offered and brought their offerings before the LORD, six covered wagons and twelve oxen, a wagon for every two of the leaders, and for each one an ox; they offered them before the tabernacle. ⁴Then the LORD said to Moses, ⁵'Accept these from them, that they may be used in doing the service of the tent of

meeting, and give them to the Levites, to each man according to his service.' ⁶So Moses took the wagons and the oxen, and gave them to the Levites. ⁷Two wagons and four oxen he gave to the sons of Gershon, according to their service; ⁸and four wagons and eight oxen he gave to the sons of Merari, according to their service, [under the direction of Ithamar the son of Aaron the priest.] ⁹But to the sons of Kohath he gave none, because they were charged with the care of the holy things which had to be carried on the shoulder. ¹⁰And the leaders offered offerings for the dedication of the altar on the day it was anointed; and the leaders offered their offering before the altar. ¹¹And the LORD said to Moses, 'They shall offer their offerings, one leader each day, for the dedication of the altar.'

12 He who offered his offering the first day was Nahshon the son of Amminadab, of the tribe of Judah; ¹³and his offering was one silver plate whose weight was a hundred and thirty shekels, one silver basin of seventy shekels, according to the shekel of the sanctuary, both of them full of fine flour mixed with oil for a cereal offering; ¹⁴one golden dish of ten shekels, full of incense; ¹⁵one young bull, one ram, one male lamb a year old, for a burnt offering; ¹⁶one male goat for a sin offering; ¹⁷and for the sacrifice of peace offerings, two oxen, five rams, five male goats, and five male lambs a year old. This was the offering of Nahshon the son of Amminadab.

18 On the second day Nethanel the son of Zuar, the leader of Issachar, made an offering; ¹⁹he offered for his offering one silver plate, whose weight was a hundred and thirty shekels, one silver basin of seventy shekels, according to the shekel of the sanctuary, both of them full of fine flour mixed with oil for a cereal offering; ²⁰one golden dish of ten shekels, full of incense; ²¹one young bull, one ram, one male lamb a year old, for a burnt offering; ²²one male goat for a sin offering; ²³and for the sacrifice of peace offerings, two oxen, five rams, five male goats, and five male lambs a year old. This was the offering of Nethanel the son of Zuar.

24 On the third day Eliab the son of Helon, the leader of the men of Zebulun: ²⁵his offering was one silver plate, whose weight was a hundred and thirty shekels, one silver basin of seventy shekels, according to the shekel of the sanctuary, both of them full of fine flour mixed with oil for a cereal offering; ²⁶one golden dish of ten shekels, full of incense; ²⁷one young bull, one ram, one male lamb a year old, for a burnt offering; ²⁸one male goat for a sin offering; ²⁹and for the sacrifice of peace offerings, two oxen, five rams, five male goats, and five male lambs a year old. This was the offering of Eliab the son of Helon.

30 On the fourth day Elizur the son of Shedeur, the leader of the men of Reuben: ³¹his offering was one silver plate whose weight was a hundred and thirty shekels, one silver basin of seventy shekels, according to the shekel of the sanctuary, both of them full of fine flour mixed with oil for a cereal offering; ³²one golden dish of ten shekels, full of incense; ³³one young bull, one ram, one male lamb a year old, for a burnt offering; ³⁴one male goat for a sin offering; ³⁵and for the sacrifice of

peace offerings, two oxen, five rams, five male goats, and five male lambs a year old. This was the offering of Elizur the son of Shedeur.

36 On the fifth day Shelumiel the son of Zurishaddai, the leader of the men of Simeon: [37]his offering was one silver plate, whose weight was a hundred and thirty shekels, one silver basin of seventy shekels, according to the shekel of the sanctuary, both of them full of fine flour mixed with oil for a cereal offering; [38]one golden dish of ten shekels, full of incense; [39]one young bull, one ram, one male lamb a year old, for a burnt offering; [40]one male goat for a sin offering; [41]and for the sacrifice of peace offerings, two oxen, five rams, five male goats, and five male lambs a year old. This was the offering of Shelumiel the son of Zurishaddai.

42 On the sixth day Eliasaph the son of Deuel, the leader of the men of Gad: [43]his offering was one silver plate, whose weight was a hundred and thirty shekels, one silver basin of seventy shekels, according to the shekel of the sanctuary, both of them full of fine flour mixed with oil for a cereal offering; [44]one golden dish of ten shekels, full of incense; [45]one young bull, one ram, one male lamb a year old, for a burnt offering; [46]one male goat for a sin offering; [47]and for the sacrifice of peace offerings, two oxen, five rams, five male goats, and five male lambs a year old. This was the offering of Eliasaph the son of Deuel.

48 On the seventh day Elishama the son of Ammihud, the leader of the men of Ephraim: [49]his offering was one silver plate, whose weight was a hundred and thirty shekels, one silver basin of seventy shekels, according to the shekel of the sanctuary, both of them full of fine flour mixed with oil for a cereal offering; [50]one golden dish of ten shekels, full of incense; [51]one young bull, one ram, one male lamb a year old, for a burnt offering; [52]one male goat for a sin offering; [53]and for the sacrifice of peace offerings, two oxen, five rams, five male goats, and five male lambs a year old. This was the offering of Elishama the son of Ammihud.

54 On the eighth day Gamaliel the son of Pedahzur, the leader of the men of Manasseh: [55]his offering was one silver plate, whose weight was a hundred and thirty shekels, one silver basin of seventy shekels, according to the shekel of the sanctuary, both of them full of fine flour mixed with oil for a cereal offering; [56]one golden dish of ten shekels, full of incense; [57]one young bull, one ram, one male lamb a year old for a burnt offering; [58]one male goat for a sin offering; [59]and for the sacrifice of peace offerings, two oxen, five rams, five male goats, and five male lambs a year old. This was the offering of Gamaliel the son of Pedahzur.

60 On the ninth day Abidan the son of Gideoni, the leader of the men of Benjamin: [61]his offering was one silver plate, whose weight was a hundred and thirty shekels, one silver basin of seventy shekels, according to the shekel of the sanctuary, both of them full of fine flour mixed with oil for a cereal offering; [62]one golden dish of ten shekels, full of incense; [63]one young bull, one ram, one male lamb a year old, for

a burnt offering; [64]one male goat for a sin offering; [65]and for the sacrifice of peace offerings, two oxen, five rams, five male goats, and five male lambs a year old. This was the offering of Abidan the son of Gideoni.

66 On the tenth day Ahiezer the son of Ammishaddai, the leader of the men of Dan: [67]his offering was one silver plate, whose weight was a hundred and thirty shekels, one silver basin of seventy shekels, according to the shekel of the sanctuary, both of them full of fine flour mixed with oil for a cereal offering; [68]one golden dish of ten shekels, full of incense; [69]one young bull, one ram, one male lamb a year old, for a burnt offering; [70]one male goat for a sin offering; [71]and for the sacrifice of peace offerings, two oxen, five rams, five male goats, and five male lambs a year old. This was the offering of Ahiezer the son of Ammishaddai.

72 On the eleventh day Pagiel the son of Ochran, the leader of the men of Asher: [73]his offering was one silver plate, whose weight was a hundred and thirty shekels, one silver basin of seventy shekels, according to the shekel of the sanctuary, both of them full of fine flour mixed with oil for a cereal offering; [74]one golden dish of ten shekels, full of incense; [75]one young bull, one ram, one male lamb a year old, for a burnt offering; [76]one male goat for a sin offering; [77]and for the sacrifice of peace offerings, two oxen, five rams, five male goats, and five male lambs a year old. This was the offering of Pagiel the son of Ochran.

78 On the twelfth day Ahira the son of Enan, the leader of the men of Naphtali: [79]his offering was one silver plate, whose weight was a hundred and thirty shekels, one silver basin of seventy shekels, according to the shekel of the sanctuary, both of them full of fine flour mixed with oil for a cereal offering; [80]one golden dish of ten shekels, full of incense; [81]one young bull, one ram, one male lamb a year old, for a burnt offering; [82]one male goat for a sin offering; [83]and for the sacrifice of peace offerings, two oxen, five rams, five male goats, and five male lambs a year old. This was the offering of Ahira the son of Enan.

84 This was the dedication offering for the altar, on the day when it was anointed, from the leaders of Israel: twelve silver plates, twelve silver basins, twelve golden dishes, [85]each silver plate weighing a hundred and thirty shekels and each basin seventy, all the silver of the vessels two thousand four hundred shekels according to the shekel of the sanctuary, [86]the twelve golden dishes, full of incense, weighing ten shekels apiece according to the shekel of the sanctuary, all the gold of the dishes being a hundred and twenty shekels; [87]all the cattle for the burnt offering twelve bulls, twelve rams, twelve male lambs a year old, with their cereal offering; and twelve male goats for a sin offering; [88]and all the cattle for the sacrifice of peace offerings twenty-four bulls, the rams sixty, the male goats sixty, the male lambs a year old sixty. This was the dedication offering for the altar, after it was anointed.

89 And when Moses went into the tent of meeting to speak with the LORD, he heard the voice speaking to him from above the mercy seat

that was upon the ark of the testimony, from between the two cherubim; and it spoke to him.

This extremely detailed chapter concerning the offering of the extraordinarily rich gifts given by the twelve 'leaders of Israel' (vv. 2, 84) as representatives of the tribes for the 'dedication of the altar' is one of the very late additions to the P-narrative. Its very position is striking. The 'day' of the setting up of the 'tabernacle' and of the 'anointing' and 'consecration' of all its furnishings which is mentioned in v. 1 is already in the past; according to Ex. 40.2, 17 the date of it was to be the first day of the first month of the second year of the exodus, but this date is already past in Num. 1.1, 18. This is tied up with the fact that several facts presupposed in what is recounted in Num. 7 materialize for the first time in the proceedings reported in Num. 1ff. Thus the 'leaders', active in this whole account of the bringing of offerings, are mentioned by name for the first time in Num. 1.4ff., that is a month after the setting up and consecration of the 'tabernacle' and the altar. The contents themselves raise the question of literary dependence. The references to the setting up, anointing and consecration of the 'tabernacle' and especially to the 'anointing' of the altar (vv. 10, 84) go back to elements in Ex. 40* which are even secondary there, especially to Ex. 40.9, 10. The names of the 'leaders' come, in the last resort, from the list in Num. 1.5–15, but their order of precedence is determined by the layout of the camp described in Num. 2.3–31. The reference to the duties of service on the part of the 'Levites' in vv. 5–9 which is especially concerned with the transportation of the sanctuary on the march (cf., especially, v. 9bβ) links up with the section in Num. 4.4–33 which, for its part, has already been noted as an addition (cf. above p. 41). From the point of view of content, this long chapter is not even particularly full. It deals only with the idea that the wilderness sanctuary, immediately after its erection and especially after the 'consecration of the altar', was provided, by the representatives of the Israelite tribes, with fantastically rich gifts which served for the adornment of the sanctuary and were, at the same time, evidence of Israel's piety and generosity. The late author thought he could emphasize the significance of these contents by means of painstaking detail and constant repetition. He obviously did not ask himself the question of where, in the wilderness, the 'leaders' could have acquired this wealth of

* Cf. *Exodus*, pp. 282f.

gifts, especially the large numbers of vessels made of precious metals.

[7.1–9] The whole chapter falls into two unequal parts. According to vv. 1–9, the 'leaders' first of all give wagons with oxen for pulling them; vv. 10–88 deal with the offerings for the 'dedication of the altar'. From the present wording it would seem that when the 'leaders of Israel' (v. 2) brought the 'covered wagons' (the meaning of this technical term is no longer certain, but it would seem from the context that it is to be understood in this sense) and the oxen, they had no particular purpose in mind; for it is only in vv. 4–5, resulting from a divine command, that these gifts are handed over by Moses to the Levites, specifically for the transportation of the sanctuary. The Levites are thereby relieved of the duty of 'carrying' the sacred objects on the march (4.15, 25, 31) and ox-drawn wagons are subsequently (contrary to the obvious sense of ch. 4) put at their disposal, and these in numbers which are obviously supposed to correspond to the size and weight of what is to be carried (vv. 7–8). According to v. 9, only the Kohathites were not able to share in this relief, because the particularly sacred objects entrusted to them (cf. 4.4–15) could not be loaded on to wagons, but could be carried only on human shoulders, and indeed only on Levitical shoulders.

[7.10–88] The many costly gifts brought by the 'leaders' of the twelve Israelite tribes for the 'dedication of the altar' (vv. 10, 84) come very late with respect to Lev. 9, for that chapter had already dealt with the first sacrifices which Israel offered after the setting up of the sanctuary and by means of which, at least for all practical purposes, the altar was 'consecrated'. It is, of course, no longer possible to decide whether the later author of Num. 7 overlooked the contents of that chapter or whether he felt obliged to regard the comparatively modest offerings made by Israel according to Lev. 9 as invalid for a proper 'dedication of the altar', and therefore to make that dedication binding only by means of the great offerings of Num. 7, which far outpass those first offerings. At any rate, the wealth of gifts was so great that, by divine command (v. 11), each 'leader' was allotted a particular day for the delivery of his contribution; so the 'leaders' came one after the other on twelve consecutive days in the order and precedence of the camp layout of 2.3ff. That the materials brought were always immediately sacrificed is nowhere stated, but is certainly to be understood. Every 'leader' brought the same and this is expounded with all the details in the most exhaustive repetition. The gifts served respectively as a cereal offering, with the incense that belongs to it, as described in Lev. 2.1 (vv. 13–14, etc.), as a burnt offering (v. 15, etc.), as a sin offering (v. 16, etc.) and finally as a peace offering particularly abundantly supplied with sacrificial victims (v. 17, etc.). These were all the relevant types of offering, in the opinion of the author, for which the altar that was to be 'consecrated' was destined. While the sacrificial animals were naturally brought alive, the materials for the cereal offering were brought in costly vessels of gold and silver (vv. 13–14, etc.), which certainly were to remain as consecrated gifts in the possession of the sanctuary.

[7.89] The final sentence, v. 89, very detailed and phrased, perhaps intentionally, in a very mysterious way, looks like an introduction to a divine address to Moses which, however, does not materialize. Since the individual sections of the next three chapters all have their own introductory formula with the usual stereotyped phraseology, we cannot assume that v. 89 originally belonged to one of these following sections. The suggestion that after v. 89 something has subsequently fallen out is a pure expedient of embarrassment. The strange wording, especially the mention of 'the voice' (sc. of God) which 'speaks with itself' (this is certainly the meaning of the text in the traditional vocalization), yet in such a way that it is turned towards Moses, suggests that v. 89 is intended as an independent statement and not simply as the introduction to a divine address. In that case, this sentence must surely mean that Yahweh, through the very act of speaking in the tent of meeting in the presence of Moses, is expressing the fact that he has accepted with pleasure the proffered gifts. In this case, too, v. 89 would certainly have to be regarded as a secondary addition, since its relationship with what has preceded it is all too loose and undefined.

5. FURTHER DIVINE ORDINANCES: 8.1–9.14

(a) THE SETTING UP OF THE LAMPSTAND: 8.1–4

8 ¹Now the LORD said to Moses, ²'Say to Aaron, When you set up the lamps, the seven lamps shall give light in front of the lampstand.' ³And Aaron did so; he set up its lamps to give light in front of the lampstand, as the LORD commanded Moses. ⁴And this was the workmanship of the lampstand, hammered work of gold; from its base to its flowers, it was hammered work; according to the pattern which the LORD had shown Moses, so he made the lampstand.

This section serves as an appendix to Ex. 25.31–40. There, the setting of the lamps on the lampstand that had previously been

described in detail was reported in the probably secondary v. 37b;*
here that brief notice is amplified without any new facts being added
to it. This is also true of the notice, appended to the concluding
sentence v. 3, concerning the 'manufacture' of the lampstand (v. 4),
which gives the description of the lampstand, found in Ex. 25.31–34,
in a purely summary fashion by singling out the 'bases'† and the
'flowers' as the lowest and topmost elements of the construction of
this artistic piece of workmanship. This section is intended to
emphasize that the detachable lamps, with their lips for the wick, are
always to be set on the (seven-branched) lampstand in such a way
that the light shines in front of the lampstand.

(b) APPENDIX ON THE ORGANIZATION OF THE LEVITES: 8.5–26

8 ⁵And the LORD said to Moses, ⁶"Take the Levites from among,
the people of Israel, and cleanse them. ⁷And thus you shall do to them,
to cleanse them: sprinkle the water of expiation upon them, and let
them go with a razor over all their body, and wash their clothes and
cleanse themselves. ⁸Then let them take a young bull and its cereal
offering of fine flour mixed with oil, and you shall take another young
bull for a sin offering. ⁹And you shall present the Levites before the
tent of meeting, and assemble the whole congregation of the people of
Israel. ¹⁰When you present the Levites before the LORD, the people of
Israel shall lay their hands upon the Levites, [¹¹and Aaron shall offer
the Levites before the LORD as a wave offering from the people of Israel,
that it may be theirs to do the service of the LORD.] ¹²Then the Levites
shall lay their hands upon the heads of the bulls; and you shall offer
the one for a sin offering and the other for a burnt offering to the LORD,
to make atonement for the Levites. ¹³And you shall cause the Levites to
attend Aaron and his sons, and shall offer them as a wave offering to the
LORD.

14 'Thus you shall separate the Levites from among the people of
Israel, and the Levites shall be mine. ¹⁵And after that the Levites shall
go in to do service at the tent of meeting, [when you have cleansed them
and offered them as a wave offering.] ¹⁶For they are wholly given to me
from among the people of Israel; [instead of all that open the womb,
the first-born of all the people of Israel, I have taken them for myself.
¹⁷For all the first-born among the people of Israel are mine, both of man
and of beast; on the day that I slew all the first-born in the land of

---

* Cf. *Exodus*, p. 209.

† For the meaning of this technical term, presumably originally in the plural
in Ex. 25.31, too, cf. *Exodus*, p. 208.

Noth would read both 'base' and 'flower' (both sing. in MT) as plurals. RSV
does so with regard to the latter, but not with regard to the former. Tr.

APPENDIX ON ORGANIZATION OF LEVITES: 8.5–26   67

Egypt I consecrated them for myself, 18and I have taken the Levites instead of all the first-born among the people of Israel. 19And I have given the Levites as a gift to Aaron and his sons from among the people of Israel, to do the service for the people of Israel at the tent of meeting, and to make atonement for the people of Israel, that there may be no plague among the people of Israel in case the people of Israel should come near the sanctuary.']

20 Thus did Moses and Aaron and all the congregation of the people of Israel to the Levites; according to all that the LORD commanded Moses concerning the Levites, the people of Israel did to them. [21And the Levites purified themselves from sin, and washed their clothes; and Aaron offered them as a wave offering before the LORD, and Aaron made atonement for them to cleanse them.] 22And after that the Levites went in to do their service in the tent of meeting in attendance upon Aaron and his sons; as the LORD had commanded Moses concerning the Levites, so they did to them.

23 And the LORD said to Moses, 24'This is what pertains to the Levites: from twenty-five years old and upward they shall go in to perform the work in the service of the tent of meeting; 25and from the age of fifty years they shall withdraw from the work of the service and serve no more, 26but minister to their brethren in the tent of meeting, to keep the charge, and they shall do no service. Thus shall you do to the Levites in assigning their duties.'

In this passage individual points from the section on the organization of the Levites in ch. 3–4 are taken up once more to be enlarged and emended. The first part (vv. 5–22) deals with the method of the separation of the Levites from the Israelite tribes; the second part (vv. 23–26) deals with the age for Levitical service. The position of this passage reveals it to be, generally speaking, an appendix to the substance of ch. 3–4. It would appear, however, that the literary relationship is complicated, since, on the one hand, the first part (vv. 5–22) is not entirely from a single source and, on the other, it is at least probable, as we shall see, that some of the latest elements in the complex of ch. 3–4 are of a later date than the basic form of the present appendix.

[8.5–22] In vv. 5–22 the Levites are conceived of as an offering brought by the Israelites at God's command. This is a novel idea, going beyond anything in ch. 3–4. This is not a reason for the peculiar position of the Levites, rather is that position presupposed and interpreted in the sense of their specially belonging to Yahweh, an idea which, for its part, is now based on a dedication on the analogy of a sacrifice. With its stress on belonging to Yahweh, the present section is closely related to the passage in 3.11–13 (cf. above, pp. 33f.) which, however, immediately relates this concept to the idea of a substitution for the first-born who belong to Yahweh, an idea which, in the present passage, does not make its appearance until later (vv. 16b–19) in a section which is very probably to be regarded as a later addition (cf. below, p. 69). In this respect the basic form of the present passage represents a simpler and, at the same time, certainly older stage than 3.11–13 and, therefore, is the earliest exposition of the idea of a substitution for the first-born as this is found in 3.40ff. However, no conclusions can be drawn from this assertion with regard to the literary dating of this basic form. According to vv. 6ff., everything is carried out in obedience to a detailed divine command. The Levites are first of all 'cleansed' prior to being offered (vv. 6b–7), with the expression 'clean', in itself a cultic term, also including outer cleanliness (v. 7b). 'Sprinkling' with the 'water of expiation' occurs only here; the term 'sprinkle', originally used of a rite involving the 'shedding' of blood,* is here transferred to that of a symbolic cleansing with water, and this water is designated 'water of expiation' only in respect of its intended effect rather than with reference to any particular method of preparation. In order to be able to approach the sanctuary, the Levites must bring with them the usual sacrifices (burnt offering with cereal offering, sin offering— v. 8). Before the assembled congregation (v. 9b), they are then designated as the offering of the whole people by the ritual of the 'laying on of hands'.† As such, they are then 'waved' 'before Yahweh'.‡ This is first mentioned in v. 11, with Aaron as the agent of this cultic gesture, while in v. 13b (15bβ) it is Moses who appears as agent in this act of 'waving'. V. 11 anticipates this latter statement and should be placed later for the reason that 'waving' is an action peculiar to the priesthood. According to the original form of the text, the Levites' own offering must be presented for their atonement, and this comes about through the agency of Moses (v. 12); only then could they be offered and assigned to Yahweh by being 'waved' (here, of course, in a purely figurative sense) (v. 13b), and this in such a way that they are thereby made to 'attend' Aaron and his sons (v. 13a). This latter remark is intentionally almost word for word identical with 3.6aβ, § for here there comes into play the idea

---

* Cf. *Leviticus*, p. 39.   † Cf. *Leviticus*, p. 22.   ‡ Cf. *Exodus*, p. 232.

§ This fact is obscured by RSV, which has 'cause to attend' in 8.13 and 'set before' in 3.6 as translations of the same Hebrew verb (*ha'ᵃmadtā*). The translation 'set before' is closer to the Hebrew. Tr.

expressed in 3.5–10, that the Levites are put at the disposal of the priests for 'service' (the expression 'to stand *or* be set before someone' usually includes the concept of 'serving'), an idea which is not exactly in opposition to their being assigned to Yahweh, but is nevertheless in competition with it (cf. the relationship between 3.11–13 and 3.5–10, and on this point see above, pp. 32ff.). In the present passage the reference to 'Aaron and his sons' is only incidental. The main object of interest remains the idea that the Levites belong to Yahweh, and this finds expression also in the fact that finally in v. 16a (v. 15b is a secondary repetition of the remarks of vv. 6b and 13b) the statement of 3.9b is taken over almost word for word, but is altered in this respect, namely that the Levites are to be 'given' (cf. above, p. 33), not to Aaron (as in 3.9b) but to Yahweh for his own. Vv. 15a and 16a clearly form a conclusion. Vv. 16b–19 are, therefore, seen to be a later addition. In them the statements of 3.12–13 are taken over, verbally the same but much extended (vv. 16b–18), and then (v. 19aα), in a peculiarly inconsequential fashion, the assertions of 3.7–9 are repeated. Added to this there is, in v. 19aβb, a very strange definition of the Levites' duties. Elsewhere, 'making atonement' is a priestly task, not a Levitical one, and that 'atonement' should then be necessary if the Israelites come too near the sanctuary (it remains quite obscure what in actual fact is meant by this) is an idea which never materialized. The lengthy divine instructions of vv. 6–16a (16b–19) are followed, in vv. 20–22, by a brief notice about their fulfilment which has later been expanded by an addition in v. 21 which goes back to v. 11.

[8.23–26] The brief paragraph in vv. 23–26 is a ruling, deriving from 4.2ff., on the question of the age at which the Levites were permitted to enter upon their active cultic service. While 4.2ff. states that Levites between the ages of thirty and fifty were to be active, the present passage puts the entry age at twenty-five; and while the upper limit of fifty is not altered, it is relaxed a little. This must surely be understood as a later correction. This is borne out not only by the isolated position of this passage in a series of 'appendices' but also by its contents, which can best be explained as a result of an appreciable lack of Levitical strength, as is shown above all by the fact that, according to vv. 25–26a, in spite of the continuance of fifty as the upper age-limit for 'service' proper, continued assistance —now no longer restricted as to length—is envisaged on the part of those Levites who have grown old. The original limitation of the time of service to the remarkably short period of life between the ages of thirty and fifty, which varies from the usual measurement of active life as being between the ages of twenty and sixty (cf. Lev. 27.3; Num. 1.3ff.), is to be understood as due to the fact that for the peculiarly delicate tasks allotted to the Levites, only the full maturity of life seemed appropriate.

(c) APPENDIX TO THE PASSOVER LEGISLATION: 9.1–14

9 [1]And the LORD spoke to Moses in the wilderness of Sinai, in the first month of the second year after they had come out of the land of Egypt, saying, [2]'Let the people of Israel keep the passover at its appointed time. [3]On the fourteenth day of this month, in the evening, you shall keep it at its appointed time; according to all its statutes and all its ordinances you shall keep it.' [4]So Moses told the people of Israel that they should keep the passover. [5]And they kept the passover in the first month, on the fourteenth day of the month, in the evening, in the wilderness of Sinai; according to all that the LORD commanded Moses, so the people of Israel did. [6]And there were certain men who were unclean through touching the dead body of a man, so that they could not keep the passover on that day; and they came before Moses [and Aaron] on that day; [7]and those men said to him, 'We are unclean through touching the dead body of a man; why are we kept from offering the LORD's offering at its appointed time among the people of Israel?' [8]And Moses said to them, 'Wait, that I may hear what the LORD will command concerning you.'

9 The LORD said to Moses, [10]'Say to the people of Israel, If any man of you or of your descendants is unclean through touching a dead body, or is afar off on a journey, he shall still keep the passover to the LORD. [11]In the second month on the fourteenth day in the evening they shall keep it; they shall eat it with unleavened bread and bitter herbs. [12]They shall leave none of it until the morning, nor break a bone of it; according to all the statute for the passover they shall keep it. [13]But the man who is clean and is not on a journey, yet refrains from keeping the passover, that person shall be cut off from his people, because he did not offer the LORD's offering at its appointed time; that man shall bear his sin. [14] And if a stranger sojourns among you, and will keep the passover to the LORD, according to the statute of the passover and according to its ordinance, so shall he do; you shall have one statute, both for the sojourner and for the native.'

To the Passover legislation of P (Ex. 12.1ff.), to which the present passage is very closely related with regard both to language and contents, there is added the rule that, in cases where the celebration is prevented, the Passover should be kept exactly one month after the appointed time and that 'strangers' also may celebrate the

Passover according to the same rules as apply to Israel. The secondary character of the passage relegates it to those additions to the P-narrative which certainly come from the post-exilic period. In this late period there is also the supposition, which is quite anachronistic as far as the Mosaic period is concerned, that individuals can be absent on a long journey (vv. 10–13).

[9.1–5] First of all, at the given time, i.e. at the beginning of the second year after the exodus from Egypt, it is enjoined by Moses that the Passover commanded them and celebrated by them at the exodus must be celebrated when the same date comes round again (a date given in accordance with the usual post-exilic practice of reckoning the year from the spring and of numbering the months) and every year on that date, and that both the time (even the time of day 'between the two evenings' = 'at the evening twilight')* and the rules of Ex. 12.1ff. were to be observed exactly.

[9.6–13] The exceptional case of those who are prevented from keeping the Passover is stated in vv. 6–12 in the form of a precedent arising out of an incident which occurred at the Passover of the second year and which is resolved by means of a direct divine decision sought and received by Moses (vv. 8–9)† and then considered as valid for all time (cf. v. 10ba). According to this, the valid reasons for being prevented from participating in the celebration of the Passover, a participation which is obligatory on pain of death (v. 13), are 'uncleanness' and absence. Of the many possibilities of becoming (cultically) 'unclean', there is envisaged only (as an example?) that of contact with a dead body.‡ By the expression (literally) 'far way' is clearly meant a journey 'abroad' and this presupposes that the Passover, although it is not confined to the sanctuary by P (otherwise in the deuteronomic law in Deut. 16.2, 5, 6) but is to be celebrated in families at 'home' (Ex. 12.3, 4, 7), yet could and must be celebrated only within the enclosed Israelite domain. For those who are prevented in this way, the divine decision prescribes, as a date for the celebration of the Passover, one month later in any given year (that is, on the fourteenth day of the second month). It is not clear, however, whether this later celebration was obligatory or voluntary for those who had been previously prevented. The final phrase of

* Cf. *Leviticus*, p. 169.
† For this type of 'charismatic judgment', cf. Lev. 24.10–23 and, on this point, *Leviticus*, p. 179.
‡ Cf. *Leviticus*, p. 155.

it can be taken as the continuation of what precedes it* or else as an introductory link to the following sentence ('thus shall he keep the passover to Yahweh, namely on the fourteenth day of the second month'). It is worthy of notice that in this context (v. 7 and again in v. 13) the Passover is designated as an 'offering', being thus placed, contrary to its original significance,† among the gift offerings. Even this special second observance of the Passover was to be done exactly according to the rules laid down in Ex. 12.1ff., those points of it which seemed most important to the author being specifically mentioned in vv. 11b, 12a (cf. Ex. 12.8, 10, 46b).‡

[9.14] The short note in v. 14 allows also to the 'stranger' living in Israel the right to celebrate the Passover (in his home) according to the rules that obtain (so already Ex. 12.48–49); this must mean, in view of the ordinances of Ex. 12.43–49, which deal specifically with the right of participation in the Passover celebration, that by 'stranger' is meant someone who does not belong to the circle of fully privileged Israelites, but who yet, by acceptance of circumcision, has given himself to the service of the God of Israel (that is a 'proselyte' in the terminology of a later period and, of course, still with the presupposition of a protracted sojourn within Israelite territory).

6. THE DEPARTURE FROM SINAI: 9.15–10.36

9 15On the day that the tabernacle was set up, the cloud covered the tabernacle, [the tent of the testimony;] and at evening it was over the tabernacle like the appearance of fire until morning. 16So it was continually; the cloud covered it by day, and the appearance of fire by night. 17And whenever the cloud was taken up from over the tent, after that the people of Israel set out; and in the place where the cloud settled down, there the people of Israel encamped. 18At the command of the LORD the people of Israel set out, and at the command of the LORD they encamped; as long as the cloud rested over the tabernacle, they remained in camp. 19Even when the cloud continued over the tabernacle many days, the people of Israel kept the charge of the LORD, and did not set out. 20Sometimes the cloud was a few days over the tabernacle, and according to the command of the LORD they remained in camp; then according to the command of the LORD they

---

* This is the view which Noth adopts in his translation of the text which reads: 'If any man of you or of your descendants is unclean through touching a dead body or is afar off on a journey and still wishes to keep the passover to Yahweh, then they should keep it on the fourteenth day of the second month . . .' The RSV is different both from this and from the other possibility which Noth suggests. Tr.

† Cf. *Exodus*, pp. 88ff.

‡ On these points, cf. *Exodus*, pp. 89, 91 and 101.

set out. ²¹And sometimes the cloud remained from evening until morning; and when the cloud was taken up in the morning, they set out, or if it continued for a day and a night, when the cloud was taken up they set out. ²²Whether it was two days, or a month, or a longer time, that the cloud continued over the tabernacle, abiding there, the people of Israel remained in camp and did not set out; but when it was taken up they set out. ²³At the command of the LORD they encamped, and at the command of the LORD they set out; [they kept the charge of the LORD, at the command of the LORD by Moses.]

10 ¹The LORD said to Moses, ²'Make two silver trumpets; of hammered work you shall make them; and you shall use them for summoning the congregation, and for breaking camp. ³And when both are blown, all the congregation shall gather themselves to you at the entrance of the tent of meeting. ⁴But if they blow only one, then the leaders, the heads of the tribes of Israel, shall gather themselves to you. ⁵When you blow an alarm, the camps that are on the east side shall set out. ⁶And when you blow an alarm the second time, the camps that are on the south side shall set out. An alarm is to be blown whenever they are to set out. ⁷But when the assembly is to be gathered together, you shall blow, but you shall not sound an alarm. ⁸And the sons of Aaron, the priests, shall blow the trumpets. The trumpets shall be to you for a perpetual statute throughout your generations. ⁹And when you go to war in your land against the adversary who oppresses you, then you shall sound an alarm with the trumpets, that you may be remembered before the LORD your God, and you shall be saved from your enemies. ¹⁰On the day of your gladness also, and at your appointed feasts, and at the beginnings of your months, you shall blow the trumpets over your burnt offerings and over the sacrifices of your peace offerings; they shall serve you for remembrance before your God: I am the LORD your God.'

11 In the second year, in the second month, on the twentieth day of the month, the cloud was taken up from over the tabernacle of the testimony, ¹²and the people of Israel set out by stages from the wilderness of Sinai; and the cloud settled down in the wilderness of Paran. ¹³They set out for the first time at the command of the LORD by Moses. ¹⁴The standard of the camp of the men of Judah set out first by their companies; and over their host was Nahshon the son of Amminadab. ¹⁵And over the host of the tribe of the men of Issachar was Nethanel the son of Zuar. ¹⁶And over the host of the tribe of the men of Zebulun was Eliab the son of Helon.

17 And when the tabernacle was taken down, the sons of Gershon and the sons of Merari, who carried the tabernacle, set out. ¹⁸And the standard of the camp of Reuben set out by their companies; and over their host was Elizur the son of Shedeur. ¹⁹And over the host of the tribe of the men of Simeon was Shelumiel the son of Zurishaddai. ²⁰And over the host of the tribe of the men of Gad was Eliasaph the son of Deuel.

21 Then the Kohathites set out, carrying the holy things, and the

tabernacle was set up before their arrival. ²²And the standard of the camp of the men of Ephraim set out by their companies; and over their host was Elishama the son of Ammihud. ²³And over the host of the tribe of the men of Manasseh was Gamaliel the son of Pedahzur. ²⁴And over the host of the tribe of the men of Benjamin was Abidan the son of Gideoni.

25 Then the standard of the camp of the men of Dan, acting as the rear guard of all the camps, set out by their companies; and over their host was Ahiezer the son of Ammishaddai. ²⁶And over the host of the tribe of the men of Asher was Pagiel the son of Ochran. ²⁷And over the host of the tribe of the men of Naphtali was Ahira the son of Enan. ²⁸This was the order of march of the people of Israel according to their hosts, when they set out.

29 And Moses said to Hobab the son of Reuel the Midianite, Moses' father-in-law, 'We are setting out for the place of which the LORD said, "I will give it to you"; come with us, and we will do you good; for the LORD has promised good to Israel.' ³⁰But he said to him, 'I will not go; I will depart to my own land and to my kindred.' ³¹And he said, 'Do not leave us, I pray you, for you know how we are to encamp in the wilderness, and you will serve as eyes for us. ³²And if you go with us, whatever good the LORD will do to us, the same will we do to you.'

33 So they set out from the mount of the LORD three days' journey; and the ark [of the covenant] of the LORD went before them [three days' journey,] to seek out a resting place for them. [³⁴And the cloud of the LORD was over them by day, whenever they set out from the camp.]

35 And whenever the ark set out, Moses said, 'Arise, O LORD, and let thy enemies be scattered; and let them that hate thee flee before thee.' ³⁶And when it rested, he said, 'Return, O LORD, to the ten thousand thousands of Israel.'

This comparatively extensive section comes under the general heading of 'Departure from Sinai' in spite of the great variety of its individual parts. Here the great, central theme of the Pentateuch which begins with Ex. 19.1, the theophany at Sinai, reaches its conclusion; and in this context the 'old sources' of the Pentateuchal narrative reappear for the first time after the long gap since Ex. 34.* At any rate, that is the case in 10.29–36. Everything that precedes in 9.15–10.28 undoubtedly belongs to the P-narrative or to a later addition to it. The whole section may be divided up as follows: In 9.15–23 there is a general treatment, clearly referring to the forth-coming initial departure, of the guiding function of the 'cloud' (by night with the appearance of fire) in which the 'command' of Yahweh with regard to striking or setting up camp is made manifest. The two trumpets of 10.1–10 had, therefore, now to be made in accordance

* Cf. *Exodus*, pp. 12ff.

with the divine command, since, along with their many other uses, they had to be blown as a signal for the breaking up of the camp. In 10.11–28 the process of the departure from Sinai is reported, while 10.29–36 describe the continuing journey of Israel in the wilderness.

[9.15–23] The introductory sentence, 9.15, connects up with Ex. 40, especially with vv. 2 and 34–38. The latter passage represents perhaps a secondary anticipation of the present statements;* but even the latter are part of the later additions to the P-narrative. They go back to the day when the 'tabernacle' was set up (cf. Ex. 40.17P) and suggest that the cloud of Ex. 24.15b–18P appeared over the sanctuary, giving, on the following night, the appearance of fire. The interplay of cloud and fire is already present in Ex. 24.15b–18; in the idea of the alternation between day and night, however, the old tradition about the pillars of cloud and fire in Ex. 13.21f. has been operative. This appearance was repeated continually from the day when the 'tabernacle' was set up (v. 16). This is mentioned because of the related statements which follow in vv. 17–23, where mention is made only of the cloud visible by day, from whose movements Israel was able to know the will of her God with regard to striking and setting up camp. With these statements the account of the wilderness wandering which is still to come is anticipated, for so far Israel has not yet moved from Sinai. A later author has here depicted in the greatest detail the divine guidance in the wilderness.

[10.1–10] The section on the making of the two silver trumpets in 10.1–10 also belongs to the secondary material. In the author's opinion these had to exist so that the signal could be given for striking camp. These trumpets existed in the post-exilic temple (they are represented amongst the booty from Jerusalem on the arch of Titus), almost certainly for the cultic usage of announcing the beginning and end of festivals, etc. (cf. v. 10). In the present section the author expounds a whole theory concerning the use of the trumpets. According to this, two different ways of blowing the trumpets are distinguished; the one is designated as 'to strike *or* blow' (Hebrew *tq'*) and the other as 'to sound an alarm' (Hebrew Hiph. of *rw'* or *tq' t^erū'ā*). There is certainly a link here with the already ancient use of wind instruments for summoning the army and at the beginning and end of warlike activities (this is indicated in v. 9 with reference to the future period of the conquest) as well as at certain cultic celebrations. That a sound such as was meant in the first place for human ears

* Cf. *Exodus*, p. 283.

should bring Israel into 'remembrance' before God, whether in war or in the cult (vv. 9b, 10b), certainly rests on later interpretation. In the present context the idea is of the use of the trumpets when the camp is to be struck (cf. v. 2b), and particular, yet strangely incomplete reference is made to this in vv. 5–6. According to these verses the tribal groups on the east side (following the layout of 2.3ff.) are to set out at the sound of the first alarm, and at the sound of the second the tribal groups on the south side. There is no further mention of the other two tribal groups (the obvious continuation would follow naturally).

[10.11–12] The report of the departure from Sinai begins at 10.11 and the opening passage at least (vv. 11–12) belongs to the original P-narrative. According to this, Israel, after nearly a year's sojourn (cf. Ex. 19.1)—is it chance that the period of time involved is that of twelve lunar months?—received the divine signal for departure in the lifting of the cloud which, until now, had covered the 'tabernacle of the testimony' (an expression otherwise found only in secondary P-passages and here perhaps inserted secondarily in place of an original 'tabernacle'); and this cloud led Israel into the wilderness of Paran. Here we probably have the idea that the move-ment of the cloud was, of itself, a sign for striking and setting up camp (only a later hand felt obliged, in 9.15–23, to state this in detail). As the first camping site on Israel's continuing journey (the next change of location occurs, in the P-narrative, at 20.1) the wilder-ness of Paran is mentioned. There is no certainty as to its location, especially as the P-itinerary only mentions isolated places and is scarcely based upon a definite concept of a coherent itinerary. It is difficult not to connect the name Paran with that of the *wādi fērān* in the mountainous southern part of the Sinai peninsula; this valley, which, in its upper reaches, contains a well-watered, fruitful oasis, is one of the most remarkable places in the Sinai peninsula, and it is at least probable that P, in using the name Paran, had this oasis in mind. Another question, scarcely susceptible of an answer, is whether P, in mentioning this name, has preserved an element of an older tradition (cf. 12.16), thus leading back to a basis of historical fact.

[10.13–28] The longer exposition (vv. 13–28), closely linked though it is with vv. 11–12, of what happened when the order of the march corresponding to the layout of the camp in 2.1–31 was first put into practice at the departure from Sinai, probably does not belong to the basic form of P. It follows exactly, it is true, the data of ch. 2 (including, once again, the names of the 'leaders'), but it introduces in vv. 17, 21 a new element which modifies the remark of 2.17 (which is probably secondary in any case—cf. above, p. 25) on the basis of 4.2ff.; according to this the sanctuary was carried in two separate parts, the outer construction being removed in the wake of the first tribal group so that the particularly sacred furnishings, which are removed only after the second tribal group, can find a newly erected tent as soon as they arrive at the next camping site.

[10.29–36] 10.29–36, in which, after having been long set aside, the 'old sources' find expression once more, is, in spite of its brevity, far from being a unified whole. It contains three disparate elements, first the incomplete story of the discussion with Hobab (vv. 29–32), secondly the notice about the departure with the ark in the van (v. 33 [34]) and lastly the mention of the so-called 'ark sayings'. In all three the divine name Yahweh is used, so the whole section is doubtless to be attributed to the 'Yahwist' (J); except that one has to reckon with J's having here simply juxtaposed different traditions rather than having worked them together.

[10.29–32] In v. 29 there appears, unmotivated, within the community of or in the neighbourhood of the Israelites encamped at the sacred mountain, a certain Hobab whom Moses asks to take over the leadership of the Israelites into a wilderness which was unknown to them, but with which he was familiar; he would seek out possible camping sites on the journey (this is expressed in v. 31b by means of a perceptual figure of speech), sites, that is, where there was at least some water and vegetation. According to the present text of v. 29, this Hobab was a son of the father-in-law of Moses who is mentioned in Ex. 2.18, and the two following words in the text of v. 29 stand in apposition to Reuel.* But already this is a harmonization. According to Judg. 4.11 (cf. perhaps also Judg. 1.16) there was a tradition according to which Hobab himself was the father-in-law of Moses and belonged to the tribal confederacy of the Kenites. This tradition does not agree with the tradition about Jethro, the priest of Midian (Ex. 3.1 et al.), and the originally anonymous 'priest of Midian' (Ex. 2.16) who was probably only secondarily (cf. ibid., v. 18) given the name Reuel. In Num. 10.29, 'Hobab the father-in-law of Moses', of whom it was originally a question here, has been brought second-arily into relationship with that 'Midianite Reuel'. This probably did

* The two words in question are 'the Midianite' and 'the father-in-law of Moses', taking the latter phrase as one linguistic unit. Tr.

not happen as early as J, who may well have designated Hobab more closely by some lost appositional word ('the Kenite'?), but probably at the hand of a later writer for whom the inapposite repetition of the name Moses in v. 29aα was a difficulty. There is no mention in vv. 29–32 either of a divine command to strike camp or of divine guidance. Moses informs Hobab of the decision to strike camp which is to lead them to the 'place' spoken of by Yahweh, i.e. to the promised land, and tells him that he is in need of an experienced human guide through the wilderness. As a reward he promises to do Hobab 'good' in connection with the 'good' which Yahweh has promised to Israel in an indeterminate future (vv. 29b, 32). By this, especially in the present context, can be meant only the gift of a land, in which Hobab is hereby promised a share. After his initial refusal (v. 30), Hobab allowed himself, as a result of renewed entreaties (vv. 31–32), to be prevailed upon to go with them. It is true that this is not now stated, but it must have been the original outcome of the story which, otherwise, would have had no *raison d'être*. That there was originally such a positive outcome is also shown by the fact that the final outcome of this tradition is the presence of 'Hobabites', testified to by the above-mentioned passage in Judg. 4.11, within the Israelite community in Palestine.

[10.33–34] The question as to why the story is broken off before it is finished must probably be answered by reference to the note which follows directly in v. 33 [34] about the guiding role played by the ark at the departure from the 'mountain of Yahweh'; for the precedence accorded to the ark, which at this initial departure—and presumably also at subsequent ones—sought out for the Israelites a 'resting place', i.e. a site for a temporary encampment, must have made the human guidance of Hobab unnecessary. From the literary point of view, therefore, v. 33 must belong with vv. 29–32; only, in this context, factually disparate traditions have been combined. If, then, v. 33, too, is to be attributed to J, then the word 'covenant' in the expression 'the ark of the covenant of Yahweh' must be a later deuteronomistic addition; the repetition of the words 'three days' journey' is certainly erroneous. It is never indicated in what way the ark fulfils its guiding role. Are we to think of a process similar to that in the narrative of I Sam. 6.7ff.? The strangest thing about vv. 33ff. is the sudden appearance of 'the ark (of Yahweh)', for in the form in which we now have the 'old sources' it has not so far made an appearance. The conclusion usually drawn from this is that at some earlier point, very probably within the Sinai narrative, an account of the construction of the ark, probably by Moses, must have existed and that, with Ex. 25.10–22P in mind, this had been deleted at the time when the whole Pentateuch was put together. This may be correct, but it is useless to construct purely hypothetical suppositions as to where and how the ark could have been mentioned for the first time in the 'old sources'. One must, however, also reckon with the possibility that the ark, known from the earliest days of the settlement, is introduced at this point without preamble as something already known and is mentioned at this point because, with the departure from the 'mountain of Yahweh', divine leadership was necessary (the human leadership of Hobab, proffered by an old tradition, was not sufficient), just as it had been available on the way to the 'mountain of Yahweh' through the pillars of cloud and fire of Ex. 13.21f. The significance given to the ark in v. 33 is incompatible with the role assigned by P to the cloud, that of mediating the divine will with regard to striking and setting up camp (vv. 11–12; cf. 9.15ff.). A later hand has attempted to resolve this tension by an additional reference, alongside the ark, to the 'cloud of Yahweh' appearing over Israel when they set out (v. 34).

[10.35–36] The 'ark sayings' recorded in vv. 35–36 presuppose some previous mention of the ark. This is provided in v. 33; vv. 35–36, therefore, belong, from a literary point of view, with v. 33. From the factual point of view, however, they offer a concept of the ark's significance independent of that given in v. 33, and they are added at this point simply because the ark has been mentioned (this fact is perhaps additional proof that the ark is mentioned in v. 33 for the first time). In the 'ark sayings' it is a question, not of leadership along unknown ways, but of enemies and war; and if v. 35a mentions the ark setting out, this is a setting out not on further travels but to battle with an enemy. Here Yahweh appears in close association with the ark (in v. 33 nothing is said about the relationship between Yahweh and the ark). Yahweh is addressed directly in the ark sayings as a 'warrior' (cf. Ex. 15.3) who defeats his enemies, who are identical with Israel's enemies, and puts them to flight. At the beginning of the battle Yahweh is addressed with the word 'Arise'. From this comes the idea of the ark as his throne or at least as the footstool of an imaginary seat. As a result there is the very probable and very simple conjecture for the beginning of the second saying, which is spoken when the ark 'rested', namely $\check{s}^e b\bar{a}$ = 'sit down' (instead of the present text $\check{s}\bar{u}b\bar{a}$ =

'return'). But there is no support for this conjecture in any of the ancient versions and it is hazarded, in any case, only because the second saying has obviously been defectively preserved. It would appear that after the initial imperative and vocative something has fallen out; the original continuation of the introductory summons has been lost and cannot now be replaced.* If the second saying should be rhythmically constructed exactly as is the first (and this is, to say the least, a very likely supposition), then two words (two rhythmic accents) must have followed the divine name, words which would have provided the missing link between the two parts of this saying. The last part contains two words which are normally used as numerals in Hebrew ('ten thousand thousands of Israel'), but which here are surely used in their original sense to indicate very large or fairly large numbers (cf. Gen. 24.60 and above, p. 21). The age of the ark sayings can no longer be determined; a *terminus ad quem* is provided by their inclusion in the Yahwistic work. Unfortunately the question as to whether they are as early as the period before the settlement or whether they are to be dated after the settlement cannot be determined from the contents of the sayings, nor can any deductions be made from them with regard to the question of the age of the ark itself. That they always belonged to the ark from the very beginning, as the introductory formulae in vv. 35a, 36a expressly state, is at least very likely, even if the actual wording of them says nothing on that subject. And it is equally probable that the conception of the ark which they reveal, namely as a throne or a footstool, is the oldest conception of the significance of the ark to be found in the Old Testament. That the ark could have been regarded as the abode of the invisible presence of Yahweh in battle even as early as the wilderness period, is clear from parallels from comparative religion; that it was still conceived of as such even after the settlement, is obvious from I Sam. 4.3ff.

* The reading of RSV, which inserts the word 'to' at this point, is based on an emended Hebrew text. The word 'to' is not in MT. Tr.

FURTHER SOJOURN IN THE WILDERNESS: 11.1–20.13

1. DISAFFECTION OF THE PEOPLE IN THE WILDERNESS: 11.1–35

11 ¹And the people complained in the hearing of the LORD about their misfortunes; and when the LORD heard it, his anger was kindled, and the fire of the LORD burned among them, and consumed some outlying parts of the camp. ²Then the people cried to Moses; and Moses prayed to the LORD, and the fire abated. ³So the name of that place was called Taberah, because the fire of the LORD burned among them.

4 Now the rabble that was among them had a strong craving; and the people of Israel also wept again, and said, 'O that we had meat to eat! ⁵We remember the fish we ate in Egypt for nothing, the cucumbers, the melons, the leeks, the onions, and the garlic; ⁶but now our strength is dried up, and there is nothing at all but this manna to look at.'

[7 Now the manna was like coriander seed, and its appearance like that of bdellium. ⁸The people went about and gathered it, and ground it in mills or beat it in mortars, and boiled it in pots, and made cakes of it; and the taste of it was like the taste of cakes baked with oil. ⁹When the dew fell upon the camp in the night, the manna fell with it.]

10 Moses heard the people weeping [throughout their families,] every man at the door of his tent; [and the anger of the LORD blazed hotly, and] Moses was displeased. ¹¹Moses said to the LORD, 'Why hast thou dealt ill with thy servant? And why have I not found favour in thy sight, that thou dost lay the burden of all this people upon me? ¹²Did I conceive all this people? Did I bring them forth, that thou shouldst say to me, "Carry them in your bosom, as a nurse carries the sucking child, [to the land which thou didst swear to give their fathers?"] ¹³Where am I to get meat to give to all this people? For they weep before me and say, "Give us meat, that we may eat." ¹⁴I am not able to carry all this people alone, the burden is too heavy

for me. 15If thou wilt deal thus with me, kill me at once, if I find favour in they sight, that I may not see my wretchedness.' 16And the LORD said to Moses, 'Gather for me seventy men of the elders of Israel, [whom you know to be the elders of the people and officers over them;] and bring them to the tent of meeting, and let them take their stand there with you. 17And I will come down and talk with you there; and I will take some of the spirit which is upon you and put it upon them; and they shall bear the burden of the people with you, that you may not bear it yourself alone. 18And say to the people, "Consecrate your-selves for tomorrow, and you shall eat meat; for you have wept in the hearing of the LORD, saying, 'Who will give us meat to eat? For it was well with us in Egypt.' Therefore the LORD will give you meat, and you shall eat. 19You shall not eat one day, or two days, or five days, or ten days, or twenty days, 20but a whole month, until it comes out at your nostrils and becomes loathsome to you, [because you have rejected the LORD who is among you, and have wept before him, say-ing, 'Why did we come forth out of Egypt?' " '] 21But Moses said, ['The people among whom I am number six hundred thousand on foot; and] thou hast said, "I will give them meat, that they may eat a whole month!" 22Shall flocks and herds be slaughtered for them, to suffice them? Or shall all the fish of the sea be gathered together for them, to suffice them? 23And the LORD said to Moses, 'Is the LORD's hand shortened? Now you shall see whether my word will come true for you or not.' 24So Moses went out and told the people the words of the LORD; and he gathered seventy men of the elders of the people, and placed them round about the tent. 25Then the LORD came down in the cloud and spoke to him, and took some of the spirit that was upon him and put it upon the seventy elders; and when the spirit rested upon them, they prophesied. But they did so no more. 26Now two men remained in the camp, one named Eldad, and the other named Medad, and the spirit rested upon them; they were among those registered, but they had not gone out to the tent, and so they prophesied in the camp. 27And a young man ran and told Moses, 'Eldad and Medad are prophesying in the camp.' 28And Joshua the son of Nun, the minister of Moses, one of his chosen men, said, 'My lord Moses, forbid them.' 29But Moses said to him, 'Are you jealous for my sake? Would that all the LORD's people were prophets, that the LORD would put his spirit upon them!' 30And Moses and the elders of Israel returned to the camp.

31 And there went forth a wind from the LORD, and it brought quails from the sea, and let them fall beside the camp, about a day's journey on this side and a day's journey on the other side, round about the camp, and about two cubits deep on the face of the earth. 32And the people rose all that day, and all night, and all the next day, and gathered the quails; he who gathered least gathered ten homers; and they spread them out for themselves all around the camp. 33While the meat was yet between their teeth, before it was consumed, the anger of the LORD was kindled against the people, and the LORD smote the

people with a very great plague. ³⁴Therefore the name of that place
was called Kibroth-hattaavah, because there they buried the people
who had the craving. ³⁵From Kibroth-hattaavah the people journeyed
to Hazeroth; and they remained at Hazeroth.

THIS CHAPTER consists of a short narrative, ending in the
explanation of a place-name (vv. 1–3), of a long story in
expansive style which likewise ends with the explanation of a
place-name (vv. 4–34), and of a concluding note about Israel's
itinerary (v. 35). Apart from this last verse, the chapter deals with the
factor of the people's disaffection and complaints concerning the
miseries of the sojourn in the wilderness. This factor is the main one
in the Pentateuchal theme of the journey through the wilderness.
This theme is invariably dealt with in factual, individual narratives.
The long central portion of the present chapter is not, in itself, a
unified whole. It includes two separate elements, first the people's
complaint about the lack of meat and how it was heard and answered,
and secondly Moses' complaint that alone he is incapable of bearing
the 'burden of the people' and the divine assistance in this case, too.
Not only have these two elements not been woven together, but there
is even a clean break between one section and another. We must,
therefore, reckon with literary juxtaposition, although it is not a case
of two formerly independent 'sources' having been worked together.
For the story of Moses' complaint does not stand on its own, but
presupposes the narrative of the people's disaffection, which provides
the necessary factual occasion for Moses' complaint (one can accept
quite arbitrarily the supposition that the story of Moses' complaint
had its own exposition, now completely lost). It is, therefore, difficult
to divide up the whole passage between the J and E 'sources'. One
must, rather, explain the facts on the assumption of a basic narrative,
found in vv. 4–13, 18–24a, 31–34, into which a later hand has, in
literary fashion, inserted vv. 14–17, 24b–30. This basic narrative,
connected, clearly but not very skilfully, by v. 4 to the brief narrative
in vv. 1–3, is probably Yahwistic. The insertions, which likewise use
the divine name Yahweh throughout, are among the later additions
to J and have left the basic form undisturbed, with the single exception that, between v. 13 and v. 18, they have suppressed what was
probably a brief sentence of the original narrative.

[11.1–3] The only factual element in the contents of the brief
narrative of vv. 1–3 is the place-name Taberah. Doubtless there
existed, in the wilderness between Egypt and Palestine, a locality of

that name which was still known to the Israelites in the period after the conquest. About its location we know nothing further (it is difficult to make anything of the late collection of names in Deut. 9.22f.). The original meaning of the name is likewise quite uncertain. It is possible to regard it as derived from the root $b^{\varsigma}r$ = 'to remove' (perhaps also 'to graze') or as connected with the Arabic $ba^{\varsigma}r$ = 'dung', 'dirt'. The meaning presupposed in the present passage, '(place of) burning', from $b^{\varsigma}r$ = 'to burn', is very probably secondary, but forms the basis of the whole passage. Here the 'fire of Yahweh' once burned (a fire miraculously occasioned by Yahweh); this must be derived from a measure of punishment from the period in which that locality in the wilderness could at one time have been of significance for Israel, i.e. after the exodus from Egypt. The reason for the punishment must have been the great sin of Israel at that time, disaffection and complaint. The narrator is unable to give any specific reason for such disaffection and complaint; his wording is highly unusual, while in v. 1a he compares the people with 'those who have something to complain about'* (this strange expression has perhaps a particular meaning which it is no longer possible to discover). The fire sent by Yahweh in his righteous anger reaches only the edge of the camp (Israel as a whole certainly survived this judgment) and is then withdrawn as a result of an intercessory prayer by Moses (vv. 1b-2); however, the name of the place in question, called forth by this phenomenon, has remained (v. 3).

[11.4-34] The extended narrative of the sending of the quails, which follows in vv. 4-34, is likewise determined in its present form by the explanation of the place-name at the end (v. 34). There was a place in the wilderness called *qibrōt hat-ta'awā*, concerning whose location also nothing is known, nor can anything reliable be derived from Num. 33.16f. or Deut. 9.22f. either. The original meaning could have been something like 'the graves at the boundary' or else 'the graves of the Ta'awa tribe'. That is quite uncertain; what is certain, however, is that the significance which the present writer, or the tradition recorded by him, derives from the name, namely 'the graves of desire, of craving', is forced and artificial and is not the original meaning. From this, however, it seemed clear that at this place a divine judgment ('graves') had once taken place as punish-

---

* The RSV is somewhat free at this point. A more literal translation of the Hebrew, such as Noth gives, would read: 'And the people were like those who complain of evil in Yahweh's hearing.' Tr.

ment for a sinful 'craving' and that this had happened in Israel's nomadic period after the exodus from Egypt; v. 4, with reference to v. 34, at once mentions a '(strong) craving' (*hit'awwū ta'ᵃwā*), which introduces the whole incident. This 'craving' is at once defined as consisting of a desire for meat to eat. Thus the story is brought within the great theme of the divine guidance in the wilderness, a guidance which manifested itself above all in the giving of food and drink in the midst of the unproductive terrain that lay between Egypt and Palestine. Yahweh cared for his people in this situation, but the people 'craved' again and again something more and something better, as seemed to emerge, in the present context, from the (later) naming of this place. Thus the theme of the people's murmuring is particularly firmly rooted in the present narrative.

[11.4–6] Since (in terms of the explanation of the place-name) it is a 'craving', an unjustified and sinful desire, that is dealt with here, the responsibility for this is put upon a 'rabble' (literally 'a gathering of people') which has mingled with Israel (the suffix of *qirbō* refers back to *hā'ām* of vv. 1–2, and this is evidence that, from a literary point of view, vv. 1–3 and vv. 4ff. belong together; for this idea cf. Ex. 12.38). The Israelites are affected by this disaffection and they now give concrete expression to their desire by demanding meat to eat. They express this desire by weeping 'again'. With this word 'again' reference is made to an earlier, analogous occurrence. The link is presumably with the Yahwistic manna story, to which an allusion is also made in v. 6b. There was such a story; parts of it have been worked into the P-narrative in Ex. 16 by an editor,* and there remains only the now unanswerable question as to whether J had already introduced the manna narrative before the Sinai pericope (as P has with the 'quails and manna' theme) or whether the re-daction of the entire Pentateuch under the influence of P removed the J-fragments on the manna theme and that originally J's manna story stood immediately before Num. 11. In the latter case, J would have presented an impressive intensification in the people's murmurings. Earlier, in response to the people's 'weeping', Yahweh had provided the manna on which they were to live from then on. Now they are tired of the manna (v. 6b) and they allow themselves to be led by the 'rabble' into 'weeping' 'again' and demanding meat to eat, the latter with reference to the good life in Egypt which they have had to leave behind (v. 5); there, it is true, there was no meat either, but

* Cf. *Exodus*, pp. 131f.

there was any number of fish and a pleasantly varied selection of vegetable products, in contrast to the monotony of the manna which 'leaves the throat dry',* that is, kills the appetite (v. 6).

[11.7–9] Linked with the mention of the manna, there is (vv. 7–9) a description of its appearance and use which is much more detailed than the short note in Ex. 16.31b, but which, the present context not being concerned with manna at all, must be regarded as a secondary addition. Nevertheless, there is no doubt that this is factually correct information about the manna from the 'manna-tamarisk' of the Sinai peninsula.†

[11.10–13] Moses is enraged at the people's desires (the phrase about 'Yahweh's anger' is premature and breaks the sequence of thought; it is certainly a later addition); however, he turns in the first place not to the people but to Yahweh with reproachful questions (vv. 11–13). Before he comes to the point in question (v. 13), namely that the people are demanding of him (here Moses applies to himself the general question of v. 4bβ) the fulfilment of their demand, which is impossible of fulfilment by a human agency, for meat to eat, he complains first of all in general terms that the people—with claims which are perhaps sometimes justified, but which are usually (as in the present case) unjustified in view of the difficult situation of the wilderness sojourn—are an unbearable 'burden' to him, and that by placing this burden upon him Yahweh has 'dealt ill' with him (v. 11). Bold as this statement certainly is, it is surpassed in v. 12 by the assertion, cast in the form of a rhetorical question, that he, Moses, is, after all, not the people's mother and is, therefore, not obliged to fulfil maternal duties towards them. Implicit in this is the very unusual idea that Yahweh himself is Israel's mother. In view of the usual avoidance in the Old Testament of personal concepts of the relationship between God and people, such as are known in the religions of the surrounding peoples, even the statement that Israel is Yahweh's son is rare (Ex. 4.22; Hos. 11.1). It is, however, extremely rare to express the connection between Yahweh and Israel by the idea of motherhood, thereby, even indirectly, attributing to Yahweh the concept of femininity (cf., nevertheless, expressions such as those in Isa. 49.15; 66.13). In v. 12bα the image alters slightly while Moses

---

* 'Now our throat is dry' is Noth's rendering of v. 6a. RSV has 'Now our strength is dried up'. 'Throat' is the first meaning given to nepeš in Koehler's *Lexicon in Veteris Testamenti Libros*. Tr.
† Cf. *Exodus*, p. 132.

complains that he is supposed to be the nurse charged by the mother with the care of the child (in spite of its masculine form, *'ōmēn* must, in the context, have a feminine sense). In the closing words of v. 12, the image is entirely abandoned; here it is obviously a question of an addition, which links to the term 'take (in the bosom)', 'carry', the idea of being led to the promised land.

[II.14–17] Vv. 14–15 contain a new thought, to which, so far, no expression has been given, namely that Moses cannot carry alone the burden he has to carry, otherwise he would rather be killed by Yahweh in view of his unfulfillable task. From the point of view of form, this is simply the continuation of the speech of Moses to Yahweh that was begun in v. 11, and the catchword introduced in v. 11b, namely 'this people' seen as a 'burden to be borne', controls the thought from now on. The beginning of Moses' speech in vv. 11–13 is then presupposed in vv. 14ff.; the new thought of a division of the 'burden' among many shoulders appears, therefore, as a literary addition to the old basic form of the chapter. Vv. 16–17 prepare the ground for vv. 24b–30. Moses receives the command to choose seventy 'elders' from amongst the 'elders of Israel', the latter obviously conceived of as being very numerous and amongst whom, unless something very special is meant by the expression, one must envisage the heads of the families who, therefore, originally and properly bore the title 'elder'. In the old days of the tribal 'organization' such 'elders' were simply the 'officials' (the relative clause in v. 16a, which is surely to be regarded as a secondary aside, inserted particularly unskilfully, while it designates the chosen men specifically as 'officers'—literally 'writers'—gives expression to this 'official' character of the elders on the basis of later concepts). The seventy elders chosen by Moses are now to become bearers of the spirit since, according to the present passage, the 'spirit' was the divine gift to Moses to enable him to fulfil his duties. Yahweh himself sees to the dispensing and distribution of the 'spirit'. If Moses' 'burden' is to be divided among a large number lest it become unbearably heavy, then the 'spirit', too, must be correspondingly divided. This led, among the chosen elders, to a remarkable combination of institution and charisma, of office and vocation. Furthermore, the 'spirit' is characterized in vv. 25–30 as a 'prophetic' spirit (see further on vv. 25ff. below).

[II.18–24a] The basic narrative thread is resumed in v. 18. The phraseology of the beginning of v. 18 shows that it must have been preceded by a word from Yahweh to Moses which, in answer to the latter's prayer of complaint in vv. 11–13, has promised him divine help in his affliction; because of the later insertion of vv. (14f.) 16f., which likewise contain the promise of divine help for Moses, this (probably short) element of the original narrative has been lost. In vv. 18–20 Moses announces to the people the fulfilment of their 'craving'. The very phraseology of this announcement with which Moses is charged by Yahweh shows clearly that the fulfilment will be at the same time a manifestation of the divine anger at the 'craving'; that is clear even without the reason given in v. 20b, which is seen, by its choice of words, to be in all probability a more recent addition. The people, who are to 'consecrate' themselves for the following day, as for a cultic celebration, in expectation of divine intervention (cf. Ex. 19.10),* are once again reproached with their 'weeping' (v. 18bβ) and are made to envisage a surfeit of 'fulfilment' (v. 19) such as can signify only disaster (v. 20a). Even Moses, who receives this commission, cannot imagine, from his human, earthly point of view, the possibility of this announcement's realization (vv. 21–22; cf. Mark 8.4 et al.; for the 600,000 foot-soldiers cf. Ex. 12.37); it is then stated that a miracle is to happen by the divine 'hand' which will surprise ('touch')† even Moses (v. 23). Before the narrative of this miracle, which one would expect to follow v. 24a directly, the thread of vv. 14–17 is continued in vv. 24b–30, the two narratives now no longer having any connection with each other at all.

[11.24b–30] As is envisaged in v. 16b, the gathering of the seventy elders, selected by Moses to relieve him of his burden, takes place at the tent of meeting. The tent of meeting is mentioned here, as in 12.4ff., in an otherwise pre-priestly tradition. This provides a factual, if not a literary link with Ex. 33.7–11. The connection of Yahweh with the '(pillar of) cloud' (v. 25aα) and the 'coming down' of Yahweh (or the cloud) are also found in Ex. 33.7ff.; finally, here, too (v. 30a, cf., too, 12.4b) it is presumed that the tent of meeting has been set up 'outside the camp' (this is stated specifically in Ex. 33. 7a). These elements are part of the oldest tradition we have about the tent of meeting, whose origins are shrouded in obscurity.‡ In Num. 11–12, the tent of meeting is not the central object of the tradition, as it is in Ex. 33.7–11, but only the scene of God's appearance and

---

* Cf. on this *Exodus*, p. 158.
† So Noth's translation of v. 23b, where the RSV has 'come true for'. Tr.
‡ Cf. also *Exodus*, pp. 254ff.

God's speaking. In Num. 11, all that is mentioned is the fact that God 'spoke' to Moses, in the sense that Moses is singled out in this respect, but no particular divine words are recorded. There follows, rather, the envisaged division of the 'spirit', which had hitherto been found only 'upon' Moses, amongst the seventy elders, with the result that they 'prophesied' unceasingly.* The sense of the verbal expression used (the Hith. of *nb'*, the stem from which comes *nābī'* = 'prophet') is shown most clearly in the narratives of I Sam. 10.5ff. and 19.20ff., where corresponding verbal forms are found. According to these we are dealing with 'prophetic' exaltation, with a state of ecstasy from which come 'prophetic' words which are not comprehensible—or not necessarily so. This is very strange in the present context. Moses is supposed to be 'relieved of his burden' (vv. 14–17). How this goal is achieved by putting the seventy elders into a state of ecstasy is difficult to imagine; moreover, nothing is said on this subject. We may conclude that the theme of 'relief from a burden' had already been dealt with (we find it in Ex. 18.13–27 developed in a quite different and much more pertinent way) and is here being made to serve another purpose. This purpose is obviously the derivation of ecstatic 'prophecy' from the 'spirit' of Moses. It is true that it is not said that from then on this phenomenon existed in Israel; but it emerges here as a prototype for the first time in the history of Israel in direct connection with the figure, envisaged as unique, of Moses. This also shows fairly certainly that the secondary additions in Num. 11 come from circles of ecstatic 'prophecy'. To give even a comparatively exact date to this is impossible; for this phenomenon is traceable from the time of Saul until the times of Jeremiah and Ezekiel. One might be tempted to find in Num. 11.16, 17, 24b, 25 a definite historical reference, but this is surely not possible. Neither the number seventy nor the connection of prophetic ecstasy with the rank and office of the elders allows of any possibility of a link, in terms of an institutional consolidation, with what is otherwise known about the history of 'prophecy'. Therefore the figure seventy must surely be taken simply in the sense of a large number, and the selection from among the elders, which, strangely enough, is made by Moses himself, must be understood in the sense

---

* The RSV ('but they did so no more') is a correct translation of MT *welō yāsāpū* (√*ysp*). Noth emends MT (presumably on the evidence of the Targum and the Vulgate—see BH³) to read *welō yāsūpū* (√*swp*), giving the sense 'and they did not cease (*sc.* prophesying)'. Tr.

that the worthiest and most trustworthy men in Israel, on the basis
of the self-assessment of prophetic 'ecstasy', are indeed worthy of the
gift of the 'spirit'. On the other hand, a definite reference is probably
to be accepted for vv. 26-29, in which specific names are mentioned.
At any rate, this passage must be an addition, for it does not fit
smoothly with the surrounding context. No reason is given as to why
the figure seventy is really to be understood as meaning seventy-two,
nor why the names of these seventy-two were previously registered
(v. 26), nor why the two who are named had not gone out of the
camp to the 'tent' with the others. At any rate, both of them were
seized by the spirit at the same time as the others and with the same
effect of 'prophesying'. In this way the divine will—perhaps even
against the wills of those concerned—had manifested itself, in contrast
to which, the uproar in the camp (v. 27) has as little effect as has the
repudiation on the part of Joshua (v. 28), who here, in accordance
with Ex. 33.11b, functions as the 'minister' of Moses in the tent of
meeting. This rouses Moses to speech, in that he disassociates himself
from every jealousy, occasioned on his account, against the division
of the 'spirit' among many others (v. 29a) and even expresses the
wish that the whole people shared in the gift of the 'spirit' so that all
of them might become 'prophets' (this technical term is used here
explicitly). This latter wish is surely simply the expression of a general
high esteem for 'prophecy' put into the mouth of Moses. On the
other hand, there must be some definite fact behind the Eldad-Medad
episode. To counter the astonishment in the 'camp' and the dis-
approving attitude of the minister of the sanctuary, Joshua, Moses'
authority is sought on behalf of Eldad and Medad. It looks very much
as if behind Eldad and Medad there stood 'prophets' or 'prophetic'
groups who at one time or another had had to battle for recognition
in Israel and who made use of the story of the seventy elders to give
their claims literary currency. The strange, peculiar names Eldad
and Medad may well be fictitious names whose meaning we can no
longer penetrate; and there is now no need to explain any further,
even approximately, the period and circumstances of the hypothetical
background to this whole narrative episode.

[11.31-34] Vv. 31-34 bring the basic narrative of the chapter to a
conclusion. The people's 'craving' is met by the fact that Yahweh, by
means of a wind 'from the sea' (this must mean the Mediterranean,
although Ps. 78.26, referring to the same thing, mentions an 'east
wind' and a 'south wind'), brings large numbers of quails and lets

them fall on and round about the camp. This provides a link with an actual phenomenon of the Sinai peninsula. In spring and autumn flocks of quails regularly appear on the Mediterranean coast of the peninsula. The birds settle on the ground and, wearied by their flight and being, in any case, ponderous birds, they are easy to catch even without special paraphernalia for bird-catching. Yahweh had once cared for his people in the wilderness by providing quails; such must certainly have been the original tenor of the tradition (cf. also the juxtaposition of quails and manna in the P-narrative of Ex. 16). In the present J-version, the quails story appears as a probably intentional advance on the manna story as an indication of Yahweh's anger (cf. above, p. 85); the unashamed 'craving' of the people is punished by means of a surfeit of the gift. In the night of the day mentioned in v. 18 (cf. the quails 'at evening' in Ex. 16.6ff.) the quails appear in such numbers that the people are busy for two whole days and a night (v. 32a) gathering them and spreading out this enormous provision round about the camp to dry (v. 32b). The smallest amount gathered by any one individual consisted of 10 homers = c. 89 bushels. While they were enjoying this gift the people were immediately punished by Yahweh's anger with a 'very great plague'. Nothing more precise is said. The explanation of the place-name which follows in v. 34 (cf. above, pp. 84f.) shows that many died. There is no explicit connection between the eating and the 'plague', but this is suggested in v. 33; that is, it is indicated that the greedy and unrestrained eating of the 'covetous' people has brought about death. Here, too, in the last resort, there may be an element of real experience of life in the Sinai peninsula.

[11.35] In v. 35 there follows a note by J about the itinerary. According to P (10.12) Israel went direct from Sinai to the wilderness of Paran. According to 10.33, J makes Israel go first of all three days' journey from Sinai with no specified destination. In 11.1-3 Israel is in Taberah and in 11.4-34, without anything having been said about another journey, in Kibroth-hattaavah. Now they proceed to Hazeroth. It is just as impossible to identify this place with its very common name as was the case with Taberah and Kibroth-hattaavah (cf. above, p. 84).

2. MIRIAM AND AARON AGAINST MOSES: 12.1-16

12 ¹Miriam and Aaron spoke against Moses because of the Cushite woman whom he had married, [for he had married a Cushite woman;]

²and they said, 'Has the LORD indeed spoken only through Moses? Has he not spoken through us also?' And the LORD heard it. ³Now the man Moses was very meek, more than all men that were on the face of the earth. ⁴And suddenly the LORD said to Moses and to Aaron and Miriam, 'Come out, you three, to the tent of meeting.' And the three of them came out. ⁵And the LORD came down in a pillar of cloud, and stood at the door of the tent, and called Aaron and Miriam; and they both came forward. ⁶And he said, 'Hear my words: If there is a prophet among you, I the LORD make myself known to him in a vision, I speak with him in a dream. ⁷Not so with my servant Moses; he is entrusted with all my house. ⁸With him I speak mouth to mouth, clearly, and not in dark speech; [and he beholds the form of the LORD.] Why then were you not afraid to speak against my servant Moses?'

9 And the anger of the LORD was kindled against them, and he departed; ¹⁰and when the cloud removed from over the tent, behold, Miriam was leprous, as white as snow. And Aaron turned towards Miriam, and behold, she was leprous. ¹¹And Aaron said to Moses, 'Oh, my lord, do not punish us because we have done foolishly and have sinned. ¹²Let her not be as one dead, of whom the flesh is half consumed when he comes out of his mother's womb.' ¹³And Moses cried to the LORD, 'Heal her, O God, I beseech thee.' ¹⁴But the LORD said to Moses, 'If her father had but spit in her face, should she not be shamed seven days? Let her be shut up outside the camp seven days, and after that she may be brought in again.' ¹⁵So Miriam was shut up outside the camp seven days; and the people did not set out on the march till Miriam was brought in again. ¹⁶After that the people set out from Hazeroth and encamped in the wilderness of Paran.

The fact that Moses is reproached with two different things is immediately clear from the opening verses of this chapter. According to v. 1 his marriage with a Cushite woman is laid to his charge; according to v. 2, on the other hand, the reproach is to do with an unjustified claim to special privileges with regard to the reception of the divine word. This twofold reproach is certainly connected with the disunity of the narrative with regard to the role played by the persons who appear against Moses. The first reproach (v. 1) is made by 'Miriam and Aaron' (in that order). In what follows we hear of 'Aaron and Miriam' (vv. 4–5); and in vv. 9–15 Miriam appears as the principal guilty party and Aaron is on her side only in so far as he intercedes for her with Moses (vv. 10b–12). These facts are most probably to be explained as follows. The reproach with regard to the Cushite marriage actually comes originally from Miriam, who is the one who is punished for it, whereas the dispute concerning the special place accorded to Moses in matters concerning the receiving of revelation is reported as stemming from 'Aaron and Miriam', and this subject ends with a reproof from Yahweh (vv. 6–9). The two subjects of the chapter, which have in common only the fact that they deal with reproaches against Moses and that Miriam figures in both of them, are now so closely joined together that it is impossible to pursue a division into separate literary sources. One could, it is true, regard the mention of Aaron in v. 1 as an editorial addition,* but one would be confounded at once by v. 2, since here the mention of both names in v. 1 is obviously presupposed; and the later appearance of Aaron (vv. 10bff.) would remain completely unmotivated if the co-operation between Aaron and Miriam had not been mentioned right from v. 1. It must therefore be accepted that in the complex of this chapter, a complex which, from the literary point of view, can no longer be disentangled, two different strands have been combined. In this respect the reproach regarding the Cushite marriage, a reproach that is suspicious yet scarcely fundamentally significant, must be regarded, from the point of view of the history of tradition, as the primary one; and it is at least probable that it formed the point of contact for a later presentation of the unique 'prophetic' significance of Moses.

Stylistically and thematically, this latter presentation stands in obvious relationship to the insertions in ch. 11 (vv. 14–17, 24b–30); cf., on this point, p. 87 above, and pp. 95f. below. It is, indeed, not in the nature of a continuation of them, but of an expansion or even a correction of them. From a literary point of view, the present chapter in this respect presupposes these insertions in ch. 11; and if these insertions have to be reckoned as belonging to the later expansions of the J-narrative, then all the more must ch. 12 be counted as one of the secondary additions to J. It is no longer clear where the author of this addition found the motif of the reproach against Moses' Cushite marriage. Against the perhaps obvious suggestion that it existed somewhere in the original J-narrative, there is first of all the fact that J, in the form in which we now have it, nowhere else mentions such a marriage and, secondly, above all, the situation that in this case, quite exceptionally, the original J-version has not preserved, not even approximately, its original unity, but (apart from v. 1) has been tailored to fit in with the 'prophet' theme (vv. 9ff.).

* The form of the verb which stands at the head of the sentence might seem to argue for this supposition; but in Hebrew it is possible for the predicate in first position to be in agreement only with the subject which stands immediately following it.

The relationship with each other of the three personages in question remains obscure. It is not stated, and perhaps not even tacitly assumed, that they were brothers and sister, as is accepted in the later period (cf. I Chron. 6.3 (*Hebr.* 5.29), dependent on Ex. 6.20 and 15.20). It would be easier to accept a brother-sister relationship between Aaron and Miriam (cf. the statement in Ex. 15.20 which precisely excludes Moses from this relationship); but there is no hint even of that. Nor are Aaron and Miriam characterized by any kind of title or official designation. Both of them appear as well-known figures of the Mosaic period who were at least prominent enough to be made the mouthpieces of specific reproaches against Moses. From the point of view of the history of traditions, this represents a stage which still knows nothing of Aaron the 'brother' as the helper and companion of Moses.* From this it can be deduced that the present chapter, in spite of its secondary character, can not be dated too late.

[12.1] The information concerning Moses' marriage with a Cushite woman belongs with the various traditions about a non-Israelite wife of Moses (cf. Ex. 2.21 and Num. 10.29 and, on this verse, p. 77 above). The 'Cush' from which the wife mentioned here came, can hardly mean, as it mostly otherwise does in the Old Testament, the country on the southern boundary of Egypt, a country far removed from Moses' sphere of activity (as Luther, who has 'negress', seems to think),† but is probably to be identified with the 'Cushan' of Hab. 3.7, where the reference is to a tribe or confederacy of tribes mentioned as a parallel to 'Midian'. At the same time, 'Cush(an)' is obviously to be distinguished from 'Midian' and, therefore, the wife mentioned here is to be distinguished from the Midianite Zipporah (Ex. 2.16ff.), as the additional justificatory clause in v. 1b is also obviously intended to assert. What the actual objection to this Cushite marriage was is not stated; no objection is made to the non-Israelite origin of the wife in Zipporah's case. That Miriam (so originally) should raise the objection in this case is perhaps to be explained on the grounds that she was the only female figure in Moses' circle known to tradition. Aaron appears only as a result of the fusion of this fragment of tradition with the subject that follows in v. 2.

[12.2] V. 2 deals with the uniqueness of Moses as the recipient of the divine word. It is not specifically stated that Moses laid claim to

* Cf. *Exodus*, pp. 46f. on Ex. 4.13–16.
† Cf., too, the AV, which has 'Ethiopian woman'. Tr.

such uniqueness; Moses is not addressed directly at all. All, rather, that Aaron and Miriam do is to make clearly known—obviously within the Israelite camp—that, in their opinion unjustly, it appears that Yahweh speaks only to Moses. This expression of displeasure serves, in its turn, to produce the divine reproof contained in vv. 6–8. Aaron and Miriam lay claim to a position, similar to that of Moses, as recipients of the word. In Miriam's case reference is certainly, however, made to the designation of her by tradition as a 'prophetess' (Ex. 15.20). Aaron, on the other hand, is not otherwise known to tradition as a recipient of the word independently of Moses. Was he perhaps placed as the male partner of Miriam in the present context only because that seemed desirable in this case and because, as a well-known figure in Moses' sphere of activity, he was specially suited to such a role? Yahweh listens to their reproachful words and 'suddenly' (v. 4) intervenes. Moses himself, then, has neither the opportunity nor the occasion to defend himself.

[12.3] The modest reserve on the part of Moses is particularly stressed in v. 3. In any case, v. 3 is a later addition which disrupts the close connection between v. 2b and v. 4. It is not easy to ascertain what is meant by the unusual phrase 'the man Moses'; perhaps the 'humanity' of Moses is meant to be brought out and given explicit expression, so that the unique distinction accorded to this 'man' should be traced back exclusively to Yahweh's free will and be regarded as a divine gift.

[12.4–5] According to vv. 4–5 Yahweh orders the three protagonists to appear at the tent (of meeting), the place where his presence appears and makes itself known. From the point of view both of content and wording the same idea is present here as in 11.14–17, 24b–30; the tent of meeting is situated outside the Israelite camp (one has to 'go out'), Yahweh comes down in a (pillar of) cloud to speak from within the tent. Aaron and Miriam are ordered to stand forward to receive the decisive divine answer to their words of dissatisfaction while Moses, although he too is to hear the divine decision, remains in the background.

[12.6–8] God's words in vv. 6–8 are in an elevated style, yet without being rhythmically constructed. They assert that there are various ways in which the divine word is transmitted. It is not contested that God 'speaks' to a man, who is then esteemed a 'prophet' (nābî'). If Miriam, as Ex. 15.20 asserts, was a 'prophetess', and if her partner Aaron could consider himself as a 'prophet' at least indirectly (cf. Ex. 4.16), then they could already claim that God 'spoke' with them (v. 2aβ). But that did not justify their comparison of themselves with Moses, for Moses received the divine word in another, unique way. Yahweh spoke with a 'prophet' indirectly through 'dream-visions' (v. 6bβ is certainly a case of synonymous parallelism) which are certainly not real 'words' of God, but yet are, as is said at least indirectly in v. 8a, 'dark speech', necessitating an interpretation. With Moses, on the other hand, God spoke directly ('mouth to mouth') as men of equal rank speak with each other (cf. Ex. 33.11 and, based on that, Deut. 34.10, where, correspondingly, we are told of God speaking or meeting with Moses 'face to face'). This is justified in v. 7b by the position which Yahweh has given to Moses and which is compared with that of the chief slave who is at once the confidant of his master and the man to whom his master's whole 'house' is entrusted. If, in addition, the as yet unheard of and quite unique expression is hazarded that Moses is permitted to 'behold the form of Yahweh' (v. 8aβ)—otherwise in Ex. 33.18–23—then this must surely be regarded as a later addition, as is shown by the mention of the divine name within a divine address; but this addition is in line with what is being said here and could be understood as a pertinent interpretation of it. The divine teaching about the uniqueness of the relationship between Moses and God, with which Aaron and Miriam are rebuked, obviously derives, in the context of the Pentateuchal narrative, from 11.14–17, 24b–30. If, with these latter remarks, ecstatic 'prophecy' had posited the 'spirit' of Moses as its ultimate point of origin (see above pp. 89f.), then the divine address of ch. 12, which is brought about by the appearance of Aaron and Miriam, will be intended to avert the conclusion that Moses had been nothing more than an '(ecstatic) prophet'. He was *much more*; Yahweh had made him his intimate confidant.

[12.9–15] V. 9, with its note concerning Yahweh's anger, coming after the rebuke has already been administered, introduces the concluding section on the punishment. Although Yahweh's anger was directed against Aaron and Miriam, only Miriam is punished. This inequality is explained by the fact that the traditional narrative of Miriam's reproach against Moses (v. 1) is resumed. In his anger Yahweh left the place where he made his appearance and left Miriam struck by a sudden attack of leprosy (v. 10). Aaron, although not affected, declares his solidarity with Miriam (1st person plural in v. 11) and describes the grudge he and Miriam had against Moses as a 'sin', it is true, but as a sin committed only out of 'foolishness', in order to effect the removal of Miriam's punishment by means of an intercession on the part of Moses (v. 11). He compares the repulsive horror of leprosy with the outward appearance of a still-born child (v. 12), thereby producing a 'reason why the prayer should be answered'. The intercession is readily made by Moses, who takes an active part only here in the whole narrative (v. 13), and it achieves the reduction of Miriam's punishment to a seven-day exclusion from the Israelite camp (vv. 14–15). This tacitly implies that Miriam was immediately cured of her leprosy, for the full acceptance of someone cleansed of leprosy could take place only after a seven-day period of waiting (cf. Lev. 14.2ff.). Here, however, it is not a question of this period of waiting but of a punishment involving a seven-day exclusion from the camp. This is an allusion to the fact that a punishment of this sort did in fact exist, namely in cases where a girl has become guilty in some shameful way or another so that her father has 'spit in her face' (cf. the somewhat different situation in Deut. 25.9, where there is no mention of exclusion). Unfortunately the phrase in v. 14a has been handed down in apparently fragmentary form (the beginning of the divine address with 'and' is hardly original),* so that it is no longer ascertainable what kind of shameful action the author envisaged. Presumably it is the clemency of the divine decision that is being brought out, a clemency which punishes Miriam only in the way in which a girl is punished who is guilty of an offence which is shameful, true, but is yet so trivial that the comparatively lenient punishment of a seven-day exclusion sufficed, whereas Miriam had turned against Yahweh's confidant, for which she should really have been punished by a lifetime of suffering from leprosy.

[12.16] The note of the itinerary in v. 16 connects with 11.35b, but is probably editorial. It brings Israel, who according to J were at Hazeroth (11.35b), once more to the wilderness of Paran, where, according to P, they had halted after their original departure from Sinai (10.12b) and where they had remained ever since (cf. 13.3a).

3. SPYING OUT THE PROMISED LAND: 13.1–14.45

13 ¹The LORD said to Moses, ²'Send men to spy out the land of Canaan, which I give to the people of Israel; from each tribe of their fathers shall you send a man, [every one a leader among them.'] ³So

* The initial 'and' has been dropped in the RSV translation. Tr.

Moses sent them from the wilderness of Paran, according to the command of the LORD, [all of them men who were heads of the people of Israel. ⁴And these were their names: From the tribe of Reuben, Shammua the son of Zaccur; ⁵from the tribe of Simeon, Shaphat the son of Hori; ⁶from the tribe of Judah, Caleb the son of Jephunneh; ⁷from the tribe of Issachar, Igal the son of Joseph; ¹⁰from the tribe of Zebulun, Gaddiel the son of Sodi; ¹¹from the tribe of Joseph (that is from the tribe of Manasseh), Gaddi the son of Susi; ⁸from the tribe of Ephraim, Hoshea the son of Nun; ⁹from the tribe of Benjamin, Palti the son of Raphu;* ¹²from the tribe of Dan, Ammiel the son of Gemalli; ¹³from the tribe of Asher, Sethur the son of Michael; ¹⁴from the tribe of Naphtali, Nahbi the son of Vophsi; ¹⁵from the tribe of Gad, Geuel the son of Machi. ¹⁶These were the names of the men whom Moses sent to spy out the land. And Moses called Hoshea the son of Nun Joshua. ¹⁷Moses sent them] to spy out the land of Canaan, and said to them, 'Go up into the Negeb yonder, and go up into the hill country, ¹⁸and see what the land is, and whether the people who dwell in it are strong or weak, whether they are few or many, ¹⁹and whether the land that they dwell in is good or bad, and whether the cities that they dwell in are camps or strongholds, ²⁰and whether the land is rich or poor, and whether there is wood in it or not. Be of good courage, and bring some of the fruit of the land.' Now the time was the season of the first ripe grapes.

21 So they went up and spied out the land from the wilderness of Zin to Rehob, near the entrance of Hamath. ²²They went up into the Negeb, and came to Hebron; and Ahiman, Sheshai, and Talmai, the descendants of Anak, were there. (Hebron was built seven years before Zoan in Egypt.) ²³And they came to the Valley of Eshcol, and cut down from there a branch with a single cluster of grapes, and they carried it on a pole between two of them; they brought also some pomegranates and figs. ²⁴That place was called the Valley of Eshcol, because of the cluster which the men of Israel cut down from there.

25 At the end of forty days they returned from spying out the land. ²⁶And they came to Moses and Aaron and to all the congregation of the people of Israel in the wilderness of Paran, at Kadesh; they brought back word to them [and to all the congregation,] and showed them the fruit of the land. ²⁷And they told him, 'We came to the land to which you sent us; it flows with milk and honey, and this is its fruit. ²⁸Yet the people who dwell in the land are strong, and the cities are fortified and very large; and besides, we saw the descendants of Anak there. [²⁹The Amalekites dwell in the land of the Negeb; the Hittites, the Jebusites, and the Amorites dwell in the hill country; and the Canaanites dwell by the sea, and along the Jordan.'] ³⁰But Caleb quieted the people [before Moses,] and said, 'Let us go up at once, and occupy it; for we are well able to overcome it.' ³¹Then the men who had gone up with

* Noth, in his translation, reverses the order of vv. 8–9 and 10–11. See below, p. 103. Tr.

him said, 'We are not able to go up against the people; for they are stronger than we.'

32 So they brought to the people of Israel an evil report of the land which they had spied out, saying, 'The land, through which we have gone, to spy it out, is a land that devours its inhabitants; and all the people that we saw in it are men of great stature. 33And there we saw the Nephilim [(the sons of Anak, who come from the Nephilim)]; and we seemed to ourselves like grasshoppers, and so we seemed to them.'

14 1Then all the congregation raised a loud cry; and the people wept that night. 2And all the people of Israel murmured against Moses and Aaron; the whole congregation said to them, 'Would that we had died in the land of Egypt! Or would that we had died in this wilderness! 3Why does the LORD bring us into this land, to fall by the sword? Our wives and our little ones will become a prey; would it not be better for us to go back to Egypt?' 4And they said to one another, 'Let us choose a captain, and go back to Egypt.'

5 Then Moses and Aaron fell on their faces before all the assembly of the congregation of the people of Israel. 6And Joshua the son of Nun and Caleb the son of Jephunneh, who were among those who had spied out the land, rent their clothes, 7and said to all the congregation of the people of Israel, 'The land, which we passed through to spy it out, is an exceedingly good land. 8If the LORD delights in us, he will bring us into this land and give it to us, a land which flows with milk and honey. 9[Only, do not rebel against the LORD;] and do not fear the people of the land, for they are bread for us; their protection is removed from them, and the LORD is with us; do not fear them.' 10But all the congregation said to stone them with stones. Then the glory of the LORD appeared at the tent of meeting to all the people of Israel. 11And the LORD said to Moses, 'How long will this people despise me? [And how long will they not believe in me, in spite of all the signs which I have wrought among them? 12I will strike them with the pestilence and disinherit them, and I will make of you a nation greater and mightier than they.' 13But Moses said to the LORD, 'Then the Egyptians will hear of it, for thou didst bring up this people in thy might from among them, 14and they will tell the inhabitants of this land. They have heard that thou, O LORD, art in the midst of this people; for thou, O LORD, art seen face to face, and thy cloud stands over them and thou goest before them, in a pillar of cloud by day and in a pillar of fire by night. 15Now if thou dost kill this people as one man, then the nations who have heard thy fame will say, 16"Because the LORD was not able to bring this people into the land which he swore to give to them, therefore he has slain them in the wilderness." 17And now, I pray thee, let the power of the LORD be great as thou hast promised, saying, 18"The LORD is slow to anger, and abounding in steadfast love, forgiving iniquity and transgression, but he will by no means clear the guilty, visiting the iniquity of fathers upon children, upon the third and upon the fourth generation." 19Pardon the iniquity of this people, I pray thee, according to the greatness of thy steadfast love, and according as thou hast forgiven this people, from

Egypt even until now.' 20Then the LORD said, 'I have pardoned, according to your word; 21but truly, as I live, and as all the earth shall be filled with the glory of the LORD, 22none of the men who have seen my glory and my signs which I wrought in Egypt and in the wilderness, and yet have put me to the proof these ten times and have not hearkened to my voice, 23shall see the land which I swore to give to their fathers;] and none of those who despise me shall see it. 24But my servant Caleb, because he has a different spirit and has followed me fully, I will bring into the land into which he went, and his descendants shall possess it. 25[Now, since the Amalekites and the Canaanites dwell in the valleys,] turn tomorrow and set out for the wilderness by the way to the Red Sea.'

26 And the LORD said to Moses and to Aaron, 27'How long shall this wicked congregation murmur against me? [I have heard the murmurings of the people of Israel, which they murmur against me.] 28Say to them, "As I live," says the LORD, "what you have said in my hearing I will do to you: 29your dead bodies shall fall in this wilderness; and all of your number, numbered from twenty years old and upward, who have murmured against me, [30not one shall come into the land where I swore that I would make you dwell, except Caleb the son of Jephunneh and Joshua the son of Nun.] 31But your little ones, who you said would become a prey, I will bring in, and they shall know the land which you have despised. 32But as for you, your dead bodies shall fall in this wilderness. 33And your children shall be shepherds in the wilderness forty years, and shall suffer for your faithlessness, until the last of your dead bodies lies in the wilderness. [34According to the number of the days in which you spied out the land, forty days, for every day a year, you shall bear your iniquity, forty years, and you shall know my displeasure."] 35I, the LORD, have spoken; surely this will I do to all this wicked congregation that are gathered together against me: in this wilderness they shall come to a full end, and there they shall die.' 36And the men whom Moses sent to spy out the land, and who returned and made all the congregation to murmur against him by bringing up an evil report against the land, 37the men who brought up an evil report of the land, died by plague before the LORD. 38But Joshua the son of Nun and Caleb the son of Jephunneh remained alive, of those men who went to spy out the land. 39And Moses told these words to all the people of Israel, and the people mourned greatly. 40And they rose early in the morning, and went up to the heights of the hill country, saying, 'See, we are here, we will go up to the place which the LORD has promised; for we have sinned.' 41But Moses said, 'Why now are you transgressing the command of the LORD, for that will not succeed? 42Do not go up lest you be struck down before your enemies, for the LORD is not among you. 43For there the Amalekites and the Canaanites are before you, and you shall fall by the sword; because you have turned back from following the LORD, the LORD will not be with you.' 44But they presumed to go up to the heights of the hill country, although neither the ark [of the covenant] of the LORD, nor Moses, departed out of the camp. 45Then the Amalekites and the Canaanites

who dwelt in that hill country came down, and defeated them and pursued them, even to Hormah.

The narrative about spying out the land is the first indication of the conquest theme. The contents are clear and simple. Men are sent from Israel into the promised land to look around. Their report on the strength of the inhabitants and their towns disheartens the Israelites, with the result that they want to return to Egypt. This lack of trust in the powerful guidance of their God is punished by God's decision that the present generation of Israelites should not enter the land, but should remain in the wilderness and die there. Only those among the spies who had been sent out and had, in contrast to the majority of their comrades, issued a summons to confident trust, are to share in the gift of the land. This narrative is presented in great detail. The reason for this is that several literary sources have been conflated and that these sources have then been expanded by later additions. Two versions are clearly distinguishable. The twofold nature of the narrative emerges clearly from a series of striking doublets (cf. 13.21 with 13.22ff.; 13.27f. with 13.32f.; 14.11ff. with 14.26ff.). Then we find differences of fact. On one occasion the wilderness of Paran is mentioned as the starting point (13.3, 26), on another it is Kadesh (13.26). According to 13.21, the whole country from north to south was reconnoitred; according to 13.22ff., the spies only reached as far as the neighbourhood of Hebron. In 14.24 only Caleb, on the basis of 13.30, is exempt from God's punishment; in 14.6ff. and 14.38 Joshua takes precedence over Caleb. It is comparatively easy to recognize the existence of a P-version by the phrases and expressions characteristic of P (e.g. 'Moses and Aaron and the whole congregation of the Israelites'); only in a few particulars can the attribution to P be doubted. The P-version consists of 13.1–17a, 21, 25, 26, 32, 33; 14.1–3, 5–10, 26–38 (secondary additions within this P-version will be discussed in the course of the detailed exegesis). According to P the whole country was reconnoitred from the wilderness of Paran by twelve 'leaders', and amongst these twelve it was Joshua and Caleb who encouraged the people. All this shows that the P-narrative is a late literary stratum. The remaining contents of the two chapters appear in the main to be part of an older version; and the facts as we have them suggest that these contents have once again not been put together from several comprehensive 'sources', but are, as elsewhere in this part of the Pentateuchal narrative, to be attributed to the 'Yahwist'(J). In addition we must notice that J has been preserved in a substantially complete condition, but has undergone in a few places, as is usual, some slight abbreviation in favour of the P-narrative which, from a literary point of view, is the basic one. On the other hand, the J-narrative, too, reveals a few expansions (especially in 14.11–25) which will be discussed later. There is yet a third version of this narrative, a 'deuteronomistic' one, in Deut. 1.20–45. As one would expect, this does not yet reveal the peculiarities of P, but is an independent variation of the theme based on the J-version and can at times help to clarify the contents and wording of J; the details of this will be indicated later.

The J-version is not the oldest form of the tradition behind this story; it is, however, the oldest known literary form of the material, going back to a traditional (oral) narrative. The development of the tradition goes back from P through J and beyond into the pre-literary sphere. In P the whole narrative, with its preference for Joshua over Caleb, who is the one singled out by the tradition, and its extension of the reconnoitring to cover the whole country, is determined by the concept of the joint conquest of the land by all Israel. J, on the other hand, lets the spies reach only the rich vine-growing area of Hebron and makes Caleb the one who encourages Israel to take possession of the land. If one takes into consideration the fact that, after the conquest, Hebron and its surrounding territory belonged to the 'Calebites' (cf. Josh. 15.13–14; Judg. 1.20), then it becomes clear that the narrative has this goal in view and, from the point of view of the history of traditions, it is from there that it starts. Now J, too, gives this story an all-Israelite framework, thereby explaining, as does P later, Israel's long sojourn in the wilderness before they started on the long detour east of the Jordan into the promised land. But in the J-version it still remains clear that originally the field of vision was restricted to the Judaean or even only the south Judaean hill country, and that an answer had to be found to the question of why precisely the Calebites had achieved possession of the Hebron district, distinguished as it was by its wealth of vineyards. The reason for this—so runs the answer—was that once the ancestor Caleb, in contrast to the ancestors of the more or less neighbouring tribal alliances, had trusted the God of Israel, so that he was allowed to achieve this possession. This would indicate that originally here we have a special Calebite tradition. The continuing expansion of the field of vision may perhaps be due to the different starting-points of the undertaking. According to P, this lay in the distant and presumably only vaguely located 'wilderness of Paran' (13.3); according to J, Israel was at that time at Kadesh (13.26), which is to be reckoned as on the southernmost frontier of Palestine. The mention of Hormah (14.45) presumably comes in the long run from the pre-literary tradition and leads directly to the edge of the south Judaean hill country.

[13.1–17a] According to P, the sending out of the twelve 'spies' results from an express command of Yahweh (13.2a). P consistently makes the divine guidance of Israel appear in unequivocal commands of Yahweh. From such a standpoint a prior human reconnoitring of the land that was to be possessed was indispensable. Here P is taking over an earlier piece of tradition and inserting it into the framework of his total conception. From each of the twelve tribes one 'spy' is to be chosen (13.2bα). This clashes with the remark that each of them is to be a 'leader' (13.2bβ), for the office of 'leader' was definitively allocated as early as 1.5ff. and could not be taken on from time to time in an *ad hoc* fashion. The phraseology of v. 2bβ sounds as if there were in each tribe a supply of 'leaders' from among whom a choice could be made. The whole passage about the 'leaders' (apart from v. 2bβ, v. 3b and, above all, the list of names in vv. 4–16 belong to it) is, therefore, probably a secondary addition to the P-narrative. In contrast to the list in 1.5–15, the present list gives the impression of being freely composed. The tribal enumeration follows, on the whole, the pattern of 1.5–15; only in the cases of the pairs of tribes Manasseh/Ephraim and Naphtali/Gad, has the order been reversed (an attempt to restore the proper sequence of Ephraim/Manasseh may have caused the textual confusion in vv. 8–11). As far as the names themselves are concerned, the appearance of Caleb (for Judah) and Joshua (for Ephraim) shows that the list has been constructed on the basis of the 'spy' story, of which Caleb and (according to P) Joshua were necessarily part. That no names compounded with the divine name Yahweh appear in the list is due here (probably otherwise in 1.5–15; cf. above, p. 18) to the conscious reflection that Moses' contemporaries could not yet have such names, since they were born before the revelation of the divine name Yahweh (Ex. 6.2–3). In the case of Joshua, who had to be included in P's list of 'spies', but who had a name containing a 'Yahweh' element, the artificial suggestion is made that he was originally called 'Hoshea' (v. 8) and that his name was changed by Moses, for some unspecified reason, to 'Joshua' (v. 16b). Among the rest of the names there are lacking those demonstrably very old formations such as we have in 1.5–15 (cf. above, p. 18); only the name 'Ammiel' (v. 12) could be classified as such. The compiler of the list has certainly simply gathered together a number of names that to him appeared archaic. The fact that the list of names (vv. 3b–16) is a secondary insertion is supported by the fact that in v. 17aα the beginning of v. 3a is repeated, thus taking up once again the interrupted thread of the narrative.

[13.17b–20] The J-narrative begins at v. 17b. The break between v. 17a and v. 17b is brought out by the fact that in v. 17b there is suddenly no further mention of spying out the (whole) 'land of Canaan', but only of the 'Negeb' (i.e. the wilderness territory stretching to an unspecified extent to the south of the Palestinian hill country) and of its adjoining 'hill country'. Israel already was 'here in the Negeb' and the territory to be reconnoitred was, as is clear from vv. 22–24, the (south) Judaean 'hill country' as far as the Hebron region. Prior to v. 17b the beginning of the J-narrative has been removed by an editor in favour of P. If it is reproduced, at least as far as the contents are concerned, in Deut. 1.19bff. (cf. above p. 102), then according to J Moses, at Kadesh, is said to have summoned Israel to take possession of the land that had been promised them, but the Israelites had wanted to spy out the land beforehand and Moses had thereupon sent out twelve men for that purpose. It is with this commission that the J-narrative begins in v. 17b. They are to 'see' (v. 18a) the territory to be reconnoitred with regard to the strength and number of its inhabitants (v. 18b), to its general nature (v. 19a), to the layout of its settlements (v. 19b) and to its fertility (v. 20).

[13.21–24] The carrying out of this task is reported twice, once in the brief assertion of v. 21 which proves, from both wording and content, to be a direct continuation of v. 17aP, and then in the longer exposition of vv. 22–24 which just as clearly connects directly with vv. 17b–20J. In v. 21 the 'land of Canaan' (vv. 2a, 17a) from south to north is particularized by the mention of two place-names, the significance given to which by the author is difficult to determine. The 'wilderness of Zin' is to be sought, according to Josh. 15.3 = Num. 34.4, to the east of the oasis of Kadesh-barnea (cf. below pp. 248f.), and probably for P it was precisely that wilderness territory which included this oasis (cf. Num. 27.14 = Deut. 32.51, also Num. 33.36) and he means it to be taken, not inappropriately, as the most southerly frontier of the 'land of Canaan'. The northern frontier is described by the expression *rḥb lbw' ḥmt*. Whatever the original meaning of this expression may have been, *lbw' ḥmt* must have been understood by P as meaning 'at the entrance to Hamath' and by this the great depression between Lebanon and Antilebanon (*beqāʿ*) must have been meant, through which lay an important point of access to the town 'Hamath' (*ḥama* on the Orontes). This assertion helps to locate *rḥb*, which is certainly meant to be taken as a place-name ('Rehob'). This 'Rehob' cannot, with any certainty, be identified with the place of the same name known elsewhere in the Old Testament, but it can with the 'Beth-rehob' of Judg. 18.28 which, for its part, is difficult to locate, supposing that the latter is to be sought in the region of the source of the Jordan, that is at the southern exit from the *beqāʿ*. This is a clear indication of the northern frontier of the 'land of Canaan' which for P was restricted to the west bank of the Jordan. According to J (vv. 22–24), the 'spies' moved northwards through the Negeb to Hebron, at the summit of the Judaean hill country. Of Hebron it is first of all stated that there lived there the three 'descendants of Anak' (*yᵉlīdē hāʿᵃnāq*), called by unusual names which occur also in Josh. 15.14 and Judg. 1.10. Of the various forms used in the Old Testament for 'Anakites', the present one (*yᵉlīdē hāʿᵃnāq*) must surely, because of its rarity, be the original; its use of the article in *hāʿᵃnāq* is particularly striking and this is evidence that we are dealing here not with a proper name but with an appellative which is obviously, to say the least, to be equated with the word *ʿᵃnāq* = 'necklace' (Judg. 8.26; Prov. 1.9). It remains, of course, obscure what may have been meant by the designation 'necklace descendants'. At any rate it seems to indicate figures of a legendary period, of whom a local tradition from Hebron purported to tell, powerful 'giant-like' figures (cf. v. 33aβ)* who, for strangers who wished to try to capture the town of Hebron, were forbidding and frightening. The remarkable note about the town of Hebron's having been built seven years before Egyptian Zoan (Tanis is the Greek rendering of the name) in the north-eastern part of the Nile delta, is to be understood to refer to the prehistoric origin of the town and to its particular permanence. It is not even probable that this note contains a piece of original authentic information. It starts, rather, from the concept of Zoan's particularly great antiquity and makes Hebron a little older. The men who were sent out certainly did not enter the 'ancient' town with its terrible 'necklace descendants',

* The RSV translates the Hebrew *nᵉpīlīm* as a proper name. Noth translates it by the word 'giants', as does, e.g., the AV. Tr.

but confined themselves to the 'Valley of Eshcol' (vv. 23–24), which is to be sought in the neighbourhood of Hebron, but cannot be located any more precisely, since its name seems to have been retained by no place at all, a fact that is all the more understandable since it is merely descriptive, with the meaning of 'valley of clusters'. Within the surroundings of Hebron, surroundings which are generally fertile and particularly rich in vines, the 'Valley of Eshcol' is most probably to be found to the south, since it was from the south that the Israelite visitors came. The name, which probably stuck naturally to a valley particularly rich in grapes, is traced back in v. 24 to a large cluster of grapes which the Israelites at that time took with them as a symbol of the richness of the land ..nd which was so big that, in order to carry it undamaged, they had to lay it on a pole carried by two bearers (most likely a kind of wooden bier such as is envisaged in 4.10, 12 for the carrying of the sacred lamp and other sacred vessels) and which they brought back along with a vine-branch and a few pomegranates and figs taken as samples from their reconnoitring.

[13.25–33] The report brought back by the spies exists in two versions. First of all P's introduction mentions the return itself and also briefly notes that the spies brought with them some of the fruit of the land, an element which appears in P only in this brief note (vv. 25–26). This passage has suppressed J's report of the return which must have stood before v. 27. Of this report only one word has been inserted by an editor into the P-text because it appeared factually significant, namely the place-name 'at Kadesh' in v. 26 which, from the point of view both of form and content, clashes with the immediately preceding statement 'in the wilderness of Paran'. That the spying out of the land began, according to J, from Kadesh may be deduced also from Deut. 1.19b, 46 (cf. also Josh. 14.6). This Kadesh (or Kadesh-barnea, to distinguish it from other places of the same name, so, too, Deut. 1.19b) is to be identified with the region of the present-day spring ʿēn qdēs which lies about forty-six miles as the crow flies south-south-west of Beersheba, perhaps including the region of other and more abundant springs lying five or six miles to the north-west. The old name still survives in the name ʿēn qdēs. According to J, the spies make their report to Moses (cf. the 2nd person singular in v. 27aα).* But their information concerning the strength of the inhabitants and their fortified cities in the rich and fertile land and concerning the presence of the 'necklace descendants'

* This is, of course, not noticeable in the RSV. Tr.

(v. 28) is overheard by the people and agitates and discourages them. The latter fact is not explicitly stated, but is tacitly assumed in v. 30, according to which Caleb alone among those who had been sent out (cf. v. 31) 'quieted' the people by stating as his opinion that they would nevertheless be able to conquer this land. Here there appears in J a narrative element which first makes its appearance in P at 14.6ff. With its description of the division of the different national elements that exist in the country and with the remarkable statement that the Canaanites dwell on the one hand on the coast and on the other in the Jordan valley—cf. Josh. 11.3—v. 29 hardly fits into the spies' report and is to be regarded as a later addition. In v. 30a what is perhaps being said is that Caleb spoke to Moses, but in such a way that the people, too, could hear. Yet the expression 'before Moses', which fits badly in the context, is presumably a later addition. In vv. 32–33, P, in direct connection with v. 26, states once again what J has already reported in v. 28. There is no longer any mention of the wealth of the territory reconnoitred (cf. v. 26bβ), but only of its dangerous character. The statement that it is a 'land that devours its inhabitants' (v. 32bα) probably means that it is full of warlike dissensions (cf. Ezek. 36.13f., also Lev. 26.38). The peculiarly Hebronite tradition of the 'necklace descendants', employed by J, is generalized in P to the statement that the whole population of the land consists of 'men of great stature' (v. 32bβ), that even 'giants' (otherwise only in Gen. 6.4) were to be seen (v. 33).* The addition in v. 33aβ makes a subsequent identification of these 'giants' with the 'Anakites' (so here in contrast to vv. 22aβ, 28bβ).†

[14.1–10] The negative reaction of the people to the report is described in great detail in 14.1–10. The bulk of this section belongs to P. Only in v. 1aβb and in v. 4 do we find short elements of the J-narrative which are proved to be such by the fact that they are doublets to what has already been stated. According to them, the people did not listen to Caleb's 'quieting' speech (13.30), but rather to the discouraging words of his companions (13.31) and resolved, in their despair (14.1aβb), to return to Egypt (14.4). With the unusual Hebrew expression in v. 4bα, probably Neh. 9.17 is to be compared, and the translation of it, therefore, would be: 'Let us set up a head', i.e. act defiantly and of our own free will (not, as would certainly

---

* Cf. footnote on p. 105 above. Tr.

† The Hebrew phrase in v. 33 is *benē ʿanāq* ('sons of Anak'), in contrast to *yelīdē hāʿanāq* ('necklace descendants') in these other two places. Cf. above p. 105. Tr.

also be possible from the wording: 'Let us choose a captain', i.e.
someone other than Moses).* According to P the congregation rebels
in its grief (v. 1aα), first of all against Moses and Aaron (v. 2), but
also against Yahweh (v. 3), so that Moses and Aaron can, in their
despair, only throw themselves to the ground (v. 5). Here, for the
first time in P, Joshua and Caleb come on the scene (v. 6), praise the
goodness of the land (v. 7) and point out that Yahweh, if he so wills,
can lead Israel into the land (v. 8), a fact with which Israel should
console itself and on which it should trust, since, in these circumstances, were Yahweh to remove the protecting 'shadow' (i.e.
perhaps the support of the local gods) from the inhabitants of the
land (v. 9bα), then they would be delivered to Israel for 'bread'
(v. 9aβ; v. 9aα is a later addition scarcely suited to the context). The
congregation, however, refused to be impressed any longer by these
encouraging words and would almost have stoned Joshua and Caleb
had Yahweh not timeously intervened, through the appearance of
his glory in the tent of meeting (v. 10), to pass a judicial sentence
which is not stated until vv. 26ff.

[14.11–25] Before that, in vv. 11ff., J takes over again with an
address by Yahweh to Moses which reacts to the people's defiant
self-will (v. 4) with a punishment. By their behaviour, the people
have 'despised' Yahweh; and Yahweh will endure this no longer. So
Yahweh's address begins in v. 11aβ. What follows in vv. 11bff. is so
strongly permeated by deuteronomistic conceptions and turns of
phrase that we must conclude that this is an extensive later addition to
the J-narrative. It begins—according to the awkward and still later
insertion, v. 11b—with a reference to the miraculous divine 'signs'
which had happened within Israel and which ought to have led
Israel to an unconditional trust in her God. Then there follows a
dialogue between Yahweh and Moses which, from the point of view
here and there of content, has its verbal counterpart in the deuteronomistic passage Ex. 32.9–14. Yahweh intends to destroy Israel (v. 12a)
and in their place to create from the descendants of Moses a new,
'greater and mightier' nation, whereupon Moses objects that
Yahweh's reputation among the nations would then be at stake (vv.
13–16). Moses therefore asks for Yahweh's forgiveness (vv. 17–19),
which is then granted (v. 20), although with the reservation that the
present generation of Israel, as a punishment for their lack of faith,

* It will be noted that the RSV gives this latter translation. Noth, in his translation, has the former, 'Let us act of our own free will'. Tr.

should not see the land (vv. 21–23a). In this section the text is, in places, far from smooth, due, certainly, to the insertion of later additions. This is true of the beginning of Moses' speech (vv. 13–14), which, in its present form, is remarkably awkward. There the thought that the Egyptians, who have followed Israel's fate after the 'bringing up', would report to the inhabitants of the promised land that Yahweh had done away with his people in the wilderness (vv. 13b, 14a), has probably been added later and thus the original beginning of Moses' speech has been lost. It may have run something like this: What will the 'nations' say to this, after they (v. 14b) have heard of the divine presence in Israel (the reference in v. 14bβ to the pillars of cloud and fire has been borrowed literally from Ex. 13.21)? The request for forgiveness (v. 19) is an appeal to Yahweh's mighty power (v. 17), preceded by some words taken from Ex. 34.6–7 (v. 18). Yahweh's final judgment on the present generation of Israel is expressed, in vv. 22–23a, in a manifestly deuteronomistic fashion (the figure ten applied to Israel's sins in v. 22bα is certainly to be understood as a round number). Since there is a clear break between v. 23a and v. 23b, the 'deuteronomistic' insertion which began at v. 11b is to be regarded as concluding with v. 23a. The original J-narrative reappears at v. 23b with a verbal reference to its last appearance (v. 11aβ); of course, a sentence must have been suppressed, due to the insertion between v. 11aβ and v. 23b, a sentence which mentioned the promised land which, according to v. 23b, none who 'despised' Yahweh would enter (vv. 22–23a in the insertion have already mentioned this). Only Caleb, who according to 13.30 was not among those who 'despised' Yahweh, is to set foot again in the land which he has entered in the course of the reconnoitring expedition (v. 24bα), i.e. the region round Hebron, and receive it as a possession for his descendants. This promise brings the whole narrative, according to its original contents (cf. above, p. 102), to its proper conclusion. What is praised in Caleb in v. 24a, is expressed in an unusual way. The word 'spirit' (rūaḥ) appears here almost in the sense of a 'disposition' which 'accompanies' a man; Caleb has, therefore, (literally) 'done fully (to go) behind Yahweh'. This latter expression plainly characterizes Caleb's behaviour in stereotyped fashion (cf. in addition Deut. 1.36; Josh. 14.8, 9, 14; Num. 32.11, 12; and, with a different reference, I Kings 11.6). The secondary remark of v. 25a concerning the dwelling-places of the Amalekites and the Canaanites, a remark which is not quite in agreement with the statements of 13.29 and is in direct contradiction to those of 14.45a and which, in addition, is quite out of place in the middle of a divine address, is followed in v. 25b by a final instruction from Yahweh which connects the Caleb-Hebron story directly once more with the theme of Israel's sojourn in the wilderness. Israel is sent back into the wilderness and told to take the way to the 'Sea of Reeds',* thereby beginning that detour to the east of the Jordan envisaged by the whole Pentateuchal narrative in its various strata. For by 'Sea of Reeds' is quite unambiguously meant here—as also elsewhere where the context is clear (cf. above all I Kings 9.26; Jer. 49.21)—the gulf of el-ʿaqaba.

[14.26–38] In v. 26 the P-narrative, in relation to v. 10, resumes at that point reached by the J-narrative in v. 11, here, too, with the question 'How long?' (v. 27, cf. v. 11aβ). Yahweh intends no longer to endure the 'murmurings' of the 'wicked congregation' (the sentence of v. 27b comes after the event and is an addition) and commands Moses (in spite of the 'Moses and Aaron' of v. 26, Moses alone is addressed in v. 28) to communicate his judgment to them, namely that all the adults, as these have been 'numbered' according to 1.2ff. (the women are passed over in silence), are to die in the wilderness, with the exception of Joshua and Caleb (according to vv. 6–9). Only the children who are still small are to enter the country (v. 31) and these only after a forty-year nomadic period in the wilderness (v. 33) through which they must still atone for the apostasy ('faithlessness') of their fathers. The period of forty years is, in the Old Testament conception, the life-span within which a man participates in the life of the community with full powers and full rights. After a forty-year sojourn in the wilderness the constituents of the community will be completely changed. In v. 34 the forty-year period is set in a not particularly illuminating relationship to the forty-day duration of the spying expedition (cf. 13.25). One might wonder whether v. 34 is not a speculative element only added later. The frequency of repetition in this section in general poses the question as to whether other later expansions are not to be established too. At any rate (v. 34 apart), v. 30 must certainly be an addition, since it begins with remarkable abruptness and mentions Caleb before Joshua. Vv. 31–32 could also, however, be part of this addition. This would be significant in so far as, with this presupposition, the original P-narrative, which otherwise shows no interest in the theme of the conquest, would not, in this

* This is Noth's usual translation of what appears in EVV as the 'Red Sea'. Cf. *Exodus*, p. 11 footnote. Tr.

context either, have mentioned the future entry into the land. In line with this would be the fact that in vv. 36–38, too, where the report is made of the sudden killing, brought about by Yahweh, of the spies who had been sent out (here, as in v. 6, there is no designation of them as 'leaders'; cf. above p. 103), it is said of Joshua and Caleb, who are, of course, exempted from this punishment, only that they 'remained alive' and not, however much one would expect this from the trend of the narrative as a whole, that they were to have a share in the distribution of the land. Naturally, even for P, the forty-year-long wanderings of the rising generation (v. 33) would have to be followed by the crossing into Canaan, but it is significant that nothing is said about this.

[14.39–45] In vv. 39–45 the J-narrative, after it has briefly noted that Moses has communicated to the people the divine judgment of vv. 11a . . . 23b, 24, 25b (v. 39), has a sequel. With the confession that they 'have sinned' (v. 40bβ) the people insist on going up to 'the heights of the hill country' and carry out this resolve in spite of Moses' warning of the unalterable nature of the judgment already delivered by Yahweh (v. 41), with the result that they are defeated and pursued as far as Hormah (v. 45), while Moses and the 'ark of Yahweh' (the word 'covenant' has been added later under the influence of deuteronomistic usage), which appears here once more within the Pentateuchal narrative in a military context (cf. 10.35–36 and, on this point, pp. 79f. above), have not participated in the undertaking. The numerous factual details in this section, such as the mention of the 'heights of the hill country' (vv. 40a, 44a) as well as 'the Amalekites and the Canaanites who dwelt in that hill country' (v. 45a) and the mention of the place-name Hormah (v. 45b), indicate that there stands behind this piece of narrative a definite local tradition of an Israelite settlement in the region of the southern edge of the Judaean hill country. The transformations through which, from the point of view of the history of traditions, the 'spy' story has passed, afford no definite answer to the obvious question, which is perhaps to be answered in the affirmative, as to whether the event mentioned here did not belong to the original, pre-literary form of the Caleb-Hebron tradition. According to v. 45b, the event must have taken place to the north of Hormah, which, according to Josh. 15.30, belonged to the 'province' of Beersheba and is probably to be located on *tell el-mšāš* to the east of Beersheba. In that border-land between cultivated land and desert, 'dwelt', in the southern foothills of the Judaean 'hill country', nomadic Amalekites and settled Canaanites, both uniting to repel attacking Israelites. Something like this may have been the nucleus of the tradition. Should there have existed an original connection with the Caleb-Hebron story, then it may have been narrated that Caleb, through his courageous trust, was able to put himself in possession of Hebron, while the others, who only subsequently decided on action, suffered a defeat somewhere in south Judah. Within the framework of the J-narrative, the episode serves to make clear the irrevocable nature of the divine judgment.

4. VARIOUS APPENDICES OF A CULTIC-RITUAL NATURE: 15.1–41

15 ¹The Lord said to Moses, ²'Say to the people of Israel, When you come into the land you are to inhabit, which I give you, ³and you offer to the Lord from the herd or from the flock an offering by fire or a burnt offering or a sacrifice, to fulfil a vow or as a freewill offering or at your appointed feasts, to make a pleasing odour to the Lord, ⁴then he who brings his offering shall offer to the Lord a cereal offering of a tenth of an ephah of fine flour, mixed with a fourth of a hin of oil; ⁵and wine for the drink offering, a fourth of a hin, you shall prepare with the burnt offering, or for the sacrifice, for each lamb. ⁶Or for a ram, you shall prepare for a cereal offering two tenths of an ephah of fine flour mixed with a third of a hin of oil; ⁷and for the drink offering you shall offer a third of a hin of wine, a pleasing odour to the Lord. ⁸And when you prepare a bull for a burnt offering, or for a sacrifice, to fulfil a vow, or for peace offerings to the Lord, ⁹then one shall offer with the bull a cereal offering of three tenths of an ephah of fine flour, mixed with half a hin of oil, ¹⁰and you shall offer for the drink offering half a hin of wine, as an offering by fire, a pleasing odour to the Lord.

11 'Thus it shall be done for each bull or ram, or for each of the male lambs or the kids. ¹²According to the number that you prepare, so shall you do with every one according to their number. ¹³All who are native shall do these things in this way, in offering an offering by fire, a pleasing odour to the Lord. ¹⁴And if a stranger is sojourning with you, or any one is among you throughout your generations, and he wishes to offer an offering by fire, a pleasing odour to the Lord, he shall do as you do. ¹⁵For the assembly, there shall be one statute for you and for the stranger who sojourns with you, a perpetual statute throughout your generations; as you are, so shall the sojourner be before the Lord. ¹⁶One law and one ordinance shall be for you and for the stranger who sojourns with you.'

17 The LORD said to Moses, 18'Say to the people of Israel, When you come into the land to which I bring you 19and when you eat of the food of the land, you shall present an offering to the LORD. 20Of the first of your coarse meal you shall present a cake as an offering; as an offering from the threshing floor, so shall you present it. 21Of the first of your coarse meal you shall give to the LORD an offering throughout your generations.

22 'But if you err, and do not observe all these commandments which the LORD has spoken to Moses, 23all that the LORD has commanded you by Moses, from the day that the LORD gave commandment, and onward throughout your generations, 24then if it was done unwittingly without the knowledge of the congregation, all the congregation shall offer one young bull for a burnt offering, a pleasing odour to the LORD, with its cereal offering and its drink offering, according to the ordinance, and one male goat for a sin offering. 25And the priest shall make atonement for all the congregation of the people of Israel, and they shall be forgiven; because it was an error, and they have brought their offering, an offering by fire to the LORD, and their sin offering before the LORD, for their error. 26And all the congregation of the people of Israel shall be forgiven, and the stranger who sojourns among them, because the whole population was involved in the error.

27 'If one person sins unwittingly, he shall offer a female goat a year old for a sin offering. 28And the priest shall make atonement before the LORD for the person who commits an error, when he sins unwittingly, to make atonement for him; and he shall be forgiven. 29You shall have one law for him who does anything unwittingly, for him who is native among the people of Israel, and for the stranger who sojourns among them. 30But the person who does anything with a high hand, whether he is native or a sojourner, reviles the LORD, and that person shall be cut off from among his people. 31Because he has despised the word of the LORD, and has broken his commandment, that person shall be utterly cut off; his iniquity shall be upon him.'

32 While the people of Israel were in the wilderness, they found a man gathering sticks on the sabbath day. 33And those who found him gathering sticks brought him to Moses and Aaron, and to all the congregation. 34They put him in custody, because it had not been made plain what should be done to him. 35And the LORD said to Moses, 'The man shall be put to death; all the congregation shall stone him with stones outside the camp.' 36And all the congregation brought him outside the camp and stoned him to death with stones, as the LORD commanded Moses.

37 The LORD said to Moses, 38'Speak to the people of Israel, and bid them to make tassels on the corners of their garments throughout their generations, and to put upon the tassel of each corner a cord of blue; 39and it shall be to you a tassel to look upon and remember all the commandments of the LORD, to do them, not to follow after your own heart and your own eyes, which you are inclined to go after wantonly. 40So you shall remember and do all my commandments, and be holy

to your God. ⁴¹I am the Lord your God, who brought you out of the land of Egypt, to be your God: I am the Lord your God.'

It is not quite clear why this rather unsystematically arranged collection of various cultic-ritual ordinances should have found a place at this particular point in the Pentateuchal narrative; presumably, in view of the mention of the wilderness at the beginning of vv. 32–36, it has been added to ch. 13–14, at the end of which Israel is condemned to a further sojourn in the wilderness. The individual parts of this collection have no connection with each other. Some of them tie up with older laws and provide expansions of these. On the whole this collection ought to be considered one of the very latest sections of the Pentateuch; there is nothing definite to go by in order to date either the whole collection or the individual parts of it.

[15.1–16] In vv. 1–16 there is exact legislation about the cereal and drink offerings accompanying every kind of animal sacrifice, and the quantities of what is to be expended on the cereal and drink offerings for every single animal that is sacrificed are laid down exactly. This legislation is valid only for the period after the conquest (v. 2b); it surpasses the sacrificial rituals of Lev. 1–7 (which, as rituals, are, moreover, quite differently orientated) in this respect that, besides the animal sacrifices and the cereal offerings, it knows of the drink offering, not, of course, as an independent offering, but as one that accompanies the other offerings. The quantities in the cases of the cereal and drink offerings are measured not with regard to the type and purpose of the sacrificial action in question, but with regard solely to the relevant sacrificial animal. The scale of values of the sacrificial animals rises from the (male) sheep, via the ram to the bull, and the quantities demanded for the respective cereal and drink offerings rise commensurately (vv. 4–10). For the cereal offering, only that type designated in Lev. 2.1–2 is envisaged, namely the offering of uncooked fine flour mixed with oil (there is no mention here of the accompanying incense that is mentioned as well in Lev. 2). The quantity of fine flour is measured according to the dry measure, the ephah (= *c*. one bushel); at least this unit of measurement is not expressly mentioned—it is, however, tacitly assumed in the mention of the 'tenth'.* For the quantity of oil demanded with the cereal offering, as well as the quantity of wine in the drink offering, the relevant measure is the liquid one 'hin' (= *c*. 11 pints). According to

* The RSV has expressed this 'tacit assumption' by inserting the word 'ephah' in its translation. Tr.

vv. 4–5, each sheep that was offered was to be accompanied by a cereal offering of a tenth of a bushel of fine flour with 2¾ pints of oil, and a drink offering of 2¾ pints of wine. According to vv. 6–10, these quantities increase from the sheep via the ram to the bull, in the case of the fine flour in a ratio of 1:2:3, and in the case of the oil and the wine in a ratio of 1:1·3:2. Probably it is a question only of approximations, for the relationship of flour, oil and wine would need to be to some extent constant. We learn nothing of the method of presenting the drink offering (in Lev. 1ff. there is, as we have mentioned, no ritual for the drink offering); presumably the wine was poured out in front of the altar. The whole section is expressed in a very disorderly way; it is partly impersonal, partly in the form of direct speech, without its being possible to recognize any system in it. There is certainly no justification for 'reconstructing', from the point of view of textual criticism, a unified form of expression. At the end, it is again stressed in great detail that, with regard to this legislation, there is to be no difference made between natives and strangers; such detail is evidence that this was an important matter and that there were, therefore, strangers ('sojourners') in some considerable numbers. This would suggest that by 'strangers who sojourn with you' is meant 'proselytes', i.e. people of non-Israelite origin who have attached themselves to the Jerusalem cult and taken upon themselves certain given obligations.

[15.17–21] The short section vv. 17–21, which is concerned with an ordinance proclaimed with regard to the forthcoming period in Palestine and concerning a particular offering 'to Yahweh', i.e. to the sanctuary or its priest, is difficult because the meaning of the most important word in it, *ʿariṣā*, is not definitely known. It occurs also in Ezek. 44.30 and Neh. 10.38 (EVV 10.37), always in the plural and always in relation to *rēʾšit* ('the first of . . .'), and every example is concerned with the offering of this first-fruit. It probably means something like 'groats' or 'coarse meal', something which, according to v. 20a at any rate, can be made into a 'cake'. In v. 20b, reference is made to a comparable offering from the 'threshing floor', that is to an offering of the threshed grains of corn. The obligation of this latter offering is taken as being in force although nowhere in the Old Testament does it appear laid down in this form. The present section adds to the obligation of offering the first of the threshed corn an additional, obviously new offering, that of the first of the coarsely ground grain. The terms 'heave', 'heave offering' are used as technical terms for 'offering'.* Originally these presumably indicated some particular way in which the gift was offered;† later—and this is the case here—these evolved into alternative, general terms for 'offer', 'offering'.

[15.22-31] Vv. 22-31 have no introductory formula of their own, nevertheless they are not a continuation of the preceding passage, since their contents are quite different and self-contained. They deal with the atonement for offences committed unintentionally, inadvertently, 'unwittingly' against a divine command. The section has two subdivisions, of which the first (vv. 24-26) takes into consideration an offence involving the whole congregation, while the second (vv. 27-28) deals with a lapse on the part of an individual. It is a question, therefore, of the same cases as in Lev. 4.13-21 and 27-35. But the interest here is not in the actual atonement ritual, which is central to Lev. 4, but to which reference is made here only in a few general phrases (vv. 25a, 28); rather is the purpose of the present section to expand on Lev. 4, especially with regard to the sacrifices that are to be offered. The general presupposition (as in Lev. 4) is the unintentional nature of a violation of the law (vv. 22-23), for which the technical expression is the word $\check{s}^e g\bar{a}g\bar{a}$, which is constantly and intentionally repeated in this section. Cultic atonement can take place only with this presupposition. There is no atonement for a conscious, intentional violation (for which the technical term is 'with a high hand', v. 30); it could be punished, as is expressly stated in the closing verses, 30-31, only by an exclusion from the community effected by putting to death. How an unintentional offence happened within the community (vv. 24-26), unnoticed by it (v. 24aα, similarly Lev. 4.13) is not stated, nor are any definite details given at all concerning the type or content of such an offence. It is, however, a fact that the congregation has incurred (objective) 'guilt' and is in need of atonement. V. 24aβb, going beyond Lev. 4.13ff., lays down that for atonement it is not just that a young bull is to be offered as a sin offering, but that a young bull is to be offered as a burnt offering, along with the cereal offering and the drink offering that go with it (v. 24aβ) and, in addition, a male goat is to be offered as a sin offering (v. 24b). For the atonement of an individual Lev. 4.27ff. demanded a female goat or lamb (the choice was open;

* Noth uses these terms in his original translation. The Hebrew terms are the Hiph. of *rwm* and the noun *t^erūmā*. Tr.
† Cf. *Leviticus*, pp. 61f.

according to 5.7ff. even dove offerings or offerings of fine flour were admissible for the poor); here only a female goat a year old is mentioned (v. 27b) without the mention of cereal and drink offerings. In both of these subsections the 'sojourner' is again specifically included in the legislation (vv. 26aβ, 29), in v. 26b for a reason which is difficult to understand, but which probably means that 'sojourners', too (cf. above, p. 115), are part of 'the whole population' and on this account shared in the 'guilt' incurred by all and therefore had to be included in the atonement.

[15.32-36] In vv. 32-36 a divine ordinance is given by bringing forward a particular occurrence as a precedent on which at first no judgment can be given due to the lack of available legal provision; but a divine instruction given to Moses passes a judgment which will henceforth—this is not stated, but is, of course, the intention and meaning of this passage—be determinative. With regard to its form this passage is related to Lev. 24.10-23 and Num. 9.6-12 (on this cf. p. 71 above). According to it the gathering of wood on the sabbath was punishable by death. The obvious question is whether this action is to be understood only as one of many possibilities of violating the general commandment about resting from work on the sabbath or whether it is a special prohibition in relation to the sabbath, which is certainly regarded here as the regularly recurring seventh day. Since the gathering of wood can scarcely be intended as anything other than the preparation for lighting a fire, a comparison may be made with Ex. 35.3, where kindling a fire is specifically forbidden on the sabbath day. One is tempted to regard as primary this specific prohibition for the sabbath over and against the general prohibition of work, but one must bear in mind that it is attested only in two very late passages in the Old Testament. Yet if it had preserved something original, then it would be important for an examination of the basic significance of the sabbath.

[15.37-41] The command to make 'tassels' (*gᵉdilim*) at the 'four corners' of their outer garment (what must be meant are the four corners of a large piece of cloth worn as a cloak) is already found in the deuteronomic law (Deut. 22.12). In the present section, vv. 37-41, the word *ṣiṣit* is used for 'tassel', first of all (v. 38) as a common noun, and then (v. 39aα) in the technical sense which is explained in this very section. It is certain that the 'tassels' with their blue cords, attached to the tassels in some unspecified way (v. 38b), originally had a magic, apotropaic significance (cf. the blue lace on the high priest's turban according to Ex. 28.37); the alteration in its significance to a means of 'remembering' which can be 'looked upon' in order to remind one of the divine commandments (v. 39aβb), is artificial (the corners of garments do not exactly lend themselves to being 'looked upon') and obviously secondary, an attempt, within the framework of the religion of Yahweh, to deprive of its power a custom which originally had a magical significance.

5. THE REBELLIONS OF KORAH AND OF DATHAN AND ABIRAM: 16.1–17.11

16 ¹Now Korah the son of Izhar, son of Kohath, son of Levi, and Dathan and Abiram the sons of Eliab, [he was the son of Pallu,] the son of Reuben,* ²took men; and they rose up before Moses, with a number of the people of Israel, two hundred and fifty [leaders of the congregation, chosen from the assembly,] well-known men; ³and they assembled themselves together against Moses and against Aaron, and said to them, 'You have gone too far! For all the congregation are holy, every one of them, and the LORD is among them; why then do you exalt yourselves above the assembly of the LORD?' ⁴When Moses heard it, he fell on his face; ⁵and he said to Korah and all his company, 'In the morning the LORD will show who is his, and who is holy, [and will cause him to come near to him;] him whom he will choose he will cause to come near to him. ⁶Do this: take censers, Korah and all his company; ⁷put fire in them and put incense upon them before the LORD tomorrow, and the man whom the LORD chooses shall be the holy one. [You have gone too far, sons of Levi!'] ⁸And Moses said to Korah, 'Hear now, you sons of Levi: ⁹is it too small a thing for you that the God of Israel has separated you from the congregation of Israel, to bring you near to himself, to do service in the tabernacle of the LORD, and to stand before the congregation to minister to them; ¹⁰and that he has brought you near him, and all your brethren the sons of Levi with you? And would you seek the priesthood also? ¹¹Therefore it is against the LORD that you and all your company have gathered together; what is Aaron that you murmur against him?'

12 And Moses sent to call Dathan and Abiram the sons of Eliab; and they said, 'We will not come up. ¹³Is it a small thing that you have brought us up out of a land flowing with milk and honey, to kill us in the wilderness, that you must also make yourself a prince over us? ¹⁴Moreover you have not brought us into a land flowing with milk and honey, nor given us inheritance of fields and vineyards. Will you put out the eyes of these men? We will not come up.' ¹⁵And Moses was very angry, and said to the LORD, 'Do not respect their offering. I have not taken one ass from them, and I have not harmed one of them.' ¹⁶And

---

* The incomprehensible text is surely to be corrected on the basis of 26.5, 8; cf. BH.

Moses said to Korah, 'Be present, you and all your company, before the Lord, you and they, and Aaron, tomorrow; [17]and let every one of you take his censer, and put incense upon it, and every one of you bring before the Lord his censer, two hundred and fifty censers; you also, and Aaron, each his censer.' [18]So every man took his censer, and they put fire in them and laid incense upon them, and they stood at the entrance of the tent of meeting with Moses and Aaron. [19]Then Korah assembled all the congregation against them at the entrance of the tent of meeting. And the glory of the Lord appeared to all the congregation. [20]And the Lord said to Moses and to Aaron, [21]'Separate yourselves from among this congregation, that I may consume them in a moment.' [22]And they fell on their faces, and said, 'O God, the God of the spirits of all flesh, shall one man sin, and wilt thou be angry with all the congregation?' [23]And the Lord said to Moses, [24]'Say to the congregation, Get away from about [the dwelling of Korah,] Dathan, and Abiram.' [25]Then Moses rose and went to Dathan and Abiram; and the elders of Israel followed him. [26]And he said to the congregation, 'Depart, I pray you, from the tents of these wicked men, and touch nothing of theirs, lest you be swept away with all their sins.'

27 So they got away from about [the dwelling of] Korah, [Dathan, and Abiram;] and Dathan and Abiram came out and stood at the door of their tents, together with their wives, their sons, and their little ones. [28]And Moses said, 'Hereby you shall know that the Lord has sent me to do all these works, and that it has not been of my own accord. [29]If these men die the common death of all men, or if they are visited by the fate of all men, then the Lord has not sent me. [30]But if the Lord creates something new, [and the ground opens its mouth, and swallows them up, with all that belongs to them, and they go down alive into Sheol,] then you shall know that these men have despised the Lord.' [31]And as he finished speaking all these words, the ground under them split asunder; [32]and the earth opened its mouth and swallowed them up, with their households [and all the men that belonged to Korah and all their goods.] [33]So they and all that belonged to them went down alive into Sheol; and the earth closed over them, and they perished from the midst of the assembly. [34]And all Israel that were round about them fled at their cry; for they said, 'Lest the earth swallow us up!' [35]And fire came forth from the Lord, and consumed the two hundred and fifty men offering the incense.

36 Then the Lord said to Moses, [37]'Tell Eleazar the son of Aaron the priest to take up the censers out of the blaze; [then scatter the fire far and wide.] For they are holy, [38][the censers of these men who have sinned at the cost of their lives;] so let them be made into hammered plates as a covering for the altar, for they offered them before the Lord; therefore they are holy. Thus they shall be a sign to the people of Israel.' [39]So Eleazar the priest took the bronze censers, which those who were burned had offered; and they were hammered out as a covering for the altar, [40]to be a reminder to the people of Israel, so that no one who is not a priest, who is not of the descendants of Aaron,

should draw near to burn incense before the LORD, lest he become as Korah and as his company—as the LORD said to Eleazar through Moses. 41 But on the morrow all the congregation of the people of Israel murmured against Moses and against Aaron, saying, 'You have killed the people of the LORD.' ⁴²And when the congregation had assembled against Moses and against Aaron, they turned toward the tent of meeting; and behold, the cloud covered it, and the glory of the LORD appeared. ⁴³And Moses and Aaron came to the front of the tent of meeting, ⁴⁴and the LORD said to Moses, ⁴⁵'Get away from the midst of this congregation, that I may consume them in a moment.' And they fell on their faces. ⁴⁶And Moses said to Aaron, 'Take your censer, and put fire therein from off the altar, and lay incense on it, and carry it quickly to the congregation, and make atonement for them; for wrath has gone forth from the LORD, the plague has begun.' ⁴⁷So Aaron took it as Moses said, and ran into the midst of the assembly; and behold, the plague had already begun among the people; and he put on the incense, and made atonement for the people. ⁴⁸And he stood between the dead and the living; and the plague was stopped. ⁴⁹Now those who died by the plague were fourteen thousand seven hundred, besides those who died in the affair of Korah. ⁵⁰And Aaron returned to Moses at the entrance of the tent of meeting, when the plague was stopped.

17 ¹The LORD said to Moses, ²'Speak to the people of Israel, and get from them rods, one for each fathers' house, from all their leaders according to their fathers' houses, twelve rods. Write each man's name upon his rod, ³and write Aaron's name upon the rod of Levi. For there shall be one rod for the head of each fathers' house. ⁴Then you shall deposit them in the tent of meeting before the testimony, where I meet with you. ⁵[And the rod of the man whom I choose shall sprout;] thus I will make to cease from me the murmurings of the people of Israel, which they murmur against you.' ⁶Moses spoke to the people of Israel; and all their leaders gave him rods, one for each leader, according to their fathers' houses, twelve rods; and the rod of Aaron was among their rods. ⁷And Moses deposited the rods before the LORD in the tent of the testimony.

8 And on the morrow Moses went into the tent of the testimony; and behold, the rod of Aaron for the house of Levi had sprouted and put forth buds, and produced blossoms, and it bore ripe almonds. ⁹Then Moses brought out all the rods from before the LORD to all the people of Israel; and they looked, and each man took his rod. ¹⁰And the LORD said to Moses, 'Put back the rod of Aaron before the testimony, to be kept as a sign for the rebels, that you may make an end of their murmurings against me, lest they die.' ¹¹Thus did Moses; as the LORD commanded him, so he did.

It is abundantly clear from the present text that in this complex of traditions several different elements have been united, not in the sense that different traditions have come together but rather that

several, already fixed, literary 'sources' have been worked together by
a redactor. In the case of 16.1–35 three versions can, in several respects, be clearly established. Different persons are involved and they
have in common only the fact that they rebel against something or
other. On the one hand the rebels are named as Dathan and Abiram
(particularly in the self-contained section vv. 12–15 and also in vv.
25–34, a section which is only very slightly mixed with extraneous
material); on the other, a certain Korah appears, but in two different
roles, either as the leader of 250 'well-known men' (so especially in
vv. 2aβb, 3) or else as the spokesman of 'Levitical' opposition (vv.
8–11). Furthermore, the direction of the rebellion is variously expressed; according to v. 3 *et al.*, it is 'against Moses and against
Aaron', according to v. 11b against Aaron alone and according to vv.
12–15 against Moses alone. Finally, the objects of the reproaches that
are made are different; in v. 3b Moses and Aaron are reproached
with having 'exalted themselves above the assembly of Yahweh',
according to v. 10b it is a question of the privileges of the priestly
office, and in vv. 13–14 of the lack of success in Israel's leadership.
The literary element in which Dathan and Abiram are the rebels can
be separated and defined with comparative ease. Their names are
first mentioned in a complicated context in v. 1; then they, and they
alone, appear in vv. 12–15 in a discussion with Moses, and their names
finally appear at the end of v. 24, vv. 25–34 dealing fairly consistently
(Korah's name appears only in v. 27a and v. 32b) with their punishment by a divine judgment. They had denied to Moses both the
ability and the right of leadership. Rightly, this element is generally
considered to be the oldest narrative strand in the chapter; it probably comes from the 'Yahwist'(J). The analysis of those sections in
which Korah appears is much more difficult. It is certainly clear that
there exist two different versions whose juxtaposition is most evident
in vv. 2–11. According to vv. 2–7a, Korah joins up with 250 respected
men to challenge the privileged position enjoyed by Moses and Aaron,
while in vv. 8–11 Korah, together with other 'Levites', demands
priestly rights over against Aaron's privileges. In what follows it is
only with difficulty that these two versions can be neatly and consistently distinguished, although several doublets appear and at the
same time individual statements can be allocated to one or the other
version. This is also the case in vv. 16–24abα. The punishment is
mentioned only in a single sentence, v. 35, and this mentions the
'250 men'. It is particularly difficult to establish the relationship of

these two versions to each other. That both belong to the sphere of the 'Priestly writing' (P) is generally accepted and is probably correct (cf. the use of language, e.g. the constant repetition of the word 'congregation'). Questions of priority and dependence with regard to the two versions are, however, doubtful. In our opinion arguments from the point of view of content do not lead to any certain decision. Literary considerations, especially the sequence of vv. 2–11, argue for the priority of the '250 men' version; and the impossibility of being able to follow the versions side by side with any certainty from v. 16 on, as well as the fact that the punishment is mentioned only once (v. 35), would lead us to suppose that the 'Levites' version is not a self-contained, independent element which has subsequently been worked into the '250 men' version, but that the former is, rather, a secondary addition to the latter. 16.36–17.11 is probably to be judged in a similar way. Of its subsections, 16.41–50, which makes a close connection between Moses and Aaron, betrays a certain affinity with the '250 men' version, while 16.36–40 and 17.1–11, with their emphasis on Aaron's priestly privileges, seem rather to belong to the 'Levites' version. In no case, however, is it a question of necessary or even likely continuations of one of the versions of 16.1–35. Thus one may probably suppose that these passages have been added successively, in the order in which we now have them, to the P-element in 16.1–35 (either before or after this was merged with the Dathan-Abiram story).

[16.1] At the beginning, the persons concerned in the various strata are introduced together by name in the context of an unusual verbal clause which should probably be considered as part of the oldest form of the narrative. Korah is given a genealogy going back to Levi which most probably belongs to the 'Levites' version of the Korah stratum. One is tempted to suppose that originally Korah was credited with different ancestors; against this, however, is the fact that, independently of the present narrative, Korah has a definite place in the (late) Levitical genealogy (cf. Ex. 6.21, 24) and therefore must surely from the first have been considered a 'Levite'. Concerning the Reubenites Dathan and Abiram nothing is otherwise known in the Old Testament; they are mentioned only in Deut. 11.6 and Ps. 106.17 with reference to the present story, in Deut. 11.6 with a genealogical note which presumably arises from an original text of Num. 16.1; this suggests that the very oddly phrased introduction of the tribal name Pallu is a later addition based on Num. 26.5bβ.

[16.2] The fact that v. 2aα is in the plural suggests that it probably belongs basically to the Dathan-Abiram stratum and reports in a quite general way the 'shameless'* 'rising up' of these two, thereby preparing the way for vv. 12ff. The Korah stratum (cf. v. 5) begins in v. 2aβ with the mention of the '250 men' who joined Korah in turning against Moses and Aaron (v. 3). The numerous appositions in v. 2b are perhaps not all original; especially remarkable is the incorrect use of the technical term 'leader' (cf. above, p. 19) as well as the strange and, from the point of view of content, quite obscure mention of them as 'chosen from the assembly'.

[16.3] According to v. 3 the reproach is directed against Moses and Aaron because they 'exalted themselves' above the 'assembly of Yahweh', i.e. above the totality of fully authorized Israelites (for this expression cf. already Micah 2.5 as well as Deut. 23.2–4), who maintain that they alone are 'holy' and have Yahweh 'among them' and therefore are able to 'come near' Yahweh (cf. v. 5b) and believe that they are 'chosen' (cf. v. 5b) by him. Unfortunately it cannot certainly be proved by textual criticism that in v. 3 the vocative 'sons of Levi' belonged to the original text.† The essential difficulty of this vocative could argue for its originality, since this would explain its subsequent omission from the text. What would emerge from this, then, would be that Moses and Aaron are here addressed as 'Levites'. Since Korah himself in all probability (cf. above) was considered to be a 'Levite', then we have here a dispute within the Levites which certainly has a real background in specific conflicts, otherwise unknown to us, from the time of the writer (P). By the following divine judgment a decision is made against a group of opposition 'Levites' whose spokesman was Korah, who for his part had made common cause with a number of 'respected men' of the 'congregation' to contest the privileges of another group, represented by Moses and Aaron, on the grounds that, as such, they were not possessed of any special 'holiness' but only shared in the holiness and the relationship with God that were common to the whole congregation. Behind Moses and Aaron there can scarcely be concealed anything other than the Jerusalem priesthood itself, on whose behalf not only the authority of

---

* The opening word of 16.1 in Hebrew, *wayyiqqaḥ*, is translated in the RSV by 'took' (v. 2). Noth suggests, however, that it is to be derived from a root *yqḥ = Arabic *waqaḥa*='to be shameless'. This is what is found in his translation ('behaved shamelessly'); hence this reference in the commentary. Tr.

† In his translation Noth points out that the words 'You have gone too far, sons of Levi' are out of place in v. 7b and he accordingly amplifies the phrase 'You have gone too far' in v. 3 with the addition of 'sons of Levi'. Tr.

Aaron but also that of the still greater figure of Moses are cited. The contempt for the Levites, whose actual existence is presumed, corresponds to a tendency, known elsewhere, on the part of P (cf. above, p. 33).

[16.4–7] The opposition group described in v. 3 is rejected by a divine judgment for which Moses prepares the way (vv. 5–7a), on the basis of a command of Yahweh's which he receives when he turns towards Yahweh in humility (this is stated in v. 4). Yahweh himself, by his own 'choice', will decide 'who is his' and 'who is holy'. Korah with all his followers, i.e. those 250 men of v. 2aβ, are addressed in v. 5. These followers are described, here and in what follows, as 'his congregation'*, the word with which P usually describes the '(cultic) congregation' of Israel. The use of this word here must surely be intentional. With his company Korah has arbitrarily created a caricature of a 'congregation' and believes that he can thereby speak for the real congregation as a whole. The divine judgment to which Korah and his 'congregation' have to submit will take place on the occasion of an 'incense offering' which is to be made ready for the following day (vv. 6–7a). This 'incense offering' is to be carried out 'before Yahweh' by the simple use of shovel-type censers held in the hand (P knows of no particular incense altar in the sanctuary).† In this respect there is the notable assumption that even the 'laity' (Korah's 250 companions) are permitted to take part in this activity. Or is this summons perhaps a *reductio ad absurdum* of the general claim to 'holiness' on the part of this questionable 'congregation' (v. 3aβ)? In any case Yahweh, by the way in which he receives this 'incense offering', will make known his 'choice' and will decide the question of 'holiness'.

[16.8–11] In v. 8 Moses begins another address to Korah. Without what has been said in vv. 3–7 this address would be left hanging in the air; on the other hand this new address is abrupt, and the subsequent statements made by Moses do not at first follow easily on the summons of vv. 6–7a and in vv. 16f. they finally turn into a repetition of that summons. This is borne out by the fact that in vv. 8–11 the question at issue is expressed differently from in v. 3, with the result that vv. 9–11 can, at a pinch, only be understood as an answer to v. 3. From all this it follows that vv. 8–11 are to be con-

---

* This is a more accurate rendering of the Hebrew 'adātō. RSV paraphrases with 'his company'. Tr.

† Cf. *Exodus*, pp. 234f.

sidered as a later addition to vv. *1, 2aβb, 3–7a. The set-up in vv. 8–11 is as follows: Korah is a spokesman for a group of Levites (v. 8b) who desire the priestly office (v. 10) that is held by Aaron (v. 11b), not on his own authority but according to the will of Yahweh (v. 11a). Moses stands over against the contestants; he points out to Korah and his followers, who in v. 11aα, too, are described as his 'congregation' (as in vv. 4aα, 6bβ), that through being entrusted with the Levitical service in 'the tabernacle of Yahweh' they have been given preferential treatment over the other members of the 'congregation of Israel' (the use of the term 'separation' for the special position of the Levites is found also in 8.14) and that they are not justified in desiring, in addition, something which Yahweh has reserved for Aaron. It is not clear from the wording of the text whether the idea is that all the Levites belonged to Korah's followers or only a particular opposition group of Levites; the fact that this is a secondary addition to vv. *1–7 would suggest the latter. Behind this whole passage there is certainly once again the fact of a party, represented by Korah, in opposition to the Jerusalem priesthood, a party which does not, as in vv. *1–7, simply question the special privileges of that priesthood but rather demands a share in them. However, Aaron's priestly rights rest on Yahweh's personal decision; therefore any opposition to Aaron is, as Moses makes abundantly clear (v. 11), in reality a rebellion against Yahweh.

[16.12–15] In vv. 12–15 there follows the first continuous section of the Dathan-Abiram story (J). All that has already been given of this story is the mention in v. 1 of the names of the two rebels, and possibly the remark in v. 2aα that they 'rose up before Moses'. It is completely unknown how in particular these two otherwise completely unknown Reubenites came to rebel against Moses, thereby becoming spokesmen of a discontentment with Moses. The tradition must at one time have been meant to relate more of a disaffection within Israel connected with the names of Dathan and Abiram. It is clear from v. 12 that these two did not address themselves directly to Moses, but spread their evil talk within Israel so that Moses summons them to him to hear what it is they have to say. They simply refuse to obey (v. 12b), pointing out that his leadership has proved to be disastrous (v. 13a) —the expression 'a land flowing with milk and honey' is applied, unusually, to Egypt—and that he is therefore quite unjustified in acting the 'prince' (v. 13b). With the unfulfilled promise of bringing Israel into a good and fruitful land (v. 14a), he is only 'blinding' his people (v. 14ba). The more general theme of the anger of an Israel that has had to spend a longish period in the wilderness (cf. Ex. 16.3; 17.3; Num. 14.2; 20.4 in different contexts) appears here with no particular reason given. The reaction of the 'angry' Moses is strange in that it does not appear to answer the particular content of the reproach, but mentions rather that he has neither harmed nor ill-treated any single one of them (v. 15b). One has to accept that this is a general and frequent way of expression with which it is customary to defend oneself against the reproach of 'lordly' behaviour and the misuse of a position of leadership (cf. I Sam. 12.3). The punishment of the rebels which Moses requests of Yahweh, that Yahweh should no longer 'respect' (i.e. receive as well-pleasing) their 'offering' (*minḥā* certainly here in this original, general sense) seems extremely mild (it is by far surpassed by the punishment which, according to vv. 31–33, is actually inflicted), but does signify an exclusion from the Israelite community. It remains uncertain whether the phrase in vv. 12b, 14bβ ('come up') means that Moses was on some raised position or whether what is meant is simply an approach to someone 'in a higher position of authority' (cf. on this Deut. 25.7).

[16.16–24] V. 16 sees the resumption of the Korah-narrative (P) following on v. 11. In vv. 16–24abα, with its numerous repetitions, the '250 men' version is closely interwoven with the 'Levites' version; it is scarcely now possible to make a clear division, since editorial and secondary additions have also to be taken into account. At any rate, the instructions of vv. 6–7a are repeated for the 'Levites' version in vv. 16–17 (after the introductory formula of transition in v. 16aα) in continuation of vv. 8–11 (the additional contrast between Korah and his followers on the one hand and Aaron on the other in v. 16b is perhaps a later attempt to clarify the situation, while the mention of the '250 men' and the juxtaposition once again of Korah and Aaron at the end of v. 17 represents a fusion of the two versions, with the supposition that Korah's 'Levite' followers had also run to 250 men). There follows in v. 18 the carrying out of the given instructions, one version only without a doublet; the intention of the supplementary mention of Moses and Aaron (v. 18b) is to ensure their participation, too, in the preparations for the expected divine judgment (cf. already vv. 16b, 17b). Before, however, the divine judgment that is now due is reported, there follows first of all, in vv. 19–24, another episode which involves the 'whole congregation' in the affair. Korah, who has emerged in v. 3 as the spokesman for the would-be

claims of the whole 'congregation' against Moses and Aaron, summons, on his own initiative, the 'whole congregation' to the spot where
the divine glory is to appear (v. 19). The aim of what follows is that,
besides Moses and Aaron, the whole congregation, too, is exempted
from any collective punishment. First Moses and Aaron are instructed
by Yahweh to remove themselves from among the assembled crowd
(vv. 21–22), so that they might be exempt from the approaching
divine judgment of destruction. Thereupon they ask of Yahweh that
the whole congregation summoned by Korah should also be spared,
since only 'one man' (the small group of Korah's followers are thereby
ignored, small that is in comparison with the whole congregation)
has sinned (v. 22), whereupon Yahweh also permits the whole congregation to withdraw, thereby exempting them from the punishment
(vv. 23–24abα). Yahweh thus makes a decision, in accordance with
the objection of Moses and Aaron, in favour of 'individual requital'.
In v. 22 God is addressed in a very unusual way. Instead of the usual
divine name, we find the old appellative 'ēl ('God'), which appears as
a proper name as early as the Ugaritic texts as well as in poetic texts
in the Old Testament, but which is striking in the present context.
The appositional phrase 'God of the spirits of all flesh' occurs also in
27.16; by it God is addressed as the creator of life (rūaḥ, in the plural
here, is to be understood in this sense) and asked not to destroy without special reason the life created by him. At the end of v. 24 the
Korah story is quite incongruously mixed up with the Dathan-
Abiram story. The mention of 'the dwelling of Korah' is out of place,
for Korah and his company are in front of the tent of meeting (vv.
18bα, 19a), not in his 'dwelling'; this statement (from the point of
view of content, not of wording) comes from the story of Dathan and
Abiram, who, according to vv. 27bff., are inflicted with the divine
punishment in front of their tents. The mention of 'the dwelling of
Korah' as well as the sudden mention of the names 'Dathan and
Abiram' must be a completely secondary fusion of the two narrative
variants, at a place where once more we encounter the change-over
from one variant to the other.

[16.25–34] For in vv. 25–34 we find the continuation and the conclusion of the Dathan-Abiram story. V. 25 connects directly with v.
15. Since Dathan and Abiram had refused to obey Moses' summons
(vv. 12b, 14bβ), Moses in person, together with the elders as representatives of Israel as a whole, goes to Dathan and Abiram (v. 25)
and first of all has 'the people' (the text has 'the congregation' which

comes, however, from the language of P and therefore from the Korah variant and has suppressed an originally different expression, presumably 'the people') move away from the dwellings and from all the possessions of those two 'wicked' men, lest the divine judgment descend upon anyone other than the guilty parties. V. 27a is yet another editorial addition linking Korah and Dathan-Abiram and is almost a literal repetition of v. 24b; there then follows a continuous section of the Dathan-Abiram story. Dathan and Abiram react to the arrival of Moses and the elders by coming and standing boldly and defiantly outside their tents, together with their whole families (v. 27b). And now Moses proclaims a divine judgment—without any previous declaration on the part of Yahweh, but, rather, clearly on the basis of a power within himself—a judgment which will confirm his 'mission' and refute any suspicion that he is acting of his own accord (v. 28). The divine judgment will be 'recognizable' (v. 28aα) by the fact that Dathan and Abiram will not die a 'natural' death (v. 29), but that rather Yahweh will do to them something new and hitherto unheard of (with the result that they will die). In v. 30aα that term is used which is specially reserved for the productive, generating action of God ('creation'); as wonderful as the work of creation will be what Yahweh will do in the sight of all men to punish those who 'despise' him (v. 30b), those who have attacked the authority of his appointed servant Moses. One can at least ask whether the exact prediction of the expected miracle in v. 30aβ belongs to the original form of the narrative or is not rather an addition by a later writer who wanted to have Moses know everything exactly beforehand, while the narrative to begin with had perhaps reserved both type and method of the realization of Moses' announcement to the power of Yahweh. In any case, hard on the heels of Moses' announcement came the miracle that Dathan and Abiram, together with their families and all their possessions, were swallowed up by the earth's opening beneath them (vv. 31–33; v. 32b is, from the point of view both of content and wording, an obvious addition which again introduces the Korah story, but anticipates v. 35 in a completely unthinking way). So Dathan and Abiram disappeared 'without trace' (v. 33bα) from the earth and from the midst of the Israelite community and went, still alive (v. 33a), into the world of the dead (šᵉ'ōl) that was thought of as being under the earth (normally one goes there only after one has died a 'natural' death). Quite understandably 'all Israel' immediately fled in fear of this place of terror (v. 34). The Dathan-

Abiram story contains no data about this place. In the whole story there is no mention of a place-name and no reference to the place where these events occurred. Nor is there any mention of any possible traces left behind by this terrible judgment. What, rather, v. 33bα seems to be saying is that after the earth had closed up again there was nothing more to be seen of what had taken place. This lack of localization is remarkable. According to the narrative as we now have it, the main interest of the tradition was in the puzzling figures of the two Reubenites and the horrible fact of their disappearance without trace.

[16.35] V. 35 contains the remarkably succinct conclusion to the Korah story. The divine judgment, expressed by a fire coming forth from Yahweh, passes sentence on the rebellion against (Moses and) Aaron, i.e. against the Jerusalem priesthood and its privileges. Strangely enough there is no mention of Korah, but only of his '250 men'. This type of divine judgment recalls Lev. 10.1–2. Here, however, there is no mention, as in Lev. 10, of 'unholy fire', i.e. of an inadmissible offering; rather were the 250 men simply carrying out an express command of Yahweh (vv. 6–7a). Or was this command from the very beginning meant in this sense: Try, you 'laymen', with nothing more than an incense offering and see what will happen? And was Korah, although spokesman of this group, not affected by the disaster because he was, after all, a 'Levite' (cf. also 26.11) and did this not refute the idea that his followers lost their lives? These questions are perhaps to be answered in the affirmative; but such a laconic conclusion to the narrative, which at any rate belongs to the '250 men' version and has no doublet, permits of no certain decision.

[16.36–40] The appendix in vv. 36–40 (Hebr. 17.1–5) has at any rate already understood the affair in this way, that the men who had presented the incense offering were not 'authorized' to do so (in spite of the divine command in vv. 6–7a), because they did not belong to the Aaronites (v. 40a), and here Korah is included amongst those 'unauthorized' persons (v. 40b). In addition this appendix tries to arrive at an explanation of the origin of a thin bronze overlay on the altar (by this general reference to an 'altar' pure and simple can be meant only the altar of burnt offerings in the Jerusalem temple). According to Ex. 27.2b this altar had a bronze overlay from the start. The present narrative agrees with this (it is difficult to think of a double overlay), while it suggests that the overlay was provided only at this point by way of a warning. Basic here is the idea that materials used in a sacrifice, even if used for an illegitimate sacrifice, have become 'holy' and must be kept from any possible misuse, either cultic or profane. Thus the sacrificial fire must be made unusable by being scattered (v. 37aβ is, of course, probably secondary, since the idea is not taken up in what follows) and some legitimate cultic use has to be found for the bronze of the censers.

[16.41–50] The second appendix, vv. 41–50 (*Hebr.* 17.6–15), has subsequently to justify explicitly the harsh treatment of Korah and his followers by Moses and Aaron. There occurs a revolt of 'all the congregation of the people of Israel' because Moses and Aaron have allegedly killed 'the people of Yahweh' (in reality it is only Korah's followers; v. 41). Yahweh, who appears in the usual way in P (v. 42), turns to Moses and Aaron with the resolve that he will immediately destroy the whole rebellious 'congregation' and spare only Moses and Aaron (v. 45a). And already the sentence of destruction begins in the form of a deadly 'plague' (of what kind it was is not mentioned); then Moses, after falling on his face before Yahweh (v. 45b), can feel justified in sending Aaron amongst the 'congregation' with an incense offering and, by means of the apotropaic effect of this offering, in bringing the ravages of the 'plague' to a standstill, so that, having begun at one end of the camp, it was unable to spread any further (cf. v. 48a). Nevertheless, the 'plague' had already claimed a considerable number of victims (v. 49a; measured by the total number given in 1.46, just under one-fortieth of the whole population had died). Thus severely did Yahweh punish a rebellion against those men commissioned by himself, Moses and Aaron.

[17.1–11] The story of 'Aaron's rod' in 17.1–11 (*Hebr.* 17.16–26) recounts a miraculous occurrence which once for all should make an end of all rebellions on the part of the Israelites against the Aaronites (v. 5b), by reason of the fact that it provides a constantly available 'sign' that, according to the will of Yahweh, Aaron and his descendants have a privileged position over all other Israelites; that this is dealing with the question of the position of the Aaronites as the sole legitimate priests is so self-evident that it needs to be neither stated explicitly nor even hinted at. Here Aaron, in the list of Israelite tribes, is simply the representative of the tribe of Levi as if, besides the Aaronites, there were no other 'Levites'; the latter are simply ignored. The story of Aaron's rod is therefore somewhat along the lines of the '250 men' version of 16.1–35, without however forming any necessary or even expected continuation of it. It is phrased in

the style of P, but is probably of somewhat later origin. The twelve
rods (v. 2a) for the twelve tribes are to be conceived of as bare
branches. It is not clear from the text what names Moses wrote on the
rods (v. 2b), the names of the tribes or the names of the 'leaders'. V.
3a would suggest the former. V. 3a likewise clearly presupposes a
system of twelve tribes that included the tribe of Levi (on this cf.
above, pp. 18f.). V. 3b proves that Aaron, on whom the main interest
of the whole story is focused, must represent the tribe of Levi, since
the number twelve envisaged for the rods did not allow of a special
rod for Aaron besides the rod of Levi. The sentence in v. 5a anticipates in a jarring fashion the nature of the miracle that is expected,
thereby diminishing the surprise expressed in v. 8aβb; the sentence is
probably an addition with the intention once again (cf. above p. 128
on 16.30aβ) of having Moses informed of everything in advance.
While the other rods, being of no further significance, are given back
after the miracle (v. 9), Aaron's rod, as the point of the whole story
demands, is preserved. Here it must be assumed that it was also part
of the miracle that the leaves and blossom and fruit of the rod (v. 8b)
remained unwithered. The place where it was preserved was somewhere 'before the testimony', i.e. in front of the 'ark of the testimony'
(Ex. 25.21f. et al.) in the tent of meeting. The possibility that it was
placed in the ark (so Heb. 9.4) is specifically excluded by the present
phraseology. It is difficult to imagine that Aaron's rod ever really
existed, even symbolically. Probably the opinion of this late narrative
is that, meanwhile, on some occasion or another, it had finally been
destroyed.

6. THE RELATIONSHIP OF PRIESTS AND LEVITES
TO THE REST OF THE ISRAELITES: 17.12–18.32

17 [12]And the people of Israel said to Moses, 'Behold, we perish, we
are undone, we are all undone, [13]Every one who comes near, who
comes near to the tabernacle of the LORD, shall die. Are we all to
perish?'
18 [1]So the LORD said to Aaron, 'You and your sons and your fathers'
house with you shall bear iniquity in connection with the sanctuary;
and you and your sons with you shall bear iniquity in connection with
your priesthood. [2]And with you bring your brethren also, the tribe of
Levi, the tribe of your father, that they may join you, and minister to
you while you and your sons with you are before the tent of the
testimony. [3]They shall attend you and attend to all the duties of the

tent; but shall not come near to the vessels of the sanctuary or to the altar, lest they, and you, die. ⁴They shall join you, and attend to the tent of meeting, for all the service of the tent; and no one else shall come near you. ⁵And you shall attend to the duties of the sanctuary and the duties of the altar, that there be wrath no more upon the people of Israel. ⁶And behold, I have taken your brethren the Levites from among the people of Israel; they are a gift to you, given to the LORD, to do the service of the tent of meeting. ⁷And you and your sons with you shall attend to your priesthood for all that concerns the altar and that is within the veil; and you shall serve. I give your priesthood as a gift, and any one else who comes near shall be put to death.'

8 Then the LORD said to Aaron, 'And behold, I have given you whatever is kept of the offerings made to me, all the consecrated things of the people of Israel; I have given them to you as a portion, and to your sons as a perpetual due. ⁹This shall be yours of the most holy things, reserved from the fire; every offering of theirs, every cereal offering of theirs and every sin offering of theirs and every guilt offering of theirs, which they render to me, shall be most holy to you and to your sons. ¹⁰In a most holy place shall you eat of it; every male may eat of it; it is holy to you. ¹¹This also is yours, the offering of their gift, all the wave offerings of the people of Israel; I have given them to you, and to your sons and daughters with you, as a perpetual due; every one who is clean in your house may eat of it. ¹²All the best of the oil, and all the best of the wine and of the grain, the first fruits of what they give to the LORD, I give to you. ¹³The first ripe fruits of all that is in their land, which they bring to the LORD, shall be yours; every one who is clean in your house may eat of it. ¹⁴Every devoted thing in Israel shall be yours. ¹⁵Everything that opens the womb of all flesh, whether man or beast, which they offer to the LORD, shall be yours; nevertheless the first-born of man you shall redeem, and the firstling of unclean beasts you shall redeem. [¹⁶And their redemption price (at a month old you shall redeem them) you shall fix at five shekels in silver, according to the shekel of the sanctuary, which is twenty gerahs.] ¹⁷But the firstling of a cow, or the firstling of a sheep, or the firstling of a goat, you shall not redeem; they are holy. You shall sprinkle their blood upon the altar, and shall burn their fat as an offering by fire, a pleasing odour to the LORD; ¹⁸but their flesh shall be yours, as the breast that is waved and as the right thigh are yours. ¹⁹All the holy offerings which the people of Israel present to the LORD I give to you, and to your sons and daughters with you, as a perpetual due; it is a covenant of salt for ever before the LORD for you and for your offspring with you.' ²⁰And the LORD said to Aaron, 'You shall have no inheritance in their land, neither shall you have any portion among them; I am your portion and your inheritance among the people of Israel.

21 'To the Levites I have given every tithe in Israel for an inheritance, in return for their service which they serve, their service in the tent of meeting. [²²And henceforth the people of Israel shall not come near the tent of meeting, lest they bear sin and die. ²³But the Levites

shall do the service of the tent of meeting, and they shall bear their iniquity; it shall be a perpetual statute throughout your generations;] and among the people of Israel they shall have no inheritance. 24For the tithe of the people of Israel, which they present as an offering to the LORD, I have given to the Levites for an inheritance; therefore I have said of them that they shall have no inheritance among the people of Israel.'

25 And the LORD said to Moses, 26'Moreover you shall say to the Levites, "When you take from the people of Israel the tithe which I have given you from them for your inheritance, then you shall present an offering from it to the LORD, a tithe of the tithe. 27And your offering shall be reckoned to you as though it were the grain of the threshing floor, and as the fulness of the wine press. 28So shall you also present an offering to the LORD from all your tithes, which you receive from the people of Israel; and from it you shall give the LORD's offering to Aaron the priest. 29Out of all the gifts to you, you shall present every offering due to the LORD, from all the best of them, giving the hallowed part from them." 30Therefore you shall say to them, "When you have offered from it the best of it, then the rest shall be reckoned to the Levites as produce of the threshing floor, and as produce of the wine press; 31and you may eat it in any place, you and your households; for it is your reward in return for your service in the tent of meeting. 32 And you shall bear no sin by reason of it, when you have offered the best of it. And you shall not profane the holy things of the people of Israel, lest you die." '

17.12f. (*Hebr.* 17.27f.) provides a loose connection between, on the one hand, the ordinances that follow in ch. 18 concerning the tasks and right of the priests and Levites and, on the other, the narratives of ch. 16–17 in which the 'congregation' were represented as having on several occasions come into deadly danger through encroaching on the realm of the 'holy' (16.19ff.; 16.41ff.). However, this connection is not entirely suitable, for there had never been any mention in ch. 16–17 of the Israelites having come too near the 'tabernacle of Yahweh' (17.13). But the internal disputes of the Levites, with the subsequent catastrophic judgments on the part of Yahweh, could have given rise to the insertion at this point of statements about priestly and Levitical functions, especially since these statements arise from the fact that the priests and Levites had to endure the danger of that familiarity with the sanctuary which is part of their office, as a 'potential iniquity' (18.1, [23aβ]). Originally the compilation that is ch. 18 was certainly an independent unit, not intended from the outset for the present context. This unit comprises, first of all (vv. 1–7), a brief formulation of the duties which the priests (Aaron and

his descendants) with the assistance of the Levites have to fulfil
towards Israel in the cultic sphere, and then provides (vv. 8–32) a
survey of the gifts which they may claim from Israel 'in return' for
their services. From the point of view both of language and subject-
matter, this section belongs to the late period. It is dominated by
expressions and technical terms characteristic of P; but this composition, clumsily and inconsequentially and carelessly put together as
it is in many respects, certainly does not belong to the original
P-narrative. This is also borne out by its subsequent connection with
the P-narrative by means of all kinds of secondary additions.

[**18.1–7**] Right at the beginning (v. 1) an immediate distinction is
made between Aaronites ('Aaron and his sons') and Levites ('fathers'
house', according to late usage, in the sense of 'tribe'); all the Levites,
of whom, of course, the Aaronites were also a part, are involved in
general in the 'sanctuary' and in the 'danger' connected with it, the
Aaronites, in addition, in the heightened 'danger' of the priestly
service itself. The Aaronites are stationed directly in front of the
'tent of the testimony' (this expression occurs otherwise only in the
gloss of 9.15 and in 17.7f.), while the Levites form only their ancillary
retinue and are not permitted to approach the holy vessels or the altar
(of burnt offerings) (vv. 2–4). The way in which the relationship of
the Levites to the Aaronites is expressed contains an interpretation of
the name 'Levi' (Niph. of *lwh* = 'to be joined to'; the same derivation
of the name Levi occurs in Gen. 29.34, but with a quite different
foundation). The priests must pay particular attention to the fact
that they alone are permitted to provide the service at the altar (of
burnt offerings); otherwise divine 'wrath' might once 'more' come
upon the Israelites (v. 5). There is obviously the fear that if unauthorized persons were to break the taboo of what is holy, especially
the taboo of the altar, this would bring divine judgment in its train.
The insertion of the word 'again' 'once more'* is noteworthy. It is
obviously intended to remind us of 16.1–35, although in that section
there was no question of any violation of the holiness of the altar
having occurred, at the most only of an evil intention in that direction (v. 10b). As in 17.12f., the connection with ch. 16–17 is not very
precise. In vv. 6f. the duties of priests and Levites are defined once
again by means of the term 'gift'. The priestly office is a 'gift' to the

---

* In the RSV translation this word has been put in the negative by being
amalgamated with the negative of the verb. Hebrew *welō* . . . *'ōd* = 'and not . . .
once more' = RSV 'no more'. Tr.

Aaronites (v. 7ba). The Levites, too, are a 'gift' to the Aaronites, chosen from the ranks of the rest of the Israelites (v. 6aba)—so, too, 3.9; 8.19—and yet are, at the same time, 'given' to Yahweh—so, too, 8.16 and the general purport of 3.11–13 (for the technical term 'given' cf. above, p. 33). Amongst the special duties of the priests there is included, in v. 7aβ, also the 'service' 'within the veil'. Since, according to the other occurrences of the word 'veil', what must be meant is the entrance to the 'holy of holies' of the post-exilic temple, then it is a question here of service in this 'holy of holies'. Since, according to Lev. 16.2–4, 34a, the 'holy of holies' could be entered only by the high priest and only on a particular occasion 'once a year', this special high-priestly function is thought of in the present passage as being included in the 'gift' of the 'priesthood', for it is difficult to conceive that a new element is being introduced here whereby all the priests could have been active continually in the 'holy of holies'. Vv. 6f. produce a disjointed effect and might be regarded as a later addition, were it not for the fact that the whole of vv. 1–7 is so disordered and lacking in unity that one can scarcely expect any consistency of thought.

[18.8–32] There follows, in vv. 8–32, a list of what priests and Levites receive in return for taking upon themselves the 'danger' of cultic action for and on behalf of the Israelites. In this context cultic technical terms are used in a very debased way. This is especially true of the terms 'heave offering' 'heave', which fundamentally designate a particular gesture accompanying the offering (cf. Lev. 7.14),* but which are to be understood here in the quite general sense of 'offering'. The term 'most holy' ('holy of holies') is also used in an extremely loose way, on one occasion for the sacrificial offerings (v. 9) and then again for a place that is not precisely defined (v. 10). Nevertheless, the whole section can be divided up tolerably consistently into a series of subdivisions.

[18.8–10] Vv. 8–10 deal with those portions of the actual sacrifices which belong to the sanctuary and which are to belong to the priests in the narrower sense, i.e. to the (adult) male members of the Aaronite family and which are to be consumed by them in the sacred precincts (v. 10). The types of sacrifice in question are enumerated in v. 9; the burnt offering is excluded, since this was completely burned on the altar (the skin of the sacrificial animal is overlooked; on this cf. Lev. 7.8), likewise the sacrifice proper, since those parts of

* Cf. on this point *Leviticus*, pp. 61f.

it which were not offered on the altar were destined for the sacrificial meal.

[18.11–18] Vv. 11–18 deal with those offerings of the Israelites which are from the realm of nature, and these, too, are assigned to the priests, in this case to use as they wish within their families, in so far as the members of these are ritually clean, and with no restriction to the sacred precincts (vv. 11aβb, 13b). These offerings are described in v. 11aα as 'wave offerings'; here again we have a technical term for a specific mode of presenting an offering* being levelled down into a general expression for 'offerings'. First of all the produce of olive-yards, vine-yards and fields is dealt with (v. 12a); it remains obscure whether the 'first' or the 'best' of this produce was to offered (the word rē'šīt in v. 12b can mean both, in v. 12a the figurative use of the term 'fat' obviously means the 'best', while v. 13a speaks quite unequivocally of the 'first fruits'),† perhaps, however, these alternatives are irrelevant, since it was believed fundamentally that the 'first' is at the same time the 'best'. V. 14 includes 'devoted things' in this context, as if the possibility still existed of a 'holy war' in which the booty was to be put under the 'ban' (yet, cf. too, Lev. 27.28f.).‡ In vv. 15–17 it is the turn of the first-born of animals; they, too, are assigned to the priests. In this respect there is to be observed the rule about the redemption of the first-born of man and of unclean animals, i.e. animals which cannot be sacrificed (cf. Ex. 34.19, 20a, et al.); this 'redemption' originally had to be effected by means of the substitute offering of an animal that could be sacrificed (Ex. 34.20a, et al.). In the present passage, however, in an addition (v. 16 proves to be such by its unfortunate position between two verses, 15 and 17, which belong together) a 'redemption' by a money payment is envisaged (on this example of the progressive 'commercialization' of the character of the cult cf. Lev. 5.14–6.7 (Hebr. 5.14–26) and 27.2ff.;§ the expression beʿerkekā occurs also in Num 18.16). According to v. 17 the first-born of 'clean' animals assigned to the priests were not simply to be received by them but had to have their blood sprinkled and their fat burned on the analogy of sacrifices (cf. Lev. 3.2b–5), except that in this case the whole of the rest of the flesh came to the priests, not, as

* Cf. Exodus, p. 232.
† The RSV has rendered rē'šīt in v. 12b as 'first fruits' and ḥēleb ('fat') in v. 12a as 'the best'. Bikkūrīm ('first fruits') has become 'first ripe fruits' in RSV (v. 13a), presumably to distinguish it from the translation of rē'šīt in v. 12b. Tr.
‡ Cf. on this point Leviticus, p. 207.
§ On these two passages see Leviticus, pp. 46f. and 204.

in normal sacrifices, only certain parts of it (cf. Lev. 7.30f., 34f.).

[**18.19**] In the concluding section, v. 19, the rights of the priests are described as a 'covenant of salt' concluded in perpetuity. This expression occurs elsewhere only in II Chron. 13.5 with reference to a covenant between Yahweh and the house of David, and in Lev. 2.13 there is, with the phrase 'salt of the covenant', an allusion to a 'covenant of salt' between Yahweh and people. The fundamental concept here is that through the common eating of salt a 'covenant' relationship between the partners is brought about.* In the present passage the reference is, strangely enough, to a 'covenant' made with the Aaronic priesthood 'before Yahweh' (any expression in which Yahweh figures as partner of a covenant is avoided).

[**18.20–24**] After a new introductory formula, there follows in vv. 20–24 legislation about what the Levites are to receive. With reference to their lack of territorial inheritance (in v. 20, as in v. 1a, Aaron appears as the representative of the whole tribe of Levi), to them are assigned all the 'tithes' to be paid by Israel (vv. 21a, 24a) in return for their cultic services which spare the Israelites the risk of approaching the 'dangerous' sanctuary (vv. 22–23). While the deuteronomic law (Deut. 12.18f.; 14.27) makes the 'Levite' only one of those who shared in the 'consumption' of the tithes and included him only every third year among those *personae miserabiles*, at whose disposition all of the tithes gathered were to be placed (Deut. 14.28f.), in the present passage the Levites are made the sole, normal recipients of all the tithes of Israel (i.e. the tax representing 10 per cent of the total produce of farming and cattle-breeding). Presumably this rule was practised in a late period which can no longer be precisely determined.

[**18.25–32**] Finally, the concluding section, vv. 25–32, regulates the relationship between priests and Levites with regard to these gifts, and in this respect the Levites appear in a strange intermediate position between priests and 'laymen'. On the one hand they are, as cultic personnel, recipients of dues, of the tithes; on the other hand they are, in turn, obliged to pay dues to the priests who are the real representatives of the sanctuary. All that they have, according to vv. 20–24, is the 'tithe of the people of Israel'; they are then to pay to the priests the 'tithe of the tithe' (vv. 26b, 28b). This tithe-levy is to be treated like the 10 per cent levy on the natural products of the Israelites (vv. 27, 30bβ) and must then be used by the priests in

* Cf. *Leviticus*, p. 29.

accordance with the rule laid down in vv. 12–13, without reference to the fact that the basis of this tithe is already a cultic levy, the whole being, therefore, according to its cultic quality, almost 'a tithe squared'. This latter is what is obviously meant by the somewhat puzzling appearance of the expressions in v. 32. Vv. 30–32, which begin with a new introductory formula (v. 30a), are, in contrast to vv. 25–29, where the Levites are addressed through Moses, directed at the priests and give instructions as to how the priests are to use the 'tithe of the tithe' which can be demanded from the Levites; in this respect the term 'heave' is used in the sense of 'take from' or 'demand', whereas earlier it had the sense of 'give'. One might wonder whether this particularly badly expressed section, vv. 30–32, is not a later addition.

7. PREPARATION AND USE OF A SPECIAL WATER OF PURIFICATION: 19.1–22

19 ¹Now the LORD said to Moses and to Aaron, ²'This is the statute of the law which the LORD has commanded: Tell the people of Israel to bring you a red heifer without defect, in which there is no blemish, and upon which a yoke has never come. ³And you shall give her to Eleazar the priest, and she shall be taken outside the camp and slaughtered before him; ⁴and Eleazar the priest shall take some of her blood with his finger, and sprinkle some of her blood toward the front of the tent of meeting seven times. ⁵And the heifer shall be burned in his sight; her skin, her flesh, and her blood, with her dung, shall be burned; ⁶and the priest shall take cedar wood and hyssop and scarlet stuff, and cast them into the midst of the burning of the heifer. ⁷Then the priest shall wash his clothes and bathe his body in water, and afterwards he shall come into the camp; and the priest shall be unclean until evening. ⁸He who burns the heifer shall wash his clothes in water and bathe his body in water, and shall be unclean until evening. ⁹And a man who is clean shall gather up the ashes of the heifer, and deposit them outside the camp in a clean place; and they shall be kept for the congregation of the people of Israel for the water for impurity, [for the removal of sin.] ¹⁰And he who gathers the ashes of the heifer shall wash his clothes, and be unclean until evening.

'And this shall be to the people of Israel, and to the stranger who sojourns among them, a perpetual statute. ¹¹He who touches the dead body of any person shall be unclean seven days; ¹²he shall cleanse himself with the water on the third day and on the seventh day, and so be clean; but if he does not cleanse himself on the third day and on the seventh day, he will not become clean. ¹³Whoever touches a dead person, the body of any man who has died, and does not cleanse himself, defiles the tabernacle of the LORD, and that person shall be cut off from Israel; because the water for impurity was not thrown upon him, he shall be unclean; his uncleanness is still on him.

14 'This is the law when a man dies in a tent: every one who comes into the tent, and every one who is in the tent, shall be unclean seven days. 15And every open vessel, which has no cover fastened upon it, is unclean. 16Whoever in the open field touches one who is slain with a sword, or a dead body, or a bone of a man, or a grave, shall be unclean seven days. 17For the unclean they shall take some ashes of the burnt sin offering, and running water shall be added in a vessel; 18then a clean person shall take hyssop, and dip it in the water, and sprinkle it upon the tent, and upon all the furnishings, and upon the persons who were there, and upon him who touched the bone, or the slain, or the dead, or the grave; 19and the clean person shall sprinkle upon the unclean on the third day and on the seventh day; thus on the seventh day he shall cleanse him, and he shall wash his clothes and bathe himself in water, and at evening he shall be clean. 20But the man who is unclean and does not cleanse himself, that person shall be cut off from the midst of the assembly, since he has defiled the sanctuary of the Lord; because the water for impurity has not been thrown upon him, he is unclean. 21And it shall be a perpetual statute for them. He who sprinkles the water for impurity shall wash his clothes; and he who touches the water for impurity shall be unclean until evening. 22And whatever the unclean person touches shall be unclean; and anyone who touches it shall be unclean until evening.'

In the present context this chapter is an addition, having no reference to the surrounding material. It is an originally independent unit which has been inserted immediately before the Pentateuchal narrative is resumed once more in 20.1. The heart of the chapter is formed by the instructions, contained in vv. 1–10a, for the preparation of the ingredients for a 'water of purification'. Behind these instructions lies a firm belief in the magical effect of a substance prepared in accordance with a specific prescription, a substance which can be kept (v. 9b) to be used at need, mixed with 'running water' (v. 17b), for cultic purification. This practice, which is presumably of great antiquity, though nothing more specific can be said as to its age, was obviously still current in the late period, as is shown by the probably late acceptance of this chapter into the Pentateuch. According to the present text, Moses and Aaron (v. 1) are the recipients of the divine instructions (in what follows the usage is not consistent, sometimes singular, sometimes plural); the person directly involved in these instructions, however, is, in the first place, 'Eleazar the priest' (vv. 3, 4), later however, simply 'the priest' (vv. 6, 7). There can be no doubt that originally it was 'the priest' who was mentioned (of a

certain sanctuary or of several different sanctuaries) and that Moses
and Aaron and, as the priest concerned in this instance, Aaron's son
Eleazar were introduced only to fit the present context. In vv. 14–22
instructions are given for the use of the 'water of purification' made
with the substance that has been described; it is to be used for the
removal of 'uncleanness' caused by contact with a dead body. In
between, in vv. 10b–13, there has been inserted a brief exposition of
the compelling necessity for the 'cleansing' of an Israelite who has
become unclean through contact with the dead.

[19.1–10a] The awkward phraseology of vv. 1, 2abα presumably
arises from the amalgamation of an older superscription (v.2a; cf. v.
14aα) with the stereotyped introductory formula of vv. 1 and 2bα.
According to v. 2b, there is needed for the preparation of the magic
substance a young heifer, without defect in the cultic sense and as yet
unprofaned through having been used as a working animal (cf. Deut.
21.3) and whose red (reddish-brown) colour is obviously considered
to be important for the intended effect (there is nothing in the Old
Testament with which to compare this last point). The slaughter of
this heifer is not part of a sacrificial action; it does, it is true, take
place in the presence of the priest, who, however, only has to perform
the subsequent 'sprinkling' of the blood (v. 4), but outside the
sanctuary (v. 3). The sevenfold 'sprinkling' of some of the blood of
the slaughtered animal towards the front of the sanctuary (the killing, then, took place outside the sanctuary, but in 'front' of it) is
presumably to be understood as signifying a dedication of the blood
and thereby of the slaughtered animal as a whole (cf. Lev. 4.6 et al.).*
The burning of the whole animal is done by someone (cf. v. 8), again
in the presence of the priest, but without his participation (v. 5); the
priest then has to add to what results from this burning the items
enumerated in v. 6, items which, according to Lev. 14.4, 7, play a
part in the cultic purification of a leper and which, according to the
basic concept of that passage, had a magical, purificatory effect.
Finally, 'a man who is clean (from the cultic point of view)' had to
gather up the resultant mixture and deposit it somewhere 'outside' in
a 'clean place' (cf. Lev. 6.11 (Hebr. 6.4); it is not said whether this
place had to be previously 'cleansed' or whether it simply had to be
free of peculiarly cultic 'uncleanness'), so that it could be kept there
ready, in cases of need, for the preparation of the water of purification (literally: 'water of impurity', i.e. water for cases of impurity).

* Cf. on this Leviticus, p. 39.

The note at the end of v. 9, 'for the removal of sin' (lit. 'it (the heifer) is a sin offering'), is left hanging in the air and is all the more surprising since a sacrificial action has precisely not taken place. It must be an addition to which, indeed, reference back is made by the phrase in v. 17a. One must therefore ask whether vv. 14–22, at least in their present form, are not to be regarded as secondary vis-à-vis vv. 1–10a. All who have participated in the preparation of this purificatory substance have become, for the day in question, 'unclean' because they have had to do with things imbued with a 'taboo' (the original affinity between 'holy' and 'unclean' is clear here) and have therefore to undertake certain washings (cf. Lev. 16.28); this is obligatory for the priest (v. 7) as well as for the vaguely defined person who has carried out the burning of the heifer (v. 8) and for the 'man' who is differentiated from the last mentioned and is described as being 'clean' at the outset and who has gathered together and deposited the substance (v. 10a). The co-operation of so many different people is strange and it arouses the suspicion that it is not original. Thus the introduction of the priest could already represent a more advanced stage at which this material, to begin with of a quite factually magical character, has been brought into at least an outward connection with the legitimate (Yahweh) cult. This might also seem to be borne out by the fact that in the section about the use of the water of purification there is no mention of the priest at all, but the essential actions are again performed simply by 'a clean person' (vv. 18–19).

[19.10b–13] The section concerning the cleansing of someone who has become 'unclean' through contact with a dead body (vv. 10b–13) has only a very tenuous connection with the context in which it is set and is probably an addition; it does, it is true, refer to the 'water for impurity', but only in a subordinate clause (v. 13b) which is probably a further, subsequent addition to this material, added with the specific aim of effecting a connection with what precedes. Legislation which is applicable to Israelites and 'strangers' alike (v. 10b) (cf. on this pp. 72, 115 above) provides for the case where, however it has come about, contact with a dead person (this is explicit in vv. 11a, 13aα, where, therefore, dead animals are not under consideration), in view of the uncleanness which issues from the sinister 'dead body', necessitates a 'cleansing' on the third and the seventh day (v. 12). Whoever does not undergo such cleansing represents in Israel an element of 'uncleanness' by which, according to v. 13a, the 'tabernacle of Yahweh', which is within Israel, is also affected, and he must therefore be 'cut off', something which could come about only through his being put to death. After the final complex sentence of v. 13a, there stands, after the event, v. 13b; here it is noted, in the form of an addition, that the cleansing must be carried out by means of the water of purification of v. 9bα, and, furthermore, mention is made of a continuing 'uncleanness' with no possibility of 'cleansing', in such a way as if the whole case had not already been settled by the 'cutting off'.

[19.14–22] In contrast to vv. 10b–13, it is difficult to regard vv. 14–22 as anything other than the continuation of vv. 1–10a. For in this section we have first of all the necessary information regarding the use of the substance that had been 'stored away' described in vv. 1–10a. It is noteworthy that here there is no mention of participation by a 'priest' (cf. above, pp. 139f.). A difficulty is created by the fact that at an important juncture (v. 17a) reference is made to the obviously secondary mention of the 'sin offering' in v. 9bβ. In view of this, it is difficult to escape the hypothesis that in vv. 14–22 a basic form, belonging from the start to vv. 1–10a, has been subsequently worked over, without there now being any possibility of making a distinction between primary and secondary material. In vv. 14–16 there are mentioned cases where it is possible for one to become unclean through contact with a dead body, resulting in a seven-day 'uncleanness'. There follow, in vv. 17–18, instructions as to how such cases are to be treated. Here the preparation of the 'water for impurity', mentioned in v. 9bα only as a future possibility, is described for the first time; the substance described in vv. 1–10a, from the stock of which (v. 9bα) part is to be taken, is to have 'running water' (i.e. spring water) poured on it in a vessel (v. 17), and with this liquid, using a bunch of hyssop, everything that has become unclean is to be sprinkled (v. 18). This sprinkling is to be carried out by 'a clean person'. The result of sprinkling with this efficacious liquid will be the restoration of 'cleanness'. The juxtaposition of the seven-day period of vv. 14, 16 and the action of vv. 17–18 is probably to be understood in the sense that the action is to be undertaken after the expiry of that period. There is, of course, a certain tension between these two ideas, in so far as the fact that this period is mentioned implies that its expiry will be effective, and on the other hand the action, whenever it is carried out, is to be understood as being directly and immediately effective. Two different methods for the restoration of cleanness are therefore combined here. In vv. 19–22 unevennesses and repetitions suggest subsequent reworking. V. 19abα refers back to v. 12, and v. 19bβ anticipates v. 21b. V. 20 repeats v. 13, partly with altered wording and partly literally. V. 21b must have belonged to the original material, for, according to it, association with the 'water for impurity' makes a person 'unclean' for the day in question (cf. vv. 7, 8, 10a). On the other hand, the general remarks about the 'contaminating' quality of uncleanness are additional, as is already clear from their position at the end (v. 22).

The ritual of purification with the 'ashes of a heifer', to which reference is made in Heb. 9.13, is one of the remnants of magical concepts and practices which survived in Israel until the late period without even an attempt being made to draw them into the quite differently orientated Old Testament belief in God.

8. ONCE AGAIN WATER FROM THE ROCK: 20.1–13

20 ¹And the people of Israel, the whole congregation, came into the wilderness of Zin in the first month, and the people stayed in Kadesh; and Miriam died there, and was buried there.

2 Now there was no water for the congregation; and they assembled themselves together against Moses and against Aaron. ³And the people contended with Moses, and said, ['Would that we had died when our brethren died before the LORD!] ⁴Why have you brought the assembly of the LORD into this wilderness, that we should die here, both we and our cattle? ⁵And why have you made us come up out of Egypt, to bring us to this evil place? It is no place for grain, or figs, or vines, or pomegranates; and there is no water to drink.' ⁶Then Moses and Aaron went from the presence of the assembly to the door of the tent of meeting, and fell on their faces. And the glory of the LORD appeared to them, ⁷and the LORD said to Moses, ⁸'Take the rod, and assemble the congregation, you and Aaron your brother, and tell the rock before their eyes to yield its water; so you shall bring water out of the rock for them; so you shall give drink to the congregation and their cattle.' ⁹And Moses took the rod from before the LORD, as he commanded him.

10 And Moses and Aaron gathered the assembly together before the rock, and he said to them, 'Hear now, you rebels; shall we bring forth water for you out of this rock?' ¹¹And Moses lifted up his hand and struck the rock with his rod twice; and water came forth abundantly, and the congregation drank, and their cattle. ¹²And the LORD said to Moses and Aaron, 'Because you did not believe in me, to sanctify me in the eyes of the people of Israel, therefore you shall not bring this assembly into the land which I have given them.' ¹³These are the waters of Meribah, where the people of Israel contended with the LORD, and he showed himself holy among them.

The principal content here is the narrative of a water-miracle which Yahweh brings about after being reproached by the people that they have been brought into a waterless country. This narrative has two different results; on the one hand the announcement that Moses and Aaron are not to enter the promised land of Israel (v. 12), and on the other an explanation, partly explicit and partly clearly enough hinted at, of the names 'Meribah' and 'Kadesh' (v. 13). Even in the heart of the narrative two parallel strands may be seen, as is particularly clear from the remarkable juxtaposition of doublets (cf. especially v. 4 with v. 5 and v. 3a with vv. 2b and 3b). The basic form comprises a narrative strand whose choice of vocabulary and way of looking at things are clearly indicative of the 'Priestly writing' (P); it appears in vv. 2, 3b, 4, 6, 7, 8aβbβ, 10, 11b, 12. The rest exhibits such close and in many respects literal conformity with Ex. 17.1–7 that we cannot avoid the idea that a later hand has subsequently inserted into the P-narrative at this point the essentials of the narrative of the water-miracle of Ex. 17. In the 'old sources'* a place was found for the story in the first part of the account of the wilderness wanderings; P has placed it right at the end of the series of stories about the wanderings, since it was supposed to provide the reason why Moses and Aaron were denied entry into the promised land. In Num. 27.14a = Deut. 32.51(P), specific reference is made to the present passage when intimation is made of Moses' death. At the same time as this secondary reworking on the basis of Ex. 17, some other secondary material has also been introduced; this is true, amongst other places, of the final verse (v. 13) and partly also of the opening verse (v. 1).

[20.1] The details of time and place at the beginning (v. 1aα) correspond to the style of P, but are probably editorial. The juxtaposition (repeated in v. 22) of 'people of Israel' and 'the whole congregation' is scarcely original. The indication of place must surely be saying that the Israelites who, according to 10.12; 13.3 P, had in the last instance settled in the wilderness of Paran, now turned to the southern border of the promised land, from which point the 'spies' had earlier accomplished their mission (13.21 P). The indication of time lacks the main item, the designation of the year. This leaves open the question as to whether the forty years of 14.33 had meanwhile elapsed without anything having been said about it. The lack of any mention of the year in this presumably editorial passage is an indication of the fact that the present narrative is in no way related to

* On this cf. *Exodus*, pp. 138ff.

14.26ff.; Moses and Aaron and the congregation are spoken of in such a way that it seems still to be a question here of the group which had emerged from Egypt. In v. 1aβ one of the 'old sources' finds expression ('the people'). According to 13. 26¶ J, the last place the Israelites had been was Kadesh (cf. on this p. 106 above) and according to 20.14, 16 they remained there for a time. The facts given in 20.1aβ, if they come from an old source and are not simply editorial with reference to the above-mentioned texts, have meaning only if there is something to report about the sojourn of the Israelites in Kadesh. This is, in fact, the case if v. 1b is the continuation of v. 1aβ. It is therefore at least probable that in front of 20.14ff. there stood, in J, a brief note concerning the death and burial of Miriam in Kadesh. This presumably reproduces a tradition that knew of a grave of Miriam in Kadesh. J, in which Miriam appears in Ex. 15.20f.; Num. 12.1ff., has nothing more precise to report than that.

[20.2–6] The narrative of the water-miracle begins in vv. 2–4 with the usual complaint and accusation on the part of the people. Here v. 3a is taken literally from Ex. 17.2aα and v. 5, at least as far as its opening words are concerned, literally from Ex. 17.3bα. According to P, 'the congregation' flocked together against Moses and Aaron (v. 2) to rouse them both to speech by a reproachful question (v. 4) which, with its introductory 'and',* is graphically depicted as arising out of an animated discussion. The question of v. 3b, which, from the point of view both of form (gwʿ) and content, goes back to 17.27f., is surely an editorial addition. With regard to the accusation, Moses and Aaron can only turn to Yahweh, who then appears to them (not to the whole congregation) in the tent of meeting in his glory, according to the usual expression in P (v. 6) and addresses them (v. 7).

[20.7–12] In the passage that deals with the actual miracle (vv. 7–11), two versions go side by side; in one Moses' 'rod' plays the really decisive role, while according to the other, Aaron and Moses are said to summon water from a rock by addressing it. Now Moses' 'rod' doubtless comes also from Ex. 17. The statements that refer to it are again partly literal borrowings: v. 8aα is a condensed form of Ex. 17.5b and v. 8bα, as far as its meaning is concerned, originated in Ex. 17.6aβb. Only the 'twofold' striking of the rock (v. 11a) has no parallel in Ex. 17 and must therefore be an editorial extra. According

* This 'and' has been suppressed by the RSV translators and the question simply begins, 'Why have you brought . . .?' Tr.

to Ex. 17 the course of events is pretty clearly this, that Moses at God's command struck with his 'rod' a conveniently situated rock, whereupon Yahweh made water pour forth from this rock; in this presentation an originally magical action is subordinated to the will and power of the God of Israel. The essential elements of this presentation have subsequently been incorporated without any great modification in the P-narrative of Num. 20 (vv. 8aαbα, 11a); except that P (v. 8aβ) uses a different word for 'rock' (sela‘) from that used in Ex. 17 (ṣūr); the remark in v. 9, whereby the 'rod' (of Moses) seems to be identified with the 'rod of Aaron' mentioned in 17.10 (*Hebr.* 17.25) as having been preserved 'before Yahweh', is probably an editorial addition. The sequence of events is substantially less clear in the P-narrative. According to vv. 7, 8aβbβ Moses and Aaron received instructions from Yahweh to address, before the assembled congregation, the rock whose existence, following on Ex. 17, is presupposed, whereupon it will yield 'its water' (i.e. apparently the water secretly present and hidden in it) to give drink to men and animals. The change from striking with a rod (Ex. 17) to an 'address' can be understood as a conscious spiritualization of the action by P. The information given in v. 10 is then puzzling, for, according to it, Moses and Aaron, in the presence of the congregation gathered before the rock, in no way carried out the divine command of v. 8aβ, but rather put a question to the assembled people. In its present form, in which v. 10 is followed in v. 11a by a fact taken from Ex. 17, this question appears as a question put to test the congregation. In the original P-context, however, and according to the present text, which it would be arbitrary hypothetically to 'improve', and in the light of v. 12, this question must have been meant as an expression of embarrassment and doubt with a reproachful address to the 'rebels' whose behaviour has caused that embarrassment and that doubt. In any case this question would have been in place before v. 6; after the divine command and promise, however, it is quite unjustifiable. This unusual feature can be explained only by the fact that P has consciously altered this tradition of the water-miracle as it appears in its original JE form in Ex. 17 in view of the purpose with which this story is told in P, namely the necessity for an instance of 'unbelief' on the part of Moses and Aaron in order that a basis may be found for the divine decision that Moses and Aaron are not to enter the promised land. The Deuteronomist found a basis for the same decision by making Moses bear the guilt for the disobedience of the whole people (Deut. 1.37; 3.25f.); but for P the personal guilt of Moses (and Aaron) seemed essential to explain Yahweh's harsh judgment. In spite of the completely incomprehensible behaviour of Moses and Aaron, the divine promise of v. *8, namely that the rock would yield water, was, according to v. 11b, richly fulfilled. Moses and Aaron, however, still have to accept the divine punishment (v. 12). They had not 'believed' in Yahweh (i.e. they had not firmly trusted his promise; the same phraseology in Gen. 15.6 et al.) and had not therefore, as should have been the case, 'sanctified' Yahweh in the eyes of the Israelites, i.e. made clear his 'holiness' which manifests itself in mighty wonders. It is scarcely likely that in using the word 'sanctify' (Hiph. of qdš) P is making a play on the place-name Kadesh, since P makes no attempt to locate this whole story (cf. above on v. 1a). On the other hand, a later writer has in v. 13 not only taken over from Ex. 17.7 the explanation of the place-name Meribah = 'place of contention',* but has also added the remark that Yahweh 'thereby (sc. by means of the water that poured forth) showed himself holy',† thus hinting at the place-name Kadesh (cf. v. 1aβ).

* On this cf. *Exodus*, pp. 139f.
† This is Noth's version of what appears in the RSV as 'he showed himself holy among them'. Grammatically both translations are possible, though the RSV is probably the more natural of the two. Tr.

IV

PREPARATION FOR AND BEGINNING
OF THE CONQUEST: 20.14–36.13

1. REFUSAL OF PASSAGE THROUGH EDOM: 20.14–21

20 [14]Moses sent messengers from Kadesh to the king of Edom, 'Thus says your brother Israel: You know all the adversity that has befallen us: [15]how our fathers went down to Egypt, and we dwelt in Egypt a long time; and the Egyptians dealt harshly with us [and our fathers;] [16]and when we cried to the LORD, he heard our voice, and sent an angel and brought us forth out of Egypt; and here we are in Kadesh, a city on the edge of your territory. [17]Now let us pass through your land. We will not pass through field or vineyard, neither will we drink water from a well; we will go along the King's Highway, we will not turn aside to the right hand or to the left, until we have passed through your territory.' [18]But Edom said to him, 'You shall not pass through, lest I come out with the sword against you.' [19]And the people of Israel said to him, 'We will go up by the highway; and if we drink of your water, I and my cattle, then I will pay for it; let me only pass through on foot, nothing more.' [20]But he said, 'You shall not pass through.' And Edom came out against them with many men, and with a strong force. [21]Thus Edom refused to give Israel passage through his territory; so Israel turned away from him, [22]and they journeyed from Kadesh.

THIS SECTION marks the beginning in the Pentateuchal narrative of the theme of the Israelite conquest. The Israelites now leave the desert and make their way towards the promised land. The most direct route would have been to march through the middle of Edom. Hence the request to the Edomites to grant them a passage. Since this request meets with a sharp refusal, and since a forced passage is not considered, the latter no doubt because Edomite territory was not part of what was promised to Israel (this is explicitly stated in Deut. 2.2–8), Israel must first of all make a detour. Such is the essential content of this section.

In its details it contains several inconsistencies. That it is Moses who sends the messengers (v. 14a) who then speak in the first instance on behalf of a collective Israel (v. 14ba) and in what follows, in the plural, on behalf of the Israelites (v. 14bβff.), that furthermore 'the Israelites' appear to be dealing directly with Edom (v. 19aa), speaking with a collective 'I' (v. 19aβb) and being addressed with a collective 'you' (v. 20a),* is perhaps as of little importance as the fact that to begin with 'the king of Edom' appears as the opposite number in the discussion, while later Edom is addressed collectively. In all this it could be a case of variation or even carelessness in the manner of expression. More important is the existence of obvious doublets. In vv. 19f. we are certainly dealing with a doublet of vv. 17f.; at least, in the present context vv. 19f. seem to speak of a resumption of negotiations—from an objective point of view unfounded and impossible—after a refusal has already been stated (v. 18). A factual variant is perhaps to be found in the fact that according to v. 17aβ the Israelites promise not to drink well-water (did they perhaps think that they could survive, in view of the season of the year, on rainwater?), while according to v. 19aβ they promise to make suitable payment for the drinking water they need. From all this the fact must be accepted that two sources have been worked together. Since the characteristic indications of P are totally lacking, we have to reckon with J and E. This, then, is the first appearance, at least the first that can be certainly proved, of the 'Elohist' in the book of Numbers. However, the two sources J and E are so closely interwoven that it is impossible to pursue any real separation of them, not even with the help of the above-mentioned formal inconsistencies which appear in haphazard fashion. Any definite characteristics of J and E are also almost entirely lacking; one can only point to one instance of the occurrence of the divine name Yahweh in v. 16a and also to the expression 'all the adversity that has befallen us' which occurs also in Ex. 18.8 and might testify to E,† although it does occur again in Neh. 9.32. A more important indication of E is the statement of v. 16aβ that the exodus from Egypt was led by an 'angel' sent by God (cf. on this Ex. 14.19a).‡ These few points lead no further than the assertion that in this section we have a composite text of J and E in

---

* This 'you' is the 2nd person sing., a fact which is not brought out by the English of the RSV. Tr.

† Cf. *Exodus*, pp. 146, 148f.

‡ See also *Exodus*, pp. 114f.

front of us and that the two sources both seem to have contained very similar narratives.

The text is in itself clear and needs only slight elucidation. According to v. 14bα, the messengers who are sent begin the fulfilling of their commission with the well-attested messenger formula that is familiar especially from the stereotyped introduction to prophetic oracles. The comparatively complete reference to the fate of Israel hitherto and to the divine help that had been experienced (vv. 14bβ–16a) makes no impression on (the king of) Edom; it had been different, according to Ex. 18.1, 8ff., with the priest of Midian. Accompanied as it is by a threat, the rejection of this modest request is given no foundation. From the very start an inimical attitude on the part of Edom towards Israel is presupposed, although Edom is addressed (v. 14bα) as Israel's 'brother'; historical experiences of later times are certainly reflected here. In Israel's request the presupposition is made that there existed through Edom, certainly in a north-south direction, a 'King's Highway' (v. 17b) or simply a 'highway' (v. 19a). Both expressions mean the same thing, namely a road which, in places where it was necessary, had been levelled off by means of 'embankments' to such a degree that one was able to drive wagons along it, especially chariots, so that even a king (with his retinue) could use it on official expeditions. It is presupposed that at the time in question here there was already a king in Edom. Of course, Israel wanted to use the 'King's Highway' only for an easy passage 'on foot' (v. 19b).

The main problem of this section is how this passage through Edom that is being discussed is to be fitted, from the geographical point of view, into the Pentateuchal narrative as a whole. The goal of the journey was the southern part of the territory east of the Jordan to the north of the Arnon, where, starting at 21.21, the first conquest stories proper lead. It was this territory that the Israelites reached from far to the south. It was there that the Edomites lived, in the hill country to the east of the present-day *wādi el-ʿaraba*. Since passage through their country had been refused, the Israelites had to go round it; this could only be possible on the eastern side along the border between cultivated land and desert. In order to reach the territory north of the Arnon, the Israelites would also, then, have to pass in some way or another the land of the Moabites which was situated between Edom and the Arnon. In contrast to Deut. 2. 9–18⁕, there is no mention of Moab in the old sources of Num. 20–21 (on 21.10–20 cf. pp. 158ff. below). Perhaps what was meant was that the

Israelites, having been forced into an easterly detour round Edom, in consequence skirted only the desert border of Moab. Thus far the route of the Israelites bent on the conquest seems comparatively clear. The question now is, why and how they came to be anywhere on the southern border of Edom. According to vv. 14a, 16b, 22a, when they set out on the journey to the promised land they were still in Kadesh (cf. p. 106 above). Whether these details belong to J or E can no longer be determined; perhaps they reproduce the opinion of both sources. Since the E-narrative has been preserved in such a fragmentary way that the connection between the Sinai stories and the present section is no longer known, nothing further can be said about how the Elohist conceived of the Israelites' route. In the case of J, however, the fact remains that Israel had still not carried out the command of 14.25b (in spite of the 'tomorrow' that is in the text there), but had remained in Kadesh. Here, too, it is clear (cf. p. 145 above) that remarkably little account has been taken of the 'spy' story in the continuing narrative. Even the résumé of the story hitherto, that is given in vv. 15–16a, gives no hint that, according to 13.23b–24, the generation of ch. 13–14, with few exceptions, was not to enter the promised land towards which Israel now turns. The lack of connection between the wilderness stories and the preparation for the conquest from east of the Jordan is also revealed by this quite unmotivated leap from Kadesh to Edom. It is true that v. 16b states that Kadesh is a city on the edge of Edomite territory, but it is strange that the group of wells of which Kadesh is made up (for a description of it and its location cf. p. 106 above) should be described as a 'city'. This statement presupposes that the Edomite domain stretched from the *wādi el-'araba* fairly far to the west, a fact which fits neither the period which is intended here nor the period of the 'old Pentateuchal sources'. One has the impression that this information is meant to bridge the spatial distance between Kadesh with its desert domains and Edom, with the help of a statement which is not to be taken too precisely and which rests perhaps on only a vague idea of the geographical relationships involved. In order to reach Edom from Kadesh, Israel had first of all to turn in the direction of the 'Reed Sea'* (= gulf of *el-'aqaba*); this, keeping in mind the future conquest, is envisaged in 14.25b (cf. 21.4a). This presupposes that one could pass the northern end of this gulf without coming into conflict with the Edomites. At a very early period it might, in fact, have been the

* Cf. above p. 110, footnote. Tr.

case that Edomite power did not reach as far as the gulf of *el-ʿaqaba*. In any event the old Pentateuchal narrative has presented the fact in such a way that Israel, in order to reach, from Kadesh, the territory east of the Jordan as the starting-point of her conquest, first of all made the enormous detour to the southern border of Edom, without any reason being given or even being evident, and then, since the requested passage through Edom was refused, had to make a detour to the east of Edom (and of Moab, too). This makes it clear that the wilderness theme and the conquest theme in the Pentateuch have not been synchronized with each other from the very beginning, but stand side by side in relative independence and have been only loosely interwoven.

2. THE DEATH OF AARON: 20.22–29

20 ²²And they journeyed from Kadesh, and the people of Israel, the whole congregation, came to Mount Hor. ²³And the LORD said to Moses [and Aaron at Mount Hor, on the border of the land of Edom, ²⁴'Aaron shall be gathered to his people; for he shall not enter the land which I have given to the people of Israel, because you rebelled against my command at the waters of Meribah.] ²⁵Take Aaron and Eleazar his son, and bring them up to Mount Hor; ²⁶and strip Aaron of his garments, and put them upon Eleazar his son; and Aaron shall be gathered to his people, and shall die there.' ²⁷Moses did as the LORD commanded; and they went up Mount Hor in the sight of all the congregation. ²⁸And Moses stripped Aaron of his garments, and put them upon Eleazar his son; and Aaron died there on the top of the mountain. Then Moses and Eleazar came down from the mountain. ²⁹And when all the congregation saw that Aaron was dead, all the house of Israel wept for Aaron thirty days.

With the exception of the first half-verse (v. 22a) which, mentioning as it does Kadesh, belongs to one of the 'old sources' and which is simply noting Israel's departure from Kadesh which is the final outcome of the unsuccessful negotiations with Edom (vv. 14–21), with this exception the whole of this passage belongs to P, as is clearly shown both in language and content. The content is simple and clear. Aaron who, according to 20. 2–12P⁋ and like Moses, is not to enter the promised land, dies on the way and at God's command Eleazar, the elder of his two surviving sons (cf. Ex. 6.23 *et al.*), is installed by Moses in his father's office by means of the transference of the official robes. In 33.38f. a later hand has been able to give details of the date of Aaron's death and of his age which are lacking in P at this point. In the present passage vv. 23aβb, 24 seem to be additional. Moses and Aaron can scarcely have been addressed together by Yahweh before v. 25; the geographical location of Mount Hor in v. 23b is out of place, it should, if original, have stood in v. 22b; the reference to 20.2–13, in itself not inappropriate but not absolutely necessary, presupposes with its mention of the 'waters of Meribah' the addition in 20.13; the intimation in v. 24aα is an inappropriate anticipation of v. 26b.

What kind of tradition lies at the basis of this passage is very hard to say. According to it Aaron dies on a mountain, as will be the case later with Moses, too (Deut. 34.1ff.). Strangely enough there is no mention of his having been buried; this may be compared with the fact that according to Deut. 34.6 Moses was buried, but the location of his grave remained unknown. Like Moses, according to Deut. 34.8a, Aaron, too, was mourned by the Israelites for 'thirty days'. One has the impression that the report of Aaron's death in P is modelled on the story of the death of Moses, especially since both of them, according to 20. 2–12P¶, are, in dying, to suffer the same fate, namely not to enter the land promised to Israel. One might even suppose that the present narrative has simply been constructed on the analogy of the reports of Moses' death that have been preserved in the pre-priestly accounts, were it not that a mysterious location is given for the death of Aaron. This in itself is also certainly problematical. In the first place, since nothing is said about a burial and therefore a localized tradition about a burial-place is obviously not the peg on which the tradition hangs, one is not sure how the mountain in question became and remained the bearer of an Aaron-tradition. Then, too, the mountain itself is puzzling. Even its name (literally 'Hor, the mountain') is unusual, though according to 34.7f., there was another mountain of identical name in quite a different area. Yet again, there is no definite information as to the location of this mountain. The statement that it lay 'on the border of the land of Edom' is, in v. 23b, secondary and presumably rests only on the later connection of this passage with vv. 14–21; in any case it is not very precise, since it is left open which border of Edom is meant. It could, however, be approximately correct, since, according to P, Israel is on the way to the 'plains of Moab' (22.1b). In any event the mountain is to be sought outside the territory in which Israel later came to dwell. All the more inexplicable is the connection of the Aaron-tradition with this mountain in view of the fact that it cannot possibly have been even on the furthest horizon of later Israel. The assertion that it is to be located in the neighbourhood of Petra and in particular on the lofty mountain peak where the present-day sanctuary of *nebi hārūn* ('the prophet Aaron') stands, is certainly very ancient, but it rests only on a secondary interpretation of the facts presented by the Old Testament. Side by side with the present facts, there stands, unreconciled and unexplained, the statement of Deut. 10.6 to the effect that Aaron not only died but was also buried in Moserah; identical with the Moseroth of Num. 33.30f., this Moserah can no longer be located either.

3. THE CAPTURE OF HORMAH: 21.1–3

21 ¹When the Canaanite, [the king of Arad,] who dwelt in the Negeb, heard that Israel was coming by the way of Atharim, he fought against Israel, and took some of them captive. ²And Israel vowed a vow to the LORD, and said, 'If thou will indeed give this people into my hand, then I will utterly destroy their cities. ³And the LORD hearkened to the voice of Israel, and gave over the Canaanites; and they utterly destroyed them and their cities; so the name of the place was called Hormah.

The purpose of this short note is to explain the name Hormah. Hormah was a town known elsewhere in the Old Testament, which is probably to be located on *tell el-mšāš* about ten miles east of Beersheba (cf. above, p. 111). The position of this note is remarkable in every respect. In the first place it breaks the literary connection between ch. 20 and 21.4 (cf. below, p. 156). Then from the geographical point of view it does not fit into the context at all, since Hormah, on the southern edge of Canaan, is far removed from the Israelite route from Kadesh to Edom. It has obviously been inserted at a later date at this particular point, just before the final transition to the theme of the conquest east of the Jordan. Where it comes from can no longer be ascertained; it could at one time have had a place somewhere in the J-narrative and have been later transferred to its present position by an editor.

The name Hormah is explained by means of the term 'put under the ban' (RSV 'utterly destroy'; Hebrew root *ḥrm*); at one time Israel carried out the 'ban' in the region of Hormah with regard to the 'cities' that were there and their inhabitants, i.e. by killing and destroying they handed everything over to Yahweh as the real victor and owner of the booty of war (there is a similar aetiology of the name Hormah, but set in a quite different historical context, in Judg. 1.17). Otherwise the content of this note is quite vague.

Mention is made of the 'Canaanites' (a general designation for the pre-Israelite inhabitants of the country) who lived somewhere in the wide territory of the 'Negeb', that is the desert country to the south of the Palestinian hill-country, and who lived in 'cities'. The only concrete detail is that Israel arrives in this region 'by the way of Atharim'; unfortunately it is impossible to explain either linguistically or geographically this designation which occurs only here. The Israelites' vow to carry out the 'ban' in the event of victory is motivated by an initial defeat. This is what happens and the aim of explaining the name Hormah is achieved. With this explanation, the scene of this event, which is at first left very vague ('the place' in v. 3b), is made more or less definite. A further precision as to locality has been added secondarily with the mention of the 'king of Arad' (v. 1). The words 'the king of Arad' are so little suited to the context that they must be regarded as an addition. By means of them a later hand has defined and located more precisely the 'Canaanites' who were mentioned in the original text.* This more precise definition is not unsuitable, since Arad (the modern *tell 'arād*) was a pre-Israelite town not far from Hormah (*tell 'arād*) is about eleven miles north-east of *tell el-mšāš*) which is known elsewhere (cf. Josh. 12.14; Judg. 1.16).

4. THE BRONZE SERPENT: 21.4-9

21 ⁴From Mount Hor they set out by the way to the Red Sea, to go around the land of Edom; and the people became impatient on the way. ⁵And the people spoke against God and against Moses, 'Why have you brought us up out of Egypt to die in the wilderness? For there is no food and no water, and we loathe this worthless food.' ⁶Then the LORD sent fiery serpents among the people, and they bit the people, so that many people of Israel died. ⁷And the people came to Moses, and said, 'We have sinned, for we have spoken against the LORD and against you; pray to the LORD, that he take away the serpents from us.' So Moses prayed for the people. ⁸And the LORD said to Moses, 'Make a fiery serpent, and set it on a pole; and every one who is bitten, when he sees it, shall live.' ⁹So Moses made a bronze serpent, and set it on a pole; and if a serpent bit any man, he would look at the bronze serpent and live.

Once again, just before the definitive transition to the stories about taking possession of the land, we have a wilderness story. V. 5 depicts the circumstances of life in the wilderness; there is neither bread nor

* If the words 'the king of Arad' are removed from the text, then the singular 'the Canaanite' would be taken in a collective sense to refer to 'the Canaanites' as a whole. Noth, in his translation, does, in fact, have 'the Canaanites' and the following verbs in the plural. Tr.

water, only worthless food. Whether this latter statement refers, in the sense of 11.6b, to the manna or whether what is meant is rather the wretchedness and the monotony of wilderness products generally, is not clear. Any more specific localization is unnecessary and is therefore not given. For the introductory sentence of v. 4a is obviously editorial; it goes back beyond vv. 1–3 (cf. above p. 154) and links up with the mention of Mount Hor in 20.22–9P, takes from 14.25bJ a fact about the general direction of the Israelite march and, finally, makes use of the outcome of the narrative of 20.14–21JE.

This section reveals a remarkable inconsequentiality in its references to its main object; first of all (v. 6) it refers to 'fiery serpents', then (v. 7) simply to 'serpents', and the 'fiery (serpent)'* which Moses is to make (v. 8) is then referred to (twice) in v. 9 as a 'bronze serpent'. This must not make us think of dividing up the passage into different 'sources', since the narrative in itself proceeds smoothly and is free of doublets. Even the unusual juxtaposition of 'God' (v. 5) and 'Yahweh' (vv. 7, 8) is not be be explained on the grounds of different sources having been worked together. Since in the Pentateuchal narrative it is the use of the divine name Yahweh which predominates, the striking feature here is the appearance of the appellative 'God' in v. 5. This inclines one to suppose that its appearance here is original and that the use of the divine name Yahweh is a secondary accommodation to what is generally the usual practice. In that case this passage would have to be allocated to the E source.

In the narrative two elements stand side by side. One consists in the fact that, according to II Kings 18.4 in the domain of King Hezekiah (one thinks of Jerusalem and in particular of the Jerusalem sanctuary, without this being said) there was 'the bronze serpent' which is said to have been made by Moses, to which the Israelites offered sacrifices until it was removed by Hezekiah and which was called 'Nehushtan'. The other is in the idea that the desert is a place of vicious and dangerous serpents and that there, in particular, there was the 'fiery serpent' (Deut. 8.15); this 'fiery serpent', whose name can no longer be explained with any certainty, is depicted as a flying serpent. According to Isa. 30.6, the desert is a land of the 'flying serpent' and according to Isa. 14.29 a 'flying serpent' is worse than an ordinary serpent. The combining of these two elements is sufficient explanation of the inconsequentiality that has already been noted in the phraseology of the present passage. This passage provides no

* At this point the Hebrew text does not contain the word for 'serpent'. Tr.

aetiology of the 'Nehushtan' of II Kings 18.4, since it does not go on to say anything about the Israelites' having somehow taken with them the 'bronze serpent' made by Moses and having set it up later somewhere in their country. But the later existence of the 'bronze serpent' attributed to Moses was certainly the reason for the telling of the story of a plague of serpents in the wilderness, thereby linking up with the more general idea of the vicious 'fiery serpents' in the wilderness (it is not stated that 'Nehushtan' was a flying serpent, but it may be deduced indirectly from the call-vision of Isaiah, experienced probably in the Jerusalem temple, in which he sees flying seraphim* —Isa. 6.2, 6). The discrimination shown by Hezekiah against 'Nehushtan' as an idol worshipped by the Israelites is obviously not known to the author of the present passage.

[21.4b–6] The discontentment of the people with the frugal life of the desert no longer leads, at the end of the period of wilderness wanderings as it has mostly done till now, to an act of divine help, but to an act of punishment of the discontented people who have risen against God and Moses (this juxtaposition is unusual, but is repeated in v. 7; it may be compared with Ex. 14.31b, although the context there is quite different). This punishment comes about by means of the fatal bite of the fiery serpents. [21.7] A confession of sin on the part of those who are guilty enables Moses to make an intercession (v. 7) which is heard. [21.8–9] The divine promise of release from the plague of serpents is linked with the condition that Moses should make an image of a fiery serpent (in v. 9 this fiery serpent is then designated as a 'bronze serpent') and put this image on top of a pole that is to be set up so that everyone can see it and look at it with the result that the bites of the serpents should no longer be fatal. Hence, release from the fatal effects of the serpent bites is linked to a test of obedience set by Yahweh in his free judgment, a test which, at the same time, bears witness to the sovereign power of Yahweh even over the dangerous and sinister character of the desert. The strange content of the divine command is, however, explicable only if one sees behind it the idea that the measure taken by Moses is in itself effective, an idea which has only later been incorporated into the Old Testament faith in God (in the cultic

---

* The Hebrew words translated by the RSV as 'fiery serpents' are nᵉḥāšîm sᵉrāpîm and these are translated more literally by Noth, both in text and commentary, as 'seraph serpents'. In the body of the commentary I have preferred to stick to the more familiar RSV translation, but the distinctive translation of Noth needs to be mentioned here to make this reference to Isaiah's vision clear. Tr.

veneration of 'Nehushtan' according to II Kings 18.4 the original idea is still or is once again to the fore). With the concept that one can annul the power of dangerous creatures by making an image of them and offering some kind of worship to that image, one might compare I Sam. 6.4f., where, of course, already the 'God of Israel' appears as the decisive protagonist. The worship of the serpent image is confined in vv. 8bβ, 9bβ to the people looking at it in order to be released from the fatal consequences of the serpent bites. In the present story the widespread religio-historical concept of the serpent as the representation or symbol of a god of healing to which one must turn might also play a part. The observation must be made that, basically and essentially, these two concepts probably belong together.

5. CAMPING-SITES ON THE WAY: 21.10–20

21 [10]And the people of Israel set out, and encamped in Oboth. [11]And they set out from Oboth, and encamped at Iye-abarim, in the wilderness which is opposite Moab, toward the sunrise. [12]From there they set out, and encamped in the Valley of Zered. [13]From there they set out, and encamped on the other side of the Arnon, which is in the wilderness, that extends from the boundary of the Amorites; for the Arnon is the boundary of Moab, between Moab and the Amorites. [14]Wherefore it is said in the Book of the Wars of the LORD,

'Waheb in Suphah,
and the valleys of the Arnon,
[15]and the slope of the valleys
that extends to the seat of Ar,
and leans to the border of Moab.'

[16]And from there they continued to Beer; that is the well of which the LORD said to Moses, 'Gather the people together, and I will give them water.' [17]Then Israel sang this song:

'Spring up, O well!—Sing to it!—
[18]the well which the princes dug,
which the nobles of the people delved,
with the sceptre and with their staves.'

And from the wilderness they went on to Mattanah, [19]and from Mattanah to Nahaliel, and from Nahaliel to Bamoth, [20]and from Bamoth to the valley lying in the region of Moab by the top of Pisgah which looks down upon the desert.

In this section the Israelites are led further north in the territory east of the Jordan by means of an itinerary which forms the framework of the section. At the beginning (vv. 10–13) this itinerary still makes use of the stereotyped phrases about 'setting out' and 'encamping'; at the end (vv. 18b–20) it appears only as isolated words. In between are set two quotations which are occasioned, however, by the mention of a place-name, first of all (in vv. 14–15) a quotation from the 'Book of the Wars of Yahweh' and then (vv. 17–18a) the quotation of a 'song' sung by Israel. The whole, however, has, in places (esp. in vv. 14b–15), not only obviously been handed down in such a textually corrupt state that it is hardly now possible either to translate it or to understand it, but also, from the point of view of form and content, it is so far from being a unit that we can scarcely attribute it to any of the Pentateuchal sources or explain it as the product of a compilation from several sources. In addition there are obvious dependencies on other parts of the Old Testament. All this argues for the fact that we are here dealing with editorial material with which a later hand has endeavoured, as best he could, to compensate for the lack of connection of which he was aware and which really exists, between the stories already related as still taking place on the edge of the desert and the following accounts of the conquests. With regard to individual details much remains obscure.

[**21.10–11**] In v. 10 a beginning is made with what is partly a verbal borrowing from the list of camping-sites in Num. 33 (vv. 43b, 44), which although it does not fit from the geographical point of view (cf. below, p. 245) is nevertheless occasioned by the explanatory note 'in the territory of Moab' in 33.44b. Starting from the presupposition that the detour round Edom has now been completed and that therefore the eastern part of Moab has now been reached, it would appear that Judg. 11.18 has also been drawn upon for v. 11bβ and v. 13aαbα. [**21.12**] To the same subject of the passing from Edom to the east of Moab, v. 12 also belongs, with its mention of the Valley of Zered (= *wadi el-ḥesa*), which probably comes from Deut. 2.13 (the only other place where the Valley of Zered is mentioned), but which seems out of place after v. 11. [**21.13**] The (northern) frontier of Moab is reached with their arrival at the Arnon (v. 13; cf. Judg. 11.18), beyond which, as may be deduced from v. 26, lay the land of the 'Amorites'; since, however, the Israelites were fairly far to the east, they came first of all to 'the wilderness that extends from the boundary of the Amorites'. [**21.14–15**] There follows here the quotation from the 'Book of the Wars of Yahweh'. In this 'Book', which is mentioned only here, we can perhaps see, according to the title it is given, a collection of probably poetic pieces on the 'Yahweh Wars' of Israel's early period. The present quotation, occasioned probably by the catchword 'Arnon', contains at any rate nothing warlike, but continues to talk about Moab (on Ar cf. Ar of Moab in v. 28). The quotation has been transmitted in such a fragmentary and obviously, in part, incorrect fashion that it defies all explanation. [21.16–18a] A further note on the itinerary, quite without a context, mentions the place-name Beer (= 'well'; v. 16a), and this is followed by a quite general remark about a divine gift of water (v. 16b) and by the so-called 'well song' that was sung by Israel (vv. 17b, 18a). This song, which perhaps once had a definite reference and subsequently remained known in Israel, is a joyful greeting to the 'springing up' of water in a newly dug well. That nobles actually dug a well with the staves which they carried as signs of their power is difficult to accept; the statement is not to be understood literally in this way, but means no more than that the digging of the well in question had been an important undertaking carried out under higher authority. [21.18b–20] The following 'itinerary' (vv. 18b–20), phrased in quite a scant way, contains first of all a number of otherwise unknown names whose origin is completely obscure; then there follow (from 'Bamoth' on) several place-names which all appear either in the Balaam stories or in the story of the death of Moses (cf. Num. 22.41; 23.14, 28; Deut. 3.29; 34.6) and are certainly borrowed from these places (cf. esp. v. 20b with 23.28bβ). This, of course, bypasses 21.21ff. and already anticipates the historical narrative which follows that passage.

6. THE FIRST VICTORIES EAST OF THE JORDAN:
21.21–35

21   21Then Israel sent messengers to Sihon king of the Amorites, saying, 22'Let me pass through your land; we will not turn aside into field or vineyard; we will not drink the water of a well; we will go by the King's Highway, until we have passed through your territory. 23But Sihon would not allow Israel to pass through his territory. He gathered all his men together, and went out against Israel to the wilderness, and came to Jahaz, and fought against Israel. 24And Israel slew him with the edge of the sword, and took possession of his land from the Arnon to the Jabbok, as far as to the Ammonites; [for Jazer was the boundary of the Ammonites.] 25And Israel took all these cities, and Israel settled in all the cities of the Amorites, in Heshbon, and in all its villages. 26For Heshbon was the city of Sihon the king of the Amorites, who had fought against the former king of Moab and taken all his land out of his hand, as far as the Arnon.

²⁷*Therefore the ballad singers say,

'Come to Heshbon, let it be (re-)built,
 let the city of Sihon be established!
²⁸For fire had gone forth from Heshbon,
 a flame from the city of Sihon,
it had consumed the cities† of Moab,
 devoured‡ the heights by the Arnon.
²⁹Woe to you, O Moab,
 you are ruined, O people of Chemosh!
He has made his sons fugitives,
 and his daughters prisoners of the Amorite§.
³⁰But we have gained the upper hand, Heshbon is ruined
 and we have further kindled a fire against Medeba.'‖

31 Thus Israel dwelt in the land of the Amorites. ³²And Moses sent to spy out Jazer; [and they took its villages,] and dispossessed the Amorites that were there. ³³Then they turned and went up by the way to Bashan; and Og the king of Bashan came out against them, he and all his people, to battle at Edrei. ³⁴But the LORD said to Moses, 'Do not fear him; for I have given him into your hand, and all his people, and his land; and you shall do to him as you did to Sihon king of the Amorites, who dwelt at Heshbon.' ³⁵So they slew him, and his sons, and all his people, until there was not one survivor left to him; and they possessed his land.

The main part of this chapter narrates the victory over 'Sihon king of the Amorites' and the taking possession of his land (vv. 21–31). There are no cogent reasons for doubting the literary unity of this narrative. We must only keep in mind the fact that the 'song' in vv. 27–30 has been inserted into the narrative; this 'song' is a poetic passage, rhythmic in form, making consistent use of the effect of *parallelismus membrorum*, and certainly older than the present narrative. In order to fit this 'song' into the narrative, the author had to

* Noth's version of the song of the ballad singers in vv. 27–30 is so different from the RSV that it has been felt more desirable to print a different text here rather than overload the commentary with footnotes. The textual notes given at this point are Noth's own. Tr.

† Instead of *'ār mō'āb* (cf. Isa. 15.1 as well as Deut. 2.9, 18, 29), *'ārē mō'āb* should perhaps be read.

‡ In place of the strange *baᶜᵃlē*, the LXX presupposes the word *bālᵉᶜā*, which was no doubt the original reading.

§ In v. 29bβ the rhythmic symmetry has been destroyed through obvious overloading; of the last three words, only one will have belonged to the original text, the most likely one in my opinion being *'ᵉmōrī* (in the form *lā 'ᵉmōrī*).

‖ Vv. 30a and 30b are obviously parallel but, on rhythmic evidence, have been overloaded. In v. 30a *'ad-dībōn* is obviously an addition. In v. 30b *nōpaḥ* should be deleted and, for the rest, *'ōd 'ēš 'al* should be read (instead of *'ad 'ᵃšer 'ad*).

make a few explanatory remarks by way of a transition; this is what we have in vv. 25–26. In this transitional passage a repetition of what had already been said in other ways was unavoidable. This gives rise to an apparent impression of a doublet, but this does not really provide grounds for a division between sources. It is generally and correctly accepted that this passage forms part of the old Pentateuchal narrative material. There is only one point that helps to decide between J and E, namely the general designation of the pre-Israelite inhabitants of the land as 'Amorites'; for the name 'Amorites' is most probably to be understood in this broad sense and not in any kind of specialized way. This fact argues for E (J usually uses the term 'Canaanites' in this sense).

The concluding passage in vv. 33–35a agrees word for word, apart from a few minor variations in v. 35aα, with Deut. 3.1–3, except that what appears there as direct speech of Moses is here turned into narrative. There can be no doubt that the passage has been taken from Deut. 3 as an expansion of the Sihon story which the Deuteronomist tells in Deut. 2.31–37 with reference to Num. 21.21–31, yet telling it in his own fashion to round off the deuteronomistic picture of the conquest east of the Jordan, according to which the whole of what later became Israelite territory east of the Jordan was taken at one stroke from the territories of the kings Sihon of Heshbon and Og of Bashan (territories which were thought of as linked together) by the defeat of these two kings.

V. 32 contains an addition, a pre-deuteronomistic addition, which is unaware of the deuteronomistic picture of the conquest that has just been described. The ill-fitting character of this brief note argues for its having been added by an editor with reference to 32.1 (according to which the 'land of Jazer' appears in Israel's possession) in order to account for its disposal.

[21.21–24] With 'Sihon king of the Amorites', concerning whose dwelling-place and territory nothing is said at first, negotiations are first of all, according to vv. 21–23, carried on, and a report of these negotiations is given, partly in verbal agreement with 20.14–21 (cf. especially 20.14a, 17, 21a). It is remarkable, having that very agreement in mind, that the initiative is not taken by Moses (as in 20.14a) but by 'Israel'. Moses does not appear at all in the whole of vv. 21–31. It would be going too far, however, to conclude from this that according to the present source Moses was no longer there at the conquest east of the Jordan. The question as to what Israel's aim then was with this projected passage through the land of the Amorites along the 'King's Highway' (for this cf. above, p. 150) is an idle one, since on this occasion the refusal of permission to pass through leads to war and to the capture of Amorite territory; and this is precisely the point of this narrative. No reason is given as to why the threatening, war-like position taken up by the Edomites should, for its part, have made Israel withdraw (20.18b, 20b, 21b), while the same attitude on the part of the Amorites (21.23) should have led to the commence-ment of hostilities and subsequently to the defeat of the Amorites. Nothing is said of any divine command such as was later intro-duced by the Deuteronomist in this context in Deut. 2.30f. (cf. also 2.4–6, 9). From the historical outcome it may be deduced that the land of the Amorites, in contrast to Edom, was part of the territory that Israel was to conquer. The first indication of locality is given with the mention of Jahaz as the place where Sihon fought with Israel and was defeated (vv. 23aβb, 24a). This place cannot, of course, be identi-fied with any certainty; according to Eusebius it lay between Medeba and Dibon and that may be correct. This does not fit in with the information given in v. 23 that Sihon met the Israelites, who are represented as coming from the east, in 'the wilderness'; according to this, Jahaz would have to be looked for on the eastern edge of the cultivated land. The extent of the land which became Israel's as a consequence of the latter's utter defeat of Sihon is delimited at least approximately in v. 24ba; it covered the territory between the Arnon (in the south) and the Jabbok (in the north); this latter limit is supplemented by the mention of the Ammonites. The Ammonites lived in the region of the upper reaches of the Jabbok; their territory did not belong to the conquered land of the Amorites and for this reason the statement 'to the Jabbok' has this pertinent restriction. The motivatory clause in v. 24bβ, which in the context has itself no motivation and is probably secondary, is presumably an attempt, with regard to v. 32, to explain further this restriction along the lines that Israel was not to take possession even of Jazer, which lay on the Ammonite border, much less of the whole land of the Ammonites.

[21.25–26] Vv. 25–26 prepare the way for the 'song' that follows in vv. 27–30. In the latter, the city of Heshbon, along with the terri-tory it governs, occupies the central position. Therefore it is this city above all that must now be introduced. Hence, in v. 25, the general statement of v. 24ba about taking possession of the land is particu-larized to the effect that it was the cities of the Amorites in which

Israel settled and that of these cities Heshbon (modern *ḥisbān*) was the chief one to which the other cities belonged as 'daughter cities'.*
V. 26 gives the historical basis for this, namely that Heshbon had been the seat of Sihon king of the Amorites, a piece of information that is now given for the first time, and that this Sihon had taken from the first king of Moab by military force the whole country as far south as the Arnon valley. This information, which leads into the following 'song' and is supposed to give it meaning and which, in its essentials, is certainly taken from that very 'song', can, from the historical point of view, no longer be checked. It is not in itself unlikely that Heshbon was an important city in the fertile country north of the Arnon and that, at the time of the beginnings and the first gradual consolidation of the Moabite state in the plain known today as *belqa*, there existed independent city-states which from time to time exercised considerable power. It is also equally plausible that Moab, from the very beginning—the phrase 'the first king of Moab' (this is literally what is in the text) certainly simplifies the matter—as also later, had a tendency to extend its power beyond the Arnon.

[21.27–30] The events indicated in the transitional passage of vv. 25–26 now form, in fact, the principal contents of the 'song' in vv. 27b–30. To understand this passage correctly one must first of all explain its construction. It begins with a summons to (re-)build the 'city of Sihon', Heshbon (v. 27b). Justification for this summons is given in a causal clause which takes in the whole of the rest of the 'song' (vv. 28–30), concluding with the statement that Heshbon has been 'laid waste' (v. 30a) and will therefore need to be rebuilt. The causal clause begins in v. 28a with a compound noun-clause which, as such, looks back in time (to be translated, therefore, with a pluperfect); the fact expressed here forms the content of vv. 28–29, for these two verses belong together and obviously deal with the same thing. Then in v. 30 verbal clauses, with 'we' as subject, suddenly appear, and they, in contrast to vv. 28–29, refer to events of the recent past. In this 'we' it is obviously the present inhabitants of Heshbon who are speaking and it is also they who give voice to the introductory summons to rebuild the city. This introduction is essential for determining the character and purpose of the whole. It is a question of a 'summons' to the rebuilding of Heshbon, of an 'order' which is to be passed from mouth to mouth amongst those who are to be concerned

---

* This is Noth's translation, both in text and commentary, of Hebrew *beⁿōtehā* (literally 'its daughters') which the RSV paraphrases as 'villages'. Tr.

with the intended undertaking. By way of justification, a backward-looking reference is made to Heshbon's past. The information given in vv. 28–29 is furthest away in time. According to it, Heshbon was once the 'residence of Sihon'; a certain Sihon, then, had once been ruler of Heshbon. In his time 'fire had gone forth from Heshbon'. In the Old Testament this expression signifies the spread of devastation and destruction from a specific point of origin which is the active side. Under Sihon, therefore, Heshbon had spread military destruction all around. The victims of this had been 'the cities of Moab' and 'the heights of the Arnon', i.e. the Moabite settlements, or the settlements to which Moab laid claim, as far as the heights of Arnon, i.e. on the plain north of the Arnon. If v. 29 is a lament for Moab and speaks of the downfall of the people of the Moabite national god Chemosh (it is certainly he who is the subject of v. 29ba), then this is an exaggeration in so far as it obviously deals only with the Moabites north of the Arnon and not, on the contrary, with the central territory of Moab proper which lay south of that river. After Heshbon had in this way extended its rule far and wide, we have what is reported in v. 30 with the subject 'we'. According to what is at least very probably the meaning of the two verbs which stand at the beginning of vv. 30a and 30b and which must be retained as such, it is a question of the conquest of a Heshbon which had become thus significant and which at the same time included the city of Medeba (present-day *mādeba*), which lay six miles to the south. According to all the historical evidence that is available, the 'we' of v. 30 can only be Israelites who have conquered and destroyed Heshbon (and Medeba) and who now, having taken possession of Heshbon, issue a summons to rebuild this city (v. 27b). If this interpretation, developed from the construction of the 'song', is the correct one, then it follows that the author of the Sihon story in vv. 21ff. has made pertinent use of this 'song' and has correctly indicated the essentials of it in his transitional passage (vv. 25–26). He was able, in conclusion (v. 31), to formulate briefly the aim and the outcome of the whole story, namely that Israel settled in 'the land of the Amorites', i.e. in what had hitherto been the domains of the defeated 'Amorite' king of Heshbon, thereby taking the first step in the conquest within the territory that had been promised to them.

[21.32] In v. 32, which is secondary, Moses again appears as subject; he has the city of Jazer spied out and the 'Amorites' who dwelt there driven out and has Jazer therefore seized (v. 32aβ, with an expression which is out of context and incomplete, must be an addition). This information must presumably be intended as a preparation for 32.1 (on Jazer and its place in the conquest tradition see below, pp. 236f.).

[21.33-35] The deuteronomistic section, vv. 33-35, taken from Deut. 3, deals with Og king of Bashan. The Og story in the Old Testament is found only in the deuteronomistic literature. It is no longer clear how much historical reality it contains. What is meant by the land of Bashan over which Og ruled is the region of fruitful plains on both sides of and especially on the north side of the upper reaches of the Yarmuk. According to v. 33a, after the victory over Sihon, Israel went on to take possession of the land of Bashan which, according to the Deuteronomist, formed the northern frontier of Heshbon and, together with the latter, comprised the territory east of the Jordan claimed by Israel. Og and his army forced Israel to a battle at the city of Edrei (modern *der'a*) which, according to Deut. 1.4 *et al.*, was, together with Ashtaroth (*tell 'aštarta*), one of his two residencies. In accordance with a promise made by Yahweh and recorded in detail in v. 34, he lost the battle and therewith his territory which passed into the possession of the victorious Israelites (v. 35b).

7. BALAAM: 22.1-24.25

22 ¹Then the people of Israel set out, and encamped in the plains of Moab beyond the Jordan at Jericho. ²And Balak the son of Zippor saw all that Israel had done to the Amorites. ³And Moab was in great dread of the people, because they were many; Moab was overcome with fear of the people of Israel. ⁴And Moab said [to the elders of Midian,] 'This horde will now lick up all that is round about us, as the ox licks up the grass of the field.' So Balak the son of Zippor, who was king of Moab at that time, ⁵sent messengers to Balaam the son of Beor at Pethor, which is near the River, in the land of Amaw to call him, saying, 'Behold, a people has come out of Egypt; they cover the face of the earth, and they are dwelling opposite me. ⁶Come now, curse this people for me, since they are too mighty for me; perhaps I shall be able to defeat them and drive them from the land; for I know that he whom you bless is blessed, and he whom you curse is cursed.'

7 So [the elders of Moab and the elders of Midian] departed with the fees for divination in their hand; and they came to Balaam, and gave him Balak's message. ⁸And he said to them, 'Lodge here this night, and I will bring back word to you, as the LORD speaks to me'; so the princes of Moab stayed with Balaam. ⁹And God came to Balaam and said, 'Who are these men with you?' ¹⁰And Balaam said to God, 'Balak the son of Zippor, king of Moab, has sent to me, saying, ¹¹"Behold, a people has come out of Egypt, [and it covers the face of the earth;] now come, curse them for me; perhaps I shall be able to fight

against them and drive them out." ' ¹²God said to Balaam, 'You shall not go with them; you shall not curse the people, for they are blessed.' ¹³So Balaam rose in the morning, and said to the princes of Balak, 'Go to your own land; for the LORD has refused to let me go with you.' ¹⁴So the princes of Moab rose and went to Balak, and said, 'Balaam refuses to come with us.'

15 Once again Balak sent princes, more in number and more honourable than they. ¹⁶And they came to Balaam and said to him, 'Thus says Balak the son of Zippor: "Let nothing hinder you from coming to me; ¹⁷for I will surely do you great honour, and whatever you say to me I will do; come, curse this people for me." ' ¹⁸But Balaam answered and said to the servants of Balak, 'Though Balak were to give me his house full of silver and gold, I could not go beyond the command of the LORD my God, to do less or more. ¹⁹Pray, now, tarry here this night also, that I may know what more the LORD will say to me.' ²⁰And God came to Balaam at night and said to him, 'If the men have come to call you, rise, go with them; but only what I bid you, that shall you do.'

21 So Balaam rose in the morning, and saddled his ass, and went with the princes of Moab. ²²But God's anger was kindled because he went; and the angel of the LORD took his stand in the way as his adversary. Now he was riding on the ass, and his two servants were with him. ²³And the ass saw the angel of the LORD standing in the road, with a drawn sword in his hand; and the ass turned aside out of the road, and went into the field; and Balaam struck the ass, to turn her into the road. ²⁴Then the angel of the LORD stood in a narrow path between the vineyards, with a wall on either side. 25 And when the ass saw the angel of the LORD, she pushed against the wall, and pressed Balaam's foot against the wall; so he struck her again. ²⁶Then the angel of the LORD went ahead, and stood in a narrow place, where there was no way to turn either to the right or to the left. ²⁷When the ass saw the angel of the LORD, she lay down under Balaam; and Balaam's anger was kindled, and he struck the ass with his staff. ²⁸Then the LORD opened the mouth of the ass, and she said to Balaam, 'What have I done to you, that you have struck me these three times?' ²⁹And Balaam said to the ass, 'Because you have made sport of me. I wish I had a sword in my hand, for then I would kill you.' ³⁰And the ass said to Balaam, 'Am I not your ass, upon which you have ridden all your life long to this day? Was I ever accustomed to do so to you?' And he said, 'No.'

31 Then the LORD opened the eyes of Balaam, and he saw the angel of the LORD standing in the way, with his drawn sword in his hand; and he bowed his head, and fell on his face. ³²And the angel of the LORD said to him, 'Why have you struck your ass these three times? Behold, I have come forth to withstand you, because your way is perverse before me; ³³and the ass saw me, and turned aside before me these three times. If she had not turned aside from me, surely just now I would have slain you and let her live.' ³⁴Then Balaam said to the angel of the LORD, 'I have sinned, for I did not know that thou didst stand in the road against me. Now therefore, if it is evil in thy sight, I

will go back again.' ³⁵And the angel of the LORD said to Balaam, 'Go with the men; but only the word which I bid you, that shall you speak.' So Balaam went on with the princes of Balak.

36 When Balak heard that Balaam had come, he went out to meet him at the city of Moab, [on the boundary formed by the Arnon,] at the extremity of the boundary. ³⁷And Balak said to Balaam, 'Did I not send to you to call you? Why did you not come to me? Am I not able to honour you?' ³⁸Balaam said to Balak, 'Lo, I have come to you! Have I now any power at all to speak anything? The word that God puts in my mouth, that must I speak.' ³⁹Then Balaam went with Balak, and they came to Kiriath-huzoth. ⁴⁰And Balak sacrificed oxen and sheep, and sent to Balaam and to the princes who were with him.

41 And on the morrow Balak took Balaam and brought him up to Bamoth-baal; and from there he saw the nearest of the people.

23 ¹And Balaam said to Balak, 'Build for me here seven altars, and provide for me here seven bulls and seven rams.' ²Balak did as Balaam had said; and [Balak and Balaam] offered on each altar a bull and a ram. ³And Balaam said to Balak, 'Stand beside your burnt offering, and I will go; perhaps the LORD will come to meet me; and whatever he shows me I will tell you.' And he went to a bare height. ⁴And God met Balaam; and Balaam said to him, 'I have prepared the seven altars, and I have offered upon each altar a bull and a ram.' ⁵And the LORD put a word in Balaam's mouth, and said, 'Return to Balak, and thus you shall speak.' ⁶And he returned to him, and lo, he and all the princes of Moab were standing beside his burnt offering. ⁷And Balaam took up his discourse, and said,

'From Aram Balak has brought me,
    the king of Moab from the eastern mountains:
"Come, curse Jacob for me,
    and come, denounce Israel!"
⁸How can I curse whom God has not cursed?
    How can I denounce whom the LORD has not denounced?
⁹For from the top of the mountains I see him,
    from the hills I behold him;
lo, a people dwelling alone,
    and not reckoning itself among the nations!
¹⁰Who can count the dust of Jacob,
    or number the fourth part of Israel?
Let me die the death of the righteous,
    and let my end be like his!'

11 And Balak said to Balaam, 'What have you done to me? I took you to curse my enemies, and behold you have done nothing but bless them.' 12 And he answered, 'Must I not take heed to speak what the LORD puts in my mouth?'

13 And Balak said to him, 'Come with me to another place, from which you may see them; [you shall see only the nearest of them, and shall not see them all;] then curse them for me from there.' ¹⁴And he took him to the field of Zophim, to the top of Pisgah, and built seven

altars, and offered a bull and a ram on each altar. ¹⁵Balaam said to
Balak, 'Stand here beside your burnt offering, while I meet the LORD
yonder.' ¹⁶And the LORD met Balaam, and put a word in his mouth,
and said, 'Return to Balak, and thus shall you speak.' ¹⁷And he came
to him, and, lo, he was standing beside his burnt offering, and the
princes of Moab with him. [And Balak said to him, 'What has the
LORD spoken?'] ¹⁸And Balaam took up his discourse, and said,
   'Rise, Balak, and hear;
     hearken [to me,] O son of Zippor:
  ¹⁹God is not man, that he should lie,
     or a son of man, that he should repent.
  Has he said, and will he not do it?
     Or has he spoken, and will he not fulfil it?
  ²⁰Behold, I received a command to bless:
     he has blessed, and I cannot revoke it.
  ²¹He has not beheld misfortune in Jacob;
     nor has he seen trouble in Israel.
  The LORD their God is with them,
     and the shout of a king is among them.
  ²²God brings them out of Egypt;
     they have as it were the horns of the wild ox.
  ²³For there is no enchantment against Jacob,
     no divination against Israel;
  [now it shall be said of Jacob and Israel,
     "What has God wrought!"]
  ²⁴Behold, a people! As a lioness it rises up
     and as a lion it lifts itself;
  it does not lie down till it devours the prey,
     and drinks the blood of the slain.'
25 And Balak said to Balaam, 'Neither curse them at all, nor bless
them at all.' ²⁶But Balaam answered Balak, 'Did I not tell you, "All
that the LORD says, that I must do"?' ²⁷And Balak said to Balaam,
'Come now, I will take you to another place; perhaps it will please God
that you may curse them for me from there.' ²⁸So Balak took Balaam
to the top of Peor, that overlooks the desert. ²⁹And Balaam said to
Balak, 'Build for me here seven altars, and provide for me here seven
bulls and seven rams.' ³⁰And Balak did as Balaam had said, and offered
a bull and a ram on each altar.
24 ¹When Balaam saw that it pleased the LORD to bless Israel, he
[did not go, as at other times, to meet with omens, but] set his face
toward the wilderness. ²And Balaam lifted up his eyes, and saw Israel
encamping tribe by tribe. And the Spirit of God came upon him, ³and
he took up his discourse, and said,
  'The oracle of Balaam the son of Beor,
     [the oracle] of the man whose eye is opened,
  ⁴the oracle of him who hears the words of God,
     who sees the vision of the Almighty,
     falling down, but having his eyes uncovered:

⁵how fair are your tents, O Jacob,
    your encampments, O Israel!
⁶Like valleys that stretch afar,
    like gardens beside a river,
like aloes that the LORD has planted,
    like cedar trees beside the waters.
⁷Water shall flow from his buckets,
    and his seed shall be in many waters,
his king shall be higher than Agag,
    and his kingdom shall be exalted.
⁸God brings him out of Egypt;
    he has as it were the horns of the wild ox,
he shall eat up the nations his adversaries,
    and shall break their bones in pieces,
    [and pierce them through with his arrows.]
⁹He couched, he lay down like a lion,
    and like a lioness; who will rouse him up?
Blessed be every one who blesses you,
    and cursed be every one who curses you.'

10 And Balak's anger was kindled against Balaam, and he struck his hands together; and Balak said to Balaam, 'I called you to curse my enemies, and behold, you have blessed them [these three times.] ¹¹Therefore now flee to your place; I said, "I will certainly honour you," but the LORD has held you back from honour.' ¹²And Balaam said to Balak, 'Did I not tell your messengers whom you sent to me, ¹³"If Balak should give me his house full of silver and gold, I would not be able to go beyond the word of the LORD, to do either good or bad of my own will; what the LORD speaks, that will I speak?" ¹⁴And now, behold, I am going to my people; come, I will let you know what this people will do to your people [in the latter days.]' ¹⁵And he took up his discourse, and said,

'The oracle of Balaam the son of Beor,
    [the oracle] of the man whose eye is opened,
¹⁶the oracle of him who hears the words of God,
    and knows the knowledge of the Most High,
who sees the vision of the Almighty,
    falling down, but having his eyes uncovered:
¹⁷I see him, but not now;
    I behold him, but not nigh:
a star shall come forth out of Jacob,
    and a sceptre shall rise out of Israel;
it shall crush the forehead of Moab,
    and break down all the sons of Sheth.
¹⁸Edom shall be dispossessed,
    Seir also, [his enemies,] shall be dispossessed,
    while Israel does valiantly.
¹⁹By Jacob shall dominion be exercised,
    and the survivors of cities be destroyed!'

²⁰ Then he looked on Amalek, and took up his discourse, and said,

'Amalek was the first of the nations,
but in the end he shall come to destruction.'

²¹ And he looked on the Kenite, and took up his discourse, and said,

'Enduring is your dwelling place,
and your nest is set in the rock;
²²Nevertheless Kain shall be wasted.
How long shall Asshur take you away captive?'
²³And he took up his discourse, and said,
'Alas, who shall live [when God does this]?
²⁴But ships shall come from Kittim
and shall afflict Asshur and Eber;
and he also shall come to destruction.'

25 Then Balaam rose, and went back to his place; and Balak also went his way.

In its entirety, the Balaam story is part of the old Pentateuchal narrative material. P is represented only by the note on the itinerary in 22.1b (v. 1a is an editorial transitional passage) and this note does not belong to the Balaam story, but leads on to 27.12ff. (cf. Deut. 32.49; 34.1). However, the Balaam story is obviously not a unified whole. This is clear from the unmotivated change, explicable only on literary critical grounds, in the designation of God ('Yahweh' and 'God'), as well as from the existence of obvious doublets (cf. right at the beginning 22.3a//3b). We have to reckon, then, with the juxta-position of two 'sources' and, since P is not in evidence, it is a question of J and E. Thus far there is extensive agreement in the scholarly analysis of this passage. Much more problematic is the detailed separation of the two 'sources'. In general in this analysis the change in the designation of God can, of course, be taken into account; in individual parts, however, doubt remains in view of the questionable nature of the textual transmission (differences between the Massoretic Text and the ancient versions). From the point of view of content the two self-contained sections 22.41–23.26 and 23.28–24.19 present obvious doublets; the former, with two 'Balaam discourses', forms the main part of the E-version, while the latter, again with two 'Balaam discourses', forms the main part of the J-version. These two variants are linked together with secondary editorial material in 23.27, 29, 30. 24.20–24 contains obvious additions (a few more short sayings which are attributed to Balaam). 24.25 concludes the old Balaam story. The most difficult part is the analysis of ch. 22. The episode of the ass in

22.21–35, which is a unit in itself, is, of course, definitely to be ascribed to the J-narrative. The remainder of the chapter, however (on v. 1 and v. 41 see above), can no longer be divided up with any certainty; one can only point to doublets and variants and make the general assertion that this is a combination of J and E.

From the point of view of subject-matter, the Balaam story presents a series of questions which are difficult to answer. It has nothing whatsoever to do with the conquest tradition. It presupposes that Israel and Moab are living as neighbours and that this is a permanent state which is by no means altered by the appearance of Balaam, for the Balaam story does not lead to any definite 'outcome'. It is set in the district to the east of the northern end of the Dead Sea, where obviously the territories of Israel and Moab bordered on each other; and originally the whole story was confined to this region. Israel is represented by the Israelite inhabitants of the southern part of the territory east of the Jordan; initially the Balaam story must have been handed down in their circles. If the district to the east of the northern end of the Dead Sea is presumed to be Israelite-Moabite border country, then—in contrast to 21.21–30—the background is formed by a fairly early historical situation in which Israel has not yet extended its settlements and its military power at Moab's expense any further south. This assertion is valid for the origin that is to be presumed for the Balaam tradition, but not, on the other hand, for the Balaam story as it is developed in its present form.

The two principal figures are Balak king of Moab, who takes the initiative, and Balaam. Balak is probably to be regarded as an otherwise unknown personage from early Moabite history. There is nothing much to be said for the suggestion that he is merely a personification of the region of *el-belqa* (the modern name for the southern part of Transjordan, a name which is more probably of Arabic origin). It is possible that Balak was not actually 'king of Moab' but some petty king or other in the early period who was neighbour to the Israelites who lived in that southern region of Transjordan. It is probable that behind Balaam, too, there stands a figure who is, in the last resort, historical. Difficulties are created in the first place by the fact that he fills various roles in the Old Testament. While in the Balaam story he must, under divine compulsion, bless Israel and actually does bless them, he is said, according to the text of Deut. 23.4b–5 (*Hebr.* 5b–6) (cf. Neh. 13.2), to have been hired to curse Israel, but that God 'would not hearken' and 'turned the curse into blessing' (similarly, but ambiguously, Josh. 24.9b–10a). The situation is quite different in Num. 31 (from which Josh. 13.22 is derived), where Balaam was a Midianite and was killed by the Israelites in the course of a campaign against the Midianites (v. 8) for the reason that he had led Israel astray in the apostasy described in Num. 25.1ff. This latter version, to which reference is made in the New Testament in Rev. 2.14, is, from the literary point of view, attested only in very late passages and presumably does not rest on an old tradition. The reproach, too, that is made in II Peter 2.15f. (cf. Jude v. 11) and according to which Balaam went astray for the sake of vile profit is based only on a secondary interpretation, and one that is not even to the point, of the Balaam story of Num. 22–24. The brief allusion in Micah 6.5a obviously has in mind the story as recorded in Num. 22–24; and, from what has been said, this latter is the oldest literary form of the Balaam tradition and the only primary one. According to this, Balaam was a man whose word (of blessing or of curse) was regarded as endowed with an infallibly effective 'power' (cf. 22.6b) and who was therefore summoned from afar when the need for such a 'powerful' word arose. Where did he come from? The only factual information is in 22.5. The city that is mentioned here, Pethor, 'which is near the River' (i.e. according to Old Testament usage, the Euphrates) can scarcely be anything other than *Pitru*, well known from Assyrian sources, in the most northerly part of Syria, which lies on a tributary entering the upper Euphrates from the right, not far above where the two rivers join. This is in essential agreement with the statement in 23.7 according to which Balaam was brought 'from Aram' (cf. Deut. 23.4 [*Hebr.* v. 5] : 'from Pethor of Mesopotamia').* Since this Pethor appears to lie much too far from the scene of the Balaam story, it has been supposed either that in 22.5 we have a confusion between the north Syrian Pethor and some other 'Pethor' that is otherwise completely unknown, or else alternative indications of origin are conjectured by means of emendations in the text which are supposed to be more original and 'more credible' than the facts given in 22.5aα. Therefore, in 22.5aβ (although this time on the basis of very ancient textual evidence), instead of 'land of his fellow countrymen',† 'land of the Ammonites' has been read with the aim of making Balaam an

---

* This is the RSV version. Noth has 'from Pethor of Aram-Naharaim', i.e. 'Aram of the Two Rivers'. Tr.

† This is Noth's more literal rendering of Hebrew '*ereṣ bᵉnē ʿammō*. The RSV, with no apparent justification, has 'the land of Amaw'. Tr.

Ammonite, or else in 23.7 'Aram' has been emended to 'Edom', thus making Edom Balaam's country of origin. This latter emendation is generally accompanied by a reference to 'Bela the son of Beor', who appears at the head of a list of Edomite kings in Gen. 36.32 and whose name bears an unfortunate resemblance to that of 'Balaam the son of Beor'. The result is that it seems tempting to equate the two figures, thus making an Edomite origin for Balaam appear probable. But the support for this equation is weak. The similarity of two names, which in the present case is not even complete, can easily lead along the wrong track to the equation of the people concerned. There is also the fact that the Edomite king-list in Gen. 36.31–39 gives the impression of being a completely reliable historical document, and there is no reason to suggest that even only in the case of the first-mentioned king we are dealing with some legendary figure or other who has only subsequently been classified as a king. As far as Balaam is concerned, then, there remains as the only real indication of his origin that we have, only the information given in 22.5aα. Even from the name 'Balaam' no reference to any other origin can be deduced.

In any event Balaam was certainly not a Moabite, far less an Israelite. How, then, does the tradition conceive of Balaam's relationship to Yahweh? The whole story says nothing further than that Balaam acknowledges Yahweh as his divine lord whose will he must follow in all that he says and does. That Yahweh is the lord of the whole world is already a fact for the old Pentateuchal sources. That Balaam, too, acknowledges this, is meant to be understood in the sense that he, as the recipient of revelation, was aware that Yahweh ruled the whole of world history, even although he himself was not part of the 'people of Yahweh'. There is also here perhaps the possibly still older idea that when it is a question of Israel's fate, then, in any event, the will of Israel's God was decisive, a fact which even a non-Israelite man of God, who himself worshipped other gods, could and must respect. With regard to the Balaam story as we have it, the acknowledgment of Yahweh by a foreigner, who stood so high in the esteem of Israel's neighbours, was at any rate of great importance.

In the Balaam story two opposing ideas are juxtaposed. Balaam is summoned by Balak to pronounce an effective 'curse' on an Israel which had become a threat to Moab. To this summons Balaam, once he had ascertained the will of Yahweh, could react in two ways. He could either refuse to come, or else come but then bless and not curse. Both themes are treated in great detail. This is remarkable especially in view of the fact that he is unwilling to come or is not supposed to come (the extended episode of the ass belongs at this point). For he does, in the end, come, and come with Yahweh's permission. From the point of view of the history of the tradition, the theme of coming to bless instead of to curse is certainly the primary one. For the purpose of the narrative from the very beginning was, without doubt, the recording of the blessings of the famous Balaam. The refusal to comply with Balak's summons, since it never could have led to a definite outcome, can never have formed the content of an independent Balaam tradition. What, then, is the point of the lengthy treatment of the initial refusal to come, which contributes nothing to the purpose of the whole narrative and which must be secondary with regard to the original substance of the narrative? In spite of the impression of antiquity which parts of it give, it must be based on later reflection and have the aim of averting from Balaam—and from Yahweh, too —any possible reproach of having deceived Balak. It all takes place in order to make clear to Balak that his desire for a curse upon Israel will not be fulfilled. Balak's obstinacy has had the final result of making effective words of blessing the final outcome of the whole affair.

However much the Balaam story may have been elaborated in the course of time, the nucleus of it must have been formed by the appearance, in Israel's early period, of a 'man of God' by the name of Balaam, who had come from afar to one of the sanctuaries of southern Transjordan (cf. 'the top of Peor', 23.28) and of whom it would be reported that he had uttered words of blessing on neighbouring Israel.

[22.1] According to 22. [1a] 1bP (cf. above, p. 171), Israel now descended into the Jordan valley; what is at any rate meant by the elaborate phraseology is the region opposite Jericho on the east bank of the lower Jordan valley ('plains of Moab' is probably a traditional designation from a period at which Moab's sphere of influence stretched that far; cf. Judg. 3.12–30). This indication of locality is not part of the Balaam story; on the contrary, in the latter, to begin with, the question remains open as to where exactly Israel and Moab bordered on each other.

[22.2–7] There is a loose connection between 22.2 and 21.21–30; the sentence must, then, belong to E. Moab's fear at the large numbers of the Israelites is expressed twice in v. 3 (doublet). From v. 4 onwards it appears to be J that is represented; v. 4b is superfluous after v. 2E and is, therefore, to be credited to J. V. 4a deals with a careful assessment by the Moabites, expressed in the remarkable image of the grazing of a considerable herd of oxen. What the Moabites are afraid of is not exactly an attack by the Israelites but rather an 'encirclement' ('round about us') which would deprive them of any possibility of expansion. The mention of the 'elders of Midian' (in v. 4a as those addressed by the Moabites and in v. 7 as participants) is certainly secondary and rests on the late concept of the connection of Balaam with the Midianites (31.8, 16). The messengers whom Balak sends to summon Balaam, well known and famous for the 'power' of his word (v. 6b), go to the latter's home, that is to Pethor in the region of the Euphrates (cf. above, p. 173). The words in apposition to the name Pethor, 'the land of his fellow countrymen'* (for this expression cf. Lev. 20.17 et al.),† are, in the present context, intended to be a specific designation of Pethor as Balaam's homeland. It could, of course, also be that in this remark we have a variant tradition (perhaps, therefore, E) which expressly leaves open the question as to where Balaam's homeland was. In the message to Balaam reference is again made to the numerical supremacy of those people who have come from Egypt and are now settled 'opposite' Moab, in an expression which means literally 'cover the eye of the land' and which is used in Ex. 10.5J of locusts, being taken to mean that 'one can no longer see the ground'. In the present passage, too, one is surely meant to think of the image of locusts completely covering the ground. An effective curse by Balaam would—such is the tenor of v. 6—be able so to weaken the vitality of this people that Balak, in spite of inferior numbers, would perhaps be able to conquer them by force and drive them out of his vicinity, whereby Moab would once more be free to breathe. On the 'fees for divination' (an expression which is found, in these words, only here and whose meaning is derived only from the context) which the messengers take with them for Balaam, cf. I Sam. 9.7f.; it is handed over in advance, even before Balaam could have done what they asked.

[22.8–14] According to v. 8, Balaam at once makes clear to the messengers that in consequence of Balak's request he must first of all obtain a decision from Yahweh, which is apparently to be expected in a nocturnal revelation. The messengers, then, have to wait overnight; they are now described (v. 8b) as princes of Moab (the word sār is normally used of officers, especially royal officers of various ranks, and

* Cf. previous note. Tr.
† RSV 'the children of their people'; Hebrew benē ʿammām. Tr.

certainly means, in the present context, royal dignitaries). Vv. 9–12
are remarkable for the sudden, unmotivated appearance of the word
'God' (instead of the divine name 'Yahweh' which is used in v. 8 and
again in v. 13). This must, therefore, be an E-section, from which one
can conclude that E as well as J contained an account of Balak's
embassy to Balaam. A fine shade of distinction is perhaps to be noted
in the fact that, according to v. 8 J, Balak declares, immediately on
the arrival of the messengers, that he must obtain instructions from
Yahweh, while, according to v. 9E, on the arrival of the messengers
it is God who takes the initiative in addressing Balaam. Balaam provides the information in words some of which have been taken over
secondarily from the J-context of vv. 5–6 (note especially the expression 'it covers the face of the earth'), while others of which are of a
distinctive formulation (note the use of the verb *qbb* 'to execrate' in
v. 11b instead of *'rr* 'to curse' in v. 6abJ). With regard to subject-
matter, both narrative variants are parallel; Balaam is forbidden to
accede to Balak's request. This prohibition is expressed in two different ways in v. 12. According to v. 12a, Balaam is forbidden to go with
the messengers; according to v. 12b, he is told not to curse Israel,
which, for all practical purposes, means the same as not going with
the messengers. V. 12a, with its use of the word 'God', certainly
belongs to E, v. 12b, with the word *'rr* 'to curse', perhaps to J. If this
is correct, then J, too, contained an account of instructions given by
Yahweh to Balaam, an account which has been for the most part
suppressed by the E-variant. V. 13, for its part, may well have followed immediately on v. 8. At any rate, in v. 13 Balak's messengers
are informed of the divine decision which Balaam had solicited. Balak
—so the narrative continues in J—does not allow himself to be discouraged by the negative outcome of this first attempt (v. 14).

[22.15–20] He makes still greater exertions. He sends what is, in
view of the number and the rank of the dignitaries, an even more
impressive deputation (v. 15) and offers to Balaam, above all,
'honour' in whatever measure he desires (v. 17a). As v. 18 shows,
what is meant by this 'honour' is a monetary payment (the word
'honorarium' exactly fits the situation envisaged here). To this Balaam
can only answer that, irrespective of such an 'honorarium', he can
only follow the will of Yahweh, which he must first ascertain, for
which reason the ambassadors must once again (as in v. 8) wait a
night (v. 19). In v. 20 E appears again ('God') with the information
that on this occasion (in contrast to v. 12a) God takes the initiative

in giving Balaam instructions to go, but in this case to do only what God specifically commands him to do. Following on v. 12a, E, too, must have contained an account of a second embassy to Balaam. It is precisely a fragment of this narrative which appears in v. 20 and probably already in v. 17b if the use of the verb *qbb* 'to execrate' may be regarded as characteristic of E (cf. above). As far as E is concerned, the exposition of the whole story is completed with the divine instruction in v. 20.

[**22.21–35**] In the case of J, on the other hand, there now follows the episode of the ass (vv. 21–35), which is ill matched with what precedes. For if it is stated in v. 21 that Balaam, on the morning after the night (v. 19) in which he had sought to ascertain the will of God, saddled his ass and set out with the Moabite dignitaries, then it must be concluded from that, that, just as in E, according to v. 20, so, too, in J Yahweh's instructions had been to go with them. It then appears as an act of irresponsible despotism on God's part if, according to v. 21aα, Yahweh's anger at this departure suddenly burst forth. The episode of the ass must come from another, presumably older version of the Balaam story, one which was taken over by J just as it stood, in which there was no mention of the events now recorded in 22.7–20 and according to which Balaam had acceded of his own volition to the request of the Moabite ambassadors, with the result that, on the way, he learned for the first time, from the encounters with the 'messenger of Yahweh', that Balak's demand was against the will of Yahweh. It is true that this version, too, in view of the discourses of Balaam, must have ended in Balaam's going with the messengers in the long run, yet not without stressing and making explicit reference to the fact that he could say only what Yahweh would charge him with saying. This is what is said in v. 35, and with this verse the exposition of the story once again reaches exactly the same point as it has already reached in v. 20.

With its clarity, with its artistic presentation of suspense and of dramatic heightening, the episode of the ass is a masterpiece of ancient Israelite narrative art. At the heart of it lies the idea that an unprejudiced animal can see things to which a man in his wilfulness is blind; there is certainly also in this respect the presupposition that Yahweh's messenger was in himself 'visible' in the usual way, just as elsewhere in the Old Testament the messenger of Yahweh, when he appears, is thought of as visible and in human form and, in the present context, with a drawn sword held threateningly in his hand.

The messenger of Yahweh ('angel of Yahweh'), here, as elsewhere in the Old Testament, not a particular individual figure but a being of unknown origin sent by Yahweh from time to time, represents Yahweh himself and is introduced particularly at those points where too extended a speech by Yahweh was to be avoided; the messenger of Yahweh, then, acts and speaks in place of Yahweh, but always in such manner as if it were an action or speech of Yahweh himself. This is usually clear at the conclusion of such an appearance of a messenger (cf., e.g., Gen. 16 v. 13a with vv. 7–12). So, too, in the present case the concluding command of v. 35aβ is a word of Yahweh himself with the 'I' of Yahweh, although strictly it is still Yahweh's messenger who is speaking. The ass's ability to speak, with which may be compared the speaking of the serpent in Gen. 3. 1ff., is not an element that is particularly stressed or even necessary; it is, however, an integral part of the narrative and is attributed to a miracle on the part of Yahweh (v. 28a) which indicates how directly and unusually Yahweh acted in this affair of blessing or curse for Israel. That in the long run Balaam, too, recognized Yahweh's messenger, also goes back to direct intervention on the part of Yahweh (v. 31a). On the way Balaam was accompanied by 'his two servants' (v. 22bβ), i.e. by two youthful servants.* These two have no part to play in the story; they remain completely in the background and serve only to show that Balaam travelled like a man of superior rank. It would be interesting to know how, in the opinion of the narrator, the Moabite dignitaries with whom, according to v. 21b, Balaam set out and with whom, according to v. 35b, he continued his journey after his encounter with Yahweh's messenger, reacted to Balaam's experience. Were they completely unaware of it because they had gone some distance ahead or were some distance behind? Or were they silent witnesses of what transpired? In the latter case it must have become clear to them that Balaam was subject to a higher authority and that he would be unable to do or say anything on his own initiative or in obedience to any human commission. The representatives of Moab, therefore, would have to reckon from the outset with the fact that Balaam might not comply with Balak's wishes and that, therefore, Balak would not have to consider himself cheated if Balaam's word of 'power' turned out other than he expected. Probably the narrator gave no thought at

* The word translated 'servant' in the RSV (na'ar) usually means 'lad' or 'youth'. The basic meaning, according to Koehler (Lexicon in Veteris Testamenti Libros, s.v.), is 'the marriageable male as long as he is a bachelor'. Tr.

all as to the whereabouts of the Moabite dignitaries during the encounter with the messenger of Yahweh, since the episode of the ass is in any case a separate entity from another tradition (cf. above), p. 178). In the episode of the ass the tension is maintained between the concept that, according to the will of Yahweh, Balaam should not really have gone with the Moabites at all (however the incomprehensible sentence in v. 32bβ is emended and explained) and the order that is finally given that he should go, but with the stricture that in what he says he is to follow the will of Yahweh (cf. above, pp. 174f.).

[22.36–38] Balaam's arrival at Balak is narrated in vv. 36–38, obviously, in the main, according to J. Only between v. 38aα and v. 38aβb is the continuity broken; and since in v. 38aβb the word 'God' appears, one has to regard v. 38aβb as an E-fragment, according to which Balaam, immediately on arrival, informed Balak that in what he says he can only obey the divine will. According to J, Balak treated Balaam with such respect that on hearing of his approach he went to meet him at the furthest point to which Moabite power extended (v. 36). The point where they met is given only very imprecisely. Of the two relative clauses in v. 36b,* certainly only one is original, the one with the less definite content; only later has it been made more precise by means of the other relative clause. Originally, then, what was said was 'the city of Moab (which lies) at the extremity of the (Moabite) boundary' (there is no valid reason for emending the text at this point). It is, therefore, left completely open as to which route Balaam had taken from his homeland and from which direction he reached Moab. The opinion of the person who introduced secondarily the 'Arnon boundary' cannot be determined with any certainty. Since elsewhere in the Old Testament, on the basis of historical circumstances that obtained from time to time, the Arnon mostly served as the northern frontier of Moab, this idea must surely be presupposed here, too. However, this is not quite consistent with the fact that, according to the subsequent geographical data (23.14, 28), Balaam made his appearance in the territory north of the Arnon. Did, then, the person who provided this supplementary information perhaps understand the Arnon as the southern frontier and think that Balak's sphere of influence was confined to the territory north of the Arnon? He would, then, have made Balaam arrive from the

---

* The Hebrew of v. 36b contains two occurrences of the relative particle, and a more literal translation of it would be 'the city of Moab which is on the boundary formed by the Arnon, which is at the extremity of the boundary'. Tr.

south, and this fact would lend support to the theory of Balaam's
Edomite origin. This is difficult to imagine for the reason that the
Arnon, as far as we know the history of Moab, was never the southern
frontier of Moab and could never have been such. One will, therefore, have to accept that the secondary reference to the Arnon frontier has been made without any precise reflection and without taking
account of 23.14, 28 and on the basis of the fact that in Israel the
Arnon was the only 'frontier of Moab' that was known to any extent.
According to J, Balak received Balaam at the frontier, with respect,
it is true, yet with the reproach that he had taken so long to accede
to the request (v. 37), and he does not omit to refer to the projected
'honorarium' (cf. v. 17aJ).

[22.39–40] In preparation for Balaam's expected appearance,
sacrifices are first of all made. They are mentioned twice, in 22.40 and
in 23.1–2. It is probable, though this cannot be proved with any
certainty, that this twofold mention is due to the juxtaposition of the
two sources. Since 23.1–2 certainly belongs to the E-narrative, 22.40,
and certainly also 22.39, are to be attributed to the J-narrative. In
22.39 we have a definite geographical reference, Kiriath-huzoth.
Unfortunately the site of this place, which is mentioned only here, is
completely unknown. There is no evidence that it is a combination
of more or less similar-sounding names. One must therefore be content with the assertion that Kiriath-huzoth must have lain somewhere
in the region to the east of the north end of the Dead Sea (cf. on
23.28). According to 22.40 (it is otherwise in 23.1), the sacrifice which
Balak offered was a communal sacrifice. Balak invited Balaam and
the Moabite princes (those who had fetched Balaam and perhaps
others as well) to share in the sacrificial meal, although the latter
took place not at the place of sacrifice itself, but somewhere near by
(this is what the phraseology of v. 40b seems to be saying). By means
of this sacrifice Balaam is brought into the sacral community of
Moab (represented by the most prominent representatives of the
Moabite state) and brought into relationship with the god (or gods)
of Moab. This was certainly Balak's intention; this could not, of
course, annul Balaam's obligation to Yahweh.

[22.41–23.6] In 23.1ff., E presents a different view of the sacrificial action. It is Balaam who takes the initiative, and the sacrifices
that are offered are burnt offerings, the meaning of which is not
exactly apparent. It seems as if E wished to present Balak's sacrifice,
which the tradition places at this point, in as inoffensive a manner as

possible. It is remarkable that E mentions a sacrificial offering of such comprehensive proportions. In the present form of E, nothing that is not ambiguous is said about the place of the action. For the place to which, according to 22.41 E, Balaam is led by Balak on the morning after his arrival is designated in a purely general way as 'a high place of Baal'* (in the text there stands actually the plural, 'high places of Baal', which might just be acceptable, but has probably arisen from an original singular by a fairly slight textual error). That *bāmōt baʿal* is to be understood as the proper name of a place is, in spite of Josh. 13.17, quite unlikely. For even if the text in Josh. 13.17 were reliable, and a place name 'Bamoth-Baal' were to be accepted, this place would, from that context, have to be located in a region which does not fit in the present context. The 'high place of Baal' was so situated that from it the Israelite border territory ('the nearest of the people') could be seen. This fact must have been important for Balak; for, according to a widespread conception, for a curse such as Balak wanted from Balaam to be effective, it was essential to be able to see the object that was to be cursed. At the 'high place of Baal' Balaam gave instructions (23.1). It is true that the sacrifice that was to be offered was to be a sacrifice by Balak (vv. 3aα, 6a); but at it, Balaam functioned as priest (in v. 2a, where the later addition clarifies the uncertainty as to the subject, originally probably Balaam was meant to be the subject, since according to v. 1 Balak had only to prepare the sacrifice; cf. also v. 4bβ) and ensured for it an orderly procedure. In particular he first of all had seven new altars built (the 'high place of Baal', as such, must have had an altar) which were not tainted by a cultic past (is perhaps the fact that *seven* new altars were built meant to be an overwhelming contrast to the fact that there was only one older 'Baal' altar?). The main thing is that Balaam is now seeking an encounter with God in order to receive instructions as to what he should say. This transpires in the vicinity of the offering that is taking place, but apart from it, on a 'bare height' where Balaam alone awaits and receives such an encounter on a higher position which is nearer heaven. He does, it is true, refer to the sacrifice in what he says to God (v. 4b); but it is surely E's intention to put a certain distance between Balaam's reception of revelation and Balak's sacrifice.

[23.7–10] Returning to Balak, Balaam reports what God has told

* The RSV takes it as a proper name. Noth, in his German version, translates it as 'a high place of Baal'. See the following sentence. Tr.

him in the first discourse (vv. 7–10). This discourse reveals, from beginning to end, complete rhythmic uniformity (3:3) and consistent parallelism. There even seems to be an intentional division into stanzas, in so far as three groups of 3:3 lines belong essentially together (vv. 7b–8 and 9–10a), with the second group giving the reason behind the first. From the point of view of content, this discourse is extremely closely related to the Balaam narrative; it is a brief summary of what is stated in detail in the narrative. The question of priority between discourse and narrative is, in this case, not easy to decide. It could certainly be that the discourse at one time achieved independent currency as a summary of the Balaam tradition; but it is more probable that it was composed for the narrative and originated with the narrative. The statements about Balaam's origin ('Aram'//'eastern mountains') consist, in accordance with poetic style, only in allusions. By 'eastern mountains' (the same expression, but with a different significance, in Deut. 33.15)* are meant the ranges of hills that traverse all the regions of the Syro-Arabian desert; the 'land of the Aramaeans' is to be located to the north-east of Palestine in central Syria and as far as the Euphrates. These details could include the Pethor (cf. above, p. 173) mentioned by J in 22.5a; it could, however, also be that in using them E is reporting a somewhat divergent tradition about Balaam's origin. Balak's aim and Balaam's inability to act contrary to the divine will are spoken of in the two 3:3 lines of vv. 7bβ, 8 in keeping with the sense of the narrative. Here the poetic language makes use of no fewer than three different but synonymous verbs for 'curse', 'Jacob' is found in parallelism as an equivalent expression for 'Israel', and the archaic word 'ēl ('God') is found with the same meaning as the divine name 'Yahweh', which is used even in E in the solemn mode of expression employed in the Balaam discourse. The sequence of thought from the first group of 3:3 lines to the second group (vv. 9, 10a), which is joined in explanatory fashion to the first, is that Balaam, who has received instructions not to curse Israel, realizes at the sight of Israel, whom he can see (at least partly) from his elevated position (cf. 22.41b), that this Israel is obviously not 'cursed' but 'blessed' (cf. 22.12b). In giving expression to this in his discourse (the whole section contains the first person 'I' of Balaam), he endorses this actual blessedness, and to this

---

* The expressions are identical in Hebrew (harⁱrē qedem). The difference in sense is clear from the translations of the two passages in the RSV, 'eastern mountains' here and 'ancient mountains' in Deut. 33.15. Tr.

extent he, too, 'blesses' Israel. It is said of Israel that it occupies a special place among the nations (v. 9b) without it being indicated wherein this special place lies or how it is evident. What *is* evident is that Israel is blessed with a population that is quite impossible to count (v. 10a). It was this very fact that had filled the Moabites with alarm (22.3a, 4a, 5bβ) and had occasioned the appeal to Balaam for help; Balaam can only corroborate it and confirm it as the effect of divine blessing. The concluding lines in v. 10b are difficult to appraise. In the context they can mean only that the blessing which rests upon Israel is so great that the speaker can wish for himself nothing better than a fate similar to that of Israel (the comparison at the end of v. 10bβ can, as the text now stands, refer only to 'Jacob/Israel'). In itself this could be a thoroughly suitable conclusion, but in its present form it is quite unusual. The speaker can, it is true, speak of his own 'death' and 'end'; but a comparison with Israel in this respect is completely out of place. Nor is the difficulty exactly removed by re-garding these concluding lines as a later addition, a theory that is supported by the fact that they fall outside the framework of the two groups of 3:3 lines (vv. 7b, 8 and 9, 10a) and, with their personal reference, appear strange in the context of the discourse. However, it is more likely that a later hand has expanded the discourse by the addition of these unsuitable concluding lines than that the original discourse contained this strange coda.

[23.11–17] Balak is angered, from his point of view with justifica-tion, at this discourse of Balaam's (v. 11). Balaam, however, can reply to him (v. 12) that he is dependent on the will of God, a fact which he has made quite plain from the very beginning (the expres-sion used in v. 12b has already appeared literally in 22.38bE; cf. also 23.5aE). Balak makes a renewed attempt to achieve his goal of getting Balaam to curse Israel by taking him to 'another place', the reason for this being that from there Balaam will be able to see Israel (v. 13aα). Now already, on the occasion of his first discourse, Balaam had been set on a place (22.41b) from which he had been able to see at least 'the nearest of the people'. This time he is to see more of Israel, he is to see all of Israel (properly). In his first discourse Balaam had already referred to the fact that he regarded 'Israel/Jacob' as a nation that had been blessed (vv. 9, 10a). According to the narrator, it was obviously Balak's opinion that Balaam had not yet seen enough of Israel and that, if he could only see them properly, he would perhaps utter a curse instead of a blessing. Since, with regard to the words of blessing of the first discourse, a defective visual connection had existed between Balaam and Israel, this curse would then surpass in effect the blessing that had already been pronounced. A later hand has added the intervening note, which is ill suited to the context, that, from this 'other place', too, Balaam could see only the 'nearest' of Israel and not the whole of them; he was certainly of the opinion that Israel was much too numerous to be surveyed in one glance. However, with regard to this 'other place', considered by Balak as more favourable for what he wanted, a detail is given by which the scene of the Balaam story is, at least to a certain extent, made definite for the first time. Balak took Balaam 'to the field of the spies at the top of Pisgah' (v. 14a).* Nothing very definite can be deduced from 'field of spies' (the expression occurs only here in the Old Testament); what is meant is obviously a place with an extensive view. The name 'Pisgah' is, however, of some significance. Unfortunately, the places where this name occurs in the Old Testament do not provide any very exact information. It is not even clear whether this name designates a single mountain or a more or less precisely delimited mountainous region. This much, however, is clear from Deut. 3.27 (cf. 34.1) and Josh. 13.20, namely that Pisgah is to be located in the mountains to the east of the lower Jordan valley or of the northern end of the Dead Sea. From this it follows that the Balaam story presupposes a situation in which Moabite power stretched so far to the north of the Arnon that the 'Moabite king' Balak could exercise power in the region designated by the name Pisgah and that in this district there existed a confrontation between Israelites and Moabites. At this 'other place' the same preparations are made, according to vv. 14b–17, as were made on the 'high place of Baal' (cf. vv. 1–6). The phraseology is repeated almost word for word, except that it is abbreviated slightly (v. 17b is a later addition). Balaam receives a further revelation from God and he transmits the content of it in the second discourse.

[23.18–24] The second Balaam discourse (vv. 18–24) is much less self-contained and much less of a unity than the first. It is true that we find here, too, the 3:3 rhythm and the stylistic medium of parallelism (in a few places where the symmetry of form is not quite perfect, the question arises as to whether the text is intact, but there are no textual

---

* RSV 'field of Zophim'. Hebrew *ṣōpīm*, a plural Qal participle, means 'spies', and Noth translates it thus in the text. RSV retains a transliteration as a proper name. Tr.

corruptions worthy of mention). On the other hand, there is no recognizable division into stanzas. From the point of view of content, various themes are juxtaposed with no relation between them. In this discourse the question arises not only of its relationship to the Balaam narrative, but also of its connection with the third discourse in 24.3–9J. In the first four 3:3 lines which open the discourse (vv. 18b–20) reference is made to the narrative situation described in vv. 11–17. On this basis it should probably be true of this discourse, too, that it has been composed for the narrative and has originated along with the narrative. It is then easy to refer v. 23 also to the narrative. The question of the relationship to the third discourse is particularly complicated. V. 22 is identical word for word with 24.8, and v. 24—with only partial verbal agreement—provides the same imagery as 24.9a. If, in the first case, one could perhaps reckon with secondary borrowing from 24.8, the facts prohibit such a hypothesis in the second case. Then there is the question of priority between the second and the third discourse. The decision is probably to be made in favour of the third; for in 24.8, 9a the comparisons with wild beasts are found next to each other, whereas in 23.22–4 they are separated by a reference to the narrative situation. From all this there arises the hypothesis that the discourse in 23.18–24 has been composed for the Balaam narrative (E), use having been made of some material from other current 'Balaam discourses' that were ready to hand.

Balaam, who in this discourse, too, speaks in the first person (v. 20), turns to address Balak (v. 18b) to indicate to him that God is not as unreliable and as fickle as a man and that, on the contrary, his word remains unalterable (v. 19). These words are certainly to be understood as a reproof to Balak, who, according to v. 13b, entertained the possibility that, after the blessing of vv. 7–10, Balaam would still pronounce the desired curse. In v. 20 Balaam draws for himself the consequence of God's unchangeableness, namely that after he has already been commissioned to bless Israel he cannot retract that blessing. There follows, then, in vv. 21–22, a word of blessing for Israel that gives expression once again to Israel's state of blessedness and at the same time strengthens that state by means of Balaam's word of 'power'. The negative affirmation in v. 21a is followed by what is both the reason for it and the continuation of it, namely the statement in v. 21b about Israel's relationship with Yahweh as 'their God'. The 'shout of a king', i.e. the loud, undisciplined calling and shouting that greets the appearance or the presence of a king, certainly refers, in the context, to Yahweh's kingship and not to the institution of a human kingdom. This relationship of Israel's with Yahweh is, in a sentence that is identical with 24.8, based on the fact of the exodus from Egypt (v. 22a), in a circumstantial clause with the participial predicate that is characteristic of hymnic style, and with the archaic word '$\bar{e}l$ = 'God' as subject. In v. 22b the predicate is ambiguous; are the horns of the wild ox attributed to 'God' or to 'Jacob/Israel'? The former alternative (probably preferable on the basis of the present text, although the latter should probably be emended on the basis of 24.8a) leads to a statement which reminds one of the fact that in the ancient east, and especially in Mesopotamia, ox horns are known as symbols of divine power and of divinity in general. Since, however, vv. 21ff. are dealing with Israel and her state of blessedness, the phrase in v. 22b is surely referring to Israel in the sense that she, through her God, is endowed with enormous power. If, in v. 23a, Israel is designated as immune to magic and divination, and if this fact is understood as the reason ('for') for the recognition of Israel's power, then this is probably meant to be a reference to the fact that Balak's machinations have proved ineffectual with regard to Israel. The idea contained in v. 23b, which is expressed in unrhythmic form, has been added secondarily. The discourse concludes in v. 24 with a reference to Israel's terrifying strength depicted in a comparatively well-developed image of a lion (cf. 24.9a).

[23.25–26] Balak's reaction to Balaam's second discourse (v. 25) is that he will not permit Balaam to say anything more. It has now become clear to him that he cannot expect Balaam to curse Israel. He wants to hear no more words of blessing on Israel's behalf. Therefore Balaam is to say nothing more. This brings E's version of the Balaam story to an end. Balaam has the last word (v. 26); he indicates once again (cf. v. 12) that he can obey only God. The note of finality in vv. 25–26 indicates that in what follows we are no longer dealing with E. In fact, what we then have in ch. 24 is the continuation of J's narrative.

[23.27–30] What intervenes in 23.27–30 is essentially editorial and serves as the link between the two versions of the narrative. Here the editor has simply repeated 23.13–14 (cf. 23.1–2); Balaam is taken once again to 'another place' and another attempt is to be made at securing a curse (v. 28), in which connection we encounter once more the preparations (vv. 29, 30). The only new element in this whole section is the indication of locality in v. 28; this verse is obviously not editorial. It comes, rather, from J and links up quite easily with 22.39-40, i.e. with the last appearance of the J-version. It was worked into the editorial section 23.27-30 because of its relevance. After the sacrifice at Kiriath-huzoth (22.39-40) Balak took Balaam 'to the top of Peor' and there awaited the cursing of Israel that he wanted. This provides an indication of locality in J, too (cf. 23.14aE), which it is not possible to pinpoint exactly, but which fixes the scene of the action in a quite definite area. Peor is the name of a mountain which was doubtless the abode of 'Baal of Peor' (25.3, 5) and which certainly also had a sanctuary to that god. There was also a place 'Beth-peor' which must have lain in the vicinity of this mountain (Josh. 13.20 et al.). As is especially clear from Num. 25.1-3, the abode of 'Baal of Peor' is to be sought on the east bank of the lower Jordan valley. The mountain must therefore have formed part of the mountain range that lay there east of Jordan (cf. above, p. 185, on 23.14a). Unfortunately, it is not possible to locate exactly either the mountain or the place. Concerning the top of Peor it is further noted in this verse that it 'overlooked the desert'. In this connection it is not the usual word for 'desert' which is used (we find that word at the end of 24.1), but a special term ($j^e\check{s}\bar{\imath}m\bar{o}n$) which was apparently used to designate particular desert regions, thus here a part of the desert-like lower Jordan valley. The choice of this place was once again determined by the idea that Balaam should see the Israel that was to be cursed (cf. 22.41b; 23.13a), which according to 24.2 was, in fact, the case.

[24.1-2] We are not told how Balaam, after he had taken up this position, knew that Yahweh wanted Israel to be blessed (24.1aα). At any rate, according to J, he did not need first of all to seek a particular direction from his God (it is otherwise the case in 23.3-5, 15, 16E, to which reference is made in the editorial remark in 24.1aβ with the obviously derogatory statement that in those cases it had been a question of 'omens'). He looked, rather, immediately towards the 'wilderness' (cf. 23.28b) and saw Israel 'dwelling'* there. In this expression 'dwelling' there emerges the tension in the situation presupposed by the Balaam story. For the expression conjures up the picture of an Israel firmly settled in the land, while on the other hand an Israel that could be seen 'tribe by tribe' is conceivable only at a time before the conquest or at the beginning of the conquest. When

* Noth's translation of Hebrew $\check{s}\bar{o}k\bar{e}n$ is a more accurate one than RSV's 'encamping' which disguises the 'tension' which Noth is going on to discuss. Tr.

Balaam saw the object of the words he was to utter he was seized by
'the spirit of God'. This is a reference to the opening of the two discourses which follow and in which Balaam is represented as an
ecstatic prophet who utters his words under the direct influence of
inspiration. Immediately Balaam begins his discourse.

[24.3–9] The first discourse in J (in the combined narrative it is
the third discourse) in 24.3b–9 is clearly differentiated in type, as is
the next one in 24.15b–19, from the discourse of ch. 23. From the
point of view of form, it is true, the 3:3 rhythm is basic to these discourses, too (in a few places the text and the rhythm have become
subsequently corrupt), and parallelism is in evidence throughout.
Both discourses have an identical introduction of three 3:3 lines. In
the main body of the discourses which follows on this introduction,
however, it is not possible to determine any definite division. From
the point of view of content, however, the two discourse of ch. 24 reveal a particular character. They have no connection at all with the
present form of the Balaam narrative. In the introduction Balaam is
spoken of in both cases as if nothing were known about him. Thus
Balaam is spoken of in the third person, although, according to the
surrounding narrative, he himself is the speaker. In each case the
discourse proper follows this introduction and in it Balaam speaks in
the first person. In this discourse the visionary element, or at any
rate the metaphorical one, is very prominent. The content of it is
Israel's state of blessedness. It is probable that the two discourses of
ch. 24 are older than the present Balaam narrative and that they
originally existed independently of it and were handed down presumably orally as blessings pronounced over Israel by a seer by the
name of Balaam, to whose words an effective 'power' was attributed,
and concerning whose origin and appearance there was certainly
much to relate, namely more or less what was subsequently crystal-
lized in the present Balaam narrative.

[24.3–4] The introduction common to both discourses, vv. 3b–4 =
vv. 15b–16 (a subsequent gap in the text of v. 4 is to be filled from the
better-preserved text of v. 16),* introduces Balaam by name along
with the name of his father and in connection with the word 'oracle'
(ne'um), which in the Old Testament appears very frequently with
the genitive of the divine name, especially in the formulae which
appear in the middle of or at the end of prophetic oracles, but which

* This Noth does in his translation, inserting after the word 'God' in v. 4aα,
the words 'and knows the knowledge of the Most High' from v. 16aβ. Tr.

has the genitive of a human name, apart from the present text, only in II Sam. 23.1 and Prov. 30.1. Balaam is then characterized as a 'man whose eye is opened'. Unfortunately the word translated here as 'opened' occurs only here, and its meaning is uncertain. If the translation 'opened' is the correct one, then the thought is that of a visionary experience and is more or less similar to that expressed at the end of the introduction (v. 4bβ = v. 16bβ); there Balaam is depicted as 'falling down', i.e. in an ecstatic condition, robbed of the normal control of his own body, and 'having his eyes uncovered', i.e. seeing with the inner eye what is hidden from normal sight. All the predicates attributed to Balaam in v. 4 = v. 16, mostly participial, but in v. 4ba = v. 16ba in a subordinate clause, have to do with the secret experiences of Balaam the ecstatic. It is a question of a 'hearing', a 'knowing' and a 'seeing' of divine origin. In this respect use is made of archaic designations for God, 'ēl ('God'), 'elyōn ('Most High') and šadday (the basic meaning of this word is uncertain; since the Septuagint, the expedient 'Almighty' has been used as a translation). The genitives in which these designations of God are expressed are surely all to be understood as subjective genitives. At any rate, this is the case with the 'words of 'ēl', and, on this assumption, we must understand the 'knowledge' which 'elyōn gives and the 'vision' which šadday provides. Balaam was thus the recipient of divine revelation, both auditory and visionary. What Balaam became aware of in this way he declares in his own words following on the introduction, predominantly in perceptual images which appear to his inner eye.

[24.5–9] In vv. 5–7a Israel appears as if richly endowed with gifts of nature. An admirable apostrophe of the 'tents'//'encampments' of 'Jacob/Israel' in v. 5 introduces the description (the use of 'tent' is part of poetic language and does not mean that the Israelite settlement is not complete). The comparisons in v. 6 speak for themselves. Both rhythm and subject-matter suggest that in v. 6aa there is a gap in the text; in its present form the comparison is unsuitable, one would expect perhaps 'like plants in valleys'. It can no longer be said with any certainty what is meant by ''āhāl-trees',* but they must at any rate be vast, splendid trees to be set beside the famous cedars. That

* Koehler (Lexicon in Veteris Testamenti Libros) suggests that the form 'ᵃhālīm in Prov. 7.17 is equivalent to the 'ᵃhālōt of Ps. 45.9 and S. of S. 4.14 and means 'aloewood'. He lists the present word 'ᵃhālīm separately and suggests 'tufts' as a translation. The RSV 'aloes' here suggests that this is the same form as in Prov. 7.17. Noth is implicitly denying this here, but is unable to offer any precise translation. Tr.

such imposing trees had been planted by Yahweh himself Ps. 104.16 also dares to say (there of the 'cedars of Lebanon'). V. 7 marks the transition from the address to Israel to the third person address. The overflowing of the buckets is a symbol for the wealth of water in wells in the ground and in cisterns from which one draws water. This wealth of water depends on the abundance of rain which also contributes to successful sowing in the fields (v. 7aβ). V. 7b refers, without the use of metaphor, to Israel's political supremacy, and this provides an immediate transition to new subject-matter. There is a king(dom) in Israel. The name Agag can scarcely refer to anyone other than 'Agag the king of the Amalekites' known from the Saul story (I Sam. 15.8ff.). On this account, this discourse must be dated in the time of Saul; for from the period immediately following Saul even more impressive proofs of Israel's political supremacy could have been adduced. It is remarkable that the only action of Saul's that receives mention is his victory over the Amalekites and that alone (with regard to this latter point one will, of course, require to be cautious, since in the second half of the 3:3 unit of v. 7b a word has fallen out of the text, to be precise the expression corresponding to *mē'ªgag* = 'than Agag'). The reason for this could be that the narrative viewpoint of the Balaam discourses is that of southern Palestine (including the southern transjordanian territory; cf. vv. 17bβ, 18). The victory over the Amalekites is a result of the divine blessing of Israel. The relationship of Israel to her God goes back to the exodus from Egypt and this relationship gives Israel great power (v. 8a; cf. above, p. 187, on 23.22). As early as v. 8b the image of the wild ox with its horns passes imperceptibly into the image of a lion swallowing its prey and breaking its bones; v. 9a makes specific mention of the lion, couched ready to spring out on its prey, and not to be provoked. The last two words of v. 8 fall outwith the rhythmic scheme and are scarcely suitable as regards their subject-matter; a later hand has here added the remark: 'He (the lion) shatters his (the hunter's) arrows.' Since we are to think of the period of Saul, the remark about eating up the enemy nations goes beyond the bounds of historical reality. In an emphatic concluding sentence (v. 9b), which stands out on account of its 2:2 rhythm, Israel, addressed once more as at the beginning (v. 5), is regarded as a general mediator of blessing and curse (cf. on this Gen. 12.3a) in so far as one's position with regard to this Israel decides one's own fate.

[24.10–14] Balak is naturally angry at this blessing (the 'striking together of the hands' is here a gesture of the emotion of anger) and he reproaches Balaam as in 23.11 E (the last three words in v. 10 are a product of the editorial working together of the two versions of the narrative). In contrast to what transpires in E, Balak does not even make another attempt with Balaam, but, with a curt command, immediately sends him home (v. 11a), not without reminding him of the promised honorarium (cf. 22.17a) of which Yahweh has now deprived him (v. 11b). For his part, Balaam can only repeat the words with which he replied to the offer of the 'honorarium' made by Balak's second deputation (22.18J), and this he does almost verbatim in vv. 12–13 (cf. also 22.35aβJ). In the act of complying with Balak's dismissal of him and returning home, Balaam does not lose the opportunity of uttering, unbidden, yet another discourse before leaving his present position. In this way J includes the final discourse (the second in J and the fourth in the whole series of discourses) within the framework of the narrative. As a farewell present Balak is to receive a piece of advice as to how 'this people' (Israel) will deal with Balak's people in the future. The expression be'aḥᵃrît hayyāmîm can mean 'in time to come', 'at a later time', and in this sense would be quite suitable in the present context. The expression can, however, also have the pregnant sense of 'end time' (the 'eschaton'); in that case the proclamation that follows in vv. 15–17 would be interpreted 'messianically', and this would have to be regarded as a secondary misinterpretation, since the content of the original discourse had only a future reference within history.

[24.15–19] The discourse itself begins in vv. 15b–16 with an introduction identical to that of the preceding discourse in vv. 3b–4 (cf. above, pp. 189f.). There follows in v. 17abα the description of a 'vision'; the seer sees a vague future figure referred to only mysteriously with the third person pronoun (v. 17a). This figure is then (v. 17bα) compared to a rising star, a comparison which refers only in general terms to the splendour of this apparition. More informative is the further comparison to a 'sceptre', for this must mean that symbol of sovereign might known to the ancient east. It is highly probable that what is conceived of here is the future glory of King David and that it is the historical emergence of David that forms the background of this discourse. Leaving aside the complicated structure of Davidic kingship, David is depicted as a king emerging from 'Jacob/Israel'. In accordance with the proclamation of v. 14b, the discourse continues in vv. 17b–18 with the prediction of the conquest and subjection of Moab and Edom by David, facts which are explained as having been already envisaged in the divine plan and as therefore willed by Yahweh. The fact that of all David's deeds account is taken only of Israel's south-easterly neighbours indicates once again the restricted horizon of the Balaam discourses which have been handed down in the circle of those Israelites who lived in the *belqa* (cf. above, p. 172). The phraseology of v. 17bβ goes back to the use of the club as a weapon. The designation of the Moabites as the 'sons of Seth'* is unique. The connection of this Seth with the Seth who, according to Gen. 4.25f., was born as a 'substitute' for Abel, who was murdered by Cain, is, in view of the territory occupied by Cain's descendants ('Kenites'), not unlikely, but it can no longer be adequately explained. In v. 18b the 'occupation' of Edom is simply noted. The name Seir, here, designates the mountainous region to the south of the modern *wādi el-ḥesa* in which the Edomites dwelt. In vv. 18b–19 the discourse concludes with a general reference to the development of Israelite power. The text of v. 19 has been transmitted so defectively that its original wording can no longer be determined.†

[24.20–24] In vv. 20–24 several additional sayings attributed to Balaam are added by way of an appendix. These can no longer be attributed to either of the versions of the original Balaam story. The first two, which contain threatening words against the Amalekites (v. 20) and the Kenites (vv. 21–22), still remain within the field of vision of the Balaam tradition (cf. p. 191 on 24.7b and above on 24.17b–18), for the Amalekites were a confederacy of nomadic tribes on the southern edge of Palestine and the Kenites dwelt in the south-eastern part of the Judaean hill-country. The proclamation of destruction in the saying about the Amalekites (v. 20), in which the antithesis between 'beginning' and 'end' is remarkably forced and lacking in relevance, is so vague that nothing more can be said as to its origin or the occasion of it. In the saying about the Kenites (vv. 21–22), the mention of Asshur is striking; this saying can scarcely have originated in the period before the emergence of neo-Assyrian power (middle of the eighth or possibly the ninth century B.C.). Behind the unusual comparison of the Kenites to birds

---

* The identity of this name with the name 'Seth' in Gen. 4.25 *et al.* has, for some reason, been obscured in the RSV. Tr.

† Noth leaves v. 19 virtually untranslated. RSV renders MT more or less as it stands. Tr.

of prey having their nests in the rocks (v. 21b) there lies a play on words (*qayin* = Cain and *qēn* = nest). The particular occasion of this saying, too, is unknown. The last saying (vv. 23–24) is to be dated in an even later period. The text of it is obviously corrupt and the original wording can be reconstructed only hypothetically. The mention of 'Kittim' certainly belongs to the original form of the text. This name is derived from the name of the town of Kition in Cyprus and originally designates the inhabitants of that town and then, presumably, Cypriots in general. In the Old Testament it is in the long run generally used for those living near the (eastern) Mediterranean and for powers which came from that area, thus for the Macedonians of Alexander the Great and his Diadochs, and finally for the Romans (cf. Dan. 11.30). According to the present saying, there was a threat from that direction, from across the sea ('ships' of war from 'Kittim' also in Dan. 11.30), of disaster and destruction; it must therefore scarcely be earlier than the time of Alexander the Great. It is probably even later, for 'Asshur' presumably means, as it does in the language of the later period, the Seleucid empire. The text does not allow of anything more exact being said. Absolutely nothing positive can be said as to what the name 'Eber' (originally an eponym of 'Hebrews') means in this context. From the point of view of subject-matter this last saying has nothing whatsoever to do with the Balaam story. In v. 24b the prior existence of v. 20bβ is presumed.

8. APOSTASY TO MOABITE IDOL-WORSHIP: 25.1–18

25 ¹While Israel dwelt in Shittim the people began to play the harlot with the daughters of Moab. ²These invited the people to the sacrifices of their gods, and the people ate, and bowed down to their gods. ³So Israel yoked himself to Baal of Peor. And the anger of the LORD was kindled against Israel; ⁴and the LORD said to Moses, 'Take all the chiefs of the people, and hang them in the sun before the LORD, that the fierce anger of the LORD may turn away from Israel.' ⁵And Moses said to the judges of Israel, 'Every one of you slay his men who have yoked themselves to Baal of Peor.'

6 And behold, one of the people of Israel came and brought a Midianite woman to his family, in the sight of Moses and in the sight of the whole congregation of the people of Israel, while they were weeping at the door of the tent of meeting. ⁷When Phinehas the son of Eleazar, son of Aaron the priest, saw it, he rose and left the congregation, and took a spear in his hand ⁸and went after the man of Israel into the inner room, and pierced both of them, the man of Israel and the woman [,through her body]. Thus the plague was stayed from the

people of Israel. ⁹Nevertheless those that died by the plague were twenty-four thousand.

10 And the LORD said to Moses, ¹¹'Phinehas the son of Eleazar, son of Aaron the priest, has turned back my wrath from the people of Israel, in that he was jealous with my jealousy among them, so that I did not consume the people of Israel in my jealousy. ¹²Therefore say, "Behold, I give to him my covenant of peace; ¹³and it shall be to him, and to his descendants after him, the covenant of a perpetual priesthood, because he was jealous for his God, and made atonement for the people of Israel." '

14 The name of the slain man of Israel, who was slain with the Midianite woman, was Zimri the son of Salu, head of a fathers' house belonging to the Simeonites. ¹⁵And the name of the Midianite woman who was slain was Cozbi the daughter of Zur, who was the head of the people of a fathers' house in Midian.

16 And the LORD said to Moses, ¹⁷'Harass the Midianites, and smite them; ¹⁸for they have harassed you with their wiles, with which they beguiled you in the matter of Peor, and in the matter of Cozbi, the daughter of the prince of Midian, their sister, who was slain on the day of the plague on account of Peor.'

This chapter contains elements of tradition, of varied content and varied age, in a juxtaposition which is difficult to disentangle and in a presentation which is remarkably inconsequential and fragmentary. The point of departure is formed by the narrative of the Israelite apostasy to the cult of their Moabite neighbours and the punishment of that apostasy (vv. 1–5). This narrative must go back to an early period and form part of the old Pentateuchal narrative-material. However, even this brief narrative is not harmonious. To begin with the Moabite god is not named (v. 2), and then, without any warning, the name 'Baal of Peor' appears (vv. 3, 5) in the context of a quite unusual figure of speech. Concerning the punishment of the apostasy there are, in vv. 4 and 5, two instructions which are not exactly doublets but which stand side by side and strangely unconnected. There is, however, a lack of any convincing indications which would enable us to divide the narrative into various 'sources'. One might attribute this section to J, but one must also make the point that it is scarcely self-contained. On the other hand, there is the appearance of Aaron's grandson Phinehas in vv. 6ff., a fact which indicates a late period in which there was an 'Aaronite' high-priesthood with an 'Aaronite' succession. However, this is clearly not part of the P-narrative. The statements of vv. 6ff. are not independent, but presuppose the existence of vv. 1–5. On the other hand, however, these statements are not always in accordance with that section, but also refer to other narrative details which have not so far been given. Besides late phraseology, vv. 6–8 contain material that is so unusual that the question arises as to whether they, too, do not contain elements of older traditions, elements which cannot rightly be delimited. The understanding of the whole is made more difficult by the occurrence of many very unusual, even unique words and expressions whose exact meaning and field of reference can only be guessed. One must apply oneself to the exposition of the individual parts of the text and thus endeavour to ascertain its meaning.

[25.1–5] According to v. 1a, the scene of the story was the east bank of the lower Jordan valley. Shittim (also in Josh. 2.1; 3.1; Micah 6.5; Num. 33.49 has the fuller form Abel-shittim) is probably to be located at *tell el-ḥammām*, which lies at the point where the *wādi kefrein* emerges into the Jordan valley. As in the Balaam story, the presupposition is that in this region the Moabites were neighbours to the Israelites. With regard to the historical and geographical situation, a connection with the preceding Balaam story (or the J-version of it) is therefore natural, and this indication of locality in v. 1a can be regarded as a basic part of J. In this respect, the transition from words of blessing pronounced over Israel in the name of Yahweh to Israelite apostasy to the idol-worship of the Moabites, whose king had wanted to have Israel cursed, is all the more jarring. We are dealing with two independent traditions, located, it is true, in the same region and situation, but quite different as to content. The Israelites entered into adulterous relationships with Moabite women (v. 1b). These relationships had obviously no cultic background to them—at any rate, there is no mention of this—but they did have cultic consequences. According to v. 2, the Israelites accepted an invitation to Moabite sacrificial feasts which, as was usual at sacrifices, were linked with sacrificial meals and perhaps—this could well be implied—with sexual rites or excesses. In doing so, the Israelites, for all practical purposes, indulged in the worship of the Moabite 'god' (the text will also allow a translation in the plural: of the Moabite 'gods'). Only in v. 3a for the first time have these proceedings been subsequently related to a specific local cult, the cult of Baal of Peor who had his abode on Mount Peor (cf. above, p. 188). This fixing of the whole story in a particular place is presumably part of the original form of the narrative in spite of the fact that the name Baal of Peor is mentioned only after the event. There must surely be something specific in the unique expression (otherwise only in

Ps. 106.28, which is dependent on the present passage) 'to yoke oneself to' (Hebrew *ṣmd* is certainly related to *ṣemed* 'yoke'). What, however, yoking oneself to a god is actually supposed to mean, to what extent and in what sense this expression is to be understood figuratively or not, can no longer be ascertained. Yahweh's anger at the apostasy (v. 3b) leads first to a divine command to Moses to punish 'all the chiefs of the people', of whom it is not said whether they themselves participated in the apostasy or only neglected their duty of vigilance (v. 4). The type of punishment commanded is not clear, but is at any rate unusual; there is a companion piece to it in II Sam. 21.6, 9. The meaning of the verb, the Hiph. of *yqʿ*, cannot be determined with any certainty. Very often the idea of 'stocks' has been suggested. In Gen. 32.25 (*Hebr.* v. 26) we find the Qal of *yqʿ* apparently in the sense of 'be put of joint'.* One has the impression of a cruel method of putting to death which, however, probably had behind it a particular significance which is unknown to us. This putting to death happens 'for Yahweh' (so, too, in II Sam. 21.6 in contrast to II Sam. 21.9, which has 'before Yahweh') † and, in addition, 'in face of the sun', an expression which must surely be saying something more than simply that the punishment was to be carried out in (broad) daylight;‡ but in this case, too, the particular significance of the action remains obscure. As in II Sam. 21, the act is intended to effect a propitiation of Yahweh, as is expressly stated in v. 4b (the divine name in the midst of direct speech of God's is remarkable). The divine command to Moses (v. 4), the carrying out of which is not specifically noted, is followed in v. 5 by an additional measure of Moses' which involves not the 'chiefs' but those who actually became guilty through contact with Baal of Peor. Moses gives his order for putting to death to the 'judges of Israel', who are presumed to be present in force and who each had 'his men', i.e. obviously specific groups within Israel for which they were responsible (for the subject-matter, but not for the phraseology, one might compare Ex. 18.13–27E). Since v. 5 follows v. 4 without any preparation, the possibility

* This is the sense which Noth gives to the verb in his translation of the Hebrew text: 'and put their limbs out of joint for Yahweh in face of the sun'. The exegesis of the remainder of the verse is of this rendering of the Hebrew, which differs somewhat from that of the RSV. Tr.

† RSV makes no distinction between the two phrases, which are, however, distinct in Hebrew (*laʾadōnāy* and *lipenē ʾadōnāy*), and translates all three occurrences as 'before the LORD'. Tr.

‡ The RSV translation 'in the sun' would seem to suggest that this is, in fact, all that the phrase means. Tr.

has to be considered that v. 5 is an addition by a later writer who wanted to make sure that those who were actually guilty were punished and therefore added, supplementary to the divine command of v. 4, which has a note of finality about it, an additional action on the part of Moses.

[25.6–9] The Phinehas episode in vv. 6ff. links up with what precedes, but only in a loose way, with the result that a certain amount has to be read between the lines in what precedes. The situation that is presupposed is that 'Moses and the whole congregation of the people of Israel' (an expression typical of P) are assembled, weeping, in front of the tent of meeting (v. 6b). What is obviously intended, although it is not stated, is that the apostasy and its punishment, referred to in vv. 1–5, were the cause of this cultic lament. Advantage of this situation is taken by an Israelite 'man' for his nefarious action. In addition, there is suddenly mention of a (divine) 'plague' that has come upon the Israelites (vv. 8–9). This must refer to the punishment of vv. 4–5. However, the word 'plague' usually means an affliction brought about directly by God, e.g. a pestilence (II Sam. 24.21, 25 et al.), not, on the other hand, the execution of a divine judgment carried out by men. In v. 6a the 'Midianite woman' suddenly appears as if she were a familiar figure; probably it is supposed that she was one of the Moabite women of v. 1b. On this juxtaposition of Moabites and Midianites cf. the secondary expressions in 22.4, 7. According to the text of v. 6a, which is certainly unusual and of questionable authenticity, a certain Israelite, who is not described in any more detail, is said to have brought the Midianite woman presumably to his family. According to v. 8a, the pair then found themselves in a *qubbā* (a word of unknown meaning, occurring only here, translated, for wanted of anything better, by 'inner room', but probably describing something like 'wedding room'). What exactly was nefarious about the Israelite's action is not specifically stated; it can be deduced only from the connection with vv. 1–5. According to this, intercourse with a Midianite woman also meant subjection to her god or gods with, in addition, defiant disregard of the cultic lament that was actually taking place (v. 6b) and of a decree of abstinence which was probably in operation during this time. Phinehas's action (vv. 7–8a), not exactly a heroic deed but laudable as a reaction on the spur of the moment, made 'atonement' for Israel (so v. 13bβ), not only with regard to the action of the individual Israelite that had just taken place, but also with regard to

the apostasy of the 'people' narrated in vv. 1ff., so that the 'plague',
inflicted on account of the latter, which had already accounted for
numerous deaths (v. 9), could now be removed by God (v. 8b).

[25.10–18] The information about the rewarding of Phinehas by
the conferring of priestly office (very probably what is meant is the
office of high priest) on him and his descendants (vv. 10–13) provides the original point of the whole Phinehas episode and is perhaps
intended to legitimatize the descendants of Phinehas, in the face of
any possible opposition, as the true heirs to 'Aaronite' privileges. The
subsequent mention of the name of the 'Israelite' and the 'Midianite
woman' (vv. 14–15) is a later addition. It defames, for no apparent
reason, an otherwise unknown Israelite clan as well as a Midianite
tribe (cf. 31.8). The final section (vv. 16–18), in contrast to vv. 1–3a,
makes the Midianites responsible for Israel's apostasy to Baal of Peor
and leads on to ch. 31. The section is very awkwardly phrased and,
in v. 18b, presupposes the additional section, vv. 14–15; it is a late
element in the redaction of the Pentateuch.

9. ANOTHER CENSUS: 26.1–65

26 ¹After the plague the LORD said to Moses and to Eleazar the son
of Aaron, the priest, ²'Take a census of all the congregation of the
people of Israel, from twenty years old and upward, by their fathers'
houses, all in Israel who are able to go forth to war.' ³And Moses and
Eleazar the priest numbered* them in the plains of Moab by the Jordan
at Jericho, ⁴from twenty years old and upward, as the LORD commanded
Moses.

The people of Israel who came forth out of the land of Egypt, were:
5 [Reuben, the first-born of Israel;] the sons of Reuben: of Hanoch,
the family of the Hanochites; of Pallu, the family of the Palluites; ⁶of
Hezron, the family of the Hezronites; of Carmi, the family of the
Carmites. ⁷These are the families of the Reubenites; and their number
was forty-three thousand seven hundred and thirty. [⁸And the sons of
Pallu: Eliab.⁹The sons of Eliab: [Nemuel,] Dathan, and Abiram.
These are the Dathan and Abiram, chosen from the congregation, who
contended against Moses and Aaron in the company of Korah, when
they contended against the LORD, ¹⁰and the earth opened its mouth and
swallowed them up together with Korah, when that company died,
when the fire devoured two hundred and fifty men; and they became a
warning. ¹¹Notwithstanding, the sons of Korah did not die.]
12 The sons of Simeon [according to their families]: of Nemuel, the

*Reading *wayyipqōd* ('numbered') in place of *wayᵉdabbēr* ('spoke') and deleting
lē'mōr ('saying') at the end of the verse—cf. BH. MT is obviously defective and
RSV has to insert 'Take a census of the people' at the beginning of v. 4 in order to
make sense of the MT of v. 3 as it stands. Noth emends v. 3 as above. Tr.

family of the Nemuelites; of Jamin, the family of the Jaminites; of Jachin, the family of the Jachinites; ¹³of Zerah, the family of the Zerahites; of Shaul, the family of the Shaulites. ¹⁴These are the families of the Simeonites according to their number*, twenty-two thousand two hundred.

15 The sons of Gad [according to their families]: of Zephon, the family of the Zephonites; of Haggi, the family of the Haggites; of Shuni, the family of the Shunites; ¹⁶of Ozni, the family of the Oznites; of Eri, the family of the Erites; ¹⁷of Arod, the family of the Arodites; of Areli, the family of the Arelites. ¹⁸These are the families of the sons of Gad according to their number, forty thousand five hundred.

19 [The sons of Judah were Er and Onan; and Er and Onan died in the land of Canaan. ²⁰And] the sons of Judah [according to their families were]: of Shelah, the family of the Shelanites; of Perez, the family of the Perezites; of Zerah, the family of the Zerahites. ²¹[And the sons of Perez were:] of Hezron, the family of the Hezronites; of Hamul, the family of the Hamulites. ²²These are the families of Judah according to their number, seventy-six thousand five hundred.

23 The sons of Issachar [according to their families]: of Tola, the family of the Tolaites; of Puvah, the family of the Punites; ²⁴of Jashub, the family of the Jashubites; of Shimron, the family of the Shimronites. ²⁵These are the families of Issachar according to their number, sixty-four thousand three hundred.

26 The sons of Zebulun [according to their families]: of Sered, the family of the Seredites; of Elon, the family of the Elonites; of Jahleel, the family of the Jahleelites. ²⁷These are the families of the Zebulunites according to their number, sixty thousand five hundred.

28 [The sons of Joseph according to their families: Manasseh and Ephraim.] ²⁹The sons of Manasseh: of Machir, the family of the Machirites; [and Machir was the father of Gilead; of Gilead, the family of the Gileadites. ³⁰These are the sons of Gilead:] of Iezer, the family of the Iezerites; of Helek, the family of the Helekites; ³¹of Asriel, the family of the Asrielites; of Shechem, the family of the Shechemites; ³²of Shemida, the family of the Shemidaites; of Hepher, the family of the Hepherites. [³³Now Zelophehad the son of Hepher had no sons, but daughters: and the names of the daughters of Zelophehad were Mahlah, Noah, Hoglah, Milcah, and Tirzah.] ³⁴These are the families of Manasseh according to their number,† fifty-two thousand seven hundred.

35 [These are] the sons of Ephraim [according to their families]: of Shuthelah, the family of the Shuthelahites; of Becher, the family of the Becherites; of Tahan, the family of the Tahanites. [³⁶And these are the sons of Shuthelah: of Eran, the family of the Eranites.] ³⁷These are the families of the sons of Ephraim according to their number, thirty-

* Inserting *lip⁽e⁾qudēhem* ('according to their number') as in v. 18, etc.—cf. BH. Tr.

† Reading 'according to their number' instead of 'and their number' (*lip⁽e⁾qudē-hem* instead of *ūp⁽e⁾qudēhem*)—cf. BH.Tr.

two thousand five hundred. [These are the sons of Joseph according to their families.]

38 The sons of Benjamin [according to their families]: of Bela, the family of the Belaites; of Ashbel, the family of the Ashbelites; of Ahiram, the family of the Ahiramites; ³⁹of Shupham,* the family of the Shuphamites; of Hupham, the family of the Huphamites. ⁴⁰[And the sons of Bela were Ard and Naaman:] of Ard, the family of the Ardites; of Naaman, the family of the Naamites. ⁴¹ These are the sons of Benjamin according to their number,† forty-five thousand six hundred.

42 [These are] the sons of Dan [according to their families]: of Shuham, the family of the Shuhamites. These are the families of Dan [according to their families. ⁴³All the families of the Shuhamites] according to their number, sixty-four thousand four hundred.

44 The sons of Asher [according to their families]: of Imnah, the family of the Imnites; of Ishvi, the family of the Ishvites; of Beriah, the family of the Beriites. ⁴⁵[Of the sons of Beriah:] of Heber, the family of the Heberites; of Malchiel, the family of the Malchielites. [⁴⁶And the name of the daughter of Asher was Serah.] ⁴⁷These are the families of the sons of Asher according to their number, fifty-three thousand four hundred.

48 The sons of Naphtali [according to their families]: of Jahzeel, the family of the Jahzeelites; of Guni, the family of the Gunites; ⁴⁹ of Jezer, the family of the Jezerites; of Shillem, the family of the Shillemites. ⁵⁰ These are the families of Naphtali according to their number†, forty-five thousand four hundred.

51 This was the number of the people of Israel, six hundred and one thousand seven hundred and thirty.

52 The LORD said to Moses: ⁵³'To these the land shall be divided for inheritance according to the number of names. ⁵⁴To a large tribe you shall give a large inheritance, and to a small tribe you shall give a small inheritance; every tribe shall be given its inheritance according to its numbers. ⁵⁵But the land shall be divided by lot; according to the names of the tribes of their fathers they shall inherit. ⁵⁶Their inheritance shall be divided according to lot between the larger and the smaller.'

57 These are the Levites as numbered according to their families: of Gershon, the family of the Gershonites; of Kohath, the family of the Kohathites; of Merari, the family of the Merarites. ⁵⁸These are the families of Levi: the family of the Libnites, the family of the Hebronites, the family of the Mahlites, the family of the Mushites, the family of the Korahites. [And Kohath was the father of Amram. ⁵⁹The name of Amram's wife was Jochebed the daughter of Levi, who was born to Levi in Egypt; and she bore to Amram Aaron and Moses and Miriam their sister. ⁶⁰And to Aaron were born Nadab, Abihu, Eleazar and

---

* Reading (with 3 MSS and the Versions—cf. BH) lešūpām instead of lišepūpām. Tr.

† Deleting 'according to their families' (lemišpeḥōtām) and reading 'according to their number' instead of 'and their number'—cf. BH and note to v. 34 above. Tr.

Ithamar. [61]But Nadab and Abihu died when they offered unholy fire before the LORD.] [62]And those numbered of them were twenty-three thousand, every male from a month old and upward; for they were not numbered among the people of Israel, because there was no inheritance given to them among the people of Israel.

63 These were those numbered by Moses and Eleazar the priest, who numbered the people of Israel in the plains of Moab by the Jordan at Jericho. [64]But among these there was not a man of those numbered by Moses and Aaron the priest, who had numbered the people of Israel in the wilderness of Sinai. [65] For the LORD had said to them, 'They shall die in the wilderness.' There was not left a man of them, except Caleb the son of Jephunneh and Joshua the son of Nun.

This section, according to its introduction (26.1–4a), reports a census, carried out in obedience to a divine command, of all Israelite men over twenty years of age and fit for military service. The results of this census, which, according to v. 4b, included those Israelites who came forth from Egypt, are given, with a total at the end of each individual section, in vv. 5–51 in the framework of the system of twelve tribes, but in a form of that system which does not include the tribe of Levi. Attached to this, there is a passage (vv. 52–56) which relates the census results to the future division of the land that has been promised to Israel. Then follows a separate review of the number of the Levites (vv. 57–62). This separate treatment of the Levites is justified by the fact that they are not to participate in the occupation of the land and therefore could not be included in the general census. Finally something is said in vv. 63–65 about the relationship of this census to the earlier one which, according to ch. 1, had taken place in the 'wilderness of Sinai'. In all this, nothing has been said about that element which occupies the bulk of this chapter. The note of the census results for the individual tribes is in each case preceded by a detailed summary of the division of the tribes into clans (and sub-clans). Even in the separate section on the Levites this summary is in evidence. From what has been said, it follows that the whole chapter has been compiled from several, varied components which, for the most part, were probably originally independent units.

Since the list of clans making up the twelve tribes is the main component, let us begin our analysis of the whole chapter with this element. For each Israelite tribe, the name of which is mentioned at the beginning, there follows in a simple enumeration the list of clans, expressly designated as such, of which the tribe is made up; the consistent practice is for each clan to be derived from its eponymous ancestor, but these ancestors (and this, too, is consistent practice) are not brought into any kind of relationship with the eponym of the tribe (the expressions *benē re'ūbēn*, etc., should be translated as 'Reubenites', etc.).* In Gen. 46.8-27 the list in Num. 26 is used as a basis and transformed into a pure genealogical scheme. The basic form of the clan list was presumably nothing more than the mere enumeration of the clans. Later it has been added to in various ways, on one occasion some information about further subdivisions of the clans and then some references to other traditions in the Old Testament (for the details, see below, pp. 204ff.). The clan list itself, to which there is no exact counterpart in the Old Testament, must have originated at a time when the division into tribes and clans still had some significance for Israel, i.e. in the period before the appearance of a constitutional organization with its different methods of division. On the other hand, it presupposes the fact that the Israelite tribes are living together in Palestine. How such an ancient and certainly reliable 'document' survived as late as the time when Num. 26 was fixed as a literary whole is a question that can no longer be answered. The form taken by the twelve-tribe system that is at the basis of the clan list here is identical with that in Num. 1.20ff. (cf. above pp. 18f., 20f.), except that the tribes of Manasseh and Ephraim appear in the reverse order.

The clan list is used to transmit the results of a census of the men of the Israelite tribes who are fit for military service. The secondary character of the figures that are given *vis-à-vis* the clan list is clear from the fact that in each case they follow the concluding formula, as well as from the fact that the actual content of the clan list has no bearing on them, since they do not refer to the individual clans but only to each tribe as a whole. The clan list has therefore been utilized simply as a tribal register. The figures were originally an independent element of their own in the tradition. In every respect the same holds good for them as for the figures in 1.20-46 (cf. above, pp. 21ff.). The figures in ch. 26 are completely different from those in ch. 1, but the general impression and also the final total are remarkably similar, in spite of several significant differences in individual cases (the figure for Simeon in ch. 26 is significantly smaller than that in ch. 1, while in the cases of Manasseh and Benjamin it is considerably higher).

* This is not, of course, how the RSV translates them. There we find 'sons of Reuben', etc. Tr.

The suggestion that the numbers are pure invention or that they are reckoned on the basis of some numerical speculation or other is just as improbable in the case of ch. 26 as it was in the case of ch. 1. The hypothesis that the word '*elep* was understood in the sense of 'thousand' only at a later stage (cf. the total in v. 51) and was originally meant as the designation of a (military) unit ('troop' or the like) is applicable also to ch. 26; 596 'troops' comprised 5,730 men fit for military service, i.e. an average of 9–10 men to each 'troop'. The most extreme variations from this average are in the cases of Reuben (17 men per 'troop') and Issachar (exactly 5 men per 'troop') and these extremes are therefore further apart than in ch. 1. At the same time one has also to consider the possibility that, with regard to the figures in ch. 26, too, their original significance ('*elep* = 'troop') originated in Israel's early, pre-monarchical period. Ch. 1 and 26, standing side by side, will have to be attributed to different censuses, taken at different times, of the military potential of the old Israelite tribes. One can hazard a relative temporal relationship between the two censuses only with the utmost caution. The above-mentioned differences in the cases of Simeon, Manasseh and Benjamin might lead us to suppose a somewhat later period for ch. 26, in which some of the tribes in central Palestine had increased in manpower and significance, while Simeon, situated on the edge of Palestine, had decreased. The connection of the clan list with the census results could, in the suggested circumstances, already have taken place in Israel's early period.

In the section about the Levites in vv. 57–62 two different enumerations of clans stand side by side, unconnected and un-harmonized. The list in v. 57 corresponds to the division which is usual in the late period and which we find presupposed in ch. 3–4. On the other hand, the list in v. 58a is unusual and very probably older; in view of our limited knowledge of the history of the Levites any more precise indication of period is no longer possible.

The introduction in 26.1–4a, which is in the style of P and is phrased in accordance with the presuppositions of the P-narrative, belongs to the final redaction; the references to the future conquest in vv. 52–56 and vv. 62b–64 have been added later when the Pentateuchal narrative was being revised preparatory to being joined to the deuteronomistic historical work.

[26.1–4] What appears in the Hebrew text as 25.19 (RSV 'after the plague' in 26.1a) is a purely formal link with the preceding pericope (25.8, 9). The introduction (26.1–4a) is composed of the same phrases as its counterpart in 1.1–3, 18, 19, but is, on the whole, more tersely expressed. Eleazar has meanwhile succeeded to the position of his father Aaron (cf. 20.23–29) and Israel is no longer in the wilderness of Sinai but in 'the plains of Moab' (cf. 22.1b). By means of this introduction, what follows is dovetailed into the post-priestly addition to the Pentateuch. The introduction is obviously secondary *vis-à-vis* the older superscription in v. 4b which has transmitted the combination of clan list and census results (vv. 5–51) as if they were an old independent unit. This superscription had given a later interpretation to this combination, but such an interpretation is no longer suitable in the present context, as is shown by the later idea in v. 64.

[26.5–11] The original form of the section on Reuben is found intact in vv. 5b–7. Preceding it in v. 5a there is an obvious, but dispensable note which, for all its genealogical interest, does not entirely fit into the clan list. In vv. 8–11, after the concluding formula of v. 7b, there is an addition with unusually detailed reference to Num. 16. This does not appear to be a self-contained unit, but stands, rather, in a complicated reciprocal relationship to 16.1. The oldest element in this addition is probably in v. 8. In it, another son (the introductory formula uses in stereotyped fashion the plur. 'sons', although it is a question of only one son) is attributed to the Reubenite clan Pallu. This could be understood as a statement about one part of the clan Pallu having made itself independent in the course of time, and therefore an early addition which is supposed to accommodate itself to the presumed historical development of clan relationships. Perhaps, however, all that is being done is that a place is being found, by way of an addition, for the Reubenite mentioned in*16.1¶ (cf. Deut. 11.6). At any rate, this addition is presupposed in the present form of 16.1, where Eliab appears as the name of Dathan and Abiram's father and the clan name Pallu has been inserted secondarily on the basis of the present list (cf. above, p. 122). The connection thus established was the reason for the mention of the Dathan-Abiram story in vv. 9–11. V. 9a, to be sure, seems still to belong to v. 8 and to be another addition to the old clan list, since the name Nemuel cannot be derived from ch. 16. There remains, however, the suspicion that this name has slipped in inadvertently

* What Noth takes as the original version of 16.1 at this point is 'Dathan and Abiram the sons of Eliab the son of Reuben'. Cf. above, p. 118 and footnote. Tr.

from v. 12, where it appears as the name of the first Simeonite clan. At any rate, in vv. 9b–10 the combined narrative of ch. 16 is briefly summarized, partly with verbal borrowing (cf. vv. 10aα and 10bα with 16.32a and 16.35abα) and partly independently (the Hiph. of *nṣh* = 'to contend' does not appear in ch. 16. nor does the reference to the divine punishment as a 'warning'). The note in v. 11 has been added in view of the later existence of the Korahites (v. 58) and presupposes what is perhaps a later addition, namely the reference to the death of Korah (v. 10aβ) which is lacking in ch. 16 (cf. above, p. 129).

[**26.12–22**] The sections concerning Simeon and Gad in vv. 12–18 are in their original form with the enumeration of the clans and the census results. Somewhat more complicated is the section about Judah in vv. 19–22. V. 19 refers to Gen. 38.7–10, according to which Er and Onan, sons of Judah, had already died 'in the land of Canaan', i.e. before the migration of Judah and his sons to Egypt. The original clan register of the tribe of Judah begins in v. 20 after an exceptional introduction with a finite verb, occasioned by the insertion of v. 19. The problem of this section lies in v. 21aα, where this introduction with finite verb occurs again. If, on this basis, v. 21aα were to be considered an addition, then v. 21aβb would simply be the continuation of the clan enumeration of v. 20. The reason for the insertion of v. 21aα might be the fact that, according to Gen. 38, there were only the three (surviving) sons of Judah who are mentioned in v. 20, so that the two clans mentioned in v. 21aβb had to be demoted to subclans of a main clan. If, however, v. 21aα belongs to the original text, then v. 21 would have to be understood as a presumably early complement to the Judah clan list, reflecting a further development of the clan divisions (cf. above, p. 205, on v. 8).

[**26.23–34**] The sections concerning Issachar and Zebulun (vv. 23–27) appear in their original form without additions. The section concerning Manasseh, which is again very complicated, has been preceded secondarily in v. 28 by a genealogical note which goes back to the usual order of enumeration of the sons of Jacob (cf. especially Gen. 29.31ff.). The normal enumeration of the clan begins in v. 29, but is immediately interrupted by genealogical remarks. The regular formulae appear in vv. 29aα, 29b, 30aβb, 31, 32. Basically the original clan list of Manasseh is to be seen in these sections. The addition in v. 29aβ, which falls outside this framework, will go back to the fact that the expression 'Machir the father of Gilead' was probably a stereotyped phrase (cf. Josh. 17.1; I Chron. 7.14). Since, according to this expression (cf. also Gen. 50.23), Gilead appeared to have been Machir's only son, the rest of the Manasseh clans were genealogically allotted to Gilead by v. 30aα. Josh. 17.1–3 has obviously made use of the Manasseh section of Num. 26, but in an original form in which the clans mentioned in vv. 30aβb, 31, 32 have been derived from the 'rest of the sons of Manasseh'* (not great-grandchildren). According to Josh. 17.1–3, it is, to say the least, doubtful whether v. 29b was part of the original text and whether, therefore, the name Gilead appeared in the list at all; for Josh. 17 only takes account on the one hand of Machir and on the other of 'the rest of the sons of Manasseh'. On this basis, the whole of vv. 29aβb, 30aα would be regarded as having been added under the stimulus of the expression 'Machir the father of Gilead'. Whether Josh. 17 is to be preferred textually with its reading 'Abiezer/Abiezerites' instead of 'Iezer/Iezerites' cannot immediately be decided. A Manasseh clan called Abiezer is known from Judg. 6.1ff. The occurrence of the name Shechem in the clan list (v. 31b) is noteworthy. This can only refer to the well-known town of that name (situated at modern *tell balāṭa*); according to this, it was incorporated in the tribes of Manasseh and its inhabitants would enjoy the rights and privileges of a Manasseh clan. The name and personage of Zelophehad, which introduces the obviously additional v. 33, are a complete mystery. With a genealogical connection with the last-mentioned clan name, Zelophehad has, ranged under him, several names all of which have the feminine ending and are therefore designated as the names of the daughters of Zelophehad who had no sons. In actual fact these are names with some kind of topographical significance. The last name, Tirzah, is to be associated with the name of the well-known town Tirzah (probably *tell fārʿa*). The names Noah and Hoglah occur in the Samaritan ostraca (eighth century B.C.) as designations of districts, as do the names Abiezer, Helek and Shemida (this fact is a point in favour of the originality of the reading 'Abiezer' instead of 'Iezer' in v. 30aβ). From all this, it in all probability follows, first of all that all the names in v. 33b are names of places whose inhabitants have been incorporated in the tribe of Manasseh, and then also that this addition to the Manasseh clan list goes back to a relatively early period, but no earlier than the time of the incorporation of Shechem, which appears already in the original form of the list.

* So MT. RSV in Josh. 17.2 has 'the rest of the *tribe* of Manasseh'. Tr.

[26.35-50] In the section concerning Ephraim (vv. 35–37) the original form is obviously in v. 35. V. 36 is an addition which, however, may be very ancient and is intended to make allowance for the fact that part of the clan Shuthelah became independent. A similar explanation holds good for the section concerning Benjamin (vv. 38–41) where the original form of the clan list (vv. 38–39) seems to be followed in v. 40 by an addition in which two more clans are named. At any rate, the formula in v. 40a, with its finite verb, is irregular and could indicate the secondary nature of v. 40a; in that case, v. 40b would originally have been simply the continuation of vv. 38–39. In the case of Dan (vv. 42–43) it is remarkable that only one clan is introduced; at the same time the usual plural framework-formulation is retained (in v. 43a a secondary attempt is made to resolve this erroneous relationship). Behind this fact lies the smallness of this tribe (on this subject cf. Judg. 18.2), which at the same time was a full member of the Israelite amphictyony. The census result in v. 43b, with its remarkably high figure for Dan, obviously presupposes different historical circumstances. In the case of Asher (vv. 44–47) the clan list comes first in v. 44. The verdict on v. 45 depends on the opening words of that verse. If they are to be regarded as additional, perhaps even merely an inadvertent accretion to the text, then v. 45aβb would simply be the continuation of v. 44. Otherwise v. 45 would have to be seen as a presumably early addition occasioned by its subject-matter (cf. vv. 33, 36). The information about a daughter of Asher in v. 46 is a complete mystery with regard to its origin and significance. Her name appears otherwise only in places which betray a literary dependence on this passage. The section concerning Naphtali has been preserved, apparently intact and in its original form, in vv. 48–50.

[26.52-56] While the Pentateuch was being revised preparatory to being joined to the deuteronomistic historical work, the census results recorded in 26.1–51 were referred, in this section (vv. 52–56), contrary to the intention of the superscription in 26.4b, to the forthcoming conquest, with the remark that the allotment of tribal shares in the occupation of Palestine is to correspond to the numerical strength of the tribes (vv. 53–54). However, the divine command to this end (v. 52) is not compatible with the stereotyped remark in a late stratum of the deuteronomistic historical work to the effect that the tribal territories in Palestine are to be allotted in most cases not on the basis of any rational calculation but by lot (Josh, 18.6b, 8bβ, 11a, etc.). A faint attempt to smooth out this contradiction is made in vv. 55–56 by means of somewhat forced remarks which are probably meant to indicate that the lot will fall in such a way that the 'inheritance' in Palestine will correspond to some extent to the size of the tribes.

[**26.57–62**] In the section concerning the Levites (vv. 57–62) we find at the beginning, in v. 57 and v. 58a, two different 'clan' enumerations standing side by side, unrelated to each other and with no attempt at harmonization. V. 57 presents what is, in general, the usual division of the Levites into three groups (cf. 3.14ff. *et al.*); the name Kohath in vv. 58bff. links up with this division. In between, there is, in v. 58a, a different enumeration of 'Levi clans' which gives the impression of being older, first of all by reason of the fact that it is not phrased in genealogical terms but mentions only clan names, and also because it presents a simple series of five names without further subdivision. The names which occur in it all appear again in the presumably later complicated Levitical genealogy (for the 'Libnites' cf. 3.18; for the 'Hebronites' cf. 3.19; for the 'Mahlites' and the 'Mushites' cf. 3.20; for the 'Korahites' cf. 16.1a as well as Ex. 6.21, 24), yet appear here in what is still a very simple juxtaposition. It is noteworthy that at least two of the names can scarcely be understood other than as the gentilics of place-names, namely 'Hebronites' (cf. the well-known town of Hebron) and 'Libnites' (cf. Libna, which, according to Josh. 15.42, lay in a south-western province of Judah), that is the 'Levites of Hebron' or 'of Libna'. So, too, one might at least compare the 'Mahlites' with the name 'Mahlah' in v. 33. That the 'Mushites', as is often supposed, had something to do with the name Moses, is not very illuminating. One might conclude from the list in v. 58a, which has no counterpart in the Old Testament and to which there is nothing exactly comparable, that it is dealing with an early regional or local grouping of 'Levites'. For the individual details concerning the family of Moses and Aaron in vv. 58b–61, cf. especially Ex. 6.18–20. The present passage, however, is secondary from a literary point of view *vis-à-vis* Ex. 6, since here some additional relevant material has been assimilated. That Moses was of 'Levitical' origin we find in Ex. 2.1. His father Amram is therefore said to be directly descended from Kohath son of Levi (v. 58b); his mother Jochebed (the name found elsewhere only in Ex. 6.20) is likewise, in verbal reference to Ex. 2.1, said to have been of 'Levitical' origin (v. 59a). The juxtaposition of the three children in v. 59b (otherwise only in Micah 6.4) depends upon information that otherwise occurs only separately, namely that Aaron and Miriam were brother and sister (Ex. 15.20) and that Aaron and Moses were brothers (Ex. 4.14 *et al.*). The information about the sons of Aaron in vv. 60–61 agrees, completely from the point of view of subject-matter and to a large extent from the verbal point of view, with 3.2, 4aα. The statement in v. 61 goes back to Lev. 10.1–2. The figure given in v. 62a for the 'numbered' Levites is inexplicably different from the total given in 3.39 (23,000 instead of 22,000). The causal clause in v. 62b is intended to explain why, in the case of the Levites, the census was taken of those from one month old and upwards (cf. 3.15) and not, as in the case of the Israelite tribes (cf. v. 4a), only of those of twenty years old and upwards.

[**26.63–65**] The appendix in vv. 63–65 is intended to correct the impression that might be obtained from the older superscription of v. 4b, that the 'census' introduced into the Pentateuchal narrative at this point and, according to vv. 52–56, undertaken in view of the coming conquest, was still dealing with those Israelites who had come out of Egypt and, according to ch. 1, had already been 'numbered' in the wilderness of Sinai; for *those* Israelites, with the exception of Joshua and Caleb according to 14.29f., had all meanwhile perished in the wilderness.

10. A PRECEDENT CONCERNING DAUGHTERS' RIGHTS OF INHERITANCE: 27.1–11

27 ¹Then drew near the daughters of Zelophehad the son of Hepher, son of Gilead, son of Machir, son of Manasseh, from the families of Manasseh the son of Joseph. The names of his daughters were: Mahlah, Noah, Hoglah, Milcah, and Tirzah. ²And they stood before Moses, and before Eleazar the priest, and before the leaders and all the congregation, at the door of the tent of meeting, saying, ³'Our father died in the wilderness; he was not among the company of those who gathered themselves together against the LORD in the company of Korah, but died for his own sin; and he had no sons. ⁴Why should the name of our father be taken away from his family, because he had no son? Give to us a possession among our father's brethren.'

5 Moses brought their case before the LORD. ⁶And the LORD said to Moses, ⁷'The daughters of Zelophehad are right; you shall give them possession of an inheritance among their father's brethren and cause the inheritance of their father to pass to them. ⁸And you shall say to the people of Israel, "If a man dies, and has no son, then you shall cause his inheritance to pass to his daughter. ⁹And if he has no daughter, then

you shall give his inheritance to his brothers. ¹⁰And if he has no brothers, then you shall give his inheritance to his father's brothers. ¹¹And if his father has no brothers, then you shall give his inheritance to his kinsman that is next to him of his family, and he shall possess it. And it shall be to the people of Israel a statute and ordinance, as the LORD commanded Moses." '

A case brought before the congregation and its authorities, which cannot be settled on the basis of legislation given hitherto, is decided by a word from God asked for by Moses; a precedent is thereby established on which future proceedings in Israel are to be based. In this respect, the present passage may be compared with Lev. 24.10–23; Num. 9.6–14; 15.32–36. The subject-matter is the right of daughters to inherit in the case where a man has no sons. This right is affirmed by the divine decision. An appendix introduced in ch. 36 subsequently made this decision more precise and, at the same time, more limited. The case in point, which forms the point of departure, goes back to the addition to the Manasseh clan list found in 26.33, where there appears the remarkable figure of Zelophehad, who had no sons but five daughters. By its phraseology, the present passage is clearly dependent on the P-narrative (cf. esp. v. 2); it can scarcely belong to the original version of the latter, but is certainly a later addition. The legislation derived from this precedent and phrased in general terms (vv. 8b–11a) goes beyond the terms of the case in point and could, as far as content and terminology are concerned, be composed of older, traditional legal material.

The extended genealogy in v. 1 is derived from the present, probably secondary form (cf. above, pp. 206f.) of 26.28–33. That Zelophehad, the father of the five daughters, died without having had any sons, is stated succinctly in v. 3aαbβ, since it is essential for all that follows. V. 3aβbα interrupts the sequence of thought and is probably additional; it seems to be saying that Zelophehad had incurred no particular sin which might still have worked itself out on his descendants, but rather, like all the Israelites of the exodus generation, had suffered the punishment of dying in the wilderness (cf. 14.29f.), so that his daughters were in the same position as all the Israelites of their generation. The complaint of Zelophehad's daughters in v. 4 presupposes that the 'name' of a man, the continued existence of which was important and was taken seriously, could be preserved only in association with the inheritance of land by his descendants. If, then, there were no sons of Zelophehad to share in the territory of the clan in question, then at least the 'daughters of Zelophehad' should be associated with their cousins. The divine judgment in v. 7 gives the daughters of Zelophehad such a right, and the judgment is at once transformed into a ruling that is henceforth to be generally valid for Israel (vv. 8b–11a). In vv. 9–11a, this legislation transcends the case from which it developed by taking account of the possibility of a man not leaving any daughters either, that is dying childless. No account is taken of the possibility of the wife of the man in question surviving him and thus being able to enter into a so-called levirate marriage and produce a son who would bear the dead man's name (cf. Deut. 25.5–10). According to the legislation of vv. 8b–11a, there follow, with regard to rights of inheritance, after the man's own sons, who, of course, have precedence (for the particular rights of inheritance applicable to the one who is actually first-born cf. Deut. 21.15–17), first of all his own daughters and then the male relatives in an order of precedence determined by blood-relationship along patriarchal lines. From this latter point of view, the right of daughters to inherit falls outside the general scheme; it needed a special divine judgment to validate it, and this, for the reason given, is what the present passage provides.

11. INTIMATION OF THE DEATH OF MOSES: 27.12–23

27 ¹²The LORD said to Moses, 'Go up into this mountain of Abarim, and see the land which I have given to the people of Israel. ¹³And when you have seen it, you also shall be gathered to your people, as your brother Aaron was gathered, because ¹⁴you rebelled against my word in the wilderness of Zin during the strife of the congregation, to sanctify me at the waters before their eyes.' [(These are the waters of Meribah of Kadesh in the wilderness of Zin.)] ¹⁵Moses said to the LORD, ¹⁶'Let the LORD, the God of the spirits of all flesh, appoint a man over the congregation, ¹⁷ who shall go out before them and come in before them, who shall lead them out and bring them in; that the congregation of the LORD may not be as sheep which have no shepherd.' ¹⁸And the LORD said to Moses, 'Take Joshua the son of Nun, a man in whom is the spirit, and lay your hand upon him; ¹⁹cause him to stand before Eleazar the priest and all the congregation, and you shall commission him in their sight. ²⁰You shall invest him with some of your authority, that all the congregation of the people of Israel may obey. ²¹ And he shall stand before Eleazar the priest, who shall inquire for him by the judgment of the Urim before the LORD; at his word they shall go out, and at his word they shall come in, both he and all the people of Israel with him, the whole congregation.' ²²And Moses did as the LORD commanded him; he took Joshua and caused him to stand before

Eleazar the priest and the whole congregation, [23]and he laid his hands upon him, and commissioned him as the LORD directed through Moses.

The comparatively brief intimation of the imminent death of Moses (vv. 12–14) is followed by a detailed exposition of the installation of Joshua as Moses' successor (vv. 15–23). The former theme appears once again in Deut. 32.48–52 more or less word for word, but in greater detail. In view of its phraseology and of its explicit reference to *20.1–13P, the whole passage belongs in some way or another to the P-narrative, which thus, following on 20.22b–29; 22.1b, makes its appearance again and appears to have made the intimation of the death of Aaron and the death of Moses follow directly on the narrative of *20.1–13P. The relationship between Num. 27.12–23 and Deut. 32.48–52 is not exactly easy to determine. According to its position in the Pentateuch as a whole, one would expect Num. 27 to be the primary version, with Deut. 32 as a secondary repetition whose purpose seems to have been the resumption of the theme of Moses' death, especially after the later insertion of the lengthy deuteronomic law. On the other hand, this repetition is the more original of the two in that it has as its subject only the death of Moses, without going on to deal with the question of his successor. From this, the conclusion may be drawn that only 27.12–14 belonged to the original version of the P-narrative and was later repeated in Deut. 32.48–52 and that, on the other hand, 27.15–23 was added only when the Pentateuch was linked to the deuteronomistic historical work; for in the deuteronomic and deuteronomistic literature mention of the death of Moses is always linked in stereotyped fashion with information about the installation of Joshua as his successor (Deut. 3.23–29; 31.1–8; also Josh. 1.1f.).

[27.12–14] After the arrival of the Israelites in 'the plains of Moab beyond the Jordan at Jericho' (22.1bP), i.e. in the eastern regions of the lowest reaches of the Jordan valley, Moses was commanded to ascend the mountain of Abarim to see from there the promised land (v. 12) and then to die without himself setting foot in that land (v. 13). The 'mountain of Abarim' (in 33.47f. it is 'the mountains of Abarim') can no longer be located exactly and was perhaps even for ancient Israel a vague term; according to the present context, part of the transjordanian mountain range round about the north end of the Dead Sea must be meant, a situation from which large tracts of territory west of the Jordan could be seen.

Perhaps a vague reference is given intentionally by P. With the aim of greater clarification, Deut. 32.49 has the additional remark that what is meant in particular is Mount Nebo in that part of Moab that lay opposite Jericho. The presupposition—and here P is certainly following an old tradition—is that this region east of the Jordan lay outside Israelite territory (the deuteronomist has it otherwise). That Moses was not to enter this land is probably one of the oldest features of the Mosaic tradition. This circumstance is explained in P as divine punishment for an act of disobedience which Moses (along with Aaron) had committed at the 'waters of contention' in the wilderness of Zin (v. 14a). This is a reference to the story of the water-miracle in 20.1–13 which has been reworked by P precisely in the sense that Moses and Aaron had disobeyed a divine command (cf. above, p. 144). In Deut. 32.51 this occurrence is set, in dependence on Num. 20.1, at the 'waters of Meribath-kadesh'; and, in dependence on that passage, this setting has been transferred to Num. 27, too, in a later addition (v. 14b).

[27.15–17] The narrative of Joshua's installation as Moses' successor is remarkable in that the initiative is taken by Moses (v. 15) and that although Moses speaks to Yahweh (v. 15) Yahweh is not then addressed (v. 16). What is certainly intended is a sense of submissiveness towards God, who is described in the same solemn terms as in 16.22 (cf. above, p. 127). According to v. 17, after the death of Moses Israel will need above all leadership in war. 'Lead out' and 'bring in' (cf. I Sam. 18.13–16; II Sam. 5.2 *et al.*) mean, in the first instance, to command the army (v. 17a is circumstantial and broadly phrased; its two halves are synonymous); and the picture of sheep without a shepherd (v. 17b) is also used, in I Kings 22.17, for an army that has become leaderless. At the same time, in accordance with the language of P, Israel is described as a 'congregation'.

[27.18–21] Yahweh immediately grants Moses' request by commanding him to instal Joshua as his successor (vv. 18–19). Joshua is introduced by a brief description as if he were a new figure, although he has already appeared on occasion, not in P, it is true, but in the Pentateuchal narrative as a whole (Ex. 17.9f., 13; 24.13; 32.17; 33.11); in the present context it is especially the Joshua of the deuteronomistic historical work who is in mind, the future leader of Israel. The 'spirit' by whose presence Joshua is characterized (v. 18aβ) is not defined any more precisely; it means some kind of ability given by God, here certainly the ability generally to carry out his new task. The 'laying on' of the hand which Moses is to do to instal Joshua (v. 18b) is presumably to be understood as signifying the transference of the (lifelong) task; it is an act which was certainly originally thought of as magically effective, which had its roots initially in the sacrificial cult.* Moses, in all his authority, is to carry out the commissioning before the chief priest and the whole congregation (v. 19) and, with the transference of his *hōd*, effect the obedience of the congregation to Joshua (v. 20). What is to be understood by *hōd* and how the transference of the *hōd* is to come about cannot be said with any certainty. The word *hōd* is usually translated as 'majesty', is frequently ascribed to a king and then, metaphorically, also to God. It must describe something effective and perhaps even visible; the translation 'vitality'† indicates only one possible way of understanding it. The word occurs only here in the Pentateuch. Since Moses is to allow only part of his *hōd* to pass to Joshua, Joshua's relationship with the chief priest Eleazar will be different from Moses' relationship to him. This is obviously what v. 21 is saying. Moses had had no need of a priestly mediator to find out the will of Yahweh. Joshua will depend upon the priest. Perhaps in the statement of v. 21aα that Joshua is to 'stand before (Eleazar) the priest' there is also already the idea that he is to stand before the priest in a ministering capacity. It is not entirely clear who is the subject in v. 21aβ and who is indicated by the suffixes in v. 21bα.‡ Very probably the priest is meant to be the subject of 'inquire' and likewise it will then be a question of the priest's 'word' (not Yahweh's, which could, strictly speaking, also be possible) which will regulate the 'going out' and 'coming in', i.e. again, in the first place, with reference to military undertakings. The mention of the sacred lot 'Urim (and Thummim)' is intentionally archaistic. It is true that, according to Ex. 28.30; Lev. 8.8, the post-exilic High Priest still carried the 'Urim and Thummim' in the pocket of the breastpiece which was part of his official robes; but there can be no question of any practical use having been made in the late period of this technique, which operated in some way now unknown, for finding out the divine will by lot (cf. on this point Ezra 2.63 = Neh. 7.65). The abbreviation

---

* Cf. *Leviticus*, p. 22.

† So Noth's translation in the text. RSV 'authority' is not inappropriate in the context. Tr.

‡ In v. 21aβ RSV has indicated Eleazar as the subject of 'inquire' by the insertion of the relative 'who', which is not in the Hebrew. The Hebrew literally is 'and he shall inquire for him . . .' Tr.

'Urim' (instead of 'Urim and Thummim') is found already in I Sam. 28.6.

[27.22–23] According to the concluding note in vv. 22–23, Moses carried out the divine command immediately, although, according to the conceptions of the Pentateuch and the Deuteronomist, he himself, before his death (Deut. 34), still had many wide-ranging duties to carry out.

12. CULTIC CALENDAR: 28.1–29.40

28 ¹The LORD said to Moses, ²'Command the people of Israel, and say to them, "My offering, my food for my offerings by fire, my pleasing odour, you shall take heed to offer to me in its due season." ³And you shall say to them, This is the offering by fire which you shall offer to the LORD: two male lambs a year old without blemish, day by day, as a continual offering. ⁴The one lamb you shall offer in the morning, and the other lamb you shall offer in the evening; ⁵also a tenth of an ephah of fine flour for a cereal offering, mixed with a fourth of a hin of beaten oil. [⁶It is a continual burnt offering, which was ordained at Mount Sinai for a pleasing odour, an offering by fire to the LORD.] ⁷Its drink offering shall be a fourth of a hin for each lamb; [in the holy place you shall pour out a drink offering of strong drink to the LORD.] ⁸The other lamb you shall offer in the evening; like the cereal offering of the morning, and like its drink offering, you shall offer it as an offering by fire, a pleasing odour to the LORD.

9 'On the sabbath day two male lambs a year old without blemish, and two tenths of an ephah of fine flour for a cereal offering, mixed with oil, and its drink offering: [¹⁰this is the burnt offering of every sabbath, besides the continual burnt offering and its drink offering.]

11 'At the beginnings of your months you shall offer a burnt offering to the LORD: two young bulls, one ram, seven male lambs a year old without blemish; ¹²also three tenths of an ephah of fine flour for a cereal offering, mixed with oil, for each bull; and two tenths of fine flour for a cereal offering, mixed with oil, for the one ram; ¹³and a tenth of fine flour mixed with oil as a cereal offering for every lamb; for a burnt offering of pleasing odour, an offering by fire to the LORD. ¹⁴Their drink offerings shall be half a hin of wine for a bull, a third of a hin for a ram, and a fourth of a hin for a lamb; [this is the burnt offering of each month throughout the months of the year. ¹⁵Also one male goat for a sin offering to the LORD; it shall be offered besides the continual burnt offering and its drink offering.]

16 'On the fourteenth day of the first month is the LORD's passover. ¹⁷And on the fifteenth day of this month is a feast; seven days shall unleavened bread be eaten. ¹⁸On the first day there shall be a holy convocation: you shall do no laborious work, ¹⁹but offer an offering by fire, a burnt offering to the LORD: two young bulls, one ram, and seven

male lambs a year old; [see that they are without blemish;] [20]also their cereal offering of fine flour mixed with oil; three tenths of an ephah shall you offer for a bull, and two tenths for a ram; [21]a tenth shall you offer for each of the seven lambs; [[22]also one male goat for a sin offering, to make atonement for you.] [[23]You shall offer these besides the burnt offering of the morning, which is for a continual burnt offering.] [24]In the same way you shall offer daily, for seven days, the food of an offering by fire, a pleasing odour to the LORD; [it shall be offered besides the continual burnt offering and its drink offering.] [25]And on the seventh day you shall have a holy convocation; you shall do no laborious work.

26 'On the day of the first fruits, when you offer a cereal offering of new grain to the LORD at your feast of weeks, you shall have a holy convocation; you shall do no laborious work, [27]but offer a burnt offering, a pleasing odour to the LORD: two young bulls, one ram, seven male lambs a year old; [28]also their cereal offering of fine flour mixed with oil, three tenths of an ephah for each bull, two tenths for one ram, [29]a tenth for each of the seven lambs; [[30]with one male goat, to make atonement for you.] [31][Besides the continual burnt offering and its cereal offering, you shall offer them] and their drink offering. [See that they are without blemish.]

29 [1]'On the first day of the seventh month you shall have a holy convocation; you shall do no laborious work. It is a day for you to blow the trumpets, [2]and you shall offer a burnt offering, a pleasing odour to the LORD: one young bull, one ram, seven male lambs a year old without blemish; [3]also their cereal offering of fine flour mixed with oil, three tenths of an ephah for the bull, two tenths for the ram, [4]and one tenth for each of the seven lambs; [[5]with one male goat for a sin offering, to make atonement for you;] [6][besides the burnt offering of the new moon, and its cereal offering, and the continual burnt offering and its cereal offering,] and their drink offering, according to the ordinance for them, a pleasing odour, an offering by fire to the LORD.

7 'On the tenth day of this seventh month you shall have a holy convocation, and afflict yourselves; you shall do no work, [8]but you shall offer a burnt offering to the LORD, a pleasing odour: one young bull, one ram, seven male lambs a year old; [they shall be to you without blemish;] [9]and their cereal offering of fine flour mixed with oil, three tenths of an ephah for the bull, two tenths for the one ram, [10]a tenth for each of the seven lambs; [11][also one male goat for a sin offering, besides the sin offering of atonement, and the continual burnt offering and its cereal offering,] and their drink offerings.

12 'On the fifteenth day of the seventh month you shall have a holy convocation; you shall do no laborious work, and you shall keep a feast to the LORD seven days; [13]and you shall offer a burnt offering, an offering by fire, a pleasing odour to the LORD, thirteen young bulls, two rams, fourteen male lambs a year old; [they shall be without blemish;] [14]and their cereal offering of fine flour mixed with oil, three

tenths of an ephah for each of the thirteen bulls, two tenths for each of the two rams, [15]and a tenth for each of the fourteen lambs; [[16]also one male goat for a sin offering, besides the continual burnt offering, its cereal offering and its drink offering.]

17 'On the second day twelve young bulls, two rams, fourteen male lambs a year old without blemish, [18]with the cereal offering and the drink offerings for the bulls, for the rams, and for the lambs, by number, according to the ordinance; [[19]also one male goat for a sin offering, besides the continual burnt offering and its cereal offering, and their drink offerings.]

20 'On the third day eleven bulls, two rams, fourteen male lambs a year old without blemish, [21]with the cereal offering and the drink offerings for the bulls, for the rams, and for the lambs, by number, according to the ordinance; [[22]also one male goat for a sin offering, besides the continual burnt offering and its cereal offering and its drink offering.]

23 'On the fourth day ten bulls, two rams, fourteen male lambs a year old without blemish, [24]with the cereal offering and the drink offerings for the bulls, for the rams, and for the lambs, by number, according to the ordinance; [[25]also one male goat for a sin offering, besides the continual burnt offering, its cereal offering and its drink offering.]

26 'On the fifth day nine bulls, two rams, fourteen male lambs a year old without blemish, [27]with the cereal offering and the drink offerings for the bulls, for the rams, and for the lambs, by number, according to the ordinance; [[28]also one male goat for a sin offering; besides the continual burnt offerings and its cereal offering and its drink offering.]

29 'On the sixth day eight bulls, two rams, fourteen male lambs a year old without blemish, [30]with the cereal offering and the drink offerings, for the bulls, for the rams, and for the lambs, by number, according to the ordinance; [[31]also one male goat for a sin offering; besides the continual burnt offering, its cereal offering, and its drink offering.]

32 'On the seventh day seven bulls, two rams, fourteen male lambs a year old without blemish, [33]with the cereal offering and the drink offerings for the bulls, for the rams, and for the lambs, by their number according to the ordinance; [[34]also one male goat for a sin offering; besides the continual burnt offering, its cereal offering, and its drink offering.]

35 'On the eighth day you shall have a solemn assembly: you shall do no laborious work, [36]but you shall offer a burnt offering, an offering by fire, a pleasing odour to the LORD: one bull, one ram, seven male lambs a year old without blemish, [37]and the cereal offering and the drink offerings for the bull, for the ram, and for the lambs, by their number, according to the ordinance; [[38]also one male goat for a sin offering; besides the continual burnt offering and its cereal offering and its drink offering.]

39 'These you shall offer to the LORD at your appointed feasts, in addition to your votive offerings and your freewill offerings, for your burnt offerings, and for your cereal offerings, and for your drink offerings, and for your peace offerings.'

40 And Moses told the people of Israel everything just as the LORD had commanded Moses.

This great compilation describes all the sacrifices that were to be offered as such by the cultic community of Jerusalem in the course of every year, and it does so in a sequence which is determined by the calendar for the various days and cultic seasons and festivals. That there was also the possibility of private sacrifices by individual worshippers is only briefly noted at the end (29.39). This compilation, which is to be thought of, from the literary point of view, as an appendix to the Pentateuchal narrative which finds a place after the intimation of the death of Moses (27.12–14), is a final, definitive and systematic treatment of its subject. It presupposes texts which are different from the point of view of content and terminology and which are from the exilic or post-exilic period, above all the sacrificial rituals of Lev. 1–7, as well as the 'Holiness Code', especially the latter's cultic calendar in Lev. 23. It is also later than Num. 15.1–16, for what is demanded in the latter passage as something new, namely the addition of cereal offerings and drink offerings to the various animal sacrifices, is here presupposed as an effective regulation. This must, therefore, be one of the latest sections of the Pentateuch, although the period of its composition cannot be determined, even approximately.

From the literary point of view, this comprehensive section is essentially of a piece. Those phrases about the goat that is to be brought as a sin offering for atonement, which occur from time to time and which strike one as out of context, have probably been added at a later stage (28.15a, 22, 30; 29.5, 11a, 16a, 19a, 22a, 25a, 28a, 31a, 34a, 38a). They surely refer to a cultic practice which probably did not emerge until later (but cf. already Ezek. 45.23b). Secondary, too, are surely the equally stereotyped pedantic references to the fact that all sacrifices are to be offered without prejudice to the two regular burnt offerings which, according to 28.3–8, are to be made every day (28.10, 15b, 23, 24b, 31a; 29.6aβ, *11bβ, 16b, 19b, 22b, 25b, 28b, 31b, 34b, 38b). To these should be added the reference in 29.6aα to the offering on the new moon which is described in 28.11–4 and which is, of course, to be made as well on the first day of the eighth month, and the reference in 29.11ba to the sin offering of atonement which is described in Ex. 30.10. These brief phrases and references occur for the most part in juxtaposition and the fact that in a few places they appear to disrupt what originally belonged together (cf. especially 28.30, 31¶; 29.5, 6aa, 11¶) is an additional argument in favour of considering them to be later additions.

A list of those sacrifices which are to be offered regularly by the community, together with details concerning the number of sacrificial animals demanded and the quantity of the cereal offering that is to be offered along with them, is first found in that programme for the future which we have in the book of Ezekiel. The 'prince' envisaged in that programme is to see to it that certain sacrifices are offered in the new Jerusalem temple 'for himself and all the people of the land' (42.22) on the great feast days (45.21-25; 46.11), on the sabbaths and new moons (46.4-7), as well as on every day of the year (46.13-15). In actual fact, in the post-exilic period, since the office of 'prince' never became a reality, the obligation of ensuring that these sacrifices were offered regularly fell on the cultic community of Jerusalem as a whole (cf. Neh. 10.33 [*Hebr.* v. 34]). It is this community that is referred to by the words 'the people of Israel' (28.2a), who, in the text of this passage, are addressed mostly as 'you', sometimes, inconsequentially, also as 'thou'.*

In its terminology, this late passage still makes use of expressions which are, in part, old and inapposite. The sacrifices are described as God's 'food' (28.2, 24) as in Lev. 21.6, 8, 17. Somewhat less drastic, but still very inapposite, is the way in which the purpose of the 'offering by fire'† is described as being intended to produce a 'pleasing odour for Yahweh' (28.2 *et al.*)‡ The technical term 'holy proclamation'§ (28.18, 25, 26; 29.1, 7, 12) by which a day of rest from work was intimated, probably comes from the Holiness Code;|| and the term '*a*ṣeret in 29.35 ('solemn assembly'), for the last day of the great Autumn Festival, goes back to Lev. 23.36.††

[28.3-8] The regular morning and evening burnt offering (on this cf. the secondary passage Ex. 29.38-42a), consisting of a lamb

---

* Such a distinction is, of course, no longer evident in RSV. Tr.
† On '*išše*, cf. *Leviticus*, p. 24.
‡ Cf. *Leviticus*, p. 24.
§ This is probably a more accurate translation of the Hebrew than RSV's 'holy convocation'. It is the translation offered by Noth. Tr.
|| Cf. *Leviticus*, pp. 168f.
†† Cf. *Leviticus*, pp. 174f.

offering with its appropriate cereal and drink offerings (28.3–8), has a fairly long prehistory. All that is demanded of the 'prince' in Ezekiel's programme for the future is a regular morning burnt offering (cf., too, Lev. 6.8–13 [*Hebr*. 6.1–6]) with, it is true, a somewhat more generous cereal offering, but without a drink offering (Ezek. 46.13–15); but as early as II Kings 16.15 a regular morning burnt offering and a regular evening cereal offering (on the latter cf., for the state of Israel, I Kings 18.29) are presupposed for the royal sanctuary in Jerusalem. This is probably what is meant, too, when Neh. 10.33 (*Hebr*. v. 34) mentions a 'continual cereal offering' (on this cf. the 'evening cereal offering' of Ezra 9.4)* and a 'continual burnt offering'. In the present passage a burnt offering with cereal and drink offerings is required both for morning and evening.† The cereal offering obviously consisted only of dough (cf. Lev. 2.1, 2) made of roughly ground meal (the dry measure 'ephah', which is understood as the unit of measurement and is not mentioned again in what follows, was the equivalent of approximately a bushel) mixed with oil (the liquid measure 'hin' was the equivalent of approximately ten pints). For the technical term 'beaten oil' cf. Ex. 27.20; this is the oil that drips of itself from beaten olives, as opposed to the normal oil which is pressed from the olives. The historical reminiscence in v. 6 interrupts the sequence of thought and must be an addition. The same is true of the explanatory remark in v. 7b, according to which the drink offering consisted of some kind of 'strong' drink, made from barley or the like and poured out somewhere 'in the holy place'. Originally certainly wine was brought as the drink offering (thus specifically 28.14a, as well as 15.5, 7, 10) and this was so self-explanatory that in most places no specific mention of it is made. According to Ecclus. 50.15, the drink offering was of 'red wine' poured out 'at the foot of the altar (of burnt offering)'. This must have been the usual practice.

[**28.9–15**] On the sabbath, which, basically, was not a cultic feast day,‡ in addition to the daily burnt offerings, an additional burnt offering, according to 28.9[10], was to be made with double the usual quantity (in Ezek. 46.4f.—cf. 46.13f.—a much more substantial

---

* In Ezra 9.4, RSV has simply 'evening sacrifice', but the above is a more accurate rendering of the Hebrew. Tr.
† For the expression 'between the two evenings'='twilight', cf. *Leviticus*, p. 169.
‡ Cf. *Exodus*, p. 164.

sabbath offering is required), but obviously only once in the day and then presumably in the morning. The prominence given to the days of the new moon by extremely large sacrifices (28.11–15) is remarkable. Here for the first time bulls and rams appear as sacrificial animals along with the lambs, hence the exact details given in vv. 12–14 about the precise quantities for the cereal and drink offerings that are to accompany the different kinds of sacrificial animals (for the relationships between these quantities, which agree with the relationships given in 15.4–12, cf. above, pp. 114f.). These details are repeated in stereotyped fashion for the cereal offering as far as 29.15 and are thereafter replaced by a general formula; they are not repeated for the drink offering, but are certainly tacitly assumed to be still operative. The cultic emphasis on the day of the new moon, which, in Ezek. 46.6f., is distinguished from the sabbath day by a bull offering, puts it on the same level as the Feast of Unleavened Bread (which lasts, however, seven days) and the Feast of the First Fruits. The reason for this emphasis (in older passages such as Amos 8.5; Hos. 2.13; Isa. 1.13; II Kings 4.23, the new moon and the sabbath are mentioned together) remains uncertain.

[28.16–31] The framework of the section on the feast of Passover and Unleavened Bread (28.16–25) is taken almost word for word from Lev. 23.5–8, as are the references to resting from work on the first and seventh days of the feast. Appropriately, no mention is made of the Passover sacrifices, for this was not an occasion for the cultic community as a whole but for individual families. It is a different matter with the sacrifices of vv. 19–21, 24, brought on the seven days of the feast of Unleavened Bread. In contrast to the other feasts, the 'day of the first fruits' (28.26–31), for practical purposes identical with the 'Feast of Weeks' (Ex. 34.22; Deut. 16.10), to which reference is made in a brief phrase in v. 26a, is not dated (so, too, Lev. 23.9ff.). What is meant by the 'cereal offering of new grain' are the first products of the new harvest.

Most space is taken up by the feast days and feast periods of the seventh month which, according to the practice, usual in the post-exilic period, of beginning the year in the spring, falls in the autumn. This is the old Autumn Festival, at the turn of the year in the autumn, which was later elaborated. In the present cultic calendar the exact order of feasts in the Holiness Code (Lev. 23) is presupposed. [29.1–6] First of all there are the two feast days on the first and the tenth of the seventh month, with the same size of offering and the obligation to rest from work. The first day, i.e. New Year's Day proper, fixed at the beginning of a month, is called a *yōm tᵉrū'ā*, a 'day for you to blow the trumpets' (29.1b; cf. Lev. 23.24), after the loud blowing of (rams') horns (cf. Lev. 25.9) with which the new period of time is introduced. **[29.7–11]** The tenth day is characterized by 'self-affliction' (cf. Lev. 23.27, 29)* presumably by means of certain abstentions which are not specifically described. This is the 'day of atonement', *yōm hakkippūrīm* (this technical term occurs only in Lev. 23.27; 25.9), on which, according to Lev. 16, special rites were to be performed which are briefly alluded to in the addition in v. 11ba; in the original version of this section reference is made only to the burnt offerings envisaged for this special day.

[29.12–38] As far as the Autumn Festival proper is concerned, for which the burnt offerings are enumerated in great detail in 29.12–38, the exact order of feasts in Lev. 23.34–36 is presupposed. There is mention first, obviously according to original practice, of a seven-day celebration (29.12b; cf. Lev. 23.34b); there is added to this an additional eighth day as a 'solemn assembly' (29.35–37; cf. Lev. 23. 36b). In the cultic Calendar the Autumn Festival, which from earliest times was the great principal festival, is distinguished by a particularly elaborate series of sacrifices, especially of bull sacrifices. Why, in the case of the seven original feast days, the number of bulls to be sacrificed is diminished by one each day can no longer be explained with any certainty. The first day of the feast, on which rest from work is also required (29.12a; cf. Lev. 23.35), would surely have a special significance which gradually diminishes in the course of the festival week. It is true that rest from work is also required on the eighth day, the 'solemn assembly' (29.35b; cf. Lev. 23.36b); for this last day, only a remarkably small number of sacrifices is envisaged (the same number as for the first and the tenth days) and this would indicate that this particular day is a late off-shoot from the great Autumn Festival.

13. THE BINDING NATURE OF WOMEN'S VOWS: 30.1–16

30 ¹Moses said to the heads of the tribes of the people of Israel, 'This is what the LORD has commanded. ²When a man vows a vow to the LORD, or swears an oath to bind himself by a pledge, he shall not break his word; he shall do according to all that proceeds out of his mouth. ³Or when a woman vows a vow to the LORD, and binds herself

* Cf. also *Leviticus*, pp. 173f.

by a pledge, while within her father's house, in her youth, ⁴and her father hears of her vow and of her pledge by which she has bound herself, and says nothing to her; then all her vows shall stand, and every pledge by which she has bound herself shall stand. ⁵But if her father expresses dispproval to her on the day that he hears of it, no vow of hers, no pledge by which she has bound herself, shall stand; and the LORD will forgive her, because her father opposed her. ⁶And if she is married to a husband, while under her vows or any thoughtless utterance of her lips by which she has bound herself, ⁷and her husband hears of it, and says nothing to her on the day that he hears; then her vows shall stand, and her pledges by which she has bound herself shall stand. ⁸But if, on the day that her husband comes to hear of it, he expresses disapproval, then he shall make void her vow which was on her, and the thoughtless utterance of her lips, by which she bound herself; and the LORD will forgive her. ⁹[But any vow of a widow or of a divorced woman, everything by which she has bound herself, shall stand against her.] ¹⁰And if she vowed in her husband's house, or bound herself by a pledge with an oath, ¹¹and her husband heard of it, and said nothing to her, and did not oppose her; then all her vows shall stand, and every pledge by which she bound herself shall stand. ¹²But if her husband makes them null and void on the day that he hears them, then whatever proceeds out of her lips concerning her vows, or concerning her pledge of herself, shall not stand: her husband has made them void, and the LORD will forgive her. ¹³Any vow and any binding oath to afflict herself, her husband may establish, or her husband may make void. ¹⁴But if her husband says nothing to her from day to day, then he establishes all her vows, or all her pledges, that are upon her; he has established them, because he said nothing to her on the day that he heard of them. ¹⁵ But if he makes them null and void after he has heard them, then he shall bear her iniquity.'

16 These are the statutes which the LORD commanded Moses, as between a man and his wife, and between a father and his daughter, while in her youth, within her father's house.

Both from the literary point of view and from the point of view of content, this passage stands on its own. Without having any connection with what precedes or with what follows, it has been included in the series of final instructions which Moses, at Yahweh's command, gives to the Israelites. It deals with a subject which is not otherwise dealt with in the Old Testament, namely the binding nature of particular obligations which one has voluntarily taken upon oneself 'with regard to Yahweh'. In this respect two categories of obligations are permanently differentiated, namely 'vows', i.e. obligations with regard to certain positive actions (e.g. sacrifices), and 'pledges' (the technical term for this, *'issār*, occurs only here in the Old Testament), i.e. obligations with regard to certain abstentions (cf. especially v. 13a,* according to which the 'pledge' means an act of 'self-affliction'). Details concerning the actual content of such obligations are totally lacking. Only the question of their binding nature is considered. The fact that they are binding is,'of course, fundamental, and this is expressly stated by way of introduction (v. 2) and is presupposed in what follows (cf. vv. 5b, 8b, 12b, 15). The only problem—and this is the real subject of this chapter— concerns the binding nature of obligations which women have taken upon themselves. Here it is presupposed at the beginning that women have the right to undertake, on their own initiative, obligations of the kind mentioned. This they do by means of—this holds true of all cases (cf. v. 2b)—a spoken and heard word. The validity of such obligations, however, depends on the assent, given at least tacitly, of the man in question. In this respect three cases are distinguished. In the case of a girl still unmarried and living in her father's house, the father has to decide (vv. 3–5); with entry into marriage the right hitherto exercised by the father immediately passes to the husband (vv. 6–8); for the woman already married it is the decision of her husband which counts (vv. 10–15). V. 9, which establishes the validity, independent of any man, of obligations assumed by a woman who has been widowed or divorced, is an addition which disrupts the sequence of thought in an attempt to fill an obvious gap in the discussion. In all this, therefore, women are accorded cultic rights of only an indirect nature (with the exception, according to the addition in v. 9, of the widow or the divorced woman.) Nothing at all is said about the motives for the decision of the man in question; it is obviously left to his personal judgment. All that is required is that he should decide immediately, as soon as he learns of the obligation in question. It is true that this is specifically stated in v. 14 only for the case of the married woman, but surely the sense demands that it is meant to be valid for every case. What is surely meant is that the man's decision is not to be determined by lengthy reflection or by irrelevant considerations. The refusal of assent by the man (the verb used for this, Hiph. of *nw'*, in vv. 5, 8, 11, originally means 'thrust back') causes an objective state of guilt on the woman's part on account of the non-fulfilment of a promise made to Yahweh. Because the woman, dependent on the man's decision, is subjectively innocent, Yahweh will 'forgive' her; this is stated in the first two cases in v. 5ba and v.8b.

* The verse references in this chapter are all to the numbering of the EVV. The numbering in the Hebrew can be found by adding 1. Tr.

In the third case, the same remark is made again in v. 12bβ, but in the case where the man has raised no immediate objection, having prevented the fulfilling of the obligation only at a later point, then the objective guilt is laid upon the man (v. 15b); no explanation is given as to what that meant in practice. It is only in the context of the statements about the woman who, through marriage, becomes the property of a man and who, at the time of her marriage, still has to fulfil obligations which she has undertaken and which have obviously been approved by her father, that the expression 'thoughtless utterance of her lips' (vv. 6b, 8aβ) occurs with reference to the 'pledge' to a certain abstention. Is the meaning of this that a woman, looking forward to her marriage, is acting thoughtlessly if she still takes a 'pledge' upon herself?

14. WAR OF VENGEANCE AGAINST THE MIDIANITES
AND THE SUBSEQUENT DIVISION OF THE BOOTY:
31.1–54

31 ¹The LORD said to Moses, ²'Avenge the people of Israel on the Midianites; afterward you shall be gathered to your people.' ³And Moses said to the people, 'Arm men from among you for the war, that they may go against Midian, to execute the LORD's vengeance on Midian. ⁴You shall send a thousand from each of the tribes of Israel to the war.' ⁵So there were provided, out of the thousands of Israel, a thousand from each tribe, twelve thousand armed for war. ⁶And Moses sent them to the war, a thousand from each tribe, together with Phinehas the son of Eleazar the priest, with the vessels of the sanctuary and the trumpets for the alarm in his hand. ⁷They warred against Midian, as the LORD commanded Moses, and slew every male. ⁸They slew the kings of Midian with the rest of their slain, Evi, Rekem, Zur, Hur, and Reba, the five kings of Midian; and they also slew Balaam the son of Beor with the sword. ⁹And the people of Israel took captive the women of Midian and their little ones; and they took as booty all their cattle, their flocks, and all their goods. ¹⁰All their cities in the places where they dwelt, and all their encampments they burned with fire, ¹¹and took all the spoil and all the booty, both of man and of beast. ¹²Then they brought the captives and the booty and the spoil to Moses, and to Eleazar the priest, and to the congregation of the people of Israel, at the camp on the plains of Moab by the Jordan at Jericho.

13 [Moses, and Eleazar the priest, and all the leaders of the congregation, went forth to meet them outside the camp.] ¹⁴And Moses was angry with the officers of the army, the commanders of thousands and the commanders of hundreds, who had come from service in the war. ¹⁵Moses said to them, 'Have you let all the women live? ¹⁶Behold, these caused the people of Israel, by the counsel of Balaam, to act

treacherously against the LORD [in the matter of Peor,] and so the plague came among the congregation of the LORD. 17Now therefore, kill every male among the little ones, and kill every woman who has known man by lying with him. 18But all the young girls who have not known man by lying with him, keep alive for yourselves. 19[Encamp outside the camp seven days; whoever of you has killed any person, and whoever has touched any slain, purify yourselves and your captives on the third day and on the seventh day. 20You shall purify every garment, every article of skin, all work of goats' hair, and every article of wood.']

21 And Eleazar the priest said to the men of war who had gone to battle: 'This is the statute of the law which the LORD has commanded Moses: 22only the gold, the silver, the bronze, the iron, the tin, and the lead, 23everything that can stand the fire, you shall pass through the fire, and it shall be clean. [Nevertheless it shall also be purified with the water of impurity;] and whatever cannot stand the fire, you shall pass through the water. 24You must wash your clothes on the seventh day, and you shall be clean; and afterward you shall come into the camp.'

25 The LORD said to Moses, 26"Take the count of the booty that was taken, both of man and of beast, you and Eleazar the priest and the heads of the fathers' houses of the congregation; 27and divide the booty into two parts, between the warriors who went out to battle and all the congregation. 28And levy for the LORD a tribute from the men of war who went out to battle, one out of five hundred, of the persons and of the oxen and of the asses and of the flocks; 29take it from their half, and give it to Eleazar the priest as an offering to the LORD. 30And from the people of Israel's half you shall take one drawn out of every fifty, of the persons, of the oxen, of the asses, and of the flocks, of all the cattle, and give them to the Levites who have charge of the tabernacle of the LORD.' 31And Moses and Eleazar the priest did as the LORD commanded Moses.

32 Now the booty remaining of the spoil that the men of war took was: six hundred and seventy-five thousand sheep, 33seventy-two thousand cattle, 34sixty-one thousand asses, 35and thirty-two thousand persons in all, women who had not known man by lying with him. 36And the half, the portion of those who had gone out to war, was in number three hundred and thirty-seven thousand five hundred sheep, 37and the LORD's tribute of sheep was six hundred and seventy-five. 38The cattle were thirty-six thousand, of which the LORD's tribute was seventy-two. 39The asses were thirty thousand five hundred, of which the LORD's tribute was sixty-one. 40The persons were sixteen thousand, of which the LORD's tribute was thirty-two persons. 41And Moses gave the tribute, which was the offering for the LORD, to Eleazar the priest, as the LORD commanded Moses.

42 From the people of Israel's half, which Moses separated from that of the men who had gone to war—43now the congregation's half was three hundred and thirty-seven thousand five hundred sheep, 44thirty-

six thousand cattle, [45]and thirty thousand five hundred asses, [46]and sixteen thousand persons—[47]from the people of Israel's half Moses took one of every fifty, both of persons and of beasts, and gave them to the Levites who had charge of the tabernacle of the LORD; as the LORD commanded Moses.

[48] Then the officers who were over the thousands of the army, the captains of thousands and the captains of hundreds, came near to Moses, [49]and said to Moses, 'Your servants have counted the men of war who are under our command, and there is not a man missing from us. [50]And we have brought the LORD's offering, what each man found, articles of gold, armlets and bracelets, signet rings, earrings, and beads, to make atonement for ourselves before the LORD.' [51]And Moses and Eleazar the priest received from them the gold, all wrought articles. [52]And all the gold of the offering that they offered to the LORD, from the commanders of thousands and the commanders of hundreds, was sixteen thousand seven hundred and fifty shekels. [53](The men of war had taken booty, every man for himself.) [54]And Moses and Eleazar the priest received the gold from the commanders of thousands and of hundreds, and brought it into the tent of meeting, as a memorial for the people of Israel before the LORD.

It is not easy to make out what the real subject-matter of this long section is supposed to be. It is made up of a narrative about a successful campaign, undertaken as the result of a divine command, to annihilate the Midianites (vv. 1–12) and a series of ordinances concerning procedure on the return from the campaign, with particular regard to the division of the booty (vv. 13–47), as well as a concluding appendix about a sin offering brought by the soldiers on their own initiative (vv. 48–54). To begin with, we can disregard this last-mentioned concluding section, since it has scarcely any point on its own. If one were to start from a glance at the scope of the different sections, it might seem as if the principal emphasis lay on the legislation about the return and the division of booty, with the preceding report of the Midianite war serving only as a 'historical' point of anchorage. However, vv. 13–47, in spite of their large compass, are fairly thin in content, since detailed enumeration in vv. 25–47 takes up a considerable amount of space, quite apart from the fact that this section is not a literary unit, but shows traces of secondary additions (see below, pp. 230f.). The report of the Midianite war in vv. 1–12 could, then, form the nucleus of the whole passage. It, too, however, is remarkably colourless and schematized and lacking in concrete details, so that it is difficult to see in it an independent element of tradition or to accept that in it is to be found the primary form of the whole, to which the details of vv. 13ff. have been annexed at a later stage, details which are to be regarded as secondary from the literary point of view. Apart from isolated secondary expansions, there are no adequate grounds for any literary-critical separation in this chapter, and the either-or question posed above as to the object of the narrative as a whole remains unanswerable.

It is, however, certain that the chapter is one of the very late sections in the Pentateuch. It is not, even as a late addition, to be considered as part of the P-narrative, but represents a supplement to the Pentateuch as a whole, for, in its present content and scope as a whole, it presupposes that variegated chapter Num. 25 (see above, pp. 195f.). There is a link between the divine command for a campaign against the Midianites given in 25.16–18 and repeated in different words in 31.1–3. Even in 25.18 this command originates from the assertion that—contradicting the old narrative of 25.1–5 and with only a slight reference to the episode of 25.6–9—it was the Midianites who led Israel astray to the apostasy with Baal of Peor. That this is to be regarded as perhaps even an old variant of the story of Baal of Peor, which told of Midianite women rather than of Moabite women (25.1) as those who led the Israelite men astray, is not very likely, since there is no indication at all of the presence of any old elements of tradition in Num. 31. Dependence on Num. 25 is an adequate explanation of the circumstances of the narrative that is before us.

[31.1–12] The report of the Midianite war (vv. 1–12) contains little that is factual; there is not even any indication as to where this total destruction of Midian took place, only the Israelites' permanent camp being mentioned in v. 12b, in dependence on 22.1bP. According to vv. 1–2, the 'vengeance' on the Midianites was a task which Moses had to fulfil before his death, of which he had already received intimation (v. 2b refers back to 27.12–14). The drawing up of the army in thousands is done in a schematized way without reference to the individual strength of the twelve tribes (vv. 4–6a). According to v. 6b, the son of the chief priest, who proved himself in the Baal-Peor affair (25.7–8a) and as a result received a divine promise (25.12–13), accompanies the army with 'the vessels of the sanctuary' (what is meant by this remains obscure, at any rate not the ark, which one can expect them to have taken with them automatically) and 'the trumpets for the alarm' which, according to 10.1–10, served as a signal for striking camp but also to 'remind' Yahweh of Israel when the enemy was pressing. According to v. 7, the victory over Midian was so complete that the total Midianite manpower was annihilated, while, according to v. 49, not a single man of the Israelite army was lost. Since all the adult Midianite women and the male children were also subsequently killed (v. 17), from then on Midian will have entirely ceased to exist (cf., on the contrary, the role of the Midianites according to Judg. 6–8). After v. 7, v. 8 has the effect of seeming strikingly out of context. This is all the more note-worthy since v. 8, by giving the names of the five Midianite kings, contains the only detailed information in this whole section. The only other occurrence of these names is in Josh. 13.21, in literary depend-ence on the present passage; and the name Zur occurs also in 25.15 as the name of the ancestor of a Midianite clan. It is difficult to think of an old tradition in connection with this list of names, especially since v. 8 is probably an addition to what is already a very late passage. This assertion holds good also for the mention of Balaam in v. 8, which is probably occasioned by the fact that he is mentioned in v. 16 (on this see below, p. 231). The statements in vv. 9–10 con-clude this theme of the total destruction of the Midianites.

[31.13–20] The section comprising vv. 13–24 is obviously not a literary unit; several points are discussed which have no relationship to each other and which are held together only by the situation of the victorious army returning with its booty. The idea, contained in v. 13, of the army being halted and addressed by the leaders of the congregation outside the camp is surprising and unexpected after what has been said in v. 12. Vv. 19–20 appear to be part of this idea, for they seem for their part to follow rather abruptly on the statements contained in vv. 14–18. According to vv. 19–20, the soldiers, having become cultically 'unclean' through having killed men and come into contact with the dead, are to remain outside the camp to begin with and submit to certain specified but undefined measures for 'purification' (cf. 19.11f.) in which even objects of personal use are to be included, all this although the campaign was one that had been commanded by Yahweh himself. It is very probable that in vv. 13 and 19–20 we have a later addition which interrupts the original sequence of thought. Vv. 14–18, on the other hand, connect easily with v. 12 and, as opposed to the addition that has just been mentioned, have a specific relationship to the report of the Midianite war. The leaders of the army are reproached by Moses with having left the Midianite women alive and brought them back as prisoners, although it was these very women who had seduced the Israelites to Baal of Peor and had been the real reason for this war of vengeance ordered by Yahweh against the Midianites, had been, therefore, the main culprits. They had subsequently to be killed, along with the little children of the male sex, with no particular reason being given for this latter action. Thus, at any rate, it was ensured that a new generation of Midianites could not arise. Only those girls who were not yet grown up were the Israelites permitted to spare and keep for themselves (as concubines and slaves). Since the reason for these measures was unique, this ruling is presumably not meant to be understood as generally valid for the treatment of conquered peoples. The note to the effect that Israel was enticed away to Baal of Peor by 'the counsel of Balaam' (v. 16) is remarkable. It is highly improbable that in this late passage there is still contained an original variant of the old Balaam tradition. It is, rather, a question of a combination resulting from the juxtaposition of the Balaam stories in ch. 22–24 and the Baal-Peor story in ch. 25, a combination which might seem to be suggested by the fact that, according to 23.28, Balaam had gone up to 'the top of Peor' (no notice was taken, of course, of the remark made in 24.25a) and that, according to ch. 22–24, hostile intentions towards Israel could be attributed to him which, after the failure of the intended cursing of Israel resulting from divine intervention, he had nevertheless realized on another occasion.

[31.21–24] Vv. 21–24, introduced in a particularly solemn manner, have a fragmentary character. The word 'only' (Hebr. *'ak*) at the beginning of v. 22 must actually introduce a limitation or a specification of something mentioned previously, but there is no such connection with anything that precedes. Only from the context is it clear that what is being spoken of is different kinds of booty which first of all, i.e. before they use them for their own purposes, must be cultically 'purified', by fire in so far as this is possible without the destruction of the articles in question, otherwise by water (the remark that in the first case, too, the 'water of impurity' of 19.9ff. must be used is a later addition). Only the final sentence about the washing of clothes (v. 24) contains any specific allusion to the situation of those who have returned from a victorious campaign and are still outside the camp. This whole passage is an addendum, having only a slight connection with the already secondary statements of vv. 19–20.

[31.25–47] An essential element of the whole chapter is the regulations for the division of the booty which are expressly dealt with in vv. 25–47. They provide first of all for the division of the whole quantity of the booty into two equal halves, one of which goes to the men who have taken part in the campaign, amongst whom it is presumably to be equally divided, while the other remains for all the rest of the 'congregation'. One might compare with this the 'statute', which grew out of a given occasion according to I Sam. 30.24f., that, when booty is to be divided, the actual combatants and those who remained behind to watch the baggage are, as individuals (the situation is therefore somewhat different from that in the present passage), to be provided with equal shares. Since the 12,000 fighting men (cf. v. 5) were only a fraction of the number of persons in the 'congregation', they were at a great advantage in this method of dividing the booty. This is also true of the tribute from the booty that was to be offered to Yahweh. While the fighting men had to give up only the 500th part of their proceeds (v. 28), in the case of the 'congregation' it was the 50th part (vv. 30, 47). The tribute from the fighting men went to the priesthood (vv. 29, 41), while that of the 'congregation' was to be given to the Levites (vv. 30, 47). Priests and Levites, then, received a share of the booty in the ratio 1:10. This whole division of booty is now carried out in detail, with figures which hardly rest on any tradition, but have been thought up *ad hoc*.

[31.48–54] The concluding section, vv. 48–54, without having any connection whatsoever with what has gone before, mentions once again a 'heave-offering' (i.e. a solemn offering)* for Yahweh. On this occasion, it consists of costly ornaments of gold which have been taken as booty. In the main section concerning the division of the booty, in vv. 25–47, only living persons and animals were mentioned, and only in a secondary passage, v. 22, was reference made to captured metal. The reason for this offering of gold was a count of the fighting men, taken after the return home, at which it was established that not a single man was missing as a result of the Midianite war (vv. 48–49). And now an 'atonement' was necessary, probably because the count was regarded as sinful (cf. Ex. 30.11–16). This was the origin of what was, according to v. 52, the extremely costly gift of gold brought into the sanctuary of the tent of meeting (v. 54) to be there a good 'memorial' for Israel before Yahweh (the exact same phrase appears also in Ex. 30.16).† This offering for atonement consisted of the precious gold ornaments contained in the 'official'

---

* Cf. *Leviticus*, pp. 61f.

† The phrases are identical in the Hebrew, but not in the RSV, although the sense of them in the latter is the same. Tr.

booty and now handed over by the army officers. It is briefly noted in v. 53 that, besides this, the individual fighting men had each taken booty for themselves. It is no longer possible to decide whether this concluding section belonged, in spite of its lack of connection, to the primary version of the chapter, or is a later addition.

15. THE FIRST DISTRIBUTION OF TERRITORY EAST OF THE JORDAN: 32.1–42

32 ¹Now the sons of Reuben and the sons of Gad had a very great multitude of cattle; and they saw the land of Jazer and the land of Gilead, and behold, the place was a place for cattle. ²So the sons of Gad and the sons of Reuben came and said to Moses and to Eleazar the priest and to the leaders of the congregation, ³['Ataroth, Dibon, Jazer, Nimrah, Heshbon, Elealeh, Sebam, Nebo, and Beon,] ⁴the land which the LORD smote before the congregation of Israel, is a land for cattle; and your servants have cattle.' ⁵And they said, 'If we have found favour in your sight, let this land be given to your servants for a possession; do not take us across the Jordan.'

6 But Moses said to the sons of Gad and to the sons of Reuben, 'Shall your brethren go to the war while you sit here? ⁷Why will you discourage the heart of the people of Israel from going over into the land which the LORD has given them? ⁸Thus did your fathers, when I sent them from Kadesh-barnea to see the land. ⁹For when they went up to the Valley of Eschol, and saw the land, they discouraged the heart of the people of Israel from going into the land which the LORD had given them. ¹⁰And the LORD's anger was kindled on that day, and he swore, saying, ¹¹"Surely none of the men who came up out of Egypt, from twenty years old and upward, shall see the land which I swore to give to Abraham, to Isaac, and to Jacob, because they have not wholly followed me; ¹²none except Caleb the son of Jephunneh the Kenizzite and Joshua the son of Nun, [for they have wholly followed the LORD."] ¹³And the LORD's anger was kindled against Israel, and he made them wander in the wilderness forty years, until all the generation that had done evil in the sight of the LORD was consumed. ¹⁴And behold, you have risen in your fathers' stead, a brood of sinful men, to increase still more the fierce anger of the LORD against Israel! ¹⁵For if you turn away from following him, he will again abandon them in the wilderness; and you will destroy all this people.'

16 Then they came near to him, and said, 'We will build sheepfolds here for our flocks, and cities for our little ones, ¹⁷but we will take up arms, ready to go before the people of Israel, until we have brought them to their place; and our little ones shall live in the fortified cities because of the inhabitants of the land. ¹⁸We will not return to our homes until the people of Israel have inherited each his inheritance. ¹⁹For we will not inherit with them on the other side of the Jordan and

beyond; because our inheritance has come to us on this side of the Jordan to the east.' ²⁰So Moses said to them, 'If you will do this, if you will take up arms to go before the LORD for the war, ²¹and every armed man of you will pass over the Jordan before the LORD, until he has driven out his enemies from before him ²²and the land is subdued before the LORD; then after that you shall return and be free of obligation to the LORD and to Israel; and this land shall be your possession before the LORD. ²³But if you will not do so, behold, you have sinned against the LORD; and be sure your sin will find you out. ²⁴Build cities for your little ones, and folds for your sheep; and do what you have promised.' ²⁵And the sons of Gad and the sons of Reuben said to Moses, 'Your servants will do as my lord commands. ²⁶Our little ones, our wives, our flocks, and all our cattle, shall remain there in the cities of Gilead; ²⁷but your servants will pass over, every man who is armed for war, before the LORD to battle, as my lord orders.'

28 So Moses gave command concerning them to Eleazar the priest, and to Joshua the son of Nun, and to the heads of the fathers' houses of the tribes of the people of Israel. ²⁹And Moses said to them, 'If the sons of Gad and the sons of Reuben, every man who is armed to battle before the LORD, will pass with you over the Jordan and the land shall be subdued before you, then you shall give them the land of Gilead for a possession; ³⁰but if they will not pass over with you armed, they shall have possessions among you in the land of Canaan.' ³¹And the sons of Gad and the sons of Reuben answered, 'As the LORD has said to your servants, so we will do. ³²We will pass over armed before the LORD into the land of Canaan, and the possession of our inheritance shall remain with us beyond the Jordan.'

33 And Moses gave to them, to the sons of Gad and to the sons of Reuben and to the half-tribe of Manasseh the son of Joseph, the kingdom of Sihon king of the Amorites and the kingdom of Og king of Bashan, the land and its cities with their territories, the cities of the land throughout the country. ³⁴And the sons of Gad built Dibon, Ataroth, Aroer, ³⁵Atroth-Shophan, Jazer, Jogbehah. ³⁶Beth-nimrah and Beth-haran, fortified cities, and folds for sheep. ³⁷And the sons of Reuben built Heshbon, Elealeh, Kiriathaim, ³⁸Nebo, and Baal-meon (their names to be changed), and Sibmah; and they gave other names to the cities which they built. ³⁹And the sons of Machir the son of Manasseh went to Gilead and took it, and dispossessed the Amorites who were in it. ⁴⁰And Moses gave Gilead to Machir the son of Manasseh, and he settled in it. ⁴¹And Jair the son of Manasseh went and took their villages, and called them Havvoth-jair. ⁴²And Nobah went and took Kenath and its villages, and called it Nobah, after his own name.

Apart from the references at the end, in vv. 39–42, the content is fairly simple and clear. The Israelite tribes, coming from an easterly or south-easterly direction, have taken possession of certain territories east of the Jordan, and a few tribes want to settle in these territories, which appear particularly suited to the rearing of small cattle, thereby renouncing their right to a share in the territory west of the Jordan. They promise, however, to take part in the communal military conquest of the land west of the Jordan and state that they will return, with their military forces, to the inheritance they want east of the Jordan, only after the completion of this task. In details, of course, there are in this presentation numerous discrepancies and differences which are a clear indication that the whole chapter is not a literary unit, but is composed of various elements, presumably of different periods. The territory that is desired is referred to in v. 1 as 'the land of Jazer and the land of Gilead'; in vv. 26, 29, on the other hand, only 'Gilead' is mentioned. The tribes who requested it were, according to v. 1, Reuben and Gad (in that order) and, according to vv. 2ff., Gad and Reuben (that is, in the reverse order); in v. 33, in addition to Gad and Reuben, the half-tribe of Manasseh appears. In many places there appear what are clearly 'deuteronomistic' phrases and concepts (cf., e.g., v. 33); elsewhere the 'priestly' style is again unmistakable (e.g. vv. 2b, 28, *et al.*).

Now, it is beyond doubt that the basic form of the chapter is neither 'deuteronomistic' nor 'priestly'. It is fundamentally different from the deuteronomistic presentation of the conquest east of the Jordan as this is found particularly in Deut. 2.26–3.22. The priestly writer, for his part, was not at all interested in the detailed proceedings of the conquest, and neither he nor the deuteronomist would have given any weight to the wishes of individual tribes in the allocation of territorial possessions. It is, therefore, generally and correctly accepted that the basic form of the narrative goes back to the 'old Pentateuchal sources'. These are here making their last appearance in the book of Numbers and, in the present passage, introduce the theme of the conquest of the land by the individual Israelite tribes. Unfortunately they have been subject to so many revisions and additions that it is impossible to prosecute any sharp and convincing literary-critical analysis; and obviously, as a result of these revisions and additions, so much of their text has been suppressed and therefore lost that a definite answer can no longer be given to the question as to whether this 'old' source-material was a unit or was itself composite. In the latter case it would be a question of a combination of J and E; in the former one might think of J. The later components certainly do not belong to these 'sources', even in those places where we are dealing not simply with additions which have no context, but with somewhat more extensive stretches. A revision in the deuteronomistic spirit must have had the obvious aim of interpreting the conquest events depicted here in terms of the presentation of these same events within the framework of the above-mentioned deuteronomistic conquest narrative; this would happen in the course of the editorial fitting together of Pentateuchal narrative and deuteronomistic historical work. The elements in priestly style do not form a coherent P-narrative; that they are here at all is certainly due to the fact that this is the generally predominant style in the book of Numbers. From what has been said, there arises the task of going through the chapter step by step, thereby determining as far as possible the content and the literary identity of the individual statements.

[32.1] The narrative goes back to the historical fact that the tribes of Reuben and Gad, unlike the other Israelite tribes, had their territory east of the Jordan and were predominantly breeders of small cattle; according to the narrative, this was of their own volition. It is not certain whether already in v. 1, which certainly belongs to the old basic form of the narrative, there are traces of a double narrative. What *is* remarkable, however, is not only the unique word-order Reuben-Gad, which is immediately resolved in what follows by the order Gad-Reuben (and this surely on the basis of an old source-tradition) and not only the lame effect of the expression 'very great' in v. 1a,* but also the juxtaposition of 'the land of Jazer' and 'the land of Gilead', in view of the fact that in vv. 26, 29 only 'the land of Gilead' is mentioned, while it is the other way about in 21.32, where, in an addition which is obviously referring to the present narrative, only 'Jazer' is mentioned. The territories in question are to be found in the mountains east of the Jordan and to the south of the Jabbok. Jazer (Hebr. *ya'zēr*) was the name of a city whose surrounding territory was known as 'the land of Jazer'. The varied data concerning its position (especially in the *Onomastikon* of Eusebius) are best suited by locating it on the modern *tell el-'arēme*, about two and a half miles (as the crow flies) north-west of the modern place *nā'ūr*.† The land of 'Jazer' is therefore to be found in the territory at the entrance to that valley which emerges into the Jordan

* This is not apparent in the RSV. A literal rendering of the Hebrew would be: 'The sons of Reuben and the sons of Gad had a multitude of cattle, a very great one.' Tr.

† Cf. R. Rendtorff, *Zeitschrift des Deutschen Palästina-Vereins*, 76, 1960, pp. 124–35.

valley as *wādi kefrein*. The name 'Gilead' must certainly be understood here in the narrow sense which it had to begin with; it was
originally perhaps the name of a mountain and then also the name of
a place which survives in the modern *ğel'ad*, about six miles (as the
crow flies) north-east of *es-salṭ*. *Tell el-'arēme* and *ğel'ad* are about
fourteen miles apart; the lands of Jazer and Gilead can be regarded
fairly easily as neighbouring territories. The exposition contained in
v. 1 must have led to Reuben and Gad's having asked for and received the territory described as their permanent dwelling. And to be
sure, what must be intended both by the phraseology of v. 1 and also
by the historical situation which lies behind it, is the first instance of a
distribution of territory to Israelite tribes. The tradition about it
stands, unharmonized, beside the narrative of 21.21 ff., in which what
is predominantly in mind is the plateau which lies further to the
south and stretches as far as the Arnon and which was conquered and
colonized by Israel (21.31) without any mention being made of
permanent dwellings for individual tribes (only the addition in 21.32
establishes a connection with 32.1 ff.). From the point of view of the
history of traditions, the basic form of 32.1 ff. is certainly older than
that of 21.21 ff.

[32.2-4] From the literary point of view it is not at first possible
to follow the narrative thread of v. 1 any further. For in vv. 2, 4 (the
list of towns in v. 3, all of which reappear in vv. 34-38, is an obvious
gloss, with no attempt even having been made to fit it into the context)
the style of P is clearly in evidence; at the most, the opening words of
v. 2 (as far as 'Moses') and the closing words of v. 4 could go back to
a basic form in the old sources; this supposition might be supported
by the address in the singular in v. 4b,* which seems to presuppose a
shorter text in v. 2 and which is taken up again in v. 5.

[32.5-15] The new introductory formula in v. 5 argues for the
fact that a new section begins here, and in actual fact v. 5 ought to
belong with the speech of Moses in vv. 6-15. This whole passage is
late and presupposes the spy story of ch. 13-14 in its present form as
put together from various sources. It does so, not in slavish dependence on it, but with a series of phrases of its own (cf., e.g., the verbal
statements in vv. 7a, 9aβ, 13aβ) and it seems also to be familiar with
Josh. 14.6-14 (the description of Caleb as a 'Kenizzite' occurs in this
form only here in v. 12 and in Josh. 14.6, 14). It belongs, therefore,

* In 'your servants have cattle', the possessive adjective 'your' is singular in
Hebrew. Tr.

to the stage when the Pentateuchal narrative was being integrated with the deuteronomistic historical work. The fact that Moses' speech refers to the spy story supposes that Reuben and Gad's wish had its root in fear at the military conquest of the territory west of the Jordan, or at least that it must have been understood in that way by the other Israelite tribes. There is no mention of this in those elements of tradition in this chapter which are to be considered as old.

[32.16–19] The tribes east of the Jordan can counter the suspicion that their wish is motivated by fear, and hence attain the fulfilment of their wish, only by declaring their readiness to share in the military conquest of the land west of the Jordan along with the other tribes. This, then, is what happens and what is expounded in detail in vv. 16–33. In this section, too, the presence of several literary strata is unmistakable, and the contents of these exhibit different shades of meaning. By their unusual style of expression, vv. 16–19 are striking, and their subject-matter is noteworthy in so far as the statement in v. 19b sounds as if the territory east of the Jordan had already been given to the tribes who asked for it and as if participation in the war west of the Jordan were a free offer on the part of those tribes, while in what follows this participation is made a condition of the gift of the desired territory. In actual fact, vv. 16–19 contain old source-material, although this has been reworked to a certain extent (v. 17 contains deuteronomistic turns of phrase, for which cf. Deut. 3.18; Josh. 1.14; 4.12). They ignore the speech of Moses in vv. 6–15 and could be linked directly with v. 1; at any rate there would not need to be much missing in between. The tribes from east of the Jordan take the initiative in announcing that, in the territory they have chosen, they will only 'build' (obviously, therefore, with walls of stone) folds for their numerous flocks and set up fortified cities for the protection of their 'little ones' (in practical terms this must mean their families after the departure of all the men who were fit for military service) and also that they are willing to take part in the war west of the Jordan until the tribes west of the Jordan have reached their goal of occupying that territory. All the same, they are thereby creating for themselves a certain advantage over the other tribes. This completes the whole business, and further discussion has become superfluous. Everything that follows, as far as v. 33, is also then later addition in the deuteronomistic-priestly style.

[32.20–23] In the speech of Moses in vv. 20–24, the choice as to the conduct of the tribes east of the Jordan seems at first still to be

open, although, according to vv. 16–19, the decision has already been
made, as, in fact, is recognized in practical terms in v. 24 with its
reference to the phraseology of v. 16 (for the expression in v. 22aα cf.
Josh. 18.1). The reply to Moses' speech in vv. 25–27 is, in the present
context, simply a confirmation of the promise already made. Since
Moses himself will not live to see this promise fulfilled (cf. 27.12–14),
he gives to the authorities who will bear responsibility in Israel after
his death (cf. Josh. 14.1b), instructions to make the allocation of land
to the tribes east of the Jordan dependent on their actual participation in the war west of the Jordan (vv. 28–30). In this context, the
territory to be allocated is called, in v. 29, as it was already in v. 26,
'(the land of) Gilead'. What is meant by this in these late texts must
be simply the land east of the Jordan in a rather vague sense; in the
framework of these contexts, it can scarcely be accepted that we have
here the basis of an old tradition with a special significance attached
to the name Gilead (cf. above, p. 237). It is noteworthy that in v. 30
what is envisaged by way of punishment if this promise is not
eventually kept is settlement in the territory west of the Jordan ('the
land of Canaan' as a designation of the country west of the Jordan is
part of the style of 'P'; cf. Josh. 22.9ff.). Although this was, in the
first instance, the land promised to Israel, yet the guilty parties would
not, in fact, have participated in the conquest of it. All that must be
meant is that their wish was, in such circumstances, not to be granted.
According to vv. 31–32, the potential inhabitants of the land east of
the Jordan answered once again as if they had been asked once more
and as if vv. 28–30 had not, rather, been concerned with the instructions of Moses to his successors. According to v. 33, Moses finally
granted them the land even before they had fulfilled this promise.
Here at the end, the whole passage is orientated in accordance with
the deuteronomistic presentation of the conquest. Besides Gad and
Reuben, there suddenly appears the half-tribe of Manasseh; and the
territory occupied by those two and a half tribes is extended to cover
the whole of the country to the east of the Jordan, in that it is identified
with the former domains of the defeated kings Sihon and Og (cf.
Deut. 2.26–3.22).

[32.34–38] The list of towns in vv. 34–38, which provides the
actual fulfilment of the intention expressed in v. 16b, is loosely
attached. To what stage in the literary history of the chapter it
belongs cannot now be decided. Of the fourteen names listed, nine
appear in the secondary v. 3 in roughly the same order, but in a

selection that appears arbitrary and with the alteration of several names. The locations of most of the cities are known; they lie in a region that stretches from the Arnon in the south to the mountains north of modern *nāʿūr* and as far as the south-east corner of the Jordan valley, that is partly more and partly less extensive than the area described in v. 1: Dibon = *dibān*; Ataroth = *ʿaṭṭārūṣ*; Aroer = *khirbet ʿarāʿir*; Atroth-Shophan occurs only here and has not yet been identified; Jazer cf. above, pp. 236f.; Jogbehah = *ǧbēha*; Beth-nimrah perhaps = *tell el-blēbil*; Beth-haran = *tell er-rāme*; Heshbon = *ḥisbān*; Elealeh = *el-ʿāl*; Kiriathaim = *khirbet el-qurēje*;* Nebo = *khirbet el-mukhajjiṭ*; Baal-meon = *māʿīn*; Sibmah perhaps = *khirbet qarn el-kibš*. The allocation of these cities to Gad (vv. 34–36) and Reuben (vv. 37–38) is strange; according to it, Gad occupied the southern, northern and north-western parts of the whole region, while Reuben had only a part in the middle, round about modern *mādeba*. This very fact might argue for the idea that at the basis of all this there are the circumstances of actual colonization. In Josh. 13.15–28 the same region, mentioning the names of the same cities, is divided between Reuben and Gad in a totally different manner (Reuben in the south and Gad in the north). The most likely explanation of this is that the original was a list of cities lying east of the Jordan, but not compiled in accordance with tribal territories, corresponding to the lists of cities in Judah in Josh. 15.21–62; 18.21–28† and subsequently integrated with the tribal system in different ways.

[32.39–42] The appendix in vv. 39–42 provides, in stereotyped phrases, further information about the land east of the Jordan. Its origin is unknown, as is the date of its insertion at the present point. It does not seem as if it had belonged at any time to any of the narrative 'sources'. That Machir conquered and colonized (vv. 39–40) the land of 'Gilead' (understood here certainly in its broader sense) is a very general statement which, although it cannot exactly be reconciled with v. 33, occurs repeatedly in the Old Testament. There follow, in vv. 41–42, the aetiologies of two place-names. Somewhere east of the Jordan, probably on the edge of the northern part of that region, there lay a settlement called 'the villages of Jair' (the usual translation 'villages' is not at all certain; the meaning of the Hebrew word *ḥawwōt* is not now known); it was called this because a

---

* Cf. A. Kuschke, *Zeitschrift des Deutschen Palästina-Vereins*, 77, 1961, pp. 24–31; 78, 1962, pp. 139f.

† Cf. H. W. Hertzberg, *Die Bücher Josua, Richter, Ruth* (ATD 9), pp. 98f.

member of the tribe of Manasseh called Jair had once conquered it and called it after his own name. Just as uncertain is what is known of the city of Nobah which is supposed to have been called after its one-time conqueror, of whose origin nothing at all is said. The city in question is supposed to have been called Kenath before that. To identify this Kenath with the modern *qanawāt* on the western edge of the Hauran mountains (*ǧebel ed-drūz*) is difficult, since *qanawāt* was too far away to have been colonized by the Israelites. However, an identification of Nobah with the Nobah of Judg. 8.11 is obvious; Kenath-Nobah would, therefore, need to be located somewhere south of the Jabbok in the region to the west or the north-west of modern *ʿammān*.

16. THE STATIONS OF ISRAEL'S WANDERINGS AFTER THE EXODUS FROM EGYPT: 33.1–49

33 ¹These are the stages of the people of Israel, when they went forth out of the land of Egypt by their hosts under the leadership of Moses and Aaron. ²[Moses wrote down their starting places, stage by stage, by command of the LORD; and these are their stages according to their starting places.] ³[They set out from Rameses in the first month, on the fifteenth day of the first month; on the day after the passover the people of Israel went out triumphantly in the sight of all the Egyptians, ⁴while the Egyptians were burying all their first-born, whom the LORD had struck down among them; upon their gods also the LORD executed judgments.]

5 So the people of Israel set out from Rameses, and encamped at Succoth. ⁶And they set out from Succoth, and encamped at Etham, which is on the edge of the wilderness. ⁷And they set out from Etham, and turned back to Pi-hahiroth, which is east of Baalzephon; and they encamped before Migdol. ⁸And they set out from before Hahiroth, [and passed through the midst of the sea into the wilderness, and they went a three days' journey in the wilderness of Etham,] and encamped at Marah. ⁹And they set out from Marah, and came to Elim; [at Elim there were twelve springs of water and seventy palm trees, and they encamped there.] ¹⁰And they set out from Elim, and encamped by the Red Sea. ¹¹And they set out from the Red Sea, and encamped in the wilderness of Sin. ¹²And they set out from the wilderness of Sin, and encamped at Dophkah. ¹³And they set out from Dophkah, and encamped at Alush. ¹⁴And they set out from Alush, and encamped at Rephidim, [where there was no water for the people to drink.] ¹⁵And they set out from Rephidim, and encamped in the wilderness of Sinai. ¹⁶And they set out from the wilderness of Sinai, and encamped at Kibroth-hattaavah. ¹⁷And they set out from Kibroth-hattaavah, and encamped at Hazeroth. ¹⁸And they set out from Hazeroth, and encamped at Rithmah. ¹⁹And they set out from Rithmah, and

encamped at Rimmon-perez. 20And they set out from Rimmon-perez, and encamped at Libnah. 21And they set out from Libnah, and encamped at Rissah. 22And they set out from Rissah, and encamped at Kehelathah. 23And they set out from Kehelathah, and encamped at Mount Shepher. 24And they set out from Mount Shepher, and encamped at Haradah. 25And they set out from Haradah, and encamped at Makheloth. 26And they set out from Makheloth, and encamped at Tahath. 27And they set out from Tahath, and encamped at Terah. 28And they set out from Terah, and encamped at Mithkah. 29And they set out from Mithkah, and encamped at Hashmonah. 30And they set out from Hashmonah, and encamped at Moseroth. 31And they set out from Moseroth, and encamped at Bene-jaakan. 32And they set out from Bene-jaakan, and encamped at Hor-haggidgad. 33And they set out from Hor-haggidgad, and encamped at Jotbathah. 34And they set out from Jotbathah, and encamped at Abronah. 35And they set out from Abronah, and encamped at Ezion-geber. 36And they set out from Ezion-geber, and encamped in [the wilderness of Zin (that is,] Kadesh). 37And they set out from Kadesh, and encamped at Mount Hor, on the edge of the land of Edom.

38 [And Aaron the priest went up Mount Hor at the command of the LORD, and died there, in the fortieth year after the people of Israel had come out of the land of Egypt, on the first day of the fifth month. 39And Aaron was a hundred and twenty-three years old when he died on Mount Hor.]

40 [And the Canaanite, the king of Arad, who dwelt in the Negeb in the land of Canaan, heard of the coming of the people of Israel.]

41 And they set out from Mount Hor, and encamped at Zalmonah. 42And they set out from Zalmonah, and encamped at Punon. 43And they set out from Punon, and encamped at Oboth. 44And they set out from Oboth, and encamped at Iye-abarim, in the territory of Moab. 45And they set out from Iyim, and encamped at Dibon-gad. 46And they set out from Dibon-gad, and encamped at Almon-diblathaim. 47And they set out from Almon-diblathaim, and encamped in the mountains of Abarim, before Nebo. 48And they set out from the mountains of Abarim, and encamped in the plains of Moab by the Jordan at Jericho; 49they encamped by the Jordan from Beth-jeshimoth as far as Abel-shittim in the plains of Moab.

The aim of this so-called list of camping sites is to present, retrospectively and comprehensively, the Israelites' route after leaving Egypt until they arrived at the Jordan, i.e. at the frontier of the land west of the Jordan that had been promised to them. To this end it utilizes the Pentateuchal narrative in the form finally arrived at by the collation of 'sources'. It is, therefore, later than that and is thus one of the late, secondary elements in the Pentateuch. [33.1–2] According to the superscription, this list was written down by Moses himself at the end of his life. Yet the sentence contained in v. 2a, which follows awkwardly on v. 1 and has occasioned a brief summary of v. 1 in v. 2b, is certainly an addition to what is already a very late passage. In several places the list is interrupted by brief references to events which occurred at the place in question, namely in vv. 3–4, 8, 9, 38–39, 40. It is very likely that these references were added only at a later point. This is especially clear in vv. 3–4, since the beginning of v. 3 anticipates the beginning of v. 5. It must therefore be considered that the original form of the whole section was a mere list of place-names, set in a framework composed of a quite simple formula which is constantly repeated in stereotyped fashion.

The most striking and most interesting factor, and perhaps also the most important one in this list, is that besides and amongst the place-names taken from the Pentateuchal narrative there occur numerous other place-names which do not come from that narrative and which, for the most part, are found nowhere else in the Old Testament. The first of these is the name Dophkah in vv. 12b, 13a, and they continue, alternating with the names that come from the Pentateuchal narrative, to the end of the section. From this it follows that what we are dealing with here is not a series of more or less haphazard, isolated additions, but a coherent list of place-names which must surely represent an 'itinerary'. In the list of camping sites in Num. 33, therefore, apart from the Pentateuchal narrative with its information about places, another 'document' has been used, about the origin and significance of which something further will need to be said, though with great caution and reticence, since the majority of the place-names contained in it cannot be identified.

[33.3–12] The phrasing of the original beginning of the list of camping sites in v. 5a, which for the first and last time mentions 'the Israelites' as subject, comes from Ex. 12.37.* The preceding addition in vv. 3–4 also comes, from the point of view both of its sense and partly also of its phraseology, from Ex. 12, especially vv. 6, 12. For v. 6 cf. Ex. 13.20. The names in v. 7 (the statement about their having 'turned back' as well) are all to be found in Ex. 14.1, only grouped somewhat differently. In v. 8 the narrative elements, amongst which the laconic note about the fundamental event of the passage through the 'sea' is remarkable, surely represent a later addition; they combine the passage through the sea with the three days' march in the wilderness referred to in Ex. 3.18; 5.3 (cf. also

* On the city of 'Rameses', cf. *Exodus*, p. 22.

15.22) and with the Etham which, according to vv. 6b, 7a, they had reached before 'turning back'. For vv. 9–10a cf. Ex. 15.23, 27a; the note about the locality of Elim is taken literally—probably second-arily—from Ex. 15.27a (as is the unusual phrase 'and came . . . and they encamped there'). The remarkable placing of the 'Sea of Reeds'* (vv. 10b, 11a) after Elim (v. 10) is perhaps to be explained as an erroneous inference from a misunderstanding of Ex. 15.27, which states that after their arrival at Elim they 'encamped there by the water'. The wilderness of Sin (vv. 11b, 12a) comes from Ex. 16.1, where it appears as the next camping site after Elim.

[33.13–40] With the names Dophkah and Alush (vv. 12b–14a) there begins the series of names not taken from the Pentateuchal narrative. The question as to why the redactor of the list of camping sites inserts them precisely at this point is difficult to answer. Did the 'document' used by him perhaps give the appearance of having its starting-point in the Sinai region (with the wilderness of Sin, vv. 11b, 12a, one has already arrived, according to Ex. 16.1, in the Sinai region)? At any rate, the wilderness of Sinai then makes its appear-ance in vv. 15b, 16a. The names in vv. 14b–18a again come from the Pentateuchal narrative, this time from Ex. 17.1; 19.2; Num. 11.34f. They are followed, in vv. 18b–30a, by a self-contained section from the 'document' with the otherwise unknown names. Vv. 30b–34a are problematical, since the names introduced here occur in Deut. 10.6–7 in a somewhat different sequence and with partly divergent forms, in a section which, in that context, is to be regarded as a mis-placed fragment. The question remains open as to which of these two passages is to be considered primary. In the present context it does not appear to be an intrusive element. At any rate, the series of vv. 18bff. continues in vv. 34b–36a, and here, for the first time in this series, there occurs a name that is known and that can be located, namely Ezion-geber (vv. 35b, 36a), the port at the north end of the gulf of el-ʿaqaba. The mention of this place is immediately followed by an excerpt from Num. 20.1, 22ff. The narrative portions in vv. 38–39 might again be a later addition; what is remarkable in them is the information about the date of Aaron's death and about his age, facts which are found only here and whose origin is unknown. The combination of the two 'sources' of Num. 33 seems at this point to be in error (yet cf. below); it makes Kadesh come after Ezion-geber, whereas Kadesh lay west of the gulf of el-ʿaqaba (more correctly,

* Cf. above p. 110, footnote. Tr.

Deut. 1.46; 2.8; cf. also Num. 21.4a). The excerpt from Num. 20 has
subsequently been supplemented, in v. 40, by a borrowing from
21.1aα, which in the present context is quite out of place.

[33.41–49] In vv. 41b–47a, linking up with vv. 37b and 41a,
the 'document' with the unusual names is once more in evidence. In
this section, one of them can be located with certainty. Punon (vv.
42b, 43a) is to be identified with *fēnān*, an old centre of metal mining,
situated on the east side of the *wādi el-'araba* about thirty-one miles
south of the southern end of the Dead Sea. Dibon-gad (vv. 45b, 46a)
is, no doubt, the well-known Dibon = *dībān*, here accurately designated by reference to its inhabitants, who were of the tribe of Gad
(cf. 32.34). Between Punon and Dibon-gad an ascent into the
mountains east of the Jordan is presupposed. The equation, often
accepted, of Oboth (vv. 43b, 44a) with *'ēn el-wēbe*, eighteen miles
almost due west of *fēnān* on the west side of the *wādi el-'araba*, does not
fit in with this presupposition at all. The ascent takes place via the
mountains of Abarim, which divide the transjordanian plateau from
the Dead Sea. The place 'Iyim' (literally: 'ruins') must have lain
somewhere in these mountains (v. 45a), for in v. 44b it is called,
more accurately, 'Iye-abarim'. With the unknown Almon-diblathaim
(vv. 46b, 47a), with which the Diblathaim of Jer. 48.22 may be
compared, this list of names comes to an end. What follows (vv.
47b–49) must be redactional, with the aim of bringing the Israelites
to the 'plains of Moab', where they have been since 22.1b; to reach
there they had to cross the mountains of Abarim once again to the
region of Nebo (vv. 47b, 48a). The details about places in v. 49
followed from that position; Beth-jeshimoth (also Josh. 12.3; 13.20)
is surely to be located on *tell el-'azēme* near the north-east end of the
Dead Sea; for Abel-shittim cf. 25.1 and above, p. 196.

Looking back, an attempt may be made to say something further
about the list of names in vv. *12b–47a. The second part of it, where
at least a few names appear which can be located, is clearly the out-
line of a route which leads from the north end of the gulf of *el-'aqaba*,
along the east side of the *wādi el-'araba* and then into the transjordanian mountains, to the plateau north of the Arnon. According
to Num. 20.14–21 (but cf. Deut. 2.2–9), this is precisely the route
which the Israelites, coming out of Egypt, did not take. The question
arises, therefore, whether the list of names initially ever had anything to do with the historical process of the exodus from Egypt. At
any rate, it must be explained from within itself. Unfortunately, in

its present form, which is probably only a consequence of the redactional insertion of it into Num. 33 as a whole, it lacks a definite beginning and end. At the end, it disappears in the southern part of the land east of the Jordan, presumably, that is, somewhere on the edge of the territory occupied by the Israelites. More important, and at the same time more difficult to answer, is the question of where it began. The first place that can be fixed with any certainty is Ezion-geber. According to the present context, the names mentioned before that have to be located in the Sinai peninsula. The possibility, however, also exists that the route indicated led along the east side of the gulf of *el-ʿaqaba* to Ezion-geber, that is from the direction of north-west Arabia; and on this latter assumption, which at the same time might perhaps explain the strange order Ezion-geber—Kadesh in v. 36 (cf. above, p. 244), there exist, for some of the names, possibilities of identification which are not, of course, all unequivocal and are, therefore, not entirely conclusive, but which exist nevertheless.* In that case the existence of this list of names within the Israelite tradition could almost only be understood on the presupposition that Sinai lay in north-west Arabia and that what we had in front of us was the itinerary of a 'pilgrim route' (to and) from Sinai.

17. DIRECTIONS FOR THE FUTURE ALLOCATION OF LAND WEST OF THE JORDAN: 33.50–34.29

33 ⁵⁰And the LORD said to Moses in the plains of Moab by the Jordan at Jericho, ⁵¹'Say to the people of Israel, When you pass over the Jordan into the land of Canaan, ⁵²then you shall drive out all the inhabitants of the land from before you, and destroy all their figured stones, and destroy all their molten images, and demolish all their high places, ⁵³and you shall take possession of the land and settle in it, for I have given the land to you to possess it. ⁵⁴You shall inherit the land by lot according to your families; to a large tribe you shall give a large inheritance, and to a small tribe you shall give a small inheritance; wherever the lot falls to any man, that shall be his; according to the tribes of your fathers you shall inherit. ⁵⁵But if you do not drive out the inhabitants of the land from before you, then those of them whom you let remain shall be as pricks in your eyes and thorns in your sides, and they shall trouble you in the land where you dwell. ⁵⁶And I will do to you as I thought to do to them.'

34 ¹The LORD said to Moses, ²'Command the people of Israel, and say to them, When you enter the land [of Canaan] (this is the land that

* For the details see M. Noth, *Palästina Jahrbuch*, 36, 1940, pp. 5–28; J. Koenig, *Revue d'Histoire et de Philosophie Religieuses*, 43, 1963, pp. 2–31; 44, 1964, pp. 200–35.

shall fall to you for an inheritance, the land of Canaan in its full extent), ³your south side shall be from the wilderness of Zin along the side of Edom, and your southern boundary shall be from the end of the Salt Sea on the east; ⁴and your boundary shall turn south of the ascent of Akrabbim, and cross to Zin, and its end shall be south of Kadesh-barnea; then it shall go on to Hazar-addar, and pass along to Azmon; ⁵and the boundary shall turn from Azmon to the Brook of Egypt, and its termination shall be at the Sea.

6 'For the western boundary, you shall have the Great Sea and its coast; this shall be your western boundary.

7 'This shall be your northern boundary: from the Great Sea you shall mark out your line to Mount Hor; ⁸from Mount Hor you shall mark it out to the entrance of Hamath, and the end of the boundary shall be at Zedad; ⁹then the boundary shall extend to Ziphron, and its end shall be at Hazar-enan; this shall be your northern boundary.

10 'You shall mark out your eastern boundary from Hazar-enan to Shepham; ¹¹and the boundary shall go down from Shepham to Riblah on the east side of Ain; and the boundary shall go down, and reach to the shoulder of the sea of Chinnereth on the east; ¹²and the boundary shall go down to the Jordan, and its end shall be at the Salt Sea. This shall be your land with its boundaries all round.'

13 Moses commanded the people of Israel, saying, 'This is the land which you shall inherit by lot, which the LORD has commanded to give to the nine tribes and to the half-tribe; ¹⁴for the tribe of the sons of Reuben by fathers' houses and the tribe of the sons of Gad by their fathers' houses have received their inheritance, and also the half-tribe of Manasseh; ¹⁵the two tribes and the half-tribe have received their inheritance beyond the Jordan at Jericho eastward, toward the sun-rise.'

16 The LORD said to Moses, ¹⁷'These are the names of the men who shall divide the land to you for inheritance: Eleazar the priest and Joshua the son of Nun. ¹⁸You shall take one leader of every tribe, to divide the land for inheritance. ¹⁹These are the names of the men: Of the tribe of Judah, Caleb the son of Jephunneh. ²⁰Of the tribe of the sons of Simeon, Shemuel the son of Ammihud. ²¹Of the tribe of Benjamin, Elidad the son of Chislon. ²²Of the tribe of the sons of Dan a leader, Bukki the son of Jogli. ²³Of the sons of Joseph: of the tribe of the sons of Manasseh a leader, Hanniel the son of Ephod. ²⁴And of the tribe of the sons of Ephraim a leader, Kemuel the son of Shiphtan. ²⁵Of the tribe of the sons of Zebulun a leader, Elizaphan the son of Parnach. ²⁶Of the tribe of the sons of Issachar a leader, Paltiel the son of Azzan. ²⁷And of the tribe of the sons of Asher a leader, Ahihud the son of Shelomi. ²⁸Of the tribe of the sons of Naphtali a leader, Pedahel the son of Ammihud. ²⁹These are the men whom the LORD commanded to divide the inheritance for the people of Israel in the land of Canaan.'

The divine commands here are concerned with the impending conquest of the land west of the Jordan. Again, they are transmitted by

Moses before his death. The main section of them, the description in 34.1–12 of the frontiers of the territory that is to be divided up, is orientated towards specific details in the book of Joshua concerning the division of the inheritance in Canaan. The introductory section 33.50–56, is, both in content and form, strongly characteristic of the deuteronomist, but also has references to, amongst other passages, Num. 26. In 34.13–15 use is made of the deuteronomistic presentation of the conquest east of the Jordan. The list of names in 34.17–28 follows the comparable lists in 1.5–15; 13.4–15. In short, this whole section presupposes, on the one hand, the Pentateuchal narrative at an already late stage, and on the other, the deuteronomistic historical work, and is, therefore, part of the editorial unification of these two literary complexes.

[33.50–56] The general command to drive out completely the present inhabitants of the 'land of Canaan' (= the land west of the Jordan; cf. 32.30, 32) is found otherwise, especially in deuteronomistic passages (Deut. 7.2ff.; 12.2ff. *et al.*), with the justification that the 'Canaanite' cults could become dangerous for Israel, for which reason especially the 'Canaanite' cultic paraphernalia are to be removed (cf. Deut. 12.30f. *et al.*). The allocation of the land as an inheritance, which will follow the expulsion of the present inhabitants, is, according to v. 54, to be undertaken in the way that has already been envisaged in 26.53–56 (partly verbal repetition), namely by means of the lot (cf. Josh. 18.6b, 10), but keeping in mind, at the same time, a suitable relationship between the size of the tribes and the area of the tribal territories (the same inconsistency in 26.53–56). Vv. 53–54 stand awkwardly between the two corresponding sections, vv. 52 and 55–56. Within the framework of this late passage, no literary-critical conclusions with regard to vv. 53–54 can be drawn from this fact. In the case of an incomplete expulsion of the former inhabitants, those who are left of the latter will become the means of terrible persecution for Israel (for the metaphorical expressions in v. 55aβ, cf. the very similar statements in Josh. 23.13Dtr.); thus has Yahweh envisaged it (v. 56).

[34.1–12] The exact delimitation, in 34.3–12, of the entire territory west of the Jordan to be divided among the tribes, is presented entirely in the style of the 'system of tribal frontiers' in Josh. 15ff., by enumeration of points on the frontier. And not only that. The southern frontier that is laid down in vv. 3–5 is identical with the southern frontier of Judah as described in Josh. 15.1–4. It cannot be doubted that the present details are derived from Josh. 15, and indeed, throughout, the southern frontier of the most southerly tribe (Judah) is taken as the southern frontier of the entire territory. The list of frontier-points is the same as in Josh. 15 (only one frontier-point in Josh. 15 is missing, probably by mistake, in Num. 34; in another case two separate frontier-points in Josh. 15 are combined in one frontier-point in Num. 34, and this is probably factually correct); in the linking text, on the other hand, there are some variants which are not, however, of factual significance. Of the points mentioned—apart from the 'end of the Salt Sea' (= the southern end of the Dead Sea)—only three can be identified with any probability: the 'ascent of Akrabbim'* is surely to be equated with modern *naqb eṣ-ṣafa*; 'Kadesh-barnea' is to be located in the territory of *'ēn qdēs*; and by the 'Brook of Egypt' the *wādi el-'ariš* is meant. From this it follows that the southern frontier is fixed far out into the territory of the Negeb, where there are no longer any permanent settlements. As in Josh. 15.1, it is noted in v. 3, by way of introduction, that the southern frontier is to run 'along the side of Edom', that Edom, therefore, would be the frontier neighbour at this point. In v. 6 the Mediterranean coastline ('the Great Sea') is taken, summarily, to form the western frontier, as in the above-mentioned 'system of tribal frontiers'. The northern and north-eastern frontier described in vv. 7–11 is problematical, since none of the numerous frontier-points mentioned can be fixed with any certainty. All that is clear is that the line of the frontier begins somewhere on the Mediterranean coast (v. 7) and ends on the eastern shore of the Sea of Tiberias ('sea of Chinnereth'; v. 11b), and that it presumably encloses an area that is to be located in the vicinity of the uppermost reaches of the Jordan. The style of the description of this frontier, too, again corresponds entirely to that of the 'system of tribal frontiers' in the book of Joshua; however, there is no description of a comparable frontier in the book of Joshua. One would expect, by analogy with the southern frontier, that the description of the northern and north-eastern frontier of the most northerly tribe would be at the basis of this. In fact, the same list of frontier-points is found in Ezek. 47.15–18, but with numerous variants and additions, and this list appears in Ezek. 48.1–2 as the description of the frontier of the most northerly tribe, Dan. In the book of Joshua, however, the description of a frontier for Dan is lacking, in view of the fact that, at the

---

* Noth translates this place-name, 'ascent of scorpions', the Hebrew *'aqrabbīm* meaning 'scorpions'. Tr.

time of the conquest, Dan had not yet taken possession of its northern territory. From this, there emerges the supposition that, in Num. 34.7–11, we have before us part of the description of the frontier of the tribe of Dan from the 'system of tribal frontiers' which has succeeded in maintaining its position here. The point of departure at the 'Great Sea' (v. 7) establishes the connection with the western frontier. This is followed by definite frontier-points. 'Mount Hor' is to be differentiated from the place of the same name which was the scene of Aaron's death (20.22ff.). The frontier-point Lebo-hamath* is probably to be located somewhere in the region of the *biqāʿ*, the plateau between Lebanon and Antilebanon; however, the name Lebo-hamath, which, literally translated, could mean 'the place at which one enters Hamath (= *ḥama* on the middle reaches of the Orontes)', is somewhat puzzling. If this is the frontier of Dan, there can be no question of the apparently obvious equation of Zedad with the modern *ṣadad* (about thirty-one miles south-south-east of *ḥomṣ*. The place Hazar-enan marks the north-eastern point of the entire territory included here and was presumably also in the description of the frontier of Dan the most north-easterly corner; its position is unfortunately unknown. The place Hariblah (with the definite article in Hebrew) † is certainly to be differentiated from the Riblah (without the article) of II Kings 23.33 *et al.* The termination of this part of the frontier on the eastern shore of the Sea of Tiberias indicates that part of the territory east of the Jordan is included, as is certainly to be accepted in the case of the tribal territory of Dan. According to v. 12a, the Jordan was to form the eastern frontier between the Sea of Tiberias and the Dead Sea, and this corresponds to the presupposition made in vv. 1–2.

[34.13–28] For the division of the land west of the Jordan among the nine and a half tribes of that area a commission is set up, according to vv. 13–28, to supervise the distribution by lot of the tribal territories (cf. Josh. 14.1; 19.51). This commission is to comprise, besides Eleazar the priest and Joshua, the 'spokesmen' of those tribes still to be taken into consideration, and these are mentioned by name in vv. 19–28. The order of the tribes follows the geographical position of the future tribal territories from south to north and these are presupposed as having already been allocated, although the lot (v. 13) is still supposed to decide the allocation. The list of names is dependent

---

* This is the name which appears in RSV as 'the entrance of Hamath', a rendering of which Noth takes account in the second part of this sentence. Tr.

† RSV has ignored this fact and has rendered this simply as Riblah. Tr.

on the enumerations of 'spokesmen' in 1.5–15 and 13.4–15. According to the given presupposition, only ten names are mentioned. This list of names can scarcely have its basis in old traditions, although it contains some names which give the impression of being very old; these, however, are surely borrowed from an older stock of names. For the tribe of Judah, which, on account of its importance, precedes the tribe of Simeon, in violation of the geographical order, Caleb is nominated (v. 19), since he could scarcely have been omitted from this list (cf. 13.6). In the case of the Joseph tribes (vv. 23–24) we find, as, e.g., in 26.28ff., and again in violation of the principle of geographical arrangement, the order Manasseh-Ephraim.

18. LEVITICAL CITIES AND CITIES OF REFUGE:
35.1–34

35 [1]The LORD said to Moses in the plains of Moab by the Jordan at Jericho, [2]'Command the people of Israel, that they give to the Levites, from the inheritance of their possession, cities to dwell in; and you shall give to the Levites pasture lands round about the cities. [3]The cities shall be theirs to dwell in, and their pasture lands shall be for their cattle and for their livestock and for all their beasts. [4]The pasture lands of the cities, which you shall give to the Levites, shall reach from the wall of the city outward a thousand cubits all round. [5]And you shall measure, outside the city, for the east side two thousand cubits, and for the south side two thousand cubits, and for the west side two thousand cubits, and for the north side two thousand cubits, the city being in the middle; this shall belong to them as pasture land for their cities. [6]The cities which you give to the Levites shall be the six cities of refuge, where you shall permit the manslayer to flee, and in addition to them you shall give forty-two cities. [7]All the cities which you give to the Levites shall be forty-eight, with their pasture lands. [8]And as for the cities which you shall give from the possession of the people of Israel, from the larger tribes you shall take many, and from the smaller tribes you shall take few; each, in proportion to the inheritance which it inherits, shall give of its cities to the Levites.'

9 And the LORD said to Moses, [10]'Say to the people of Israel, When you cross the Jordan into the land of Canaan, [11]then you shall select cities to be cities of refuge for you, that the manslayer who kills any person without intent may flee there. [12]The cities shall be for you a refuge from the avenger, that the manslayer may not die until he stands before the congregation for judgment. [13]And the cities which you give shall be your six cities of refuge. [14]You shall give three cities beyond the Jordan, and three cities in the land of Canaan, to be cities of refuge. [15]These six cities shall be for refuge for the people of Israel, and for the stranger and for the sojourner among them, that any one who kills any person without intent may flee there.

16 'But if he struck him down with an instrument of iron, so that he died, he is a murderer; the murderer shall be put to death. [17]And if he struck him down with a stone in the hand, by which a man may die, and he died, he is a murderer; the murderer shall be put to death. [18]Or if he struck him down with a weapon of wood in the hand, by which a man may die, and he died, he is a murderer; the murderer shall be put to death. [19]The avenger of blood shall himself put the murderer to death; when he meets him, he shall put him to death. [20]And if he stabbed him from hatred, or hurled at him, lying in wait, so that he died, [21]or in enmity struck him down with his hand, so that he died, then he who struck the blow shall be put to death; he is a murderer; the avenger of blood shall put the murderer to death, when he meets him.

22 'But if he stabbed him suddenly without enmity, or hurled anything on him without lying in wait, [23]or used a stone, by which a man may die, and without seeing him cast it upon him, so that he died, though he was not his enemy, and did not seek his harm; [24]then the congregation shall judge between the manslayer and the avenger of blood, in accordance with these ordinances; [25]and the congregation shall rescue the manslayer from the hand of the avenger of blood, and the congregation shall restore him to his city of refuge, to which he had fled, and he shall live in it until the death of the high priest who was anointed with the holy oil. [26]But if the manslayer shall at any time go beyond the bounds of his city of refuge to which he fled, [27]and the avenger of blood finds him outside the bounds of his city of refuge, and the avenger of blood slays the manslayer, he shall not be guilty of blood. [28]For the man must remain in his city of refuge until the death of the high priest; but after the death of the high priest the manslayer may return to the land of his possession.

29 'And these things shall be for a statute and ordinance to you throughout your generations in all your dwellings. [30]If any one kills a person, the murderer shall be put to death on the evidence of witnesses; but no person shall be put to death on the testimony of one witness. [31]Moreover you shall accept no ransom for the life of a murderer who is guilty of death; but he shall be put to death. [32]And you shall accept no ransom for him who has fled to his city of refuge, that he may return to dwell in the land before the death of the high priest. [33]You shall not thus pollute the land in which you live; for blood pollutes the land, and no expiation can be made for the land, for the blood that is shed in it, except by the blood of him who shed it. [34]You shall not defile the land in which you live, in the midst of which I dwell; for I the LORD dwell in the midst of the people of Israel.'

The directions for the future division of the inheritance of land west of the Jordan (ch. 34) are now followed by certain special laws; they are concerned, first of all, with the gift of cities of residence for the Levites, since they were not to receive a self-contained tribal territory (vv. 1–8), and then with the setting up of cities of refuge as places to which a killer could flee who, even if he had acted without evil intent, found himself exposed automatically to the rule of blood vengeance (vv. 9–34). These two disparate subjects, the second of which has nothing to do with the theme of the allocation of territory in Palestine, are held together by the fact mentioned in v. 6, namely the identity of the cities of refuge with a part of the Levitical cities of residence. Again, this identification goes back to the present final form of Josh. 21. Yet not only in this one point, but in its whole compass, the present chapter is clearly dependent on Josh. 20.1–21.42. Just as this section of Joshua follows Josh. 14–19, so, analogously, does Num. 35 follow Num. 34. The present passage, then, also belongs to the redactional unification of Pentateuchal narrative and deuteronomistic historical work. What, according to the Joshua narrative, was later carried out, had already been commanded the Israelites by Moses on the basis of divine direction.

[35.1–8] Contrary to the order in Josh. 20–21, the Levitical cities are dealt with first in vv. 1–8. The Israelite tribes are to 'give' to the Levites, who receive no tribal territory of their own and who are certainly not to live in a closely knit community, but are thought of as living scattered throughout the whole country, cities with adjoining pasture lands, and in this way to care for them. How, in this case, the conditions of ownership are to be regulated is not clearly stated. The emphasis on the fact that the cities are to be for the Levites 'to dwell in' (vv. 2–3) suggests that they are to have the use of them, but not to own them, and, correspondingly, this would also apply to the pasture lands. In addition it would appear from the wording that the idea was that the cities in question were to be inhabited exclusively by Levites, and that the latter were not simply to be fellow citizens with the members of the tribe to which the cities belonged. Against this suggestion is the fact that there is a ruling for the measuring out of a quite definite area for the pasture land (vv. 4–5), for here the tacit assumption is that the fields round the town must sometimes have been more extensive, with the result that one has to imagine an area in excess which could then be used by non-Levites. These considerations are perhaps, however, superfluous, since the whole passage is purely theoretical, as is clear from the prescriptions for the schematic measuring out of the pasture lands. According to these, the 'city' with its 'wall' must have been only a point without extension (v. 5). The idea of cities of residence for the

Levites must, in itself, go back to deuteronomic-deuteronomistic ideology (so, too, surely the original form in Josh. 21); the present elaboration is a very late product. Nothing is yet said about the actual selection of Levitical cities of residence. As a guiding principle, all that is laid down, on the basis of Josh. 21, is that the cities of refuge which are to be discussed in the next section—six in all—are part of them (v. 6a) and that the total is to be forty-eight (vv. 6b–7) and that the Israelite tribal territories are to participate in 'handing over' Levitical cities (v. 8) in proportion to their size (on content and phraseology cf. 26.54). The latter statement refers to the allocation of Levitical cities among the individual tribal territories that is given in Josh. 21, but again this is purely theoretical, for there can be no question in Josh. 21 of any correspondence between the size of the tribal territory and the number of cities to be handed over.

[35.9–15] The command to set up cities of refuge (vv. 9–34) must have Josh. 20 in mind. In this regard, no account is taken of the fact that the deuteronomic law also contains instructions for the setting apart of cities to which the killer can flee (Deut. 19.1–13), in which passage, however, there is no technical term for 'city of refuge'. These instructions, which are essentially connected with the deuteronomic demand for the centralization of the cult, have behind them Josh. 20, which, for its part, shows evidence of several literary strata. The final literary form of Josh. 20 has then been utilized for the present section. The expression 'city of refuge' (there is no longer any certain derivation for the words 'ir miqlāṭ) is also found in Josh. 20.2, 3. The future cities of refuge are not fixed at this stage (in Josh. 20.7–8 their names are mentioned); on the basis of Josh. 20, the guiding principle is established that there are to be three east of the Jordan and three west of the Jordan, that is six in all (vv. 13–14; in v. 14 once again, as already in v. 10, 'the land of Canaan' as a special designation of the land west of the Jordan). The person who has killed a man without premeditation is to be able to flee to one of these cities in order to escape the blood vengeance, which does not inquire into the motive of the deed. The practice of blood vengeance is presupposed here, as is the fact that the potential avenger of blood has to respect the right of asylum in the city in question. Now, the person who commits a murder with intent could, of course, abuse this institution. Therefore a trial must still take place 'before the congregation' (v. 12bβ), who certainly have to decide the rights or wrongs of the claim for refuge and then, if occasion arises, make the provisional residence in the city of refuge definitive. The function of the 'congregation' (so, too, Josh. 20.6aα) appears unrealistic (what must surely be meant is the whole congregation of Israel); what is certainly a more original version has been preserved in Josh. 20.4–5, according to which the elders of the city of refuge in question had to decide the right to asylum.

[35.16–29] From v. 16 onwards there follow individual statements concerning the theme of whether a killing has been done intentionally or not. Whether they always belonged to vv. 9–15 or have only been added later cannot definitely be decided. In favour of the latter possibility there is the fact that the word *rōṣēaḥ* ('killer') which, in vv. 11–12, designates the 'killer' (without evil intent), now occasionally means specifically the conscious 'murderer', exactly as if it were a technical term (cf. especially vv. 16–21). It remains questionable, of course, whether one can claim as much for the consistency of the terminology in this chapter. According to vv. 16–21, the murderer had to be refused the right of asylum. He 'shall be put to death'. At the first impression, this phrase sounds like an official judgment and sentence. According to vv. 19, 21b, however, the killing of the murderer is left to the avenger of blood. Here, then, we have a combination of the practice of blood vengeance and regulated, legal procedure. The indications noted in vv. 16–23 as to whether the killing was premeditated or not are concerned partly with the method of the killing and partly (overlapping here) with the previous relationship between the killer and the slain (for this subject cf. already the Book of the Covenant in Ex. 21.12–14). The legal decision of the 'congregation' (v. 24) leads to the definitive acceptance of the killer into the city of refuge (v. 25a; *rōṣēaḥ* here again in the sense of 'killer') and thus to the barring of the avenger of blood. This ruling is valid until the death of the high priest, i.e. until the termination of a high priest's term of office (vv. 25b, 28; cf. Josh. 20.6aβb); for with this termination the right of blood vengeance obviously expires. In this respect the high priest—as is the case, too, with the anointing mentioned specifically in v. 25bβ—must have taken over the role formerly played by the king, and this must be a reference to the fact that a general amnesty was, or at least could be, bound up with a change in the occupancy of the throne. An earlier, irresponsible departure from the city of refuge meant for the killer (*rōṣēaḥ* in this sense) a renunciation of protection and the risk of falling into the hands of the avenger of blood (vv. 26–27).

[35.30–34] There follow, in vv. 30–32, a few more, loosely attached, additional statements, first of all in v. 30 the ordinance that at least two witnesses are necessary to convict someone as a murderer (*rōṣēaḥ* in this sense; cf. Deut. 17.6f.; 19.15), that, therefore, the matter is to be dealt with according to the principle of *in dubio pro reo*; then, in v. 31, the prohibition of accepting ransom money for the forfeited life of a murderer (*rōṣēaḥ*); and finally, in v. 32, the prohibition of granting, for ransom money, i.e. by way of a bribe, protection to someone who has no right to it (that seems to be the sense of the somewhat obscure text).* The closing remarks, in vv. 33–34, are a warning to take the question of bloodshed very seriously, since the whole land—not just any land, but the land in which Israel lives and in which Yahweh himself 'dwells' in the midst of Israel—would become polluted by any blood shed anywhere within it. Expiation can be effected only by the killing of the murderer (v. 33b; cf. Gen. 9.5–6). Strangely enough, this assertion takes no account of unpremeditated killing and the granting of asylum.

19. APPENDIX ON DAUGHTERS' RIGHTS OF INHERITANCE: 36.1–13

36 ¹The heads of the fathers' houses of the families of the sons of Gilead the son of Machir, son of Manasseh, of the fathers' houses of the sons of Joseph, came near and spoke before Moses and before the leaders, the heads of the fathers' houses of the people of Israel; ²they said, 'The LORD commanded my lord to give the land for inheritance by lot to the people of Israel; and my lord was commanded by the LORD to give the inheritance of Zelophehad our brother to his daughters. ³But if they are married to any of the sons of the other tribes of the people of Israel then their inheritance will be taken from the inheritance of our fathers, and added to the inheritance of the tribe to which they belong; so it will be taken away from the lot of our inheritance. ⁴[And when the jubilee of the people of Israel comes, then their inheritance will be added to the inheritance of the tribe to which they belong; and their inheritance will be taken from the inheritance of the tribe of our father.]'

5 And Moses commanded the people of Israel according to the word of the LORD, saying, 'The tribe of the sons of Joseph is right. ⁶This is what the LORD commands concerning the daughters of Zelophehad, "Let them marry whom they think best; only, they shall marry within

---

* Noth's translation of v. 32 is somewhat different from that of RSV: 'Neither shall you accept ransom money for permitting someone to flee to his city of refuge and then to return to live in the land at the time of the high priest's death.' Tr.

the family of the tribe of their father. ⁷The inheritance of the people of Israel shall not be transferred from one tribe to another; for every one of the people of Israel shall cleave to the inheritance of the tribe of his fathers. ⁸And every daughter who possesses an inheritance in any tribe of the people of Israel shall be wife to one of the family of the tribe of her father, so that every one of the people of Israel may possess the inheritance of his fathers. ⁹So no inheritance shall be transferred from one tribe to another; for each of the tribes of the people of Israel shall cleave to his own inheritance." '

10 The daughters of Zelophehad did as the LORD commanded Moses; ¹¹for Mahlah, Tirzah, Hoglah, Milcah, and Noah, the daughters of Zelophehad, were married to sons of their father's brothers. ¹²They were married into the families of the sons of Manasseh the son of Joseph, and their inheritance remained in the tribe of the family of their father.

13 These are the commandments and the ordinances which the LORD commanded by Moses to the people of Israel in the plains of Moab by the Jordan at Jericho.

This is an appendix to 27.1–11, which has been included at the very end of the book of Numbers. Again, as in 27.1–11, the daughters of that Zelophehad who was mentioned in 26.33 and who had no sons, serve to present a precedent concerning the right of daughters to inherit in cases where there is no male heir. This right to inherit was affirmed in 27.1–11. Here there is added the further condition that daughters who have rights of inheritance may be married only within their own tribe, in order that the total inheritance of the Israelite tribes should remain unaltered. This presupposes that the inherited property of daughters would pass, in the event of their marriage, into the possession of the husband and his tribe, and would remain there. The reference to the year of jubilee in v. 4 is, from both the literary and the factual point of view, out of place. It breaks the sequence of thought and suggests that in the year of jubilee everything remained unaltered; one would expect, rather, that in the year of jubilee the original conditions of possession would beʳ reinstated, although no reference is made to the present case in Lev. 25. V. 4 is an irrelevant addition. The subject of Num. 36 is fairly simple and clear; it is stated in great detail. First of all the precedent is introduced (vv. 1–3, 5–7); then there is derived from it a general rule which is to be valid from now on (vv. 8–9). Finally, there is a report of its being implemented, thus concluding the precedent (vv. 10–12). The text of vv. 3, 6b, 7, 8, 12 suggests that daughters who inherited could be married only within their own tribe, though not necessarily within their own clan. It is a question of maintaining unaltered the heritable property of the tribes as a whole; within the clans of a tribe, alterations in the conditions of heritable property could take place. In practical terms, this whole legislation contemplates a marriage within the circle of a woman's cousins (in the broad sense; v. 11b).

The concluding formula in v. 13 does not belong specifically to the present chapter, but generally to the final sections of the book of Numbers.